A brilliant new book ... In *Who Only Cricket Know*, David Woodhouse writes a compelling account of a historic series marked by tantrums and turmoil, racism and riots, class conflicts and colonialism – and some great cricket.
ROGER ALTON, *THE SPECTATOR*

Superb ... Wide-ranging ... Woodhouse gives full flavour to the complex issues of race and class, without which Caribbean cricket of the time cannot be understood ... If you like cricket, the Caribbean and history then *Who Only Cricket Know* is a fine place to start.
MIKE ATHERTON, *THE TIMES*

Bodyline has long been recognised as the most controversial of all tours, certainly of all England tours, but a new reappraisal makes a persuasive case for an England tour of West Indies to take the title. We think Joe Root has plenty on his shoulders ... This fascinating account makes it clear that Len Hutton had plenty more on his.
SCYLD BERRY, *THE DAILY TELEGRAPH*

Brilliant ... Of all the books written about MCC and English tours over the last century (including the Bodyline series) this book is one of the truly outstanding ones. It is gripping and exciting and just demands to be read.
ANTHONY BRADBURY, *MENSA CRICKET SPECIAL INTEREST GROUP*

We are big on West Indies cricket beyond the boundary and this book is a political, social, cultural and economic tour de force. You'll want to pour yourself a cup of tea and really take this one in.
CARIBBEAN CRICKET PODCAST*

Woodhouse's writing shows great skill and he is an accomplished wordsmith who clearly has a sense of humour ... Bringing up the rear of this splendidly written and well-illustrated book are the scorecards of the Tests, the tour statistics, a comprehensive bibliography and a very fine index ... Pretty much perfect.
MARTIN CHANDLER, *CRICKETWEB*
(5-star review – 'Martin wanted to give this one six stars')

It is hard to believe that a tour book could be much better than this ... The author's research is meticulous and remarkable ... It is riveting stuff and while the account of the cricket is excellent, the background to it is what makes this book such a tour de force. This book is an absolute gem and deserves its place among the very best that I have read.

STEVE DOLMAN, *PEAKFAN BLOG*

This is a notably well-informed and enjoyable account of a highly absorbing series. Although it took place so long ago it feels as if the author was himself on tour with England in '53/54. As a young newspaper employee at the time, I recall the tensions which sprang out of the daily reports. What we read then was a convenient narrative. David Woodhouse has neatly unveiled the complexities of a sensational cricket tour.

DAVID FRITH, AUTHOR OF *BODYLINE AUTOPSY* **AND** *PADDINGTON BOY*

David Woodhouse's immaculate book is a piece of modern history shown through a cricketing lens ... It is deeply and lovingly researched, and then crafted like a batmaker working on his Grade A willow. One for the purists, in every respect.

JON HOTTEN, *WISDEN CRICKET MONTHLY*

Truly wonderful ... And what a really beautiful object the book itself is!

ANDY IRVINE, MUSICIAN AND SINGER-SONGWRITER

Authoritative ... While the English-centric record of events has always concentrated primarily on the "who said what to whom" and who was most to blame, Woodhouse aims for a far more balanced and expansive view, foregrounding Caribbean voices and revisiting complex and even contradictory characters ... Seven years of research and writing allowed him to place the full gamut of detail within a rich social, racial and political history.

EMMA JOHN, *THE GUARDIAN*

David Woodhouse's compelling account of the controversial English tour of the West Indies in 1953/54 represents the culmination of a revolution in cricket history ... He conveys a vivid sense of place; he offers psychological insights (cricket being of course a game played largely in the mind); and throughout he is aware of the bigger social and cultural picture ... Our cricket remains in some fundamental ways the prisoner of history. But at least we now have in this fine book a sure guide to an important slice of that history.

DAVID KYNASTON, *TIMES LITERARY SUPPLEMENT*

A superb chronicle of an often overlooked chapter in cricketing history, written not only with a deep and intimate love of the game but a rare social and cultural perspective.
JONATHAN LIEW, *GUARDIAN* SPORTSWRITER

The characters and the plot ... make for a fascinating tale. But Woodhouse achieves far more than the standard tour book by placing the series in its historical context in a scholarly, yet accessible way. *Who Only Cricket Know* is a tour de force, and *Wisden*'s Book of the Year.
VIC MARKS, *WISDEN CRICKETERS' ALMANACK 2022*

Balanced and sympathetic ... With impressive insight and immaculate research, Woodhouse creates a grippingly entertaining tale of touring intrigue that shows how sport can never be insulated from the wider social and political circumstances in which it is played ... Here is a very specific, and beautifully written, example of the calamities that can befall any sporting team that fails to 'read the room'.
PETER MASON, *MORNING STAR*

What are the greatest books on cricket? Lovers of the game have long debated this topic ... Now we have another contender. This book by David Woodhouse will surely make the short lists for a host of annual awards. It will deserve to do so on literary merit, supported by rigorous research and a balanced quest for the truth about a tour that perhaps surpasses Bodyline for the contention and ill-feeling it provoked.
DOUGLAS MILLER, *THE CRICKET STATISTICIAN*

There can be no more fitting title for a book that pulls off the remarkable trick of making its readers feel more intelligent with every passing page. Sport exists ineluctably hand in hand with politics, and David Woodhouse grippingly illustrates that truth in this profoundly absorbing and masterfully written tale. A genuinely stupendous achievement.
DANIEL NORCROSS, *TEST MATCH SPECIAL* COMMENTATOR

A really remarkable book ... A major work of political, economic, social and cultural history ... It says a lot about the present as well as the past.
OBORNE AND HELLER ON CRICKET

A page-turner ... Completely compelling ... Serious history writing applied to cricket ... A book that matters.
REVERSE SWEPT RADIO

David Woodhouse's account of Len Hutton's tour of the Caribbean in 1953/54 is a beautifully told and important story of cricket and politics, unavoidably and fascinatingly mixed, with echoes that reverberate as much today as they did nearly 70 years ago, perhaps more so.

SIR TIM RICE, LYRICIST

The best cricket book I have read in ages. Buy it, read it, savour it …
A rare and magnificent gem.

ARUNABHA SENGUPTA, *CRICKETMASH*

An excellent resource … The cricketing events of 1953/54 are entirely beyond my memory but this book brings the passions simmering in Guyana, or British Guiana as it was known back then, and indeed the wider West Indies, and entrenches them in the field of play and beyond. On the field, the author positions himself behind the umpire and off the field he observes from behind the colonial officials who ran the colony after suspending the Constitution and jailing some of its political leaders. Two chapters – Chapter 12, 'British Guiana' and Chapter 13, 'Third Test (Bourda)' just by themselves are worth the price of the book.

DR TULSI DYAL SINGH, BERBICE CRICKET BOARD SPONSOR

This is a superb book. It does for Len Hutton's turbulent tour of the West Indies what David Frith's *Bodyline Autopsy* did for Douglas Jardine's Australia campaign.
It is the last word.

SIMON WILDE, *SUNDAY TIMES* CRICKET CORRESPONDENT

A masterful retelling of an historic tour and so much more besides. Woodhouse brings alive the time, the characters and the matches with great skill and flair.

DEAN WILSON, *DAILY MIRROR* CRICKET CORRESPONDENT

A wonderful story, very smartly told. Proof of the old saying that there is nothing as new as the history we do not know.

ROBERT WINDER, CHAIR OF JUDGES, THE CRICKET SOCIETY AND MCC BOOK OF THE YEAR AWARD 2022

First published by Fairfield Books in 2021
Reprinted in 2022 with minor revisions

fairfield books

Fairfield Books
Wildfire Sport
Bedser Stand
Kia Oval
London
SE11 5SS

Typeset in Garamond
Typesetting by Rob Whitehouse

This book is printed on paper certified
by the Forest Stewardship Council

© 2021 David Woodhouse
ISBN 978-1-909811-59-1

A CIP catalogue record for is available from the British Library

Printed by CPI Group (UK) Ltd

WHO ONLY CRICKET KNOW

Hutton's Men in the West Indies 1953/54

BY DAVID WOODHOUSE

For my wife Mariya
…l'amor che move i sole e l'altre stelle
and my mother and father, Melba and Frank
…da lingua che chiami mamma o babbo

CONTENTS

PART III: THE AFTERMATH

STATISTICAL AND REFERENCE SECTIONS

NOTES ON THE TEXT

REFERENCES

If you like to check references as you read, you can have the printed book open at the same time as the accompanying website who-only-cricket-know.uk, which includes all the footnotes and a bibliography. I have made suggestions for further reading at the back of the book but the website has more detail, ranging from audio and video resources accessible on the internet to more rarefied printed material.

LANGUAGE

Clyde Walcott once observed that 'the pages of *Wisden* don't mention a man's colour'. I have tried to write this book in the same spirit. Nonetheless, because one of its subjects is the racial politics of the 1950s, a person's colour sometimes has to be mentioned and the terms used matter now as they mattered then. Grossly offensive epithets were still prevalent in the period – I have decided not to expunge them in five of my quotations – and even in polite discourse there were conventions we would now find unacceptable. In Britain, the word 'black' was considered objectionable and the words 'Negro' or 'coloured' appropriate. In the Caribbean, people of mixed race could be opprobriously sub-categorised as 'octaroon', 'quadroon', 'mulatto' and so forth, while the term 'local white' could include people of darker skin who were considered absorbed into elite society. When forced to generalise myself, I will use the word 'black' to mean African-Caribbean, the no doubt imperfect word 'brown' for the important and heterogenous component of Caribbean society that is mixed-race, another imperfect word, 'Indian', for those whose ancestors migrated (mainly from Uttar Pradesh and Bihar) to work as indentured labourers (mainly in Trinidad and British Guiana), and the term 'local white' for caucasian settlers and British expatriates.

Difficulties are also presented by anachronistic political terminology. I hope it will be understood why the term 'colony' has been left to stand, because an important distinction was still made in the 1950s between the Dominions of the Commonwealth, especially the 'kith-and-kin' Dominions such as Australia and New Zealand, and the remaining colonies, which included the territories in the 'British West Indies'. Even that term conglomerated a set of disparate islands by defining their location and status in relation to their imperial master, although I will be using it without inverted commas in a cricket book. While I have used the adjective 'Guyanese' throughout, I have referred to Guyana as 'British Guiana' or 'BG' in any context before independence in 1966. I have also let stand the complications that arose at the time from cricket being the 'English' game played in the 'British' empire, the interchangeability of 'England' and 'Britain' remaining as contentious today.

CONVENTIONS

Two of my interviewees, Sir Everton Weekes and Alan Moss, have died during the writing of the book, but it feels right that these fine men should sometimes speak in the present tense when I quote from their interviews.

Acronyms appear in the form 'MCC' not 'M.C.C.' and quotations are silently conformed. To distinguish between cricket seasons played in the English summer and the English winter, I have, like *Wisden,* tried consistently to use the form '1953/54' for the latter, even if the relevant cricketing event obviously falls within a single calendar year.

SCORECARDS

The Test scorecards are based on the original scorebooks held by MCC at Lord's, re-scored using the 'vertical' method and drawing on contemporary newspaper reports in order to calculate deliveries faced by each batsman. I have still occasionally had to make educated guesses about the rotation of the strike arising from byes and leg byes.

INDEX

I have tried to tell a few jokes in the index, but I am not seeking to mock English amateurs or white West Indian cricketers and administrators by using their initials instead of their first names: this is just the most economical way of registering distinctions which were still considered important in 1954 (even if the index to that year's *Wisden* used initials for everybody).

INTRODUCTION

George Headley	Len Hutton
Jeffrey Stollmeyer	Willie Watson
Frank Worrell	Peter May
Everton Weekes	Denis Compton
Clyde Walcott	Tom Graveney
Garry Sobers	Trevor Bailey
Gerry Gomez	Godfrey Evans
Denis Atkinson	Jim Laker
Sonny Ramadhin	Tony Lock
Alf Valentine	Fred Trueman
Frank King	Brian Statham

These composite teams selected from players who appeared in the series between West Indies and England in 1953/54 may not reflect the first-choice sides at that precise moment in history. But there are many names to conjure with here.

The series was bookended by the final appearance of one legendary West Indies figure, Headley, in the first Test and the debut of another, Sobers, in the last. Worrell, Weekes and Walcott, the great Barbadian triad better known then as the 'W formation' and now as the 'Three Ws', all scored big hundreds. The 'little pals' Ramadhin and Valentine, immortalised by the calypso which celebrated the first win by West Indies on English soil in 1950, continued to cast a spell over some of the visiting batsmen.

England had famous spin twins of their own, Laker and Lock, even if the ghost of Johnny Wardle, who played in two of the Tests, might still be heard grumbling he should have played more. The young fast bowlers, Trueman and Statham, would evolve into one of the most celebrated new-ball pairs in Test cricket. Hutton and Compton were the two greatest English batsmen from the generation whose careers spanned the Second World War; May and Graveney were two of the finest from the next generation. Many of the players who graced the series could still be considered now for all-time XIs, even after the passage of nearly 70 years and more than 2,000 Tests.

The cricketers on both sides will remain at the heart of this book. But they are not the only reason the 1953/54 tour should be remembered. Before a ball was bowled, the expedition led by Hutton set some notable precedents. It was the first time an MCC team had been sent overseas under a professional captain. It was the first time they had made the outward journey by air. And it was the first time the West Indies had been visited by a side ostensibly representing England's best.

Having just presided over the first home Ashes victory since 1926, Hutton came to the Caribbean with a squad almost at full strength. The only notable omission was Alec Bedser, rested in view of the next winter's tour to Australia. While there was always a sense of Hutton treating the series in the Caribbean as a dry run for that challenge, he had played on losing sides against West Indies away in 1947/48 and at home in 1950. He badly wanted to beat them. For their part, despite a setback on their recent tour to Australia, West Indies had never been defeated in a series on their own soil. The press on both sides understandably built up the contest as the unofficial 'world championship of cricket'.

The series lived up to its billing. The play, if sometimes attritional, was almost always gripping. There were three individual double-centuries, eight hundreds and 28 other scores over fifty, but also four spectacular collapses where a total of 19 wickets fell for just 59 runs. There were some stunning catches. There were run-outs sublime and ridiculous. And yet, in the words of John Arlott, 'this tour was, in impact, so much more than a matter of batting, bowling and fielding that its events and the constituents of its atmosphere would fill several books'.

Arlott came to this conclusion in the 1955 *Wisden*, reviewing the two books by English journalists which emerged in the immediate aftermath of MCC's visit: E.W. Swanton's *West Indian Adventure* and Alex Bannister's *Cricket Cauldron*. Swanton lamented 'a tragedy of misunderstanding and muddle mattering far more than the result of the games'. Bannister regretted that 'almost from first to last a wave of prejudice, acrimony and undeniable bitterness made the tour the most unpleasant and unfortunate experience in cricket since the visit of D.R. Jardine's MCC team to Australia in 1932/33'. The general view, reflected by *The Times*, was that 1953/54 ranked as 'the second most controversial tour in cricket history'. Some of the protagonists were prepared to go even further. Tom Graveney felt Hutton's tour 'might go down as the most unpleasant, the most controversial of all time'. Clyde Walcott believed the series caused a greater 'storm' than Bodyline.

It may be more than a coincidence that full records did not survive for either tour in the Lord's archives. Yet, while Bodyline has inspired a large body of literature, no full-length account of the other extraordinary chapter in cricket history, and late-colonial history, has been produced since Swanton and Bannister.

> What do they know of cricket who only cricket know?
> C.L.R. James, *Beyond a Boundary* (1963)

Arlott's suggestion that events on the field were less than half the story anticipates this celebrated aphorism from what he was to call 'the finest book' about the game. *Beyond a Boundary* was first published the year after James's home island of Trinidad gained independence. Its rhetorical question is so often quoted that it has become a cliché, sighted on T-shirts at a quiet day's county cricket and cited in articles shelved in the dustier nooks of academic libraries.

The question's original context is James's analysis of West Indies cricket against the political background of 'nationalist passions and gains' during the period when the Caribbean islands were 'in the full tide of the transition from colonialism to independence'. The 1953/54 tour features prominently in this account. Indeed, the robust criticism of Hutton and his men in *Beyond a Boundary* provides a running commentary, from a West Indian perspective, on the carefully worded tour report in the 1955 *Wisden*.

The umpiring – as so often in the age before neutral officials – was a persistent issue. *Wisden* confessed: 'To a man the MCC team recognised their responsibilities as ambassadors of sport, but, being human, the less phlegmatic did not always hide their annoyance and displeasure.' James observed more briskly that one of the reasons the English team became 'actively disliked' was 'unsportsmanlike behaviour by individuals'.

Wisden was pained to admit that the tour was marred by 'controversy and uneasiness', ascribed partly to 'the constant emphasis upon victory which the MCC players found to be stressed by English residents in the West Indies'. James was more categorical. Hutton's team 'had given the impression that it was not merely playing cricket but was out to establish the prestige of Britain and, by that, of the local whites'.

Merely in cricketing terms, Test matches had more importance when there were far fewer of them and no one-day internationals. David Frith was working in a Sydney newspaper office in 1954 and remembers being on tenterhooks for news of his idol Hutton as the scores were cabled across. His sense that 'in those days Test series stood out so wonderfully' is supported by the fact Hutton's tour was sometimes on the front page of newspapers in Britain and always on the front page in the West Indies.

Many of the headlines were lurid. There were so many incidents on and off the field that Reg Hayter, the journalist who wrote up the tour for *Wisden*, found he had exceeded his Reuters word limit halfway through the series. This caused him immediate issues in an age where newswires were expensive and newsprint still rationed. But he was more concerned about a decline in 'the principles of sportsmanship' and the way modern Test cricket was becoming so deadly serious.

From other perspectives, cricket could seem gloriously, or ridiculously, trivial: 'One sunny afternoon, whilst Peter May is making a century at Lord's against Middlesex ... and the old men are dozing in the Long Room, a hydrogen bomb may explode.' The Yorkshire-born theatre critic Harold Hobson made this observation later in the decade, but 1954 has often been described as the year of the H-Bomb, the moment when it became clear that the second generation of nuclear weapons could annihilate humankind.

The Cold War was undeniably a constituent of the tour's atmosphere. Four months before British Guiana hosted the third Test, Winston Churchill's government was so disturbed by the Communist tendencies of the colony's democratically elected nationalist leaders that it placed some of them under house arrest, suspended the constitution and shipped in a battalion of the Argyll and Sutherland Highlanders. Graveney and Hutton – perhaps with some help from their ghostwriters – later reflected that the MCC team had been thrown into a 'vat of unrest' and an 'impossible vortex'. If the cricketers on both sides really were playing for national prestige, it had become an intense and complex thing.

'A race has been freed, but a society has not been formed'

Lord Harris, Governor of Trinidad (1848)

The third Lord Harris made this remark a decade after the abolition of slavery in the British West Indies took practical effect in 1838. In the century between Emancipation and the Second World War, not much changed for the former slaves except their legal status. The islands essentially remained sugar 'monocultures', the very term suggestive of what the St Lucian poet Derek Walcott called a 'malarial enervation', and an economic dependence on one export crop now subject to the vagaries of the world economy. In the 1930s a ton of sugar sometimes sold for less than a cricket ball, circumstances which led to serious labour unrest across the region. The complete findings of the 1938 Moyne Commission, sent out from London to investigate the causes, were not published for the duration of the war because of their potential propaganda value to the Germans.

Cricket arguably played a more central role in the formation of West Indian society than any sport anywhere in the world. The fourth Lord Harris, born in Trinidad while his father was Governor, promoted the idea that nothing which 'ever came out of England has had such an influence on character and nation-building as this wonderful game of ours'. As *éminence grise* of MCC from the last years of Victoria to the eve of Bodyline, he believed that cricket had a crucial role in 'connecting together every part of the British Empire' and, in theory at least, connecting all races and classes within each Dominion and colony. Pelham Warner, also born in Trinidad, assumed both Harris's role at MCC and his faith in cricket's civilising mission. He took pleasure in the way the game was loved by 'the whole population' of the West Indies and suggested that any Governor of Barbados should have played cricket for his public school. The image the British cultivated of themselves, as benevolent trustees teaching 'backward' races the rules of the constitutional game, was reinforced by the way the politicians negotiating independence, whether they were white, brown or black, were also sometimes Blues.

From the perspective of the governed, the only respectable routes for aspirational browns and blacks were to marry up, to cram up or to pad up. C.L.R. James, who took all three, liked to quote the words of his friend and fellow Trinidadian Learie Constantine: cricket was one of the few ways to prove 'they are no better than we'. James believed his people, playing it on the beaches and playing it on the streets, had found not only a means of self-expression but also a potent symbol of 'national' consciousness, which he trusted would be realised in a Federation of independent islands. Tony Cozier's observation that cricket 'is the one West Indian endeavour which has endured without fragmentation' is intended as a tribute to this vast cultural investment in the game. But it also invites an inference drawn by his father Jimmy: 'Unity is not the strongest feature of the West Indian character.'

West Indies cricket has always been literally insular. During and after the war, its fiercely competitive inter-island rivalry improved the level of play but also heightened the level of parochialism. Furthermore, cricket's ability to serve as the game of the empire and the game of the people was coming under increasing strain. Not only did its encouragement of racial integration and social mobility usually stop at the boundary edge, but the sport itself preserved discrimination in its own structures, most notably in the unwritten rule about the captaincy of the West Indies team. In 1953/54, Jim Laker might not have been thinking just about his own side when he regretted that 'the issue became one of white man versus the coloured man rather than a game of cricket'.

> 'Great Britain has lost an empire and has not yet found a role'
> Dean Acheson, former US Secretary of State (1962)

Acheson touched a raw nerve with this observation, made when Britain's remaining colonial holdings, including the major ones in the British West Indies, were being liquidated on a more bracing timetable than previously envisaged. Towards the end of the war, Britain still ruled nearly 800 million people outside her own borders. After the handover of Hong Kong in 1997, the number remaining was calculated at 168,075. Back in 1964, James Bond, a new configuration of the English gentleman created by Ian Fleming in Jamaica, was taking a quantum of solace in the qualities which had withstood the wind of change: 'The liberation of our Colonies may have gone too fast, but we still climb Everest and beat plenty of the world at plenty of sports.'

At the point of Hutton's tour, in the winter after the Coronation and the conquest of Everest, Britain still hoped that relations with what the Queen had called her 'Imperial family' would represent a managed continuation rather than a scuttling repudiation of empire. While statues of Viceroys had been coming down in India since 1947, during Coronation year statues went up in London to General Gordon and David Livingstone. The Duke of Edinburgh also unveiled the Imperial Memorial Gallery at Lord's. It is true that in April 1954 the Movement for Colonial Freedom was formed, its treasurer Anthony Wedgwood Benn describing the ending of empire as 'a moral challenge parallel with the moral challenge of slavery in the last century'. But, later in the same year, Enoch Powell was among the Tory MPs who formed the Suez Group in an attempt to keep British troops in the canal zone, and so restore 'faith in Britain's imperial mission and destiny'.

At home, mainstream opinion fell somewhere between these two ends of the spectrum. The people who still believed most strongly in an imperial destiny, and in beating the world at sports, were the settler minorities in the remaining colonies. If Hutton's men came home traumatised by their experience of the 'colour question', this was due not just to the hostility of nationalists who wanted independence from Britain but also to the desperation of loyalists who did not. Player-manager Charles Palmer recollected that 'every day on the tour we were being invited to social functions, invariably with the white people'. They kept telling him that beating the West Indies cricket team was 'a matter of life or death'. Palmer, far from seeking to establish the prestige of local whites as James suggested, became disillusioned with the stakes being attached to the series: 'We wanted to win, but not for them.'

English players and journalists were also informed, at certain functions, that a black captain would spell 'the end of Test cricket in the West Indies'. If many had arrived without a grasp of how colour permeated every nuance of status in the Caribbean, they were more familiar with the attitudes of the local elite who 'thought it was a humiliation for them to be the first to have a professional captain sent out from England'. As that first professional captain, Hutton quickly realised he was not qualified to deal with all the issues confronting him. He was better acquainted with another intransigent elite, the Marylebone Cricket Club, working behind his back in London. On the 1953/54 tour, the imperial mindset and the amateur ethos were dancing one of their last duets.

Who Only Cricket Know is in three parts. Part I has three pairs of chapters on the background to the series, beginning with the two Test victories which, through the established power of radio in the West Indies in 1950 and the emerging power of television in England in 1953, seemed so symbolic of national prestige. On the other hand, the selection of the two teams in 1953/54 tended to highlight divisions of race and class, sharpened in the Caribbean by insular rivalry, in England by the north-south divide, and in both cases by the distinction between amateurs and professionals. The two captains, Jeffrey Stollmeyer, the amateur, and Len Hutton, the professional, provide striking examples of the interplay between individual personalities and historical forces which makes the 1953/54 series so fascinating.

At the heart of Part II are the five Test matches. They all have remarkable storylines in their own right, even before we try to eavesdrop on the confidences of the dressing rooms and try to understand the complexities of each host island.

Part III looks at the aftermath of the tour. Its first two chapters draw on the Lord's archives to show how MCC sought to punish Trueman, Bailey and Hutton for perceived breaches of the amateur ethos (even though Bailey was technically an amateur). Its last two trace the reverberations of the 1953/54 series in the West Indies, up to the point when Frank Worrell triumphed as the first tenured black captain of the cricket team, just as the political project of Federation was collapsing.

PART I

THE BUILD-UP

Two Balcony Scenes

CHAPTER 1

LORD'S 1950

> I can hear them now, clearly as if it were yesterday. The
> excited, pleasure-drunk voices, the humming music of
> the steel percussion band … they come back to me
> with vivid clarity. For this was our greatest moment, the
> occasion for which West Indies cricket had waited and
> worked, hoped and played, for so long.

Clyde Walcott began his autobiography with an evocative account of
the celebrations following West Indies' first Test victory on English
soil at Lord's in 1950. When he wrote a second set of memoirs
nearly 50 years after the event, he lingered again over this 'symbolic
moment in our lives and in the lives of millions of our countrymen',
the moment Clive Lloyd would call 'VE Day'.

Walcott had batted with heroic intensity to help set England
an impossible target of 601. In a dressing room crowded with
opponents, officials and well-wishers, he raised a ceremonial glass
of champagne, graciously laid on by MCC. Victory was then toasted
even more appropriately. Captain John Goddard, whose family's
business interests in Barbados included a rum distillery, had brought
eight cases to England, duly impounded by Customs and Excise.
Goddard, perhaps tempting fate as his spinners began to get on top,
had taken some bottles out of bond. Walcott was not a seasoned
drinker but went with the flow:

> And all the time, as 'Goddard's Gold Braid Rum' sank
> – and our spirits rose, unbelievably, higher – we kept
> repeating to each other that we had won, not at Lord's,
> but at *Headquarters*. That was the thing which made
> the victory so wonderful to us.

Walcott's italics reinforce the significance of the long-awaited moment coming at the physical home of the Imperial Cricket Conference and at the spiritual home of cricket. The West Indians felt they had been cheated in the first Test by a doctored ash-heap of a wicket at Old Trafford. But this made even sweeter their breakthrough victory on the sacred sward of Lord's.

The voices of the players wafting across the balcony were answered by a group of supporters who had congregated in front of the pavilion. The steel percussion band Walcott enjoyed was improvised out of dustbin lids, cheese graters and bone discs on wire. There remains some debate about how many West Indian supporters were actually there, how robustly the police and MCC staff reacted to what Godfrey Evans called their 'joyous – rather riotous' progress across the Lord's turf, how their commemorative calypso was composed and how many times they lapped the statue of Eros in Piccadilly Circus during their procession through London.

Usually less debated is the status of the calypso as the most famous song written about the game. *Victory Test Match*, better known as 'Cricket, Lovely Cricket', was released by Lord Beginner (Egbert Moore), although Lord Kitchener (Aldwyn Roberts) also claimed paternity rights. Their Lordships had both come to Britain on the *Empire Windrush* in 1948. Whatever their precise contributions, the calypso celebrated a moment of uncomplicated joy ('People shout and jump without fear') where any insular rivalries were set aside ('West Indies voices all blended'). The song took care to namecheck players from all of the 'Big Four' colonies which then made up the cricket team: Barbados, British Guiana, Jamaica, Trinidad. The famous description of Ramadhin and Valentine as 'those little pals of mine' proposed a close connection between player and fan, but also celebrated the fact that two cricketers from Trinidad and Jamaica were 'pals' across national and ethnic divides. Ramadhin was the special hero of 1950 because he was the first player of 'East Indian' origin to be selected for West Indies.

The team's own celebrations continued long into the night, moving on to the Kingsley Hotel, where the flags of the 'Big Four' had been hastily raised. The party ended up in Room 326, a number which happened to tally with the margin of victory. Vice-captain Jeffrey Stollmeyer, the only survivor from the previous Lord's Test of 1939, confessed to not remembering much about the festivities. He did recall being pleased to see four of the pre-war tourists joining in: 'It was as much their day as ours.'

Stollmeyer was conscious that 1950 was the golden jubilee of the first West Indies tour of England. However well they had performed at home since gaining Test status in 1928, their record in the 'mother country' had been chastening: played 9, lost 6, drawn 3. Walcott's thoughts also turned to the 'great names' of this first phase of West Indies cricket: George Challenor, Learie Constantine, George Headley.

Walcott had attended the same school in Barbados as Challenor but it is still striking that, at least in 1950, he accepted without much strain a rich white amateur's status as the founding father of West Indian batsmanship. Challenor, who held his own playing against Grace, Ranji and MacLaren, was perceived to be the link between the golden age of imperial cricket and the emergence of a more indigenous West Indian style exemplified by the Three Ws. But he had been well past his best on the 1928 tour to England, when West Indies' inaugural Tests were all lost by an innings.

The Trinidadian Constantine, the most exciting all-rounder in inter-war cricket, had won a match at Lord's on that tour, against Middlesex, virtually on his own and virtually on one leg. He or his father had taken part in every West Indies tour to England before the Second World War, and he was there to celebrate the victory as a BBC commentator. Constantine was an A-list one-day cricketer in an age when one-day cricket was not considered List A. He had been the pioneer for West Indians plying their trade, and honing their skills, as professionals in the northern leagues. But in international cricket Constantine had become disillusioned by what he called the 'dead hand' of prejudice, feeling he had sometimes been 'manipulated' out of the side. He stated repeatedly that West Indies must be prepared to appoint a black captain in order to fulfil the team's potential at Test level.

Headley, the first great black specialist batsman and the first great Jamaican cricketer, scored centuries in both innings to set up West Indies' first Test victory over England at home in 1929/30. He repeated the feat, this time in a losing cause, at Lord's in 1939. Headley, if less overtly than Constantine, had also tired of the prevailing system. It was alleged he had been manouevred out of the 1950 tour by the West Indies Cricket Board of Control. He supported the team by telegram and by attending some of the games played in the north. But during the Lord's Test he was otherwise engaged – by Bacup in the Lancashire League.

There is a strong sense that the 1950 team felt they were revenging previous humiliations, and also refuting what Arlott called 'the widespread and mildly disapproving generalisation that West Indian cricketers are too "carefree" to win Test matches'. Everton Weekes had been irritated by references in the English press to 'a bunch of calypsonians'; Stollmeyer by the way they seemed more interested in 'the amount of rum we had brought with us' than the team's cricketing credentials. The victory at Lord's, and equally heavy wins in the final two Tests, exploded other stereotypes. England were defeated not by the battering pace already associated with West Indian teams, but by paralysing spin. The measured opening partnerships of Stollmeyer and Allan Rae, preparing the ground for 'daddy' hundreds from all Three Ws, proved that Caribbean batsmen could play with discipline as well as flair.

According to the typecast, West Indian team spirit would fall apart under pressure. For Weekes, another to consider the Lord's triumph the highpoint of his career, the togetherness of the side was its great achievement: 'We were a mixed race team, the only one of its kind in Test cricket, Indians, blacks, whites, Jews, Portuguese, we had everything.' In the particular case of Lord's in 1950, Weekes was one of the blacks, the Indian was Ramadhin, the white was Goddard and the players of Jewish and Portuguese heritage were Stollmeyer and Gerry Gomez. By the time West Indies next returned to England in 1957, the rum-magnate Goddard, controversially recalled as captain despite the stronger claims of Frank Worrell, Stollmeyer and Rae, proved a divisive figure. But in 1950 the West Indies dressing room achieved a unity as precious as it was fragile.

A delegation of the British West Indies and British Guiana Sugar Association happened to be in London for another round of protracted negotiations with the Colonial Office on the guaranteed quotas still crucial to the region's economy. Its leader was Albert Gomes, sometimes described as Trinidad's 'largest export' because of his voracious appetites. Gomes may have timed the visit so that he could take in the cricket and other sporting events. He admitted he succumbed 'to the festive inducements' at the Derby on a later trip, and in 1950 he joined the celebrations in the Lord's dressing room with characteristic enthusiasm. He trusted that governments in the islands back home would show 'sufficient imagination' to declare public holidays:

> The victory has done more for the morale of West
> Indians in the West Indies, and for his prestige in
> Britain, than all the speeches and achievements
> of politicians at home in the British West Indies
> and abroad. I sincerely hope it will sweeten the
> negotiations.

This risked being just another speech. Gomes, once a beacon of resistance to colonial rule in pre-war Trinidad, was now thought by many to have sold out his principles for the plumage of political office. But his belief that a Federation of West Indian islands provided the best path to independence was at that point shared by a younger generation of budding politicians, who had all studied at the London School of Economics after the war: Errol Barrow of Barbados, Forbes Burnham of British Guiana, Michael Manley of Jamaica. Manley, who seems to have watched a lot of cricket in 1950, later remembered that the Lord's victory felt like 'the proof that a people was coming of age'.

Back home, the power of cricket combined with the power of radio to produce an outpouring of joy and pride which seemed to sweep across all classes and races. West Indians had been receiving uninterrupted ball-by-ball commentary long before the British. In 1950, particularly as a rights dispute deprived them of newsreel footage, they followed short-wave radio coverage obsessively.

In Trinidad, Philip Thomson, like Stollmeyer a member of the elite Queen's Park Cricket Club, would time his lunch-hours to listen to the closing overs on the Radio Rediffusion box nailed to his living-room wall. He sometimes arrived back at work late on the grounds that the cricket 'easily outweighed in importance' any emergency at his insurance practice. Out in the sugar fields, Tony Deyal's family were probably less able to extend their lunch-breaks. But among his earliest memories were the Lord's calypso and the celebrations of his father and uncle 'coming home high on victory and the spirits of the cane they grew and reaped', boasting about their ex-workmate Ramadhin.

In Jamaica, a Kingston councillor noted that 'radio commentary of the match has drawn from even the conservative element … high sounding superlatives'. *The Daily Gleaner*, usually part of that element, published a cartoon of Hutton cowering beneath Valentine's sword-arm.

In British Guiana, a 15-year-old Lance Gibbs crouched close to his crackling wireless 'to hear what was going on'. He remembered being 'extremely proud' of 'Walcott making 168 at Lord's and the calypso coming out: "Those little pals of mine…"'

In Barbados, Sir Alan Collymore, president of the island's Cricket Association as well as its Chief Justice, could not listen to the commentary because he was presiding over a murder trial. But he made 'certain arrangements' to have the scores passed to him at seemly intervals. 'We won! We won it at Lord's!' Collymore is supposed to have blurted out as everyone in the court cheered, 'none more loudly than the accused'. Sir Alan played a prominent part in the celebrations when the Barbados contingent arrived home. A public holiday was duly declared. There is no record of whether the defendant was free to participate but, according to Walcott, 'half the population of Barbados seemed to be on the quayside' before a motorcade took the players to a reception in Trafalgar Square.

The emphasis in Collymore's official circles was on the invaluable role played by 'cricketing ambassadors' in 'fostering and cementing diplomatic relations between the Mother Country and the West Indies'. Weekes took more pleasure from the 'the natural joy and happiness on the faces of our people'. Either way, the ethos of the cricket team could provide a blueprint for multicultural societies moving towards independence.

If Walcott thought about the achievement of 1950 in terms of cricketing traditions and the reaction back home, he was also well aware of its importance to West Indians migrating to Britain: 'In those days, coloured people or black people, whatever you want to call them, were more or less given a hard time. And they said how … proud they felt to go into work the next day or the Monday or whenever it was, having beaten England.'

The next day was actually a Friday. Llewelyn Barrow, who had collapsed into bed fully clothed, probably stayed there. But the experiences of watching the victory from the G Stand at Lord's, and the ensuing bacchanal led by Lord Kitchener, gave him exactly the sense of self-worth described by Walcott: 'We was proud of the cricket team, of course, but we was proud of weself too.' Barrow had left Trinidad for Kilburn in 1949. The joy he took in beating England 'bad-bad, at the cradle of cricket' provided some reparation for the welcome the Windrush generation often received, 'a real Arctic feeling, bad-bad-indifferent and even enemy hostile'. That hostile environment was infamously recreated by a 21st-century British government. Back in the early 1950s, two of the celebrants at Lord's, Kitchener and Constantine, were already bearing witness to it.

'London is the place for me', Kitchener sang for a Pathé newsreel after disembarking zoot-suited from the *Windrush*. But this ideal of a 'magnificent' and 'comfortable' life in Britain quickly gave way to calypsos recording a reality which left the migrant 'sorry' and 'crying'; the general sentiment 'English people are very much sociable' to the personal experience of 'my landlady's too rude'.

Constantine was one of many West Indians who had supported the British war effort, not least by appearing in morale-boosting cricket matches at Lord's. But on one such occasion, in 1943, he was refused accommodation he had pre-booked at the Imperial Hotel in Russell Square. Its Irish manageress explained it would be impossible to take in 'niggers' while American servicemen were staying there. Constantine won a landmark court case, if only for breach of contract, and would continue to trust in what he called the British 'sense of fair play' by becoming one of the first members of the Race Relations Board in the 1960s. But in his 1954 book, *Colour Bar*, he starkly catalogued the humiliations of life as a 'Negro-in-England'.

Bullying at the workplace, discrimination at the guesthouse, hostility (at least from English men) at the dancehall: these experiences were also brought to life in two novels published in the mid-1950s, *The Lonely Londoners* by Sam Selvon and *The Emigrants* by George Lamming. Just as Kitchener and Beginner shared a passage on the *Windrush*, Selvon and Lamming sailed together to Britain only weeks before the cricketers arrived in 1950. It would be trite to call them the Ramadhin and Valentine of Caribbean literature, which flowered as vibrantly as Caribbean music and Caribbean cricket after the war. But Lamming trusted that he and Selvon, respectively the direct descendants of an enslaved African and an indentured Indian, could become symbols of 'political unity and creative pride'.

For Lamming, the Test team was another symbolic portent of a brave new world. Like Weekes, he trusted its distinctive rainbow of 'Indian, Negro, Chinese, White, Portuguese mixed with Syrian' demonstrated how traditional divisions in West Indian society might be bridged. Selvon's short story *The Cricket Match* also showed, with mordant comedy, how enthusiasm for the game could act as a bridge into English culture for the Windrush generation.

However, for them cricket became less about making friendships than making statements. Lamming recognised the paradox that 'no islander from the West Indies sees himself as a West Indian until he encounters another islander in foreign territory'. It needed a journey of 3,000 miles for people from islands sometimes a few miles apart to take a collective pride in the West Indies and in its first federated institution – the cricket team.

In a related paradox, the racial assumptions that had underlain the empire were being more starkly exposed now that its subjects were coming to live in the 'mother country'. Lord Kitchener encapsulated the disorientation of migrants, accustomed to intricate social gradations based on skin colour, discovering a binary distinction in Britain: 'You can never get away from the fact | If you not white you considered black.' In *Colour Bar*, Constantine made this point in broader terms, warning British readers that racism was not only a recruiting officer for Communism but might one day unite the 'whole coloured world'. Here are the seeds of the more monochrome consciousness given expression in the Black-Power activism of the late 1960s, the cricketing Blackwashes of the mid-1980s and the Black Lives Matter movement of today.

As a Jamaican character in *The Emigrants* put it, most of the 1950 team was out 'to prove something', to beat the old master at his own game. The refrain Weekes used to celebrate – 'London Bridge is falling down' – had been sung on the plantations. And the historian Hilary Beckles tells the story of a Barbadian migrant who went to work on the buses, in a hired tuxedo, the day after the victory at Headquarters:

> Winning the series 3-1, the first time we beat them wasn't the big thing. It was Lord's, son – going in to their own backyard and taking their chickens out of the coop and frying them on the front lawn. For me son, the empire collapse right there; not Churchill or Wellington could bring it back.

CHAPTER 2

THE OVAL 1953

Whether or not England regained the Ashes in 1953, the nation was guaranteed one balcony scene that year – at Buckingham Palace. On the early evening of 2 June, nearly 16 million people were still congregated around their television sets, or more likely the set somebody in their street had just bought or rented, to see the newly crowned Queen wave to the massed throngs in The Mall.

Roy Strong was one of two Edmonton County Grammar schoolboys selected to be bussed into central London for the Coronation procession. It struck him as 'glittering, glamorous, effulgent', an awe-inspiring contrast with the monochrome grey of bomb-cratered, smog-choked, teeth-chattering austerity: 'This was the England I fell in love with, a country proud of its great traditions and springing to life again in a pageant that seemed to inaugurate a second Elizabethan age.'

England captain Len Hutton remembered tapping into this 'swell of popular sentiment'. At the start of the season, Neville Cardus of the *Manchester Guardian* told him to 'go and win' the Ashes for the new Queen. At the start of the series, Geoffrey Green of *The Times* told him to come out showing 'the Elizabethan spirit'. Hutton also recalled that the Test matches were played out against the backdrop of 'momentous' events in other fields. Perhaps 1953 marks the moment when the concept of the 'Summer of Sport' entered the national consciousness as well as the social diary.

Green was the *Times* correspondent at the Empire Stadium, on the first Saturday of May, covering what became the 'Matthews Final'. After two previous Wembley heartaches, the 38-year-old Stanley Matthews finally fulfilled a promise made to his late father by helping orchestrate Blackpool's extraordinary comeback from 3-1 down to beat Bolton Wanderers 4-3 in added time. Green correctly predicted that the match would go down in folklore, partly because of the wizardry of Matthews, partly because of 'the magic screen of television' and partly because of the magic link with monarchy:

'Here in the presence of the Queen and the Duke of Edinburgh, the game of football … was crowned with all felicity in this year of Coronation and national rejoicing.'

Coronation Day itself, which *The Times* described as 'the nation's feast of mystical renewal', was further enriched by the efforts of its correspondent, James Morris, to get a coded telegram through in time for the newspaper to report the conquest of Everest that morning. The triumphant Commonwealth expedition fitted perfectly into the Queen's own fresh narrative of 'an equal partnership of nations and races'. But the attainment of the last great geographical prize on the planet was still unmistakably a 'British victory', led by Colonel John Hunt for the Alpine Club. The club had helped organise nine previous British expeditions, including the one in 1924 led by General Bruce where Mallory and Irvine had died attempting the summit. The way Hunt had combined old-fashioned Corinthian spirit with state-of-the-art British technology provided 'no better omen for the beginning of a new Elizabethan age'.

Four days later, on the first Saturday in June, came the 'Richards Derby'. Gordon Richards, despite riding more winners than any other British jockey, had endured nearly three decades of failure in the most important classic. Now he prevailed at last before a crowd of more than half a million on Epsom Downs. Richards noted the added 'piquancy' of beating into second a horse owned by the Queen, who had just knighted him in her Coronation Honours List.

The fight for the Ashes was therefore built up, like all three of the events which had preceded it, as a quest for the ultimate prize after repeated, bitter disappointments. Twenty years had elapsed since England had last won a series against Australia – even that triumph carrying a moral asterisk because of Bodyline – and 27 since they had last won at home. The post-war score measured in individual Tests stood at Australia 11 England 1. And the one had been in a dead rubber. English supporters were long overdue some unrationed joy as well as some unrationed tea.

The West Indies had played an innocent role in the coincidence of Coronation year and Ashes year. 'Gubby' Allen, captain of the singularly unsuccessful MCC tour there in 1947/48, returned home convinced that the international schedule needed to be changed so that England teams could be better prepared. One result of his initiative was that the Australians' next visit was pushed back from 1952 to 1953.

The optimism generated by the Coronation preparations made Jack Fingleton quickly realise that 'interest in England in a coming series has never approached this, not even in Bradman's days'. Fingleton had played under the Don in 1938 and reported on his all-conquering tour in 1948. The fact that Bradman would now be sitting alongside him in the press box gave the English genuine belief they could at last regain the Ashes. The breathing space engineered by Allen was also helpful: Trueman, Statham and Lock had all emerged in the interim, while the formidable combination Hutton referred to as 'Lindwall-Miller-Johnston' was not getting any younger.

England's best bowler, Alec Bedser, noticed a 'tremendous upsurge' of support for cricket all over the country in Coronation year. He attributed this to the evolving medium of television but coverage of the game in the more established media was as extensive as ever. Beginning his *Test Match Diary* for 1953, Arlott pointed out that cricket lovers could now follow the game in four ways – as 'spectators, listeners, viewers or daily readers'. All of these angles were brought to life in a play originally written for BBC television by Terence Rattigan. *The Final Test* was remade as a feature film for release in early 1953 to cash in on Ashes fever, with cameo appearances by Hutton and other England players. Its situations included a capacity Oval crowd hoping rain will deny Australia victory; a group transfixed by Arlott's commentary on the pub radio; an eminent writer caught by his secretary watching the cricket on his new television; a visiting American senator alarmed by the newspaper headline 'England May Collapse Today'.

It did not rain much in the film but it rained on the Coronation and on a lot of the cricket in 1953. Paradoxically, the English weather was the final factor which created such interest in the series. The draws it caused only added to the drama. In stark contrast to the Bradman era, the Tests were low-scoring affairs with no team total above 400. What Swanton called a 'war to the knife' made for what Arlott called a 'magnificent, somersaulting, unpredictable Test series'.

There were capacity crowds at the first four days of the Lord's Test, Fingleton noting that 'some left the ground merely to queue up again' through the night. The game broke records for aggregate receipts and aggregate attendance. This was despite the stands being less full on the fifth day, when Australia seemed certain to win. That final day has gone into folklore as England's cricketing Dunkirk. It also inspired the legend that the nation downed tools to share in what Cardus described as 'the intense strain' of the match-saving partnership between Willie Watson and Trevor Bailey.

With the series still locked at nil-nil, anticipation had reached fever pitch by the time of the deciding contest at The Oval. According to some reports, 2,000 people slept outside the ground in an attempt to guarantee a first-day ticket. A 14-year-old Brian Luckhurst, later to feature in another Ashes climax, took the last bus from Sittingbourne to join the queue. The historian David Kynaston has collected some rich anecdotes to show how 'compelling' the match became, one of which involves Denis Thatcher. Having wisely paid to sit in the covered stand at the Coronation, Thatcher managed to secure a place for the opening day at The Oval. He proved impossible to contact for several hours after his wife gave birth to twins.

Conversely, those who were unable to attend in person kept in obsessive contact with the match. Michael Parkinson watched the game on a miniscule television set with a magnifying glass strapped to the front. Harold Pinter, alone in a kitchen in County Galway, was glad to find some radio coverage. John Major retired to the wireless more reluctantly. He had walked back to Brixton in tears after finding his pocket money did not stretch to the prices of the ticket touts.

The BBC radio broadcast received higher audience appreciation ratings than its coverage of the Coronation. Those following the game at home seem to have been as riveted by its twists and turns as those closer to the action. Peter West watched on from the television gantry: 'I can hardly believe that we shall ever endure again quite the same tension, the same drawn-out agonies.' Peter May had been brought back into the England side on his home ground: 'I do not remember anything like the tenseness of that Test match.'

On the first day, Australia were reduced to 118 for five, only to recover to a respectable 275. On the second, Hutton's dismissal for

82 precipitated England's decline from 154 for two to 235 for seven. As we shall see, at this crucial point of the most important game in a generation, the England captain was then required by MCC to spend the evening in a long meeting with its selection committee for the West Indies tour. On top of these distractions, Hutton worried that the odds were 'certainly in Australia's favour'. His nerves were wearing because he knew the pitch was wearing. He felt anything above 250 would be extremely difficult to chase down.

It was on the third day that Bailey acquired one of his nicknames – Barnacle – for clinging on long enough to take England into a precious first innings lead of 31. Hutton put Lock and Laker on after five overs. A.A. Thomson, working in Whitehall for the Ministry of Information, was updated by calls on the internal telephone system from a fellow civil servant:

> 'Hello?'
> 'Fifty-nine for two. It's Hole.'
> Pause and ping.
> 'Hello? Who is it?'
> 'Sixty for three. It's Harvey.'
> 'Hello. Who is it?'
> 'Sixty-one for four. It's Miller.'
> Short pause and ping-ping.
> 'Hello? Who is it now?'
> 'Sixty-one for five. Now it's Morris. They're on the run.'
> …
> 'Who is it now?'
> 'The Foreign Office,' replied a slightly outraged voice,
> 'if you have no objection'.

Over the course of four-and-a-half matches, the sides had been locked in what West called a 'long tug of war'. Now Australia had suddenly lost their grip – and four wickets in 14 minutes. They were not done with: the young players in their lower-middle order launched a spirited counter-attack. English supporters had to suffer another bout of palpitations until Lock came back to rocket through the tail.

England were 38 for one overnight, requiring another 94 to win. There are parallels with the series of 1926 and 2005 when, after similar periods of hurt, the exhilarated feeling that the Australians were finally about to be beaten was accompanied by the nagging doubt that they could ever be beaten. Hutton had uncharacteristically managed to run himself out. But, by his standards, he was now reasonably relaxed. Australia had neglected to include a genuine spinner in their team.

Television coverage in 1953 was restricted to the 15 minutes before lunch and portions of the final session, because of the perceived threat to live attendances, especially at county matches running concurrently with the Tests. MCC had 'regretfully refused' BBC's request to cover every ball at The Oval because of its duty to protect the County Championship. For the final day the governing body caved in to popular demand rather more easily than the Australians. Johnston and Lindwall made England fight for every run and were taken out of the attack only when the end was in sight.

At 2.53pm on 19 August, Denis Compton pulled an Arthur Morris long hop down towards the gasholders for four. This is almost certainly the most replayed stroke in the history of English cricket, not least because it was used for years by BBC engineers in trade-test transmissions. But it would have been replayed anyway, in schoolboy re-enactments and adult imaginations, because it brought such a long era of cricketing misery to an end. Swanton was old enough to remember the scenes in 1926, when 'the crowd let themselves go as though a reproach had been wiped away'. This time, in a pitch invasion even more exuberant than that of the West Indians at Lord's, policemen were almost knocked over in the rush to engulf Compton and his partner Bill Edrich.

It was fitting that the two Middlesex batsmen were at the crease at the moment of victory. Their buccaneering partnerships in the vintage summer of 1947 were credited with brightening up not just English cricket but English life. 'There were no rations in an innings by Compton', as Cardus put it in an oft-quoted phrase which itself brooked no rationing.

Yorkshiremen pointed out that, as in 1926 when Herbert Sutcliffe and Wilfred Rhodes played leading roles, victory would not have been possible without Hutton's sober virtues. He said the view from the pavilion balcony was 'something I will never forget'. Many never forgot their image of him. He was described by *The Times* as 'a workmanlike cricketing figure', smoking a cigarette in shirt sleeves and Yorkshire CCC tie. But for Fazal Mahmood, on a reconnaissance mission for Pakistan's entry into Test cricket the next year, 'watching him, it felt as if he was the victor of the whole world and that a whole sea of humanity had knelt in front of him'.

A.A. Thomson, moonlighting as a journalist, wrote a piece on the unalloyed joy of the moment: 'Here on the balcony stands the captain Len Hutton, as surely the architect of victory as Trevor Bailey is its most honourable bricklayer.' Thomson hailed the way Hutton had treated criticism 'with a decency and dignity that Lord Hawke could not but have admired'. The allusion was to a Hawke speech of 1925, made as Yorkshire president and MCC mandarin, which still reverberated through the game: 'Pray God that no professional shall ever captain England!'

As Hutton observed – playing himself in *The Final Test* – the world had 'moved on a bit'. Thomson's article implied that it was indeed moving on in a reassuringly gradual way. He painted a portrait of a clean-living family man who had stayed true to the 'hard school' of Yorkshire cricket but lived up to the standards expected of an England captain, 'neat as a new pin, whether in flannels, lounge suit or dinner jacket'.

When two sociologists, Edward Shils and Michael Young, talked of a 'great nation-wide communion' brought about 'through radio, television and press and in festivities', they were talking about the Coronation not the Ashes. But readers of an influential article they published in December 1953 did not have to wait long for references to the cricket:

> Something like this kind of spirit has been
> manifested before – during the Blitz, the Fuel Crisis
> of 1947, the London smog of 1952, even during the
> Watson-Bailey stand in the Lord's Test or Lock's final
> overs at the Oval...

The sociologists were contributing to a debate, which continues to this day, about the degree of consensus in post-war British society.

They were convinced that the people's deep-seated urge to knit together as a cohesive 'family' ultimately prevailed over political, social and regional differences. This had been one of the underlying messages of Rattigan's script for *The Final Test*. The *News Chronicle*, in an editorial after the real final Test, had also mused on 'the curious power of Test cricket to unify; to provide a shared experience of the human spirit, making the secret and inner thoughts of the Mile End Road comprehensible to Mayfair, and vice versa'.

Although Young was a socialist and Shils an American, they gladly extended the idea of 'family' to the Commonwealth and empire, pointing to the enthusiasm of the crowds for the colonial contingents in the Coronation procession. The balcony speeches at The Oval were certainly full of Commonwealth bonhomie. Hutton paid tribute to his twinkling opposite number Lindsay Hassett, 'who has done so much for the game, not only in Australia, but in all parts of the world'. Hassett graciously reciprocated, professing that there had 'not been one incident out of place' in such a hard-fought series.

Cricket's power to serve as the quintessence of national unity and imperial solidarity could easily be found spurious as well as curious. In victory Hutton tried to rise above 'the pinpricking criticisms of my supposed caution from predictable quarters' ('predictable' his code for both 'amateur' and 'southern'). When Hassett came off the balcony, he congratulated himself on holding his tongue 'considering Lockie threw us out'. Yet the historian Peter Hennessy reminds us that it is now difficult to appreciate first 'how easy and natural it was to get a touch carried away in 1953' and second 'how powerful a grip cricket exerted on the collective sporting *mentalité* of the English in the early postwar years'.

In one of the many felicitous coincidences of Coronation year, the Oval decider was the first Test C.L.R. James saw in the flesh since McCarthyism had driven him back to Britain from America. The last game he attended before his departure in 1938 was probably the timeless Test on the same ground. Then he had witnessed the previous transcendent moment of English cricket: Hutton's Test-record score of 364. This marathon effort restored national pride after years and years of Bradman. Even allowing for press exaggeration at a time when global conflict seemed inevitable, it also captured the imagination of millions throughout the empire.

The poet Edwin Brock suggested Hutton's innings was so talked about that it 'became the year before the war'.

For another poet, Dannie Abse, the year 1953 meant '*Vivat Regina* and the linseed willow-sound | of Compton and Edrich winning the Ashes'. James concluded, after seeing how the country 'stopped work to witness the consummation', that cricket was even more 'a part of the national activity than it used to be'. He realised this was partly because of the 'highly developed media of mass communication'. But the euphoria also confirmed his view that the 'dramatic intensity' of the game raised great cricketers to the status of admirable national types. Hutton may have cut less of a New Elizabethan figure than Compton or Edrich, but he still embodied the strong feelings of relief and reclamation which had emerged after the war. Whether he liked it or not, he would be carrying this emotional cargo with him to the West Indies.

Two Selection Processes

CHAPTER 3

PREPARATIONS IN THE WEST INDIES

Christopher Nicole, Guyanese-born novelist and cricket historian, remembered that 'throughout the summer of 1953 West Indians looked forward to the greatest trial of strength ever to be experienced in these waters'. Both the Coronation and the Coronation Ashes, followed avidly by radio in the Caribbean, were whetting the appetite for the series ahead.

Many Trinidadians took pride in Willy Richardson joining commentators like Arlott and Rex Alston on the BBC's Coronation broadcast, and the event being celebrated in a popular calypso by another of their countrymen, Young Tiger. The Coronation procession included, admittedly some way down the marching order, detachments from the Big Four colonies who would host the next winter's Tests: the Jamaica Battalion, the Barbados Regiment, the British Guiana Volunteer Force and the Trinidad Armed Police.

Meanwhile, the West Indies Cricket Board of Control announced its captain and vice-captain for the English visit as early as mid-July. At the end of that month, just after the fourth Ashes Test, MCC revealed the first tranche of its touring party, making it obvious the big guns would be sent out. Expectation continued to build and, by the late autumn, Caribbean newspapers were full of advertisements for match tickets, radio sets, binoculars and suitable refreshments endorsed by players from both sides.

Minutes of the Board of Control's meetings as it prepared for MCC's visit have never been made available. But it seems clear enough that there were internal trials of strength going on, between the different islands and between the Board and some of the players.

In 1950 the Jamaican journalist Jack Anderson lamented that 'insular prejudice had gnawed at the very core of West Indies first class cricket for generations'. Even in that year, when Goddard's triumph seemed to offer such promise of a more united future, the colonies which made up the international team were still sometimes sinking their teeth into each other. The British Guiana Cricket Association nearly boycotted the whole enterprise, after an almighty row with the Board of Control about the omission of their fast bowler John Trim. When Jamaicans celebrated the victory at Lord's on the streets of Kingston, they made a pointed reference to their absent hero: 'George or no George we win the match.' For MCC's tour in 1953/54, the itinerary, let alone the composition of the team, provoked fierce debate.

It was customary for Tests in the West Indies to be played over six days, each of five hours. The original plan for 1953/54 was a four-match series starting in Trinidad, with the other major centres taking a Test each. The Big Four, backed by the largest sugar interests, jealously guarded their first-class status against the other islands in the British West Indies, to the point that some in the smaller territories found it hard to rally round the cricket team.

At least the MCC schedule included two-day games in Antigua and Grenada (the first for a representative English side since the era of Lord Hawke). But there was little chance of players from those centres being considered for selection, especially after the promising Antiguan quick Hubert Anthonyson injured himself in the Test trial in British Guiana. An arguably faster bowler, Frank Mason of St Vincent, also played in that game. He was rated by Worrell and Weekes but apparently not by the selectors, despite the fact the West Indian pace reserves looked unusually bare.

The first of two significant alterations to the original itinerary also disappointed the islands outside the Big Four. A preparatory leg of the tour was introduced before Christmas in Bermuda, not traditionally considered a part of the British West Indies, nor considered to be rich in cricket tradition. No less than eight days of play were envisaged there, on the understanding the Bermudans would meet all expenses.

The second change was not universally well received either. The Test series was extended to five matches, with Jamaica now hosting the first and last games. Whether measured by size or population,

Jamaica was nearly bigger than all the other British islands put together. This was one reason for what the historian Gordon Lewis called its 'notorious psychological alienation' from the eastern Caribbean. The other was that Port-au-Prince, Havana and Miami are much closer to Kingston than Port of Spain, Georgetown and Bridgetown.

The award of the extra Test sparked a predictable spat between Jamaica, the largest island, and Trinidad, which thanks to its oil reserves was now the least impoverished. Offence was also taken in Barbados, 25 times smaller than Jamaica but confident that its cricket traditions were several times stronger. Meanwhile, the Guyanese, from the only British colony on the mainland of South America, felt – with some justification – that their significant contribution to West Indies cricket was always underestimated.

In 1953/54, each colony's press, particularly in its sports pages, tended to spend as much time obsessing about the faults of its 'foreign' neighbours as about the colonial system which kept them looking more towards London than to each other. Among the various stereotypes in such diatribes, Jamaicans could be caricatured as too fiery, Barbadians as too starchy, Trinidadians as too laid-back and Guyanese as too backward.

The British and Irish Lions provide an imprecise analogy for an international team drawn from four nations, ostensibly united by a common cause and language but potentially divided by different traditions and accents. A side drawn from the diverse environments of the Welsh valleys, the Scottish borders, the English public schools and the Irish universities had to be well managed, as was the case on their tied tour of South Africa in 1955 (although the appointment of an Irish captain and the number of Welsh players in the party had been questioned beforehand). The differences between the Big Four colonies in the Caribbean were arguably more pronounced, partly a matter of size and history, as shown in the table overleaf, but also environmental and temperamental. There were, for example, several reasons why slave revolts had been most frequent in Jamaica, but one explanation was the protection its mountainous interior offered to guerrillas.

MCC tour of the West Indies 1953/54

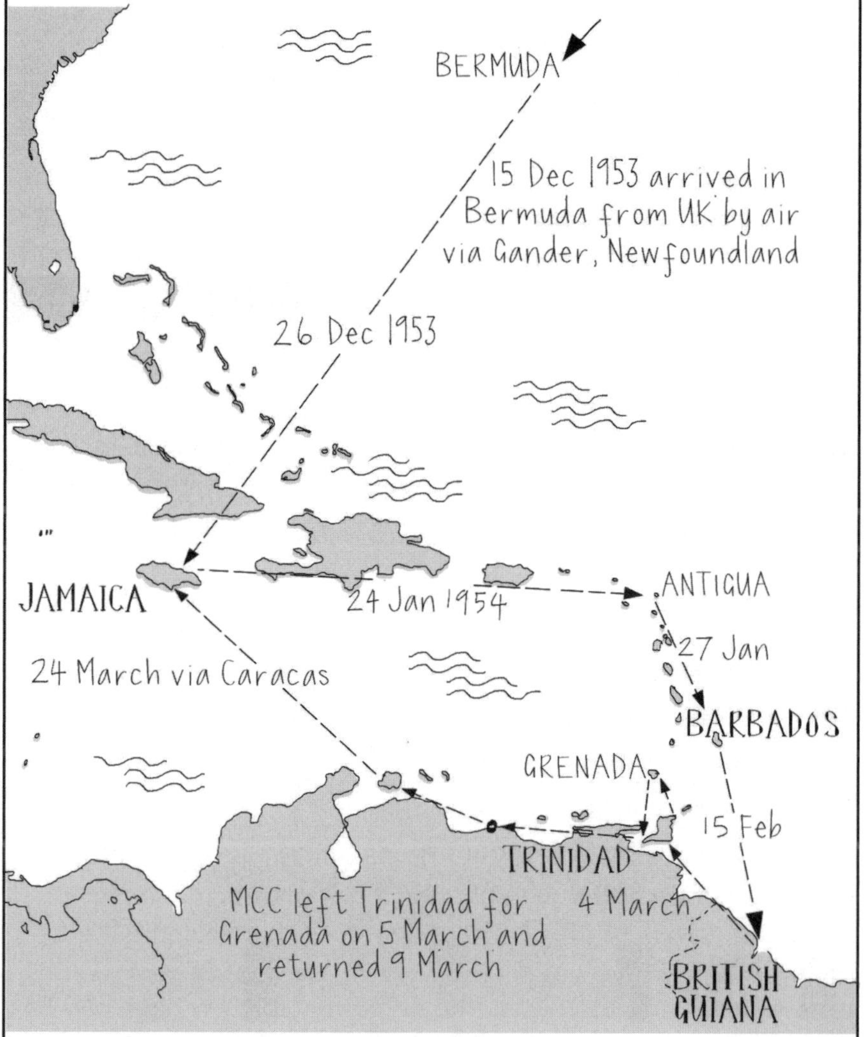

BERMUDA

15 Dec 1953 arrived in Bermuda from UK by air via Gander, Newfoundland

26 Dec 1953

JAMAICA

24 Jan 1954

ANTIGUA

27 Jan

24 March via Caracas

BARBADOS

GRENADA

15 Feb

TRINIDAD

MCC left Trinidad for Grenada on 5 March and returned 9 March

4 March

BRITISH GUIANA

FIRST TEST   Jamaica 15-21 Jan
SECOND TEST   Barbados 6-12 Feb
THIRD TEST   British Guiana 24 Feb-2 Mar
FOURTH TEST   Trinidad 17-23 Mar
FIFTH TEST   Jamaica 30 Mar-3 Apr

	JAMAICA
Area (mi²):	4,240
Roughly equivalent to:	Yorkshire
Population c.1954:	1,520,000
Equivalent c.1954:	Birmingham plus Nottingham
Date of British colonisation:	1655
Date of universal suffrage:	1944
Date of independence:	1962
British Governor in 1954:	Hugh Foot
Sugar production in 1954 (tonnes):	363,303
Population mix c.1954 Black Indian Brown White Other	78% 2% 18% 1% 1%
Adult literacy rate (post-war census):	76%
Emigrants to UK in 1950s (as % of home population):	9.2%
Test cricketers up to 1954 with more than two caps:	10

BARBADOS	BRITISH GUIANA	TRINIDAD
167	83,000 (coastal plain: 1,000)	1,981
Isle of Wight	British Isles (coastal plain: Oxfordshire)	Lancashire (pre-1974)
225,000	465,000 (90% on coastal plain)	717,000
Coventry	Bristol	Manchester
1627	1814	1802
1950	1952	1945
1966	1966	1962
Robert Arundell	Alfred Savage	Hubert Rance
178,960	238,922	172,769
77% 0% 17% 5% 1%	36% 46% 11% 1% 6%	45% 36% 15% 2% 2%
93%	79%	77%
8.1%	1.3%	1.2%
19	6	15

43

Trinidad had been awarded two Tests in West Indies' first five-match home series against India the previous winter. Jamaicans will have lobbied for an appropriate gesture in return, especially as they were still rebuilding after a devastating hurricane in 1951. The upcoming general election of 1955 may have been another factor. Modern political consciousness, or at least a nascent two-party system along Westminster lines, had evolved most quickly in Jamaica. The Jamaica Labour Party (JLP) was led by the buccaneering Alexander Bustamante. Despite its name, the JLP was to the right of the People's National Party (PNP), led by Bustamante's cousin, the Rhodes scholar Norman Manley. Bustamante had won the first election under universal suffrage in 1944 by playing on the black majority's fears that 'self-government meant brown man rule'. The success of this strategy carried some irony, given that the party leaders were brown men under the local definition.

Both parties were aware of the importance of sport in nation-building (and vote-winning). Donald Sangster, the JLP's Minister for Finance, had captained his parish cricket team in 1949. He helped arrange the first Australian tour to the West Indies, scheduled for the year after MCC's visit. His opposite number in the PNP, Noel 'Crab' Nethersole, had once captained Jamaica. On his home island's Cricket Association, Nethersole had long advocated the game's role in racial integration: one of the local cup competitions was named after him. On the West Indies Board of Control, he was perhaps the strongest proponent of regional solidarity.

If Jamaica was the main breeding ground of West Indian nationalism, it had initially played a peripheral role in the evolution of West Indian cricket. It never participated formally in inter-colonial competition because of the distances involved: Kingston is nearly as far away from Georgetown as London is from Moscow. And, before the emergence of Headley, Jamaica tended to lose heavily to visiting English sides and to have only token (and usually white) representation on West Indian tours.

Although by 1953 Jamaican cricket was much more developed, the other islands felt the allocation of two Tests was still disproportionate to its cricketing strength. At a more practical level, critics of the decision were not convinced that the ground would always be full at Sabina Park, whereas they believed capacity crowds could be guaranteed at the Kensington and Queen's Park Ovals in Barbados and Trinidad. One letter to the *Trinidad Guardian* huffed that Jamaica 'should play their own cricket, as they have too high an opinion of their prowess'.

As the presidency of the Board of Control had recently transferred from the Jamaican Karl Nunes to the Trinidadian Sir Errol dos Santos, there was a natural assumption that Jamaica had gained the extra Test by promising to make concessions elsewhere. The selectorial process had always been characterised by horse-trading about the precise 'quotas' from each colony and the question of the captaincy. MCC's previous visit, in 1947/48, provided a particularly striking example.

In that series, Headley became the first black captain of West Indies (Constantine had skippered the side temporarily when white captains were off the field). For Headley to lead out the team in Barbados, the most reactionary of the Big Four colonies, might have appeared a watershed moment. But he was appointed on the basis that he would step down for Jeffrey Stollmeyer for the second Test in Trinidad and John Goddard for the third in British Guiana, only resuming the leadership for the final game on his home island.

Headley's main advocate within the Board of Control was Crab Nethersole. Yet there was obvious resistance to the initiative, from insular forces in other colonies and from reactionary forces in Jamaica. In his understated way, Headley remembered being not 'altogether a popular appointment'. As it turned out, he played only in Barbados because he was struggling with a back injury. Many suspected that he was struggling more with the prospect of returning to the ranks under less experienced officers. Then Stollmeyer pulled a hamstring and was denied the chance to fulfil his already transparent ambition to skipper West Indies. His close friend and cricket lieutenant Gerry Gomez took over in Trinidad, but it was the Barbadian Goddard who led West Indies to victory in the final two matches of the series and cemented his position as captain.

Goddard might be likened to Brian Close without the cricket brain. At his best, he led by example: a fearless close fielder, a determined batsman in a crisis and a useful bowler in two styles (off-cutters and off-spinners). Stollmeyer occasionally acknowledged his 'abundance of guts' but consistently criticised his 'deep-seated and nonchalant disregard for tactical forethought and strategic planning'. This contempt was fuelled partly by his own aspirations, and partly by an inter-island jealousy which Clyde Walcott thought was 'always' in play between the captains of Trinidad and Barbados.

When Stollmeyer sniffed that Goddard 'on his own admission, had never read a cricket book', he revealed another side to the rivalry. Stollmeyer was not by British West Indian standards the worst of snobs but he looked down on Goddard, the product of a family of underprivileged 'redleg' whites who had made their fortune in trade.

The cracks in team solidarity, which success had papered over in England in 1950, widened like a fifth-day pitch during Goddard's tour of Australia in 1951/52. The West Indies Board lost £4,000 and the West Indies team lost 4-1. Gomez concluded that 'we could easily have won the series if only our chaps had settled down to sane and intelligent cricket'. The tourists were betrayed at crucial moments by dropped catches, indisciplined batting, poor tactics and a patent breakdown in team spirit.

Goddard carried the can, although it is difficult to know the precise chain of events. He certainly announced, towards the end of 1952, that he was 'through with Test cricket'. It was widely reported that the Board of Control had issued him with a multi-year ban for criticising its organisation of the Australian tour. However, Goddard told a journalist that he was back in contention for the captaincy at home to India in 1952/53, as one of three candidates along with Stollmeyer and the Jamaican Allan Rae.

Stollmeyer got the job and kept it for Hutton's tour. Before MCC's arrival, he sought to put an end to the long tradition of each host venue having the biggest say in selection for its own Test match. Instead of a committee of Big Four selectors with a revolving chairman, Stollmeyer appears to have insisted on leading a three-man panel made up of his vice-captain and one selector designated at each home venue. This no doubt had something to do with the power struggle between Stollmeyer and Goddard, who as Barbados captain and an accredited selector was still lurking in the wings. It was also a genuine attempt to achieve more continuity from Test to Test. Stollmeyer was right to say the previous system 'merely encouraged infighting and parochialism'. But if his initiative might temper inter-island rivalries, it would not by itself put an end to the divisions of race and class which had characterised cricket on each island.

It was customary for the Board of Control to underwrite the expenses of MCC tours, setting the budget and taking any residual profit for itself. As we shall see, this had serious ramifications for the English visitors, who were restricted in the number of players and staff they could bring and had limited say in arrangements for travel and accommodation.

The main ramification for the Board of Control was the cost of bringing back players contracted as professionals to the Lancashire and Birmingham Leagues. Trevor Bailey was not exaggerating when he opined that a team drawn from West Indians with league experience would beat a team drawn from those who played all their cricket at home. In 1953, the five most important men were all in England: Worrell at Radcliffe, Weekes at Bacup, Walcott at Enfield, Ramadhin at Crompton, Valentine at Walsall.

Before the war, the Board had banned professionals from inter-colonial competition. Uneasy accommodations had sometimes been made with Constantine and Headley to release them from league duties for Tests at home and abroad. But, for the 1948/49 tour to India, terms could not be agreed with Worrell (the precise details were contested) and in 1950 Weekes initially hesitated over an invitation for the party to England because of his Bacup contract (which was eventually fulfilled by his mentor Headley).

It was only in 1952/53 that the Board started paying professionals proper expenses for coming home – even then, the players discovered that different arrangements had been made with each of them. They always had to tread carefully if they wanted to ply their trade and still play for West Indies. Alf Valentine had gone to Walsall with the intention of qualifying for Worcestershire, but backtracked

47

once informed by the Board that a county contract would disqualify him from Test cricket.

Such treatment had close parallels with what Frank Tyson called the 'apartheid' practised against professionals in England. It was also bound up with what Gordon Lewis called the 'multilayered pigmentocracy' prevailing in the British West Indies. Distinctions based on skin colour were often made with invidious precision: the contestants of a Jamaican beauty pageant of 1955 were judged in ten groups ranging from 'Miss Ebony' to 'Miss Apple Blossom'. But the essential three-tier pyramid of the plantation, white-brown-black, had changed little since Emancipation, even if it was complicated on many islands by the immigration of Indians, Chinese and Madeiran-Portuguese to provide new sources of labour. After the war, the political power of browns and blacks was at last becoming less inverse to their numerical strength, but the same could not be said of economic power, nor of social status. If the West Indies team had the potential to dissolve racial distinctions, the structure of the cricket clubs feeding into it tended to reinforce the racial pyramid.

In the most celebrated chapter of *Beyond a Boundary*, James explained how Queen's Park topped the hierarchy of cricket clubs in Port of Spain. It was the white and wealthy 'boss' club with easily the best facilities; second in prestige came Shamrock, the club for non-elite whites, mostly Catholic; next came Maple, the club of the brown middle class for whom, generally speaking, the paler the skin the better; next came Shannon, the club of the Constantines, the black lower-middle class, full of bristling competitiveness; at the bottom was Stingo, whose members James described as 'totally black' and of 'no social status'.

James stressed that these 'caste' lines were not absolute. For the purpose of his narrative – his 'social and moral crisis' as he chose 'brown' Maple instead of 'black' Shannon – he also underplayed other factors. Separate clubs were founded by Indian and Portuguese communities and by employers such as the police and the railways. There was no precise Stingo equivalent on some islands: in Barbados, the players with no social status banded together to form the Barbados Cricket League (BCL) in 1936. But, with such provisos, club cricket in the capital cities of the other big colonies developed upon similar lines to Trinidad. In Barbados, the hierarchy ran:

Wanderers – Pickwick – Spartan – Empire. In Jamaica: Kingston CC – Kensington – Melbourne – Lucas. In British Guiana: Georgetown CC – Guiana Sports – Demerara – Malteenoes.

In the first half of the 20th century, there were many stories of injustices – Weekes called them 'atrocities' – done to players lower down the club hierarchies by national selectors who were almost always members of the 'boss' clubs. *Beyond a Boundary* included a poignant vignette of the dignity of the fast bowler George John, a 'man of the people' allegedly cold-shouldered by the patrician leaders of the 1923 tour to England. George's son Errol remembered the treatment of his father more bitterly in his play *Moon on a Rainbow Shawl*, which premiered at the Royal Court in 1958. There he created the character of a retired cricketer 'broken' by white administrators: 'The Big Ones here strangled my future, boy.'

MCC's tour of 1947/48 provided another salient example from Trinidad. Andy Ganteaume has the distinction of the highest batting average in Test cricket: 112. But this is because, after a maiden century on his home island, he was dropped for slow scoring. Ganteaume played for Maple. He placed the blame for his deselection on the shoulders of two Big Ones from Queen's Park: the injured Stollmeyer and acting captain Gomez, who happened to be his boss at a sports-equipment company as well as being a denizen of the 'boss' club.

As James put it, 'times had indeed changed, but not enough'. In Barbados, the first great working-class cricketers to emerge from the BCL both lived within sight of the elite white clubs. Weekes was born in a wooden 'chattel house' 300 yards away from Kensington Oval, Pickwick's home ground. As a youth, he volunteered to prepare the pitch because it was the only way he could get in to see some cricket. Garry Sobers came from the tough Bayland area close to the Wanderers ground, where he was sometimes allowed to play on the outfield and help operate the scoreboard. Both players knew they could never become members of the white clubs. Sobers, a teenager with an outside chance of selection in 1953/54, felt it was 'three times' as hard for a black cricketer from the BCL to break into the Barbados colony side as for a player from Wanderers or Pickwick. It was also twice as hard for him and Weekes as for Walcott and Worrell, who had been educated at the respectable secondary schools which acted as nurseries to the established clubs of Spartan and Empire.

In Jamaica, the administrator who may well have used his influence with MCC to help win the extra Test was Karl Nunes. He can be described as the Lord Harris of West Indies cricket for two reasons. First, he was on the Board of Control from its inception in 1926 until he died in harness in 1958. Second, according to Michael Manley, he hailed from 'a family that came as near to aristocracy as the colonies can produce'. Nunes had been the first West Indies Test captain. He and Constantine appear to have despised each other. Although Nunes and Headley once put on a record partnership, their relationship seemed little better. Nunes would no doubt be trying his hardest to continue the tradition of a white Kingston Cricket Club player being selected for the Jamaica Tests.

In British Guiana, the two premier batsmen in the colony would, at best, be fighting for one place in the Test side. The man in possession, Bruce Pairaudeau, was a white from Georgetown Cricket Club. The popular hero, Robert Christiani, was a brown from Demerara Cricket Club. Christiani was arguably past his best but emotions were running even higher than usual. The Volunteer Force which had attended the Coronation was now helping a British battalion enforce a state of emergency.

Dos Santos, the new president of the Board of Control, was known as the 'Great White Lord'. But, in the summer of 1953, the Board had at least made one progressive move when it invited Frank Worrell to serve as vice-captain under Stollmeyer. Although Constantine and Headley had sometimes acted as de facto vice-captains, nobody had been officially designated in that role before unless they were white.

The appointment was well received in Jamaica, where Worrell now based himself on his increasingly rare visits from England. The respected local journalist 'Strebor' Roberts suggested that he should have been made captain. The cricket establishment on his home island of Barbados was less impressed, especially when Worrell announced that he and Ramadhin would still be taking up an engagement with a Commonwealth tour to India, flying back late for the Test series with England. Goddard weighed in by saying that Worrell and Ramadhin 'should remember that they owe something to West Indian cricket'. Worrell's bad press in Barbados intensified when he could not find a plane to get him back before Christmas, and even more when he dislocated a finger playing against a Bengal

XI on Boxing Day 1953. He must have known that his performances and his conduct in the upcoming series would be under close scrutiny. By then, an even greater black cricketer would be facing a similar challenge.

———————————

When West Indians say that Bradman was the white Headley, they are responding to the presumption of things being put the other way around. But the claims have some statistical basis: Gideon Haigh calculated that Headley contributed more than Bradman to his team's totals; C.L.R. James that his average was far higher on rain-affected wickets. And Headley was not just about runs, although he scored pots of them. His compatriot Michael Manley described him as a 'revolutionary' figure who carried 'the hopes of the black, English-speaking Caribbean man'.

Manley found it significant that Headley burst onto the international scene in 1929 just after the return home to Jamaica of Marcus Garvey. Garvey was a messianic, idiosyncratic figure whose great achievement was to put a capital N on 'Negro', awaking pride in African origins, consciousness of racial equality, confidence in untapped potential. Manley's analogy between the the 'Black Moses' and the 'Black Bradman' may seem forced, yet Garvey was a cricket enthusiast and Headley, not usually a man for grand gestures, is said to have written 'African' on his immigration form when entering Australia for the 1930/31 tour. Famously dubbed 'Atlas' for carrying the West Indies team, Headley not only blasted through the traditional division of labour, where the white men did the batting, but also inverted the prevailing hierarchical pyramid by proving that black men could bear responsibility.

Headley's genius flowered in the 1930s at the same time as the first seriously organised labour resistance across the British West Indies. 'Mas George' was certainly an authentic Jamaican hero: its representative side lost only one game in which he played before the war (and that was to Yorkshire). But he had been born in Panama, where his father, a Bajan, had emigrated to work on the Canal. Lamming's first novel, set in the 1930s, suggested that 'the only knowledge' of Jamaica possessed by most Bajans was Headley.

The great batsman became not just a pan-Caribbean symbol but a symbolic working man: he followed Constantine to the Lancashire League out of financial necessity. This was a decision bound to cause him issues with the Board of Control, whose prejudice against professionals coalesced with its prejudice against blacks.

Headley became the first black captain of the Test side in 1948 just after a diplomatic conference in Montego Bay on 'Closer Association of the British West Indian Colonies'. While both events were important landmarks on the roads to further integration in cricket and independent federation in politics, they also suggested how bumpy those roads might still be. Headley confided in Ganteaume that he chose to sit out the rest of the series because he was 'finished with this shit'. Others will have muttered the same sort of thing while the British dragged their feet on full self-government during the 1950s.

As West Indies prepared for Hutton's men, Nethersole seems to have warmed to the idea of Headley answering the perennial Jamaican need for a saviour figure. The prevailing Cold-War climate had just forced the PNP to purge Marxist elements from its ranks. In this atmosphere, the Communist union leader Ferdinand Smith was not welcomed as a returning prophet when he was forcibly repatriated to Jamaica in 1952. Headley was a hero who could harness nationalist energies without offending respectable taste. A campaign to bring him home from the Birmingham League gathered unstoppable momentum.

There is a long tradition in the Caribbean of collections by the general public to support their cricketers, stretching as far back as the inaugural 1900 tour of England and as far forward as 1972, when a voluntary committee of Antiguans raised funds for Viv Richards and Andy Roberts to train at Alf Gover's indoor school in south London. Richards remembered the 'moving experience' of being funded by his fellow islanders more fondly than his earliest encounter with the English weather, but he and Roberts would become the first Antiguans to be capped by West Indies. In 1953/54, Ken Rickards was another Jamaican professional brought back from the leagues by public subscription, although he failed in the final tour match against MCC and did not make the Test side. For Headley, a figure of £1,183 0s 2d was reportedly raised, nearly four times more than

West Indies pros were paid for the entire series and more than twice what English pros received for touring.

There was one problem. Headley was now 44. He was still easily the best player in Dudley. My father Frank Woodhouse never forgot a moment of dexterity he saw in a Birmingham League game, when Headley took a rasping return catch and threw the ball to the wicketkeeper in one motion to take the sting out of his hands. But six-day Test cricket was a different proposition.

Swanton, trying to put it politely, suggested Headley was 'by tropical standards decidedly a veteran'. Weekes, one of his most fervent disciples, now compares his batting style to Steve Smith's: shuffling across, seeing the ball early, playing it late. That method relies on a good eye and even Weekes admits Headley should not 'really' have been considered for selection in 1953/54. Headley himself appears to have tacked between pride in the compliment Jamaicans had paid him and trepidation about what he had got himself into, as rumours circulated that the Sabina Park pitch might be dug up if he were not included in the Test team.

There seems to have been a split in Jamaican cricket circles between the progressive voice of Nethersole and more reactionary forces represented by Nunes and the Kingston Cricket Club. A meeting of the local Board of Control on 2 November sought to clarify its position 'in answer to the public clamour' for Headley's return. The Board had 'no objection' to his selection in the two games Jamaica would play against MCC, despite having blocked professionals from consideration in the past. But it was made clear that any 'guarantee' of a place in the side would set 'a most dangerous precedent'. Headley's age may have been subtly targeted in selection criteria based on 'physical fitness' as well as 'cricket ability'; at the same meeting the Board also initiated 'a course of physical training and fielding practice' for Jamaican players in preparation for MCC's visit.

Another batsman who may have been caught in the crossfire between Nethersole and Nunes was Rae. He had moved up the order to open for Jamaica at Headley's suggestion in 1948, an initiative which reportedly caused Nunes to fall out with both men. Rae proved an enormous success in that position on the all-conquering 1950 tour of England. In Australia, he had struggled against the short ball and continued to look out of form in the trial games before Hutton's men arrived. It was still difficult, given his long-established opening partnership with Stollmeyer, to see why the Jamaica captain was not considered a near-automatic squad member. It was less difficult to know he was a PNP supporter.

While Stollmeyer and Gomez, Ramadhin and Valentine and the Three Ws would all be certainties if fit, at least four places were up for grabs. A 'nucleus' of players including these names was announced at the end of October 1953. But there was still time for other candidates to assert themselves, and room for partisan journalists from each colony to press their claims.

CHAPTER 4

PREPARATIONS IN ENGLAND

If Hutton admitted that he 'felt rather like a head boy called to a meeting of house masters' before the selectorial panel which had taken the bold step of making him captain at home, such feelings would only be heightened when he became a candidate to lead MCC abroad. The home panel comprised Les Ames, the first professional appointed to it on a permanent basis, and three former England captains. Two of them, Bob Wyatt and Hutton's Yorkshire skipper Norman Yardley, had recently suggested in their autobiographies that the distinction between amateur and professional might be abolished. The selector with the most traditional attitudes, Freddie Brown, had led England to defeat in Australia in 1950/51 and could at least vouch for Hutton's tactical acumen and good behaviour on that tour.

The MCC selection committee for the West Indies included Wyatt and Brown. The other members were Pelham Warner, Gubby Allen and Walter Robins. All three happened to be former captains of Middlesex and were also part of what Hutton called 'the "inner circle", who direct the policy of the game'. This phrase nods to the capacity of Lord's mandarins for secrecy and intrigue. It may also conjure the idea of a socially exclusive 'magic circle', a shorthand used to characterise the Old Etonian cabal which installed Alec Douglas-Home as Conservative leader in 1963. Home was also an MCC committee man, and one of the many parallels between cricket club and political party was that important decisions tended to be made after secret processes of consultation by a select group. In the case of MCC's inner circle, Warner had been the leader, Allen was emerging as the leader and Robins wanted to be the leader.

Warner celebrated his 80th birthday in 1953 and was paid the honour of the first dinner to be held in the Long Room. He was still playing a role in the administration of the game, receiving a special tribute for his 43 continuous years' service on MCC's Cricket Sub-Committee. Although he no longer sat on the panel for home Tests, he never knowingly undersold his long record as a selector and was invited to chair the MCC committee tasked with picking the party for the West Indies.

Warner had been captain of the first overseas tour under official MCC auspices. The interests of cricket and the prestige of the club were synonymous in his mind. This is why he was permanently scarred by the 'moral and intellectual damage' he remembered suffering as manager of the Bodyline tour. Warner got off the boat at Fremantle in his best imperial form preaching 'the gospel of British fair play'. He came out of the dressing rooms at Adelaide in tears after a celebrated rebuke from the Australian skipper: 'There are two teams out there. One is trying to play cricket and the other is not.' Warner would never again be predisposed to any touring captain who placed too much emphasis on pace or too much emphasis on winning at all costs.

Allen was of that comparatively rare species: an amateur fast bowler. He was a Warner protégé and had emerged as the likely candidate to succeed him as unofficial leader of the inner circle. Warner, ever the string-puller, possibly helped engineer Allen's entrance to Eton, definitely fast-tracked him into the England side in 1930 over the heads of the other selectors and appointed him captain for the 1936/37 Australian tour, the crucial recovery mission after Bodyline. Such solicitous sponsorship engendered the rumour that Warner was Allen's biological father. Gerald Howat, Warner's biographer, gives a more credible explanation:

> Neither of Warner's sons were identified with cricket at top level. Allen, by 'adoption', might continue the lineage and heritage of which Warner, in his grander moments, saw himself a part – Harris, Hawke, Warner, Allen: all great men who would give their lives to Lord's and to MCC.

Allen had conscientiously objected to bowling Bodyline – although he was prepared to field in its leg-trap. His outburst against Harold

Larwood and Bill Voce as 'swollen-headed, gutless, uneducated miners' took place at a moment of stress on that tour, in a private letter not intended for publication. It may however be pertinent that Allen's father won a knighthood for his role in the 1926 General Strike as Commandant of the Metropolitan Special Constabulary. If, as Geoffrey Moorhouse suggests in his history of Lord's, Allen tended to 'divide the world clearly into "deadbeats" and those who are "awfully nice"', such divisions were usually drawn on the basis of social background. His mantra of 'when in doubt, play class' could therefore be read in more ways than one.

Robins was the next England captain after Allen and was later to succeed him as chairman of selectors. In the Highgate-educated Robins, Arlott sensed that 'the traditions and culture of public school are coupled with the North London Cockney alertness of mind'. An attacking leg-spinner, Robins had a temperamental streak. He once managed to get himself warned off a golf course by Enid Blyton. His playing career was badly interrupted by the war and his administrative career by hypertension. Whereas Warner and Allen were knighted and have stands named after them at Lord's, Mr Robins has to make do with a memorial bench.

Robins therefore risks being a forgotten man. Indeed, the residents of an old people's home in a play by Bob Larbey cannot remember his name, even though they can recall every other member of the Middlesex team which he captained with such panache to the Championship in 1947. But the imprint he left on the English game in the post-war period was significant, if not as significant as he would have wished. Robins was perhaps the shrillest proponent of 'brighter cricket', in the genuine belief that it led to winning cricket. He served on the 1944 MCC Select Committee which had emphasised 'the duty of captains in particular to animate their sides into enterprise'. In private notes after the war, he attributed cricket's problems to a 'lack of amateurs of the right quality', suggesting that the spirit of the first-class game might be rescued only by encouraging public schoolboys back into it.

The minutes of the relevant committees reveal that, whether by habit or design, the inner circle did not initially think it right for a professional to lead MCC in the West Indies. The first selection meeting in February, which Warner chaired with Allen and Robins in attendance, made an automatic assumption that the tour captain would be an amateur, recommending that he should receive an extra £50 on top of the proposed amateur's allowance of £175.

Minutes of the next meeting on 19 May show David Sheppard and Peter May were two of the ten batsmen asked about their availability at this early stage. They had just been named by *Wisden* as the improving young amateurs who might relieve Hutton of the captaincy in the not 'far distant' future. In 1952, Sheppard had beaten May to the honour of captaining Cambridge University and had topped the national batting averages. He was now leading Sussex with the requisite dash and was the most obvious candidate if amateur leadership was still felt essential on tour. But Sheppard ruled himself out because he was committed to a career in the church: at the end of the season he was due to start a two-year theological course at Ridley Hall in Cambridge, which meant he could play cricket only in the summer holidays.

At the start of June, another meeting concluded 'as a matter of policy' that deliberations about the tour manager should commence only once the captain had been appointed. This is perhaps the first indication that Hutton was now under consideration, on the understanding that he had a suitable chaperone. Indeed, Hutton was about to experience being chaperoned on the field of play in an Ashes Test match.

Brown, chairman of the home selection panel, allowed himself to be picked for the second Test at Lord's on the grounds that a leg-spinning all-rounder would help the balance of the side. As the Anglo-Irish cricket historian Allen Synge observed, the fact that all parties protested loudly they were comfortable with the arrangement 'reinforced rather than allayed' the impression that it was highly unusual. Synge compared Hutton's position to that of 'a middle-management executive on whom the Chairman had dropped in to see how he handles a meeting':

> On the second day, Hutton literally handled the
> agenda disastrously. As England struggled to wrap
> up Australia's wagging tail, a clearly nervous Hutton

dropped three catches and had to retire to the
pavilion for repairs to a finger damaged in the third
unsuccessful attempt. In his absence, Brown took
impressive charge. It was noticeable that players
obeyed his commanding gestures at the double.

On the other side of the ledger, Hutton backed up his worst day
as a fielder in Test cricket with a masterful century. Several England
players confirmed that Brown effaced himself with reasonable
success, even if Hutton found it hard to stop calling him 'Skipper'.
Arlott still read the selection as evidence of a 'grudging attitude' to
professional captaincy and suspected, despite official statements to
the contrary, that the authorities might ask Brown to take over the
reins for the remaining games if he did well at Lord's.

This prophecy was nearly fulfilled when Hutton had an injury
scare before the next match at Old Trafford. The MCC secretary
Ronnie Aird, in a private letter written during that third Test, certainly
seems to have been disappointed that the chairman did not drop in
for the rest of the series: 'I don't know why Freddie Brown is not
playing except that he told me before the Lord's Test Match that he
did not think a leg-spinner would be required at Old Trafford or
Leeds, why I cannot imagine.'

England had the better of a rain-affected draw in Manchester,
Hutton showing unusual panache by opening the second-innings
bowling with Laker. Whether or not this was the deciding factor –
May had been dropped after the first Test so there were few realistic
amateur candidates left standing – it was following the third Test,
on 15 July, that Hutton was finally proposed as captain for the West
Indies, subject to ratification by the main MCC Committee at the end
of the month.

MCC's attention immediately turned back to the important question
of the tour manager. Swanton tells the story that he 'happened' to be
watching the Rugby v Marlborough match with the MCC treasurer
Harry Altham during the last week of July. In the knowledge that
Swanton would shortly be covering the Roses match at Bramall

Lane, Altham asked him to have a 'quiet word' with Hutton as to the captain's preference: 'When I passed on Harry's message Len paused a moment, and then simply said, "I should like the colonel."'

The 'colonel' was Billy Griffith, whom Hutton knew well from two overseas tours and whom Swanton, rightly, considered a 'natural' for the managership. Swanton was also right to find MCC's decision to pass over Griffith, because of his duties as its new assistant secretary, hard to fathom. There is, however, one problem with what Swanton called his 'important piece of first-hand evidence'. He implies he was the crucial intermediary but the MCC archives show that Griffith had been proposed for the role two weeks earlier – and had already been ruled out within two days of that proposal.

The meeting of the sub-committee of 15 July which had recommended Hutton's appointment as captain simultaneously recommended Griffith as manager. Warner took the approval of the MCC Committee for granted and wrote a congratulatory letter to Hutton that day, predicting the 'delightful' Griffith would 'be a great help'. But the sub-committee had also minuted that Griffith's appointment 'depended on it being possible to make adequate arrangements for the distribution of his work at Lord's'.

Aird, his boss, clearly had second thoughts and convened yet another meeting, with himself and Griffith in attendance as usual, on the evening of 17 July. Despite the tabling of a message from Allen supporting the original decision, Aird gave his 'very definite opinion', after 'very careful consideration', that he could not do without his assistant for four months. So, when the approach was made at Sheffield at the start of August, Hutton was almost certainly less in the dark than Swanton and was making a final attempt to get Lord's to see sense.

Hutton wanted the 'colonel' because he had observed at first hand his man-management skills. Griffith was an excellent wicketkeeper but probably fortunate to have represented England. In 1947/48, he was appointed deputy to Allen, who had initially taken on the dual role of captain-manager in the Caribbean. An important factor was that the West Indies Board of Control had budgeted for a fixed number of tourists. Griffith, then secretary at Sussex, could double as a manager and an extra player. He proved one of the few success stories. Playing as a makeshift opener in the second

Test in Trinidad due to an injury crisis, he scored his maiden first-class hundred. That this may have come as a surprise even to himself was indicated by the one-word telegram he received from his friend Austin Matthews: 'Really!'

In 1947/48, Griffith had also proved his qualities off the pitch during an ill-fated tour where, for the first time, MCC failed to win any meaningful game. For the authorised version we can turn to Swanton: 'In terms of friendly relationships and the spirit of the cricket everything went admirably, and for this state of things Gubby Allen, with much aid from Billy Griffith, who acted as player-manager, was of course responsible.' In the unauthorised version, relations broke down almost completely between Allen and the axis of his amateur vice-captain (Ken Cranston) and his senior professional (Joe Hardstaff).

Hutton arrived as an emergency replacement mid-tour to find Griffith acting as peacemaker between the cliques. The next winter Griffith went to South Africa as vice-captain to George Mann. This proved a happy, lucky and indeed happy-go-lucky expedition where the amateur leadership gained the respect of senior professionals such as Hutton, Washbrook and Compton. Griffith was a character who had the ability both to assert his authority and to suppress his ego.

Although Aird and Griffith were comparatively new to their roles, there was no obvious reason for secretarial duties to have been heavier than usual. It does seem extraordinary that Aird, normally devoted to MCC's wider interests, felt he would be unable to muddle through. This is especially the case as he saw fit to leave Griffith on his own the next winter when he went out to Australasia with Mrs Aird, taking in two Ashes Tests before a fact-finding mission in New Zealand. Altham was also given full cover for his duties as MCC treasurer when he was appointed chairman of selectors in 1954. Perhaps Aird was remembering his own experience as assistant secretary back in 1936. He was the first choice as manager for Allen's tour of Australia, but had to stand down when it proved impossible to provide back-up at Lord's.

The next proposal was for the Yorkshire secretary, John Nash, to fill the role. Nash had been joint-manager of Brown's 1950/51 tour of Australia but it appears the approach to him was quickly rebuffed. Then came the bright idea – 'pure Gubby Allen' according to Trevor Bailey – of Charles Palmer.

Budgetary restrictions again played their part. Back in June the selection sub-committee had envisaged 'the manager may well be a player able to take his place in the team should the occasion demand', in a reprise of Griffith's dual role. Palmer was captain-secretary at Leicestershire, an increasingly prevalent arrangement to keep amateur leaders in the game. He had been on the Mann-Griffith tour to South Africa, without playing a Test, and it was difficult to make the case that he was an all-rounder of international class. But he had gone back into inner-circle notebooks after a sparkling century which almost took the Gentlemen to victory in the 1952 Lord's fixture. This earned a characteristic tribute from Warner: 'Yours was one of the best innings I have seen in a Gentlemen v Players match and I have seen a very large number.'

In 1953, Palmer had brought Leicestershire into a race for the Championship which also involved Sheppard's Sussex, both counties perceived to be playing the approved brand of 'out-to-win' cricket. He did not have a typical inner-circle background, educated at a grammar school in Halesowen and a redbrick university in Birmingham. But he had a certain cachet, like Brown at neighbouring Northamptonshire, as an enterprising leader of a county not known for its strong amateur captains. Indeed, Brown appears to have made the approach to Palmer on behalf of the tour selection committee. One irony of the situation was that Palmer had to leave his own newly appointed assistant secretary, Tony Diment, to his own devices: 'I literally walked into the office … and Charles said "I'm going. Enjoy yourself."'

Palmer was a popular figure but Hutton could hardly have been enamoured of the arrangement. As had been the case at home when Brown had been parachuted back into the side, the presence of a playing amateur with captaincy experience on tour meant that he would always have to factor in the outside possibility that he might be returned to the ranks.

Another less official but potentially sinister development was that Robins' daughter Penny was engaged to provide secretarial support to Palmer – and perhaps feedback on the conduct of the tour to her father. As it turned out, Miss Robins may not have had much opportunity to operate as a mole: she busied herself darning the players' socks, helping Swanton with his typing and, if West Indian society columns are to be believed, having a very good time. But her presence was another factor that must have done little to assuage Hutton's sense of himself as a captain 'on appro'.

From the wider perspective there were two problems with the management set-up, one structural and one human. MCC seemed not to provide any written guidance as to the responsibilities of captain and player-manager. The club's only, typically cryptic, instruction was that the composition of a tour selection committee should be left 'entirely' to Hutton, who was nevertheless 'informed that the Manager in this case was eligible to be a voting member of such a Committee'. Even if their remits had been more clearly defined, what Palmer called the 'two-fisted' nature of the manager/captain relationship, with him reporting to Hutton on the pitch and Hutton sometimes reporting to him off it, was predestined to be dysfunctional.

At the level of personal character, the combination of Palmer's affability and Hutton's diffidence was not designed for the enforcement of discipline. Swanton, who always attached great importance to the chemistry of captains and managers on MCC tours, was scathing in retrospect: 'In my experience it is just about the worst decision ever to have come out of Lord's.'

Swanton also lamented that 'to cap the performance MCC, for the only time in my memory, failed to provide Hutton with a nominated vice-captain'. He does not seem to have been privy to the decision, admittedly taken as late as 26 October, to name Trevor Bailey for this role. But Bailey did not exempt himself when he put forward the tour's management structure as one of the main reasons for it becoming so controversial: 'A captain who had never led a team abroad, a vice-captain who lacked experience and a player manager who had never even been to the West Indies.'

Touring parties were announced earlier in the season than nowadays but usually in at least two tranches. Warner preferred this custom of staggering the selection process, which may have had its origins in the quirks of amateur availability, for two reasons. He liked the main selection meeting to take place during the Gentlemen v Players match at Lord's, a fixture especially close to his heart but also recognised as a tour trial. He also preferred to take his time over the final choices because, as he put it in a letter to Hutton, 'someone may suddenly arise'.

In 1953, the first batch of eleven names, pencilled in at the same meeting which approved Hutton's captaincy, was due to be announced at the end of July. All would take part in the Ashes triumph at The Oval except Watson (Edrich played in that game instead). It was hard to argue with a middle order of May, Compton and Graveney, even if they were all having their struggles against Australia. Bailey and Evans would continue to give the team not only their estimable qualities but also its enviable balance. Trueman, Bedser, Laker and Lock were by common consent the best bowlers of their type in England.

MCC had hoped to finalise the other selections on 29 July, the day after the fourth Test at Headingley. The meeting had to be pushed back. Much to Hutton's annoyance, it was rearranged for the second evening of the Oval Test. He remembered this being a 'concession' to Warner, who had attended that day's play. Howat, who also wrote a biography of Hutton, explains that if the selection meeting were scheduled later at Lord's, Warner would have to make another (three-mile) trip from his flat in South Kensington.

All five tour selectors attended the final meeting, along with Altham and the MCC secretariat of Aird and Griffith. Hutton had spent the first part of the day completing a painstaking 82. By the evening, the most crucial home Test for a quarter of a century was delicately poised – England closed 40 behind Australia's first innings with three wickets left. It is hard to imagine Hutton being wholly focused. He says as much himself, recalling that 'the timing could not have been more inappropriate' and regretting that the process had been 'rushed'.

The main reason for the postponement of the final meeting was a separate 'consultation' after the previous one between Warner, Altham, Aird and Bedser. It is not clear whether this was at the initiative of the bowler, MCC or – as Hutton later suspected – Surrey. As early as 1951, Warner had publicly suggested that Bedser, renowned as a willing workhorse, would benefit from 'rests', a sentiment echoed in Aird's minutes confirming that all parties to the side-meeting were agreed a 'winter's rest' would be beneficial in 1953/54.

Clearly, the tour of Australia the next winter was still considered far more important than the one to the West Indies this. Given Bedser had been easily the best English bowler in the current home Ashes series, and on the two previous tours down under, the decision was understandable. In the season just finishing, made more strenuous by the fact 1953 was his benefit year, he would clock up more than 1,250 overs. His preparation the day before the Oval decider – incredible to our age of central contracts and managed workloads – was to bowl 21 overs for Surrey against Leicestershire and then drive back from Loughborough to London.

Bedser may have been briefed by his Surrey teammate Laker on conditions in the Caribbean, generally unhelpful to medium-fast seam and swing. He was also never at his best in extreme heat: on passages to Australia he often slept on deck; whenever in Adelaide, where he once withdrew to the boundary to be physically sick, he stayed with friends in the Lofty Ranges to avoid the non-air-conditioned hotels down in the city. Perhaps as importantly, Alec was inseparable from his twin brother Eric, who had been permitted to accompany him on previous tours to Australia. Overall, there is a sense of Bedser husbanding his reserves for the oldest enemy. On his retirement he said the games he enjoyed most 'were the Tests between England and Australia, for these provided the greatest thrill'. He would never make a tour as a player outside the old Dominions.

Hutton gives contradictory accounts of his own reaction. In his last set of memoirs, he says the decision upset his masterplan to bring Trueman on slowly for the 1954/55 tour of Australia. He had previously written that he already suspected Bedser's powers were waning and could now try out Trueman and Statham as new-ball partners 'without embarrassment'. Statham had played in the Lord's Test and his name was duly announced in the second tranche. But who would become the back-up fast bowler?

Derek Shackleton of Hampshire was Bedser's nominated reserve for the Players that season. His medium was presumably considered too military for the West Indies. Warner leant towards the young Surrey paceman Peter Loader, although when he canvassed Bedser's own opinion he was told Les Jackson of Derbyshire was a better bet. Jackson would take his customary 100-plus wickets in 1953, despite an early-season injury, and was higher in the national averages than any other candidate. He had not received an availability letter. Indeed, the only thing he seemed to receive from Lord's was short shrift. Whether because of his low slingy action or low mining background, it was rumoured he had been blackballed by Allen or Brown. Brown had taken Middlesex's John Warr to Australia instead (series figures: one for 281) and the selectors now plumped for another Middlesex bowler, Alan Moss.

Moss was a shade quicker than Jackson but the captain could have been thinking of someone faster still. Frank Tyson had literally made an impression on him, as a young colt in a one-day game at Redcar, with a full toss that thudded into his pads. Hutton 'remembered that bruise a few years later when we chose the squad to go to Australia'. But he had already alerted Allen to Tyson's potential and may have wanted a trial run in the West Indies. Although Tyson had to finish his qualification period for Northamptonshire in 1953, he did play against the Australian tourists, taking two early wickets and, perhaps more significantly for Hutton, hitting several of them painfully. English selectors tended not to risk young players on tour who did not have a solid season of county cricket behind them. However, Brown had taken Brian Close after a season interrupted by national service and MCC were now doing the same with Trueman.

If Hutton did not dig in his heels on the third fast bowler, he may have had to on the third slow bowler. Warner was conscious of 'bombarding' Hutton with letters after his appointment. In all but one of them he kept pressing the claims of Robin Marlar. Warner's intelligence was not restricted to the field of play: 'He will want to know fairly soon as I understand he will be going to a public school as a master at the end of September, if not selected.' Marlar's well-flighted off-breaks had taken the Gentlemen to a rare victory at Lord's and he had enjoyed an excellent season, first as Cambridge University captain and then for Sussex under Sheppard. Swanton assumed he was 'almost certain to be asked' as he gave the ball more than a 'gentle twiddle'.

However, Johnny Wardle, twelfth man at The Oval, had taken 13 Ashes wickets in the three Tests he played, had previous experience of the Caribbean and could bowl wrist-spin as well as orthodox left-arm. This might prove especially helpful as MCC had agreed for the first time, in a dry run for the tour to Australia, to covered wickets in the West Indies. It is easy to assume Wardle was Hutton's preference, although more difficult to know how hard the captain had to argue to get his Yorkshire teammate onto the tour.

It must have been a long meeting. At least the choice of deputy wicketkeeper, Dick Spooner of Warwickshire, was reasonably uncontroversial, even if Warner (and Swanton) had a soft spot for Leicestershire's Jack Firth.

This left a final and major debating point, the perennial question of Hutton's opening partner. Hutton himself always had one answer – 'Give me Cyril'. He had pressed strongly for Washbrook's selection in 1953. But he was not prepared to go out on a limb. Hutton well remembered that, before the war, Wyatt's captaincy had been fatally compromised by his once insisting on Tommy Mitchell's selection as a leg-spinner, in spite of Warner proposing Robins. Nevertheless, it was a matter of lasting regret to Hutton that Washbrook was not with him when the Ashes were won. This was partly because the alternative selections averaged 23.13. It was also because he and Washbrook had been through so much together in three hard losing series against Lindwall and Miller in their pomp.

Washbrook, not sent an availability letter, was apparently still persona non grata at Lord's because of the difficulties he caused in 1950/51. He had originally declined to go to Australia, citing his winter business commitments, before being persuaded to change his mind on condition he could fly out late and fly back early.

Edrich was probably Hutton's next preference. He was ruled out for two reasons. First, he had effectively been suspended from international cricket for three years, after Wyatt caught him out all night during a home Test, and was probably not yet trusted for a long overseas tour. Second, he always struggled against spinners who could turn the ball both ways and had appeared all at sea against Ramadhin in 1950.

By earmarking Watson as a potential opener, the selectors were following a hunch about selecting left-handers in an attempt to negate Ramadhin's leg-break and Valentine's orthodox left-arm. At the same time, they were overcompensating for a mistake on

Brown's tour when Reg Simpson, one of five opening batsmen chosen, admitted there were far too many of them. Simpson, who had been sent an availability letter, was overlooked despite Warner being a great admirer of his fielding. So were all the other openers who had enjoyed a good domestic season.

Instead, Warner had an intuition about another young left-hander who might be turned into a makeshift opener like Watson. He believed strongly that the English batsmen should have used their feet against the West Indian spinners in 1950. The result could have been different had they been prepared to 'die in the attempt' rather than suppress their 'natural ability and enterprise' in the modern fashion. Watching Sussex play Middlesex at Lord's in late May, Warner had taken a particular shine to Ken Suttle, who scored a sparkling century by giving free rein to his 'natural attacking game'.

Hutton was seemingly unimpressed by Warner's proposal of Suttle and unhappy when it was carried. Here was another indication that the chairman no longer strayed far from London, leaving the captain as the only specialist opener in the party. Hutton may also have wanted more time to discuss Palmer's appointment, rubber-stamped at the Oval meeting. The tour selection process smacks of a group of selectors trying to put up with a captain they did not think quite suitable, and of a captain having to put up with a series of selections he did not think quite right.

After the Ashes were secured, Hutton took the step of writing personally to every member of the touring party, stressing that in a tropical climate 'any surplus weight put on since the end of the county season not only would be difficult to take off but would add to the risk of early injury in the field'. An emphasis on fitness was *à la mode*. Warwickshire's all-professional side followed a physical education regime when they won the Championship in 1951; South Africa, who surprisingly pulled off a drawn series in Australia in 1952/53, had a programme created for them by Danie Craven, trainer of the Springboks rugby team. But the first professional captain of an MCC tour may also have been having a little dig at the captain of the previous expedition to the West Indies. On the outward journey in 1947/48, Allen had set the tone for a 2-0 defeat by pulling a muscle skipping on deck.

Two Captains

CHAPTER 5

JEFFREY STOLLMEYER

> Stollmeyer ... was as shrewd a captain as I came across.
> I expected he would show all the perceptive qualities
> of a cricket student, be able accurately to sum up the
> opposition, assess players and be tactically aware, but
> I confess I was surprised by the high order of those
> qualities. I also quickly discovered that his position was
> no sinecure, and he had difficulties to match my own
> on that volatile tour. In my book, Stollmeyer deserves a
> high ranking among postwar Test captains.

Although he could not suppress a snipe about how long it took his opposite number to set his field, Hutton's tribute recognised the same cricketing virtues often noted in himself. At first sight, it would seem odd to draw parallels between the English professional and the West Indian amateur. However, the two men had much in common: both were technically adept opening batsmen, both were of increasingly fragile constitution, both from bitter experience had a healthy respect for fast bowling, both developed the conviction that they were most qualified to captain their countries, both were prone to worry and sleepless nights, both believed that giving nothing away was, as Stollmeyer put it, the 'only way to win'.

They even shared the same bat sponsor: Slazenger. For reasons which will become apparent, they did not share many drinks during the 1953/54 series. But, in their later recollections, there is a sense of mutual respect and sometimes empathy for each other's problems. The main difference between them is that Hutton provides a study of a man without privilege, negotiating his way through an evolving English class system, whereas Stollmeyer provides a study of a man conscious of his privilege, negotiating his way through a society where the traditional linkages between class and race were beginning to break.

Stollmeyer recognised that he was 'fortunate' in his background and to all appearances he was a member of the most privileged caste in Trinidad. His uncle owned Stollmeyer's Castle, loosely modelled on Balmoral. This stood in a line of imposing trophy mansions known as the 'Magnificent Seven', located in a socially exclusive area of the capital Port of Spain. Jeffrey's own branch of the family owned large swathes of the Santa Cruz valley, the area later to produce Brian Lara, and lived there on the cocoa estate of Mon Valmont.

Stollmeyer was educated at the island's elite school, Queen's Royal College (QRC). He was a member of its elite cricket club, Queen's Park (QPCC). He was a Test cricketer by the age of 18, Trinidad captain at 21 and, but for injury, would have captained West Indies at 27. In his early fifties, he duly became president of the Board of Control, joining what Michael Manley tartly called an 'honour-roll of the upper echelons of the class structure of the region'.

All Stollmeyers in Trinidad are descended from the Bavarian-born Conrad Frederick Stollmeyer, Jeffrey's great-grandfather, who came to the island in 1845. Conrad's lucky break was to befriend Lord Harris, the British Governor, who granted him government supply contracts and an entrée into the development of the island's glutinous Pitch Lake, which remains one of the largest asphalt deposits in the world. Asphalt eventually made Conrad's fortune and he became a resilient if eccentric entrepreneur. While he made allowance for the 'former conditions of slavery', he would reportedly never have a 'negro' at his table.

Albert Stollmeyer, Conrad's grandson and Jeffrey's father, inherited the family's agricultural interests. Jeffrey described Albert as a 'cocoa planter to the core' and remembered him presiding assiduously over a classic estate where 'servants abounded'. Jeffrey spent countless happy hours in the expansive grounds playing at cricket, football and horse racing (which was simulated by an elaborate form of Poohsticks).

At Queen's Royal College, Jeffrey thought he received 'a secondary education second to none', and excellent cricket coaching from the expatriate masters whose nicknames could have been given to them by Brian Johnston: 'Wilkie', 'Doodles', 'Stokes' and 'Piggy'. Such was the sports-centric culture of fee-paying schools in the Caribbean that their first XIs played competitive league cricket and football against adult teams. In 1933, QRC achieved the feat, possibly unique for a secondary school anywhere in the world, of being national all-age champions at both sports.

Despite Stollmeyer having studied no science, he wangled his way into the Imperial College of Tropical Agriculture after its authorities were 'approached' and private cramming undertaken. The college was a prestigious finishing school for colonial civil servants. Its prevailing attitudes were reflected by its Yorkshire-born Professor of Botany, Sydney Harland, who believed it was 'accepted by *all* competent biologists that the negro is inferior in intelligence to the white race'. When Stollmeyer was selected for the 1939 tour of England, he was further accommodated by being set a specially written paper so that he could graduate in time to take his place on the boat: 'It was a noble gesture by the college but I have often wondered what my fellow-students thought about this unusual procedure.'

His selection was viewed by many across the Caribbean as another unusual procedure. Stollmeyer himself thought he was lucky to emerge from the trial games on his own island ahead of players such as Rupert Tang Choon, whom he described as 'perhaps the best player never to have played for West Indies' (a view certainly shared by the Chinese community in Trinidad). Jeffrey was conscious too that charges of nepotism would be inevitable given that his elder brother Victor had also been chosen. The Jamaican and Guyanese press, incensed in any case by their low representation in the party, protested that a teenage patrician had been 'pitchforked' into the team.

Nonetheless, Stollmeyer did well in England, impressing Warner as a 'beautiful stylist'. He would always be worth his place in the international side. A cricketing annual of the early 1960s, admittedly emanating from Trinidad, included him in its best-ever West Indies Test XI.

Andy Ganteaume's personal grievances may explain his view that his colony captain was merely 'seen as pretty'. But his antipathy was also driven by the fact that Stollmeyer played an 'influential part' at QPCC, the private club modelled on MCC which owned the

Test ground and which ran Trinidad cricket until as late as 1980. Ganteaume distrusted this 'Establishment', by which he meant the elite who 'ran the show for and on behalf of their own', because its amateur ethos was discriminating in more ways than one.

As vice-captain for the tour to India in 1948/49, Stollmeyer apparently took the side of the Board of Control in its decision to overlook Worrell because of recent issues relating to timekeeping and attitude: 'I have no doubt that this had a salutary and beneficial effect on Frank in the long-term.' What he omits to mention is that Worrell asked to be paid £250 for the tour rather than the notional expenses which were then customary. When the campaign for Worrell's captaincy gathered momentum in 1959, Stollmeyer opposed it because of its unfairness to the white incumbent Gerry Alexander, a position which can be read either as typical of his determination to judge every situation on its merits or illustrative of his reversion to the instincts of his caste at critical moments. Clive Lloyd later found Stollmeyer difficult to deal with on the Board of Control: 'Now I'm not saying there was a colour issue going on between us, but let's say we never quite gelled.'

Stollmeyer's attitudes outside cricket were clearly traditional. He had great affection for the 'mother country', especially as his own mother was British. His view of its elite was not unobservant but usually affectionate: 'I have a soft spot for retired English officers. They are a type but they are the stuff from which the British Empire was made.' He got on well with Rae, his opening partner on three post-war tours, but disagreed with him when they killed time in political debate. Stollmeyer attributed some of Rae's 'strangely anti-Conservative' leanings to his 'reading the wrong literature'. It was a familiar argument of those defending the status quo in the British West Indies, either side of the war, that recent agitation was as much the result of Marxist indoctrination as of genuine grievance.

The paternalistic tone of Stollmeyer's memoirs chimes with the two Trinidad-born patricians who dominated the administration of imperial cricket. There is more than a tinge of nostalgia for the 'complete mutual respect between master and servant' which prevailed at the family home during his childhood, just as Warner had fond memories of being bowled to in his nightshirt in Port of Spain by 'a native boy who did all sorts of jobs about the house and garden'. And Stollmeyer's elegy for the 'moral decline' of Trinidad after independence seems to invite juxtaposition with his earlier quotation of a purple passage from the fourth Lord Harris (son of Conrad's patron) describing cricket as a 'moral lesson in itself'.

If Stollmeyer was admired in later years for his contribution as a senator in Trinidad and Tobago's upper chamber, he was reviled in some quarters for the company directorships he cultivated. He became chairman of the local subsidiary of Barclays Bank, an institution which was gaining a special place in pan-African demonology as a prop of apartheid. He also had a seat on the board of Metal Box, another company that had South African connections and a reputation in Trinidad for victimising union activists. It is easy to see why Mighty Sparrow, in a brilliantly withering calypso on the Packer crisis, caricatured Stollmeyer as a 'cricket Sir | Controlling the Empire'.

However, Stollmeyer's contribution to Trinidadian society and West Indies cricket can easily be oversimplified. While some believed the very fact of his QPCC membership made him 'indifferent or even hostile' to progressive forces, he has also been described by the historian Natasha Barnes as a 'proud example of the best of what a reformed, multiracial, nationalist West Indian cricket environment could bring'. Stollmeyer was the type of person whose mind was conservative and enlightened at the same time, no less the one for being the other, a trait which can be traced back through the family history.

Conrad Stollmeyer told two tales about his emigration to Trinidad. The first was that he arrived with just five dollars in his pocket. The second was that he had fled the United States to escape a lynching after publishing an anti-slavery tract. Although he came to believe his black workforce was workshy, in another pamphlet on the sugar industry he asserted that 'all men are *one* common family' and sarcastically mocked the racial assumptions of 'enlightened' Europeans. Conrad was also a staunch adversary of Pelham Warner's father, Charles, who pursued an aggressive pro-imperialist policy as Attorney General of Trinidad in the mid-19th century.

Jeffrey's father Albert served as an elected member of the Trinidad Assembly between 1925 and 1928. No doubt he had vested interests to protect but he sat on a sub-committee, alongside the popular hero Captain Cipriani, which recommended labour reforms. In 1929 Albert, who traded cocoa on a forward basis, was nearly bankrupted by the Wall Street Crash. He had to rebuild from scratch, with the assistance of a loan from Barclays. Jeffrey's later association with the bank arose from other family connections but there must also have been a sense of acknowledging an important debt.

Albert therefore had to abandon the family policy of sending his sons to America for their further education. The three youngest of six brothers – Hugh, Victor, Jeffrey – remained at home. When Victor arrived at Queen's Royal College, C.L.R. James umpired him in school games, having stayed on as a master there after graduating.

There is the same fierce debate about the merits of the (very restricted) scholarship system in the Caribbean as there is about the eleven-plus in England. Its critics assert that it was designed to train a few 'native overseers' at the expense of the rest of the population; its proponents assert that the cadre it developed became a crucial force for social change, the most notable alumni of QRC being James and Dr Eric Williams, who broke the mould of Trinidadian politics when he formed the People's National Movement (PNM) in 1955.

If a QRC education was designed to instil what James described as the English 'code', it also provided an environment where staff and pupils from different backgrounds accepted each other with less strain than in wider society. The image of the Stingo fast bowler Fitz Blackett giving Stollmeyer extra net practice before the 1939 tour may smack of traditional deference, but QRC boys seem to have jumped to attention whenever the intimidating Blackett did his rounds as head porter of the school.

Every Sunday, Stollmeyer would cycle the seven miles from Mon Valmont to play club cricket on the Savannah in Port of Spain. The Savannah was fringed by symbols of privilege: QRC, QPCC, St Andrews Golf Club (until the 1930s), the Race Club and the Magnificent Seven private mansions, whose prodigious water consumption was a cause of resentment in the rest of the capital.

But the Savannah was also, rather like the Maidan in Bombay, a teeming public space where up to 60 games of cricket could be played, where political demonstrations were sometimes held and where the annual Carnival took place. The multicultural spirit of the Savannah and the Carnival filtered through, in however diluted a form, to the manicured turf of Queen's Park. Weekes was one of many to acknowledge that 'the cricket culture of Trinidad was the most liberal in the region': club rivalry was fierce but 'all the races played together in the national team in a way that seemed progressive and noble to us'.

Four of Jeffrey's five elder brothers pursued careers in business, public service or the law. His other brother Hugh found his vocation in painting and sculpture. A member of the self-styled 'Independent' group of artists, Hugh also played a role in *The Beacon*, the groundbreaking journal of the 1930s established by Albert Gomes (who featured at Lord's in Chapter 1). The *Beacon*'s express intention was to smash the prevailing 'conspiracy of silence' about institutional racism in Trinidad. In one of its early numbers James picked apart the supremacist arguments of the Imperial College's Professor Harland. Hugh Stollmeyer's rare written contributions were perhaps the most radical of all, including an impassioned poem calling for the 'self-despising' subject-races of the West Indies, African and Indian, to cast off the yoke of 'perfidious Britain'.

Hugh was defiantly bohemian, shocking Port of Spain society when he strolled down the capital's main shopping boulevard 'sparsely clad in open-neck shirt, creaseless trousers, sockless and sandalled'. Victor and Jeffrey were far more strait-laced. But they seem to have been proud of their brother's achievements. When Jeffrey toured India, some of his reactions to 'coolie' squalor were unreconstructed. Nonetheless, he took the trouble to read Nehru's autobiography and to canvass views on the British legacy: 'They felt, and quite rightly too, that it was their country and that they were being subjected to and kept down by a foreign power.'

Stollmeyer could point to his record of encouraging players from the Indian community in Trinidad, who represented a third of the island's population but were not yet fully integrated into its society or sport. When the spinner S.M. Ali was no-balled for throwing in Barbados, his Trinidad captain wore his cap inside out in protest, not a very Queen's Park thing to do. Stollmeyer also sponsored Ramadhin's selection for the 1950 tour of England on the strength of two inter-colonial games, and reportedly kept his spirits up in Australia in 1951/52 by writing new lyrics to Lord Radio's calypso 'We want Ramadhin on the ball'.

In 1956, Victor Stollmeyer seems to have been the first white man to declare support for Dr Williams. Jeffrey took the step of writing to *Time* magazine to answer the charge that the PNM was an 'all-Negro' organisation: 'In this small outpost we have a Heaven-sent opportunity to show the world how persons of different races, colours and creeds can live together, as equals, in harmony.'

The relatively liberal culture of Trinidadian cricket honed Stollmeyer's sense of fairness. It also explains some of his toughness. The pride of the Savannah was Shannon, the club of the Constantines, whose players dominated the colony side between the wars and might have dominated it even more had selection been entirely meritocratic. James soon regretted joining Maple and abjuring Shannon:

> As clearly as if it was written across the sky, their play
> said: Here, on the cricket field if nowhere else, all
> men in the island are equal, and we are the best men
> in the island. They had sting without the venom. No
> Australian team could teach them anything in relentless
> concentration. They missed few catches, and looked
> upon one of their number who committed such a crime
> as a potential Fifth Columnist.

This combination of controlled aggression and austere comradeship, which James dubbed 'Shannonism', no doubt took some of its inspiration from Australian cricket (three Shannon players toured there in 1930/31). It also adapted several qualities enshrined in the public-school code: fierce tribal pride, esprit de corps, stiff upper lip. But on another island, during the same period, one county cricket club answered to the same description, down to the details of under-representation in the national side and being particularly tough on each other with respect to the crime of dropped catches. Constantine, despite his strong allegiance to Lancashire, saw the closest equivalent to Shannon in Yorkshire, 'a real fighting *team*, welded together, cunning, steady and hardest of any English county to beat'.

It was inevitable that a cricketer with Stollmeyer's keen eye and good sense would imbibe some of the spirit of Shannonism. He also developed a devout respect for what he called Yorkshire 'guts' and 'wits'. When he outfoxed the county in a 'grim' low-scoring game at Sheffield on the 1950 tour – captaining West Indies as Goddard rested – he treasured the victory as one of his proudest moments, the 'match of a lifetime' where 'nothing was wasted'. Stollmeyer positively relished the way the 'unashamedly partisan' Bramall Lane crowd 'lived with the game and kept it alive' – although, when it was over, he was shocked to see them hurling their seat-cushions onto the playing area.

If Stollmeyer learnt his cricket in the teeth of Shannon and in awe of Yorkshire, he learnt most of all about 'sting without the venom' at the knee of Headley. He had cause to remember their first encounter during the inter-colonial matches which doubled as trials for the 1939 England tour. Stollmeyer happened to be bowling his occasional leg-breaks when Headley came to the crease, and immediately hurt himself stopping a straight drive. He was soon to learn that one of Headley's many stratagems was to render spinners less effective by trying to warm their fingers as quickly as possible.

Gerry Gomez, who had snuck into the Queen's Park pavilion during the Test of 1935 to get Headley's autograph, remembered the experience of touring England with him in 1939 only increased his devotion:

> Early in the tour I began to appreciate the cricketing
> genius of George Headley and, like Jeff Stollmeyer,
> became receptive to the stream of knowledge which
> he gave forth in a slightly embarrassed manner ... I
> remain forever in his debt for the thoughtfulness and
> consideration which he extended to us, the young ones
> of the 1939 tour. During a day's play he would take the
> trouble to sit with us and expose to our minds many of
> cricket's skills and intricacies ...

Gomez found Headley 'very modest, even introverted' but 'supremely confident' in his ability to deal with any situation on the field, and mildly impatient with those who failed to show the same dedication and focus. Gomez and Stollmeyer both remembered Headley's catchphrase of 'Him don't like to bat' whenever one of the tourists was out carelessly, delivered 'without rancour, but with a twinge of disappointment and admonishment'.

Headley remained without rancour, despite more than a twinge of disappointment, in the case of Jeffrey's brother Victor. Victor's Test average of 96 is almost as high as Ganteaume's. His only innings for West Indies was in the final Test of 1939. Headley never looked like getting out in that match – until he had made 65 when Victor managed to run him out. Victor partly redeemed himself with a fighting knock but still must have braced himself for a mixed reception when he made his own return to the pavilion. Headley slapped him on the back and congratulated him on 'a grand innings'. The Stollmeyers never forgot this act of 'radiant' magnanimity.

In the 1947/48 series with England, Headley's Trinidadian disciples performed auspiciously in the one rain-affected Test he captained. The next winter Headley again appeared in only one Test on the tour of India, after complaining of a rib injury. Even Stollmeyer eventually concluded that the great man was 'funking'; Gomez harboured 'the uncharitable thought' that Mas George, covetous of his pre-war reputation, feared he would be outscored by Weekes and Walcott. Stollmeyer and Gomez did not voice the possibility that Headley, granted paid leave from his civil-service job to ensure the tour turned a profit, preferred not to play under Goddard's captaincy.

But neither did they. Stollmeyer, who kept a diary of the tour full of mutterings about Goddard's mismanagement on and off the field, seems to have formed a troika with Gomez and Headley to stand up for the players' rights when they were denied bonuses and air travel. And, given Goddard's failure to 'tape' the opposition or form any 'definite plan', Stollmeyer called on his hero's wisdom to force the captain into the requisite strategy. Headley had become a connoisseur of negative leg-theory, having often been its target. This was the device which just saved the final Test and clinched a 1-0 series win.

The India tour confirmed Stollmeyer's opinion that Headley 'had a greater tactical sense than any cricketer with whom I have played'. It also alerted him to the know-how of the next generation of black players. He had assumed Weekes and Walcott were 'raw Bajans' but developed an admiration for them as batsmen and as people, particularly relishing the former's 'picong' (Trinidadian slang for piquant banter). Just as James always emphasised 'West Indian brains' in resistance to the stereotype of instinctive calypso cricketers, Stollmeyer took care, in his autobiography's insightful analysis of the Three Ws, to pay tribute to their strengths of intellect as well as their natural talents. He praised the cool Worrell's 'leadership qualities'; he recorded his 'unlimited respect' for Walcott, whom he judged 'a wonderful asset to a team on tour'; he remembered the way the astute Weekes 'anticipated my every move' in the field.

There may be an element of tokenism in these remarks, made when Stollmeyer was portraying himself as the elder statesman of West Indian cricket, and his admiration for the Three Ws was not always reciprocated. Walcott blamed Stollmeyer for encouraging a campaign against him in the Trinidadian press in 1952: 'To say the least, I was never his favourite cricketer.' Worrell bore the scars of his omission for India and implied that Stollmeyer withdrew from the team's 'brains trust' on the Australian tour in a selfish and disruptive way.

That said, when Stollmeyer took over at home to defeat the Indians in 1952/53, there was an inescapable sense of the new captain and his senior players uniting, in homage to Headley and in reaction to Goddard, to put an end to what Stollmeyer called 'the naïve approach to the serious business of Test cricket'.

Bruce Pairaudeau, who made his debut in that series, feels there was no comparison between Goddard and Stollmeyer on or off the pitch. Goddard was 'nowhere near the team on merit'; Stollmeyer was a 'graceful' batsman. Goddard was a 'village idiot when it came to tactics'; Stollmeyer 'knew his cricket'. Goddard was a resolute 'non-mixer'; Stollmeyer 'sang calypsos with his team'.

Pairaudeau's opinion is no doubt coloured by the disastrous tour of England in 1957, when he had a difficult time under Goddard, and might be dismissed as the view of a privileged white. Even so, it is hard to believe Goddard would have embraced Worrell's vice-captaincy in the way Stollmeyer did. For the 1954/55 series against Australia, the Board of Control saw fit to remove Worrell from that role, appointing Denis Atkinson, a Goddard protégé, in his stead. As we shall see, Stollmeyer found this decision 'preposterous', even if he then sought to manage the sensibilities of both men as best he could.

Worrell is sometimes perhaps simplistically portrayed as the Nelson Mandela of West Indian cricket. It may be even more simplistic to portray Stollmeyer as its F.W. de Klerk. But he was the most important bridging figure between the era when the West Indies captaincy was awarded on background and the era when it was awarded on merit.

There would always remain an unbridgeable distance between a Queen's Park mandarin and the Three Ws, rather like the distance between the Lord's mandarins and Len Hutton. 'Can you really envisage Frank, Clyde or I dashing up to Stollmeyer and planting an embrace around his neck?' Weekes asked in his 2007 memoirs. But, in his interview for this book, he acknowledged 'everyone was pulling together for the cause in a Jeff Stollmeyer team'.

CHAPTER 6

LEN HUTTON

After spending four months with Hutton in the West Indies, Alex Bannister concluded: 'He takes some understanding – as he himself is the first to admit.' Hutton was a man of some reserve and considerable reserves, who would have proved an enigmatic character in any event. Yet the title of his first autobiography, *Cricket is My Life*, was chosen advisedly. In his last, ghosted by Bannister, he briefly mused on whether he would have played in a different way had he been a gentleman from the Home Counties: 'But I was born in the north, and was a pro. We are what we are.'

Hutton was born in 1916 into what he called the 'exceptional environment' of Fulneck in the West Riding. The village was the first English settlement of the Moravians, an evangelical movement that could lay claim to being the first Protestant denomination. From an early age, Hutton's leanings were towards the other religion in which his family was immersed. The earliest spiritual sensation he could recall was 'just that caressing "feel" of a cricket bat'. He also kept a cricket ball in his pocket on Sundays, when games were prohibited, just in case he could find a private spot to practise his leg-breaks.

But Hutton still acknowledged the 'big impact' of his upbringing. In some ways the isolated community of Fulneck anticipated the close atmosphere of the Yorkshire dressing room: there was a similar emphasis on thrift, craft and self-reliance; a similar sense of being specially elected; a similar tendency towards gloom. Dorothy Hutton felt that her husband's austere Moravian background ensured that 'even when things were going well, Len would be looking for the down side'.

Hutton's parents did not have the means to send him to the Moravian senior school in Fulneck. But he still knew 'there were considerable advantages in being the youngest of a cricketing family living as near to the heartbeat of Yorkshire as Pudsey'. At the age of 14, Hutton made his debut for Pudsey St Lawrence in the Bradford

League, where he remembered an invaluably 'severe' early training, pitted against unrelenting adults on bad pitches in front of sarcastic crowds. Like Weekes, who would learn his cricket in the equally tough Barbados Cricket League, Hutton was taught to keep both the ball and his feet on the ground.

Hutton sometimes opened for St Lawrence with Edgar Oldroyd, the first player to score 1,000 runs in a Bradford League season after being released – prematurely in his opinion – by Yorkshire. Oldroyd was 'none too keen' on being given such a junior partner, but from the other end Hutton had the best view of a batsman described by the *Yorkshire Post*'s J.M. Kilburn as a quick-witted 'artist' on sticky wickets and a slow-scoring 'labourer' on better ones. Oldroyd was a stereotypical Yorkshire pro, an admixture of the dour and the canny, the neurotic and the bolshie. He was once politely informed by a Warwickshire dressing-room attendant that he was in a chair reserved for Captain Parsons: 'Tell him Private Oldroyd proposes to go on sitting in it.'

The story of Hutton's 'true baptism' in the Yorkshire first team, aged 17, was relished and probably embellished by Cardus. He tells the story of Arthur Mitchell, Oldroyd's successor in the county side and, if it were possible, an even harder character, passing judgement from the non-striker's end on a cavalier square cut: 'That's no _____ use.' Working out what was of 'use' and what was not became elemental to the process by which, to quote Kilburn, 'cricketers from Yorkshire underwent a subtle metamorphosis into Yorkshire cricketers'.

Initiation into the freemasonry of the professional dressing room was a hard business. Hutton remembered the only communication he received on his first introduction was a request to find out the winner of the 2.30 at Thirsk. But he now had full access to a cast of characters – more varied than the Yorkshire clichés sometimes suggest – who made him feel like 'a privileged pupil attending an advanced seminar'. He approved of the amateur captain Brian Sellers having a separate changing room because it allowed the pros to dispense their accumulated wisdom 'without hindrance'. Hutton's experiences as he learnt his county cricket percolated into his international captaincy, especially in his failure to empathise with younger players not so attuned to the rhythms of apprenticeship and the rewards of observation.

The flip side of Yorkshire CCC's artisan pride was a horror of affectation. Mitchell is involved again in another oft-told tale as he reacts to a slip fielder holding up the ball after a somersaulting catch: 'Gerrup. Tha's makkin' an exhibition o' thisen.' Richard Hoggart, the cultural commentator who grew up in the same era as Hutton eight miles away from him, recorded many other examples of Yorkshire people slapping down any hint of pretension: "E makes a lot of fuss and lah-de-dah about it.' This is actually Hoggart's mother talking about the dirty bits in D.H. Lawrence. Yet particularly applicable to cricket is his argument that northern communities had a theatrical sense of a plummy, privileged 'Them' which forged a solidarity, as much out of regional consciousness as class consciousness, in a self-respecting 'Us'.

The 'Them' against whom Yorkshire players and supporters constructed their 'Us' was not Lancashire, with whom they shared 17 out of 21 Championships between the wars and the narcissism of small differences, but Middlesex, the only champion county from the south between 1919 and 1947. In the era of Allen, Middlesex nearly cancelled fixtures with Yorkshire such was the needle of their encounters. When Sellers faced off as captain against Robins, he was as aggressive as any of his players in his intense contempt for the 'fancy-dan', the 'swash-buckle', the 'jazz-hat'. James's description of Shannon's attitude to his more socially selective Maple club could be applied to Yorkshire's approach against Middlesex: 'They were out to beat us, to humble us, to put us in our place.'

Hutton made his England debut by 1937, days after turning 21, but it was in 1938 that he awoke to find himself famous after breaking Bradman's Test-record score. The poet Edmund Blunden considered this innings – 'thirteen hours of temptation repelled' – the fruition of Hutton's 'virtuous studentship' in Yorkshire. There was indeed a Yorkshireman at the crease throughout the England innings of 903 for seven declared, supporting the view, held by Constantine among others, that only the white rose had the 'needle keenness' to match the baggy green. Hutton's tight-fisted instincts made him perfectly suited not only to the extreme acts of self-denial demanded by the Yorkshire brotherhood, but also to the extreme 'dodges' they were prepared to countenance. Less well remembered than his 364 is Hutton's attempt to keep the Australian rabbit Fleetwood-Smith on strike by deliberately kicking the ball over the boundary.

Bradman would still be there waiting for Hutton after the war to take his considerable revenge. The Oval Test may also mark the beginnings of another, internal, rivalry. After a day and three-quarters sitting with his pads on, Denis Compton scored one run. He concluded that 'Len could play the type of innings that was foreign to my nature'. If this was meant to be a compliment, Compton himself encouraged the contrast between what he called Hutton's 'joyless concentration' and his own more 'natural way of playing'.

Hutton was only 23 months older but, to judge from the comparisons often made, the age gap may as well have been 23 years. As Cardus noted, the word 'Master' was reserved for Hutton, implying a 'certain air of age and … Mandarin authority' and never for Compton, whose cricket 'always looked young, fresh and spontaneous'. Although both men were professionals, the frequent analogies of roundhead and cavalier bestowed upon Compton the amateur virtues. In retirement, these two great servants of English cricket insisted they had always been friends. Doug Insole, who played against them for Essex and the Gentlemen, was not so sure: 'To Compo, Len was a tight-fisted bloody Yorkshireman; and to Len, Compton was a Lothario.' For many northerners, Compton's status as a Brylcreemed playboy was clinched by the fact he was also a star player for Arsenal, a club despised in Yorkshire (especially in Huddersfield) as much as Middlesex.

One thing Hutton and Compton did have in common was that the war deprived them of six prime seasons. It also deprived Hutton of two inches of his left arm, after a complex double fracture suffered on army training in a York gymnasium in 1941. Hutton was too sensible a person not to put his injury in perspective: it was incurred preparing for the Dieppe raid – in which three out of five commandos were killed, wounded or captured – and one of his most beloved comrades from the great pre-war Yorkshire side, Hedley Verity, died on active service in Italy.

But, as he concluded simply, 'it was a fact of my life that my accident in 1941 left me with difficulties'. The nagging ache in his foreshortened arm was accompanied by the nagging fear of being 'put out of business for good'. It is telling how frequently Hutton measured the effectiveness of fast bowling by the amount of physical pain inflicted. In a warm-up game on the 1954/55 Ashes tour, he saw Neil Harvey taking off a pad to rub his shin after being hit by Tyson: 'It must have hurt. From that moment I knew we had a chance.'

In a similar way, Hutton remembered his first serious encounter with Ray Lindwall in terms of the excruciation of having his finger flattened onto the bat handle. After the war, the Australians recognised that Hutton would be their most reliable foe for the foreseeable future. Under Bradman's initial direction, Lindwall and Miller systematically embarked upon a decapitation strategy. Colin Cowdrey considered the barrage Hutton faced from them over the course of five series to represent 'the stiffest examination of any batsman in the history of the game'. Hutton's Yorkshire teammate Vic Wilson put it in more vernacular terms: 'He took some hammer.'

Hutton remembered particularly the 'grim time' he endured on the first post-war tour in 1946/47, when he thought Lindwall and Miller were trying to put him back 'in hospital' by targeting his arm when they were not targeting his head. Deciding to eliminate the hook shot because of his disability, Hutton ducked and weaved stoically and topped the batting averages just ahead of Compton and Edrich. But mutterings about his fortitude against pace, tending to emanate from London-based journalists, began in earnest on this tour. When he was alerted to them in Sydney by his Yorkshire confrère Bill Bowes, Hutton was reportedly so angry he launched a premeditated assault on Miller, a legendary cameo which came to an end when the bat slipped out of his weaker hand.

Back home in 1948, where he started the return Ashes series as well as any English batsman except Compton, Hutton claimed he had again 'tried to take the Aussie bowling by the scruff of the neck and failed' in the second innings at Lord's. But his backing away to leg was viewed as uncharacteristic at best and shell-shocked at worst. The cold silence of the MCC members in the pavilion indicated the latter interpretation. Their unofficial spokesman Swanton felt the ensuing decision to drop Hutton had the desired effect: 'I never saw Len flinch again for the rest of his career.'

In time-honoured fashion, for the next Test in Manchester the selectors brought in two batsmen who had just impressed for their county, on this occasion Gloucestershire, against the tourists. In equally time-honoured fashion, and in a tactic Hutton would copy in the Caribbean, the Australians may have been grooming their preferred candidates while seeking to eliminate the players they really rated. In that same fixture Tom Goddard's bowling figures were 32-3-186-0. Hutton's direct replacement was George Emmett but Yorkshiremen may have observed that their hero had also made way for Crapp.

This notorious omission is a major landmark in the long history of northern hostility to a national selection process perceived as being run from the Home Counties. A.A. Thomson was not being entirely facetious when he remembered 'riot squads out in the West Riding'. Roy Hattersley, then a 15-year-old schoolboy, remembered being 'personally affronted' by the decision and went to support Hutton in Yorkshire's next home game against Surrey. Throughout the match, the Bramall Lane crowd mercilessly heckled the visiting skipper Major E.R.T. Holmes – 'Tha couldn't pick a fine day' – believing (or pretending) he was chairman of selectors Group Captain A.J. Holmes of Sussex.

Hutton had not been given the courtesy of prior notification – he heard the news on the radio – nor a subsequent explanation. He remained 'hurt' by an experience he took care rarely to discuss in public but never to forget in private. Although two Yorkshire captains were on the committee chaired by Holmes, the Yorkshire press believed that the selector who had agitated against Hutton was Walter Robins. Robins, in fairness a brave player of fast bowling, thought backing away to leg was vulgar and 'yellow'. The Australian writer Malcolm Knox has even surmised that Robins allowed himself to be heavily influenced by the opposing captain Bradman, given the amount of time the two men spent together during the week in which the decision to drop Hutton was made.

Although Hutton was recalled after one game, his omission had a two-fold personal significance which was still resonating more than five years later in the West Indies. His already vivid respect for pace was further enlivened and he seemed never again prepared to risk his position in acts of calculated aggression. For Arlott, Hutton was now a man 'battered by cricket'. For Kilburn, his role as prop of the England batting and brunt of the opposition bowling had forced Hutton to conclude that 'the penalty of greatness is its enchainment'.

Hutton was 'badly hurt' again two years later, when MCC broke with established custom by naming a professional vice-captain for Freddie Brown's tour to Australia. Having been invited to lead the Players in the Grace Centenary match against the Gentlemen in 1948, Hutton thought he might be best equipped for the job. He assumed MCC had based their decision on 'the popularity stakes' when Compton was appointed. He may also have blamed Allen, who tended to favour southern players and had asked for Compton first in 1947/48 when Hutton was eventually persuaded to fly out to the West Indies as a replacement. In 1950, Hutton again heard the bad news on the radio, as he was driving into London with Kilburn after a round of golf:

> I felt the car slow down and Leonard gripped the wheel. 'All right, Leonard, what's up?', I asked and he said: 'As soon as I get back to London, I'm going to write the MCC a letter and tell them that I'm not going on the tour.' I made him stop the car and told him not to write that letter and told him that he would captain England long before Compton ever would.

The two players shared a cabin on the outward journey, an experience which must have been made even more difficult for the fastidious Hutton by Compton's notorious untidiness and bad timekeeping. But Kilburn turned out to be right: Hutton was served well by the comparison on that tour. Judged on simple numbers, he averaged 88.83 in the Tests; Compton 7.57. Judged on tactical contribution, he was often consulted by Brown in the big games; Compton had some difficult experiences as captain in the State games. Judged on off-field behaviour, he kept his nose clean; Compton picked up a black eye at a Christmas party. Indeed, Richard Hutton suggested that the main reason his father became a serious candidate for the England captaincy was that he 'conducted himself particularly well' on a tour where other senior players did not.

MCC's inner circle may still have felt that Hutton was, at one and the same time, too intense and too austere a figure to be appointed captain of England. His Fulneck and Pudsey background made him, at best, sergeant-major material in their eyes. But Jack Davies, the Cambridge psychologist who ran Hutton out for a duck on his first-class debut, thought he had an 'instinctively pro-traditional' mindset and enjoyed 'being accepted by, if not being an active member of, the Establishment'. There was certainly a part of Hutton fascinated by the trappings of privilege, and elements in his upbringing which cultivated a stiff upper lip more than a chip on the shoulder.

One of the striking characteristics of the Moravians, emphasised in a history of the movement by one of Hutton's uncles, was their contemplative 'stillness'. This may have helped Hutton at the crease: his son thought he always had the ability 'to be relaxed enough to be able to concentrate'. It also helped him, despite his innate shyness, in public life: Arlott described Hutton as a 'calm, worried, wise man' and it was one of his particular qualities to hold in suspension the traits of being highly strung and highly composed. He was almost incapable of the profane over-exuberance which seemed to put Lord's off a certain type of amateur leader.

Hutton also came from the 'respectable' working class, not the 'rough' end which was about to find its cricketing incarnation in Trueman. The two great breeding grounds of Yorkshire cricket were the institutions that could often be found on alternate street-corners of its urban conurbations and mining villages: the chapel and the public house. If the Moravians were not quite chapel, they were definitely not public house. And, when Hutton started training at Headingley's indoor cricket school, he found his 'ideal coach' in George Hirst, who had been born above a pub but happened to be one of the most upright characters in the history of cricket, said to have 'all Yorkshire's strength and more than Yorkshire's grace'.

Allen had been coached by Hirst at Eton and described him as 'the nicest, kindest man in the world'. As in the structures of the army battalion and naval squadron upon which the amateur ideals of leadership were largely based, MCC grandees could have genuine affection for their men and inspire genuine affection in return. The warm officer-batman relationships began with the coaches they encountered at their public schools: Warner believed his true 'headmaster' at Rugby was another Yorkshire pro Tom Emmett; at Highgate, Robins was coached by Albert Knight, the ex-Leicestershire professional and Methodist preacher who had toured Australia with Warner in 1903/04.

Hutton's early relationships with senior MCC figures were developed within this paternalistic tradition, and reflect the respect for 'the value of authority' he too thought essential in cricket. On his Test debut in 1937, an occasion when he was intimidated as much by the social as the cricketing milieu at Lord's, he remembered the generous encouragement of the chairman of selectors, Warner, and the captain Robins. He admired and befriended several other amateur leaders of England, which helped him appreciate 'the easier approach to captaincy that comes with not having to rely on the game for a living'.

Once MCC countenanced Hutton's candidature for the England captaincy, they no doubt expected him to find a sinecure and turn amateur. Edrich had done so in a transparent bid for the role. There would have been a queue of Yorkshire businessmen ready to offer Hutton something suitable. But he had observed the experiences of two men he 'hero-worshipped' when they tried to combine an ultra-professional approach to cricket with a more flexible approach to status.

In Pudsey, Hutton admitted to being initially 'terrified' of an even more formidable formative influence than Oldroyd – Herbert Sutcliffe. Sutcliffe recommended Hutton to Yorkshire and, as his senior partner in the 1930s, taught him to 'make sure your manners and bearing are better than those of the amateurs'. The drama critic Laurence Kitchin believed Sutcliffe's immaculate comportment played a major role in undermining some of the feudal arrangements established by Lord Hawke: 'His flourishing rebukes to anyone, from MCC aristocrats downwards, who dared to move behind the bowler's arm, are part of the social history of cricket.'

Sutcliffe had all the qualities of an artisan shop steward with few of the faults: he was a fine team man for Yorkshire and England, someone you would want batting for your life, and always felt it his duty to look after his fellow professionals. But some of them did make fun of his increasingly elocuted vowels and some of them turned against him when, in an extremely complicated affair of

1927 which came to nothing, he seemed prepared initially to turn amateur to become captain of Yorkshire. While Sutcliffe acquired many social graces and enjoyed the openings offered to a famous cricketer, strength was his only criterion on the field. He was among Jardine's staunchest defenders after Bodyline, which was one of several reasons Allen discarded him for the next tour of Australia.

In Test cricket, by far the biggest influence on Hutton was Walter Hammond, his captain at The Oval in 1938 and arguably his only important mentor outside Yorkshire. That said, Hammond had been coached by the Pudseyite John Tunnicliffe and, in Hutton's opinion, had 'much in common' with the Pudseyite Sutcliffe, combining an 'aura of superiority' with a ruthless will to win. Hutton enjoyed batting with Hammond more than anyone: 'He was like a man planing a piece of wood, the master-craftsman doing it for you to watch.'

Warner had always been 'potty' about Hammond's classical strokeplay and encouraged him to accept a directorship with Marsham Tyres, so that he could captain England as an amateur in 1938. But Hammond's style of leadership turned out to be less Corinthian. He had become obsessed by the fact Bradman had eclipsed him as the world's greatest batsman. Now that Bodyline was unofficially banned, he felt the only course left was to grind the Don down. 'I have never felt grimmer in my life', admitted Hammond, as he insisted on an ultra-cautious strategy after winning the toss in the timeless Test at The Oval. When Hutton played a lofted drive on about 140, his captain came out onto the balcony with instructions to 'cool it' before the ball had reached the boundary. Even after the final irony of Bradman injuring himself bowling, Hammond 'practically wanted a doctor's certificate' confirming his inability to bat before declaring.

Hammond's remorseless approach, which Hutton copied for six-day Tests in the West Indies, was thought dishonourable by the more romantic followers of the game. *Wisden* was not paying a compliment when it retrospectively called Hutton's innings 'that supreme act of cricket Fabianism'. After the war, Hammond should not have carried on and cut a somewhat tragic, cripplingly introverted figure. But he seemed to be getting the worst of both worlds. On the one hand, his captaincy was characterised as 'aloof and Olympian'. He lost heavily to Bradman in 1946/47 and also lost the dressing room, although Hutton – loyal to the end – thought Compton and Edrich should have been sent home for their unprofessional attitude to touring. On the other hand, Warner now appeared to be wondering whether a tyre salesman had been captaincy material after all.

The most militant act of Hutton's life was to refuse to gentrify himself to become England captain. When he was first sounded out about the post on his return from Australia in 1951, he made it clear that he would 'do so only as a professional'. He may have changed his accent over the years as a matter of expediency, like Sutcliffe and Hammond, but he was determined not to change his status as 'a matter of principle'.

Two players with diametrically opposed social attitudes give extra colour to Hutton's quiet assertion that the England captaincy gave him an opportunity to 'serve cricket and the professional cricketer'. Trueman opined that 'Leonard didn't really have a great deal of time for many amateurs'; Bedser thought Hutton had a 'fixation' about the game's in-built deference to gentlemen which he 'never got over'. It may be that Trueman was projecting his own contempt for authority and Bedser his own respect for it. But the fact both came to the same conclusion suggests that Hutton had more of a problem with what he called the 'prevailing system' than his airbrushed public comments indicated.

In Coronation year, the *News Chronicle* celebrated the socially binding power of Hutton's Ashes victory. But its coverage of Everest touched upon the tendency of British expeditions to treat their 'sherpas' as hired porters, an attitude which stemmed not so much from a 'colour bar' as 'the British prejudice that it was right and proper that amateur cricketers should leave the pavilion by one gate and the professionals by another, that there should be separate messes for officers and other ranks, that Jack was as good as his master – at a distance'.

This distance was closing after the war – separate gates were a thing of the past if not separate dressing rooms – but what gnawed away at Hutton was the lack of consideration, in every sense of that word, still afforded to professionals. It was reportedly his personal suggestion, although Allen sometimes took more of the credit, that professionals should be considered for honorary MCC membership once they had retired. Perhaps Hutton made the proposal after seeing Frank Woolley subjected to the indignity of having to sign in to enter the Lord's pavilion. The manager of the 1954/55 tour of Australia, Geoffrey Howard, remembered being asked not to wear his MCC tie at a social function by a captain embarrassed not to be an MCC member.

Hutton would also be on the wrong end of one of Lord Hawke's paternalistic measures at Yorkshire, the convention that most of a professional's benefit proceeds should be withheld because working men were not to be trusted with a lump sum. The county deigned to return Hutton's capital 17 years after his retirement – net of losses caused by their investment policies. Like Sutcliffe, Hutton ran a successful sports shop but he was well aware that retained jockeys, such as Sir Gordon Richards, were the exception not the rule among British sportsmen in being able to set a market rate for their labour.

The social distance between gentleman and player was still measured by the school tie. In *The New Elizabethans*, published in Coronation year, the conservative novelist Philip Gibbs noted that the new grammar schools were producing 'fine lads' who might prove officer material. He damned with fainter praise those elementary boys who had become 'as well behaved as those of the old Public Schools, though they have not as yet the same tradition, style and quality of leadership'. Tom Dollery, the first tenured professional county captain of the modern era, was one of the 'fine lads', having attended Reading Grammar School and captained its first XI before going on to lead Warwickshire to the Championship in 1951. But Dollery understood why his own son might still be reluctant to pursue a career in cricket: 'Although there has been a great advance in the attitude towards the professional, he is still faintly inferior, a person who is "not quite."'

Hutton, from Littlemoor Council School with no early experience of leadership, was made to feel more than faintly inferior when he dealt with the inner circle as England captain. He always remembered Warner's early kindnesses and his support in 1948, when Hutton's omission after Lord's was described in *The Cricketer* as 'a decision

Lord's 1950: All these photographs were staged for the press, but the drama of West Indies' first Test victory on English soil was enlivened by their supporters' pitch invasion, led by Lord Kitchener on guitar, and the calypso celebrating the 'little pals' Ramadhin and Valentine, who took 18 wickets in the match and symbolised a new feeling of West Indian unity.

'Summer of Sport' 1953: The sense of a 'New Elizabethan Age' was augmented first by the 'Matthews Final' (top left: Stanley is chaired by Mudie and Mortensen), then the conquest of Everest (top right: Colonel Hunt waves a patriotic pickaxe on his return to Heathrow with Hilary and Tensing), then the 'Richards Derby' (Sir Gordon is pictured in conversation with the owner whose horse came second).

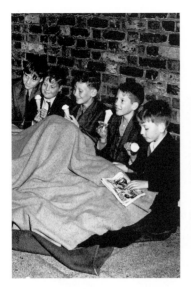

The Oval 1953: At the climax of a series which seemed to grip the nation, schoolboys queued up outside the ground all night for tickets and crowds gathered outside radio shops for commentary. Hutton never forgot the 'sea of humanity' before him when he came onto the balcony to celebrate England's first home Ashes victory since 1926.

In his immaculate pomp – the portrait on the left was taken on the 1930/31 tour of Australia – George Headley was a potent pan-Caribbean icon; a boy who began playing cricket with coconut boughs and breadfruit grew up to inscribe his name in gold at Lord's. By 1951 – and the portrait on the right – Headley was still a model league pro but it was assumed he had retired from his role as the 'Atlas' of the Test side.

Trinidad 1941: Jeffrey and Victor Stollmeyer emerging from the pavilion at Queen's Park, a bastion of elite privilege which no doubt propelled their emergence into international cricket. But the Stollmeyers became devoted disciples of 'Mas George', with whom Jeffrey is pictured in India in 1948.

The Oval 1950: Jeffrey Stollmeyer looks less elegant than usual here (the obscured wicketkeeper is Arthur McIntyre) but he averaged more than 50 as vice-captain in the 3-1 series victory. Promoted to the leadership in 1952/53, Stollmeyer was, arguably, the first captain of West Indies to be worth his place in the side and, certainly, an important bridging figure in the development of Caribbean cricket.

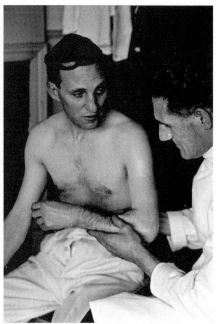

Top left: 1930 – Hutton at the lathe in the Fulneck handicraft centre. Top right: 1953 – his damaged arm is inspected by Yorkshire masseur George Alcock. One of several tensions in Hutton's cricketing personality was between the keen artisan forever learning his craft and the old pro battered by injuries and responsibilities. But his cover drive remained the best in the business, unveiled here against West Indies in 1950 (the fielders are Gomez, Walcott and Weekes).

Left to right: P.F. ('Plum') Warner, G.O.B. ('Gubby') Allen and R.W.V. (Walter) Robins, three former Middlesex captains on the tour selection committee – and also members of what Hutton called MCC's 'inner circle'.

The inner circle's bright idea of Charles Palmer (left) as player-manager impressed Hutton as little as the omission of his preferred opening partner Cyril Washbrook (pictured with him on the film-set of *The Final Test*).

Washbrook, Bill Edrich and other candidates were overlooked in favour of Ken Suttle of Sussex, whose footwork and fielding had invigorated Warner. Suttle, seen here jogging on Worthing beach in late November 1953, took Hutton's injunctions to keep fit before the tour more seriously than Hutton took his batting.

which causes one furiously to think'. This was, in Warner-speak, about the strongest criticism possible of the selection process – and also a reminder that the inner circle was never quite as united as it appeared to its critics.

However, once Hutton became captain, he sensed that Warner, like another octogenarian leader Churchill, was not only 'feeling his age' but becoming ever more set in his opinions: 'He was … a very powerful influence, and accustomed to getting his own way, albeit in an unfailingly courteous manner.' Hutton left a coded message in his retirement memoirs of 1956 in the very act of saying he had treasured their friendship: 'I have had little contact with Sir Pelham Warner during the past three years.'

Hutton was astute enough to know that Allen's influence at MCC had become 'considerable'. But he also knew Allen was never, in Swanton's words, 'altogether *simpatico*' with professionals such as Sutcliffe who had ideas above their station. When, many years later, the journalist Scyld Berry mischievously asked Hutton for an opinion on Allen, he interpreted the reply as a polite but pointed expression of distaste: '"I don't – I don't go to Lord's," Sir Len began ..."I don't go to Lord's – to see him."'

While Hutton recognised Robins to be 'an authority on Lord's', he almost certainly blamed him for being dropped in 1948 and took a dim view of the way Robins had tried to undermine the England captaincies of Hammond and Yardley. Hutton was a disciple of Hammond, a comrade of Yardley and a Yorkshireman suspicious of leg-spinners and of any collaboration with Bradman. His autobiography quietly alluded to Robins' notorious propensity for popping in for a little chat when players were in the bath or on the massage table: 'Let me say that for Selectors of the England side to be constantly visiting the dressing-room to offer advice to the captain or to any of the team could be most confusing to the players.' Hutton praised the 1952 and 1953 home selection committees for their discretion in this regard; Robins returned to that committee in 1954.

Plummie, Gubby and Robbie fitted into the stereotype of the 'pin-stripe brigade' and 'old school tie' which socialist and regional newspapers began to develop in earnest either side of the war, and which has long survived in formulations such as Ian Botham's 'gin-soaked old dodderers' and Matthew Engel's image of Lord's administrators 'behind the times and in front of the *Daily Telegraph*'. The alternative, semi-official view was given by Ian Peebles in *Wisden*: Harris, then Warner, then Allen were 'competent and devoted men', doing their best without 'material reward' to serve cricket in a 'changing world'.

The truth lies somewhere in between the egalitarian caricature and the establishment iconography. To their credit, the inner circle did not block Hutton's appointment by the progressive 1952 home selection committee. They were now so desperate to beat Australia that they seemed prepared to hold their noses. While they lamented the war's sociological effect, a weakening of deference to the officer class, they were also sensible enough to recognise its economic effects, which made it more difficult for amateurs to commit to full summer seasons or MCC winter tours. Warner never had time for those he called 'cricketing Bolsheviks' but he, Allen and Robins could all point to ways in which they had tried to improve the lot of the professional cricketer and the coaching of elementary schoolboys.

However, in the changing post-war world, elites who portrayed themselves virtuously serving wider interests came under increasing critique for their self-interest. By 1964, the social historian Rupert Wilkinson (educated at Winchester and Harvard) was pointing out the hypocrisies which had sustained what he called the British prefect class over the previous century: '*Within* the appeal to altruism, the gentleman ideal, lurked hidden appeals to egoism – the egoism of the patron.' The egoism of the patron is precisely the quality one discerns in the inner circle's relationship with Hutton, especially because the absence of material reward was more significant for them than for landed aristocrats of previous generations such as Lord Harris.

Warner had failed the Westminster entrance exam. Even though a 'vacancy was found' at another great public school, he admitted his mother endured a financial struggle to get him through Rugby and Oxford. Allen was conscious that his path through Eton and Cambridge 'meant some financial sacrifice on his father's part'. Robins owed his education to his mother talking the Highgate headmaster into reduced fees, and the headmaster then talking the school into establishing a special scholarship to enable him to go up to Cambridge. All three had day jobs which compromised their cricketing and social positions: Warner was a journalist, Allen a stockbroker, Robins an insurance underwriter.

It is perhaps understandable that the barrier of a public-school and Oxbridge education, that great Victorian pact between old and new money, became even more important to these men when they exercised their patronage. Another tendency of the leisured gentleman identified by Wilkinson, the equation of 'aesthetic manners with moral virtue', was particularly active in their attitudes to cricket, perhaps because of their own latent anxieties about being thought shabby-genteel in society.

Hutton was essentially cut from the same cloth as deferential professionals such as Hirst. Like the less deferential Sutcliffe, he had implicitly accepted the wider rules of the English game by working hard to send his own children to public school. But his insistence on remaining a professional seems, rather quickly after his appointment, to have pricked MCC complexes about social and cricketing manners.

In the 1959 Boulting Brothers film *I'm All Right Jack*, the plummy personnel manager Major Hitchcock (Terry-Thomas) has a reasonable working rapport with the Communist shop steward Kite (Peter Sellers), while remarking privately that he is 'the sort of chap who sleeps in his vest'. Hutton, once seen by his manager in Australia 'sitting up in his bed with a woollen vest on', was certainly not a Communist but he was that sort of chap.

Warner, whose pyjamas were monogrammed, was not programmed to have an elementary schoolboy at the same committee table. He reserved his most piquant observations for his private correspondence with the Australian Prime Minister Robert Menzies. Given that Hutton was called a 'silly so-and-so' by his own brother for inserting Australia at Brisbane in 1954/55, Warner might be forgiven for describing him as a 'Mutton-Head' in the context of that decision. But the preposterous observation earlier in the year that he had 'no cricket sense' reveals an ingrained attitude towards professional captains, vented in another letter to Menzies after the West Indies tour: 'I do not feel Hutton is a leader. Was Lord Hawke right?'

Even before that tour, the battle lines had been drawn. It did not take Hutton long as England captain 'to discover that the spectre of bodyline still haunted the corridors of power'. Unfortunately for him, Warner associated Bodyline not just with Jardine and Larwood but with Bill Bowes. When Bowes had the temerity to deploy a prototype for Yorkshire against Hobbs in 1932, Warner had described bouncers to a leg-side field as 'not bowling' and 'not cricket'. Hutton's reverence for pace, his close friendship with Bowes and his good relationship with Jardine were all well known.

One of the more low-key events in the 1953 summer of sport was Roger Bannister's first serious attempt to run the mile, that most imperial of measures, in under four minutes. Bannister was somewhat ruefully aware he had become a symbol of 'national prestige' in a sport where Britain had been doing very badly. The only time the national anthem had been played on the post-war Olympics track had been for Jamaican sprinters. At an invitation time-trial in the London suburbs in June, Bannister achieved the fastest time recorded in Britain, two seconds outside the barrier. It would not be recognised as an All-Comers Record by the Amateur Athletics Association because Chris Brasher, one of the pacemakers who would help Bannister under four minutes the next year, stopped to a virtual walk before joining in again.

In the same way that the AAA took great pride in Bannister's achievements, but fussed about the ways his 'coldly scientific' training methods and use of pacemakers were not 'bona fide', MCC was thrilled to beat the Australians in 1953 but still anxious that some of the methods involved were 'not cricket'. Bailey's time-wasting tactics to ensure a draw in the fourth Test were the most obvious instance, when Kilburn observed that his 'direction was notably accurate, some way down the leg-side' and Green that he 'suddenly had a lot of problems with his bootlaces'. Negative leg-theory was not quite Bodyline but, in combination with slow over-rates, it was something MCC did not want associated with teams representing the club abroad. And, with Trueman in the party, it was possible that Hutton might start leaving the same smell as Jardine.

As important was the concept of 'brighter cricket'. Cardus wrote a letter to *The Times* after the Matthews Final saying he could no longer contest its claim that football was 'the people's game'. Cricket, once the noblest of pastimes, was now 'a decaying contemporary industry'. Cardus partly attributed the 'creeping paralysis' in modern cricket to social developments such as the welfare state, but he also thought Hutton's England captaincy proceeded 'gloomily and parsimoniously, not to say unchivalrously', setting a tone which risked being 'unworthy' of the Coronation: 'The players are, so to say, always prone to drink out of the wrong glass or even eat peas off their knife.'

Lord's never took much notice of Cardus. But the inner circle was equally obsessed, with generally pure motives, about the trends which were threatening cricket's popularity as a spectator sport. Perhaps with baser motives, Brown, a member of the selection panel for the West Indies, wrote an article in the 1954 *Wisden* to address 'an almost unanimous disquiet about the lack of attack in the England batting'. Although he acknowledged the 'tremendous fillip' of the Ashes victory and paid some technical compliments to Hutton and Bailey, his critique of the 'defensive virus' in English cricket, and celebration of Australian run-rates, constituted a thinly veiled attack on them, written while they were representing their country in the Caribbean.

To the end of his days, Hutton was studiously polite in public about the role of MCC during his tenure, admitting only to a 'few scars' from attacks by traditionalists and claiming to understand he was a 'stopgap' appointment until the next suitable amateur. But Kilburn, the journalist closest to him, believed he was 'persistently anxious not to tread on corns' and that 'poor old Leonard nearly finished up in a mental home' due to the equivocations of the inner circle. What the social historian Derek Birley called Hutton's 'lonely pioneering journey through the class barrier' can be romanticised. But the class barrier arguably caused him as many problems as the colour bar when he captained MCC in the West Indies.

Two Teams

WEST INDIES

JEFFREY STOLLMEYER (captain, Trinidad)
Birthplace: Santa Cruz. **Age:** 32. **Previous Tests:** 25. **First-class debut:** 1938/39. **Test debut:** 1939.

Stollmeyer averaged over 50 as captain against India in 1952/53. But he made an inauspicious duck in a final practice game in Trinidad before MCC's arrival, having missed some of the autumn trials in British Guiana for business reasons.

At a press conference in Trinidad before leaving for the first Test in Jamaica, Stollmeyer expressed surprise that the English had left Bedser at home and reckoned his side had an even chance of victory.

....

FRANK WORRELL (vice-captain, Jamaica)
Birthplace: Bridgetown (Bank Hall), Barbados. **Age:** 29. **Previous Tests:** 19. **First-class debut:** 1941/42. **Test debut:** 1947/48.

Worrell had begun his first-class career for Barbados as a left-arm spinner batting at No.11. His exploits in wartime inter-colonial games soon moved him up the order. In 1943/44, aged 19, he scored 308* in a world-record fourth-wicket partnership of 502 with Goddard; two seasons later he put on 574 with Walcott, breaking the all-wicket world record of Holmes and Sutcliffe. Worrell then made an equally Bradmanesque start in international cricket, averaging 147 in his debut series against England and 90 on the triumphant tour of 1950. On his second Commonwealth tour of India, he captained the side – after Les Ames was injured – with the same grace and calmness which distinguished his batting.

At home, however, he was considered big-headed by the Barbados elite and a 'cricketing Bolshevik' by the Board of Control. Worrell moved to the less claustrophobic atmosphere of Jamaica. He also took the first opportunity to play Central Lancashire League cricket with Radcliffe, not just for the money but for a respite from 'sneers about my conceit'. His critics thought he looked jaded in the series against Australia and India, overlooking the fact that he was doing a lot of bowling, now at medium-fast pace.

....

DENIS ATKINSON (Barbados)
Birthplace: Bridgetown (Rockley). **Age:** 27. **Previous Tests:** 7. **First-class debut:** 1946/47. **Test debut:** 1948/49.

Atkinson had made little impression as a Test cricketer on the tours of India and Australasia. Yet, by the time of MCC's visit, he was being touted as an all-rounder who might develop into the West Indian Keith Miller. Perhaps this was optimistic with respect to his nagging off-cutters, but Atkinson bore closer resemblance to Miller as a good-looking, hard-hitting batsman and brilliant fielder.

Although Atkinson and his three brothers played for the elite Wanderers club, he described himself as a 'hard red man'. Married to Goddard's niece, he was understandably seen as a protégé, and Goddard handed over the Barbados captaincy to him in 1955. But Atkinson may have been more open-minded than some white Bajans. He had played cricket in Trinidad, where he worked for Demerara Mutual Life; he remembered having 'plenty fun' in India as a junior squad-member; he took a solicitous interest in the early career of Sobers. Richie Benaud thought Atkinson was a 'tough' customer on the field but also 'one of the most approachable and dedicated players I came across'.

....

ROBERT CHRISTIANI (British Guiana)
Birthplace: Georgetown. **Age:** 33. **Previous Tests:** 21. **First-class debut:** 1938. **Test debut:** 1947/48.

From a talented cricketing family, Christiani was revered by Guyanese as a stylish strokeplayer, the unchallenged forerunner of their great line of batsmen: Kanhai, Lloyd, Kallicharran, Chanderpaul. One of his nicknames was 'Sugarfoot' and Constantine reckoned him the best player of spin he saw in the West Indies, Headley excepted. Having been cruelly adjudged lbw for 99 on debut against Allen's men, Christiani became the first Guyanese Test centurion in India the next winter.

On tours to England and Australia, he showed flashes of brilliance, including two hundreds in a match against Middlesex, but a series of frustrating cameos in the Tests led to his being dropped in 1952/53. In later years, Christiani was not universally popular, the spinner Ivan Madray complaining that 'he lived in the white people's compound' after being employed as a coach on the Booker sugar estates. But in 1953 he was still 'Sir Robert', and a recent century against Trinidad increased Guyanese clamour for his selection.

....

WILF FERGUSON (Trinidad)
Birthplace: Longdenville. **Age:** 36. **Previous Tests:** 7. **First-class debut:** 1942/43. **Test debut:** 1947/48.

Ferguson was variously described by journalists as one of the 'ugliest' and one of the 'most likeable' men in cricket. A great local favourite, he seems to have taken all the ribbing about his looks with what Alex Bannister called 'cordial geniality'. Ferguson was the main West Indian spinner when MCC toured under Allen. He took 23 wickets in the series and a ten-for in his home Test, combating the deadness of the matting wicket at Queen's Park with big, generously flighted leg-breaks.

Ferguson failed in India but was still a surprise omission for the 1950 tour of England, having bowled well in the trials. Thenceforth eclipsed by Ramadhin, he would remain under consideration for the Trinidad Test because of his effectiveness on the mat and his useful lower-order batting.

....

MICHAEL FREDERICK (Jamaica)
Birthplace: Mile and a Quarter, Barbados. **Age:** 26. **Previous Tests:** 0. **First-class debut:** 1944/45.

Frederick was not even on the long list of 28 names drawn up by the local cricket board for the Jamaican colony side. But he scored a century in the final trial, perhaps having nudged himself into contention by captaining a recent tour to Trinidad by the West Indies Sugar Company, a subsidiary of Tate and Lyle. Frederick was a compact batsman with a vicious hook-shot, but there remained a suspicion that he was under consideration for the Tests more because of the intricacies of Jamaican cricket politics than the certainty of his defence.

The son of a clergyman, Frederick had been educated at the Lodge (the same school as Goddard) and represented Barbados at under-16 level. He then went to England in 1945, where he trained with the Fleet Air Arm, apprenticed at a sugar equipment company and played as an amateur for Derbyshire (more for the seconds than the firsts). He had relocated to Jamaica with his English wife to take up his post in the sugar industry.

....

GERRY GOMEZ (Trinidad)
Birthplace: Port of Spain. **Age:** 34. **Previous Tests:** 25. **First-class debut:** 1937/38. **Test debut:** 1939.

If Gomez had been English, he might have been described as a stout yeoman. He was a robust inside-right for Trinidad's football team and a lustily competitive all-rounder. A QRC scholarship boy, Gomez placed an emphasis on etiquette and discipline which was not to all Caribbean tastes. But, in a golden age of Trinidadian cricket, he had developed a cult following on his home island after a run of huge scores at the Queen's Park Oval between 1942 and 1948 (including 178* against Allen's men).

A peripheral figure on his first tour of England in 1939, Gomez proved himself an exemplary team man there in 1950. Conscious of a dearth of new-ball bowlers in the West Indies after the war, he worked hard on his medium-paced swingers. He took 16 wickets in India in 1948/49 and a ten-for in a losing cause at Sydney in 1951/52. Gomez had shown all his fighting qualities on the Australian tour, playing a vital hand with the bat in the only Test West Indies won. Although there were now signs of wear and tear, he remained a vital cog in Stollmeyer's team.

GEORGE HEADLEY (Jamaica)
Birthplace: Colon, Panama. **Age:** 44. **Previous Tests:** 21. **First-class debut:** 1927/28. **Test debut:** 1929/30.

Headley's return to Jamaica caused consternation in the other islands, where it was assumed he had retired from international cricket. But there was recent, if limited, evidence that he could still hold a bat. In his first season with Dudley, in 1951, he broke the Birmingham League record with 922 runs.

In his only first-class game of 1952, for a Commonwealth XI against a strong England XI, he had scored 98 (lbw to Les Jackson) and 61. Valentine, who bowled to Headley for Walsall in 1953, concluded that 'George is batting very, very well'. Back in Jamaica, Headley scored 87 in the first internal trial game for the colony side. He had clinched his place there, if not yet in the Test team.

....

JOHN HOLT (Jamaica)
Birthplace: Kingston. **Age:** 30. **Previous Tests:** 0. **First-class debut:** 1946.

Holt, christened John Kenneth like his father and his son, is less famous than either of them. His son became a celebrated reggae artist. His father, dubbed the 'W.G. of Jamaican cricket' by C.L.R. James, established Lucas CC as the first champion black club in domestic competition. Holt senior's countrymen found his repeated omission from representative sides inexplicable. Although he did tour England in 1923, he was thought too old to be selected once West Indies achieved Test status.

Jamaicans became incensed on the easy-going Holt junior's behalf when he too was overlooked in 1947/48, despite strong showings for the island. To use a Jamaican phrase, he continued to 'get himself set', touring India with Worrell's Commonwealth side in 1949/50 and spending two seasons in the Lancashire League with Headley's old club Haslingden. Strong off the back foot, Holt was a good judge of how to pace an innings but not always of when to take a run.

ESMOND KENTISH (Jamaica)
Birthplace: Cornwall Mountain. **Age:** 37. **Previous Tests:** 1. **First-class debut:** 1947/48. **Test debut:** 1947/48.

Kentish, best man at Valentine's wedding, appears to have been an upwardly mobile member of the Jamaican black middle class. Before the war, he attended the teacher-training college at Mico. At the very end of his career in 1956, he would win an Oxford Blue as a mature student. Mobility only went so far in local cricket: Kentish had turned 30 before making his debut for Jamaica. Despite being the injured Headley's nominated vice-captain in 1950, he was overlooked as skipper in favour of a white player from the Kensington club.

Kentish's accurate fast-medium had at least won him a place in the Sabina Test of 1948. Allen and Evans were among his three victims. Although Kentish captained Melbourne in Jamaica's Senior Cup competition, he had not played again for West Indies. Some thought he had lost a little nip and that he was 'a man to be carefully concealed in the field'.

....

FRANK KING (Barbados)
Birthplace: Bridgetown (Delamere Land). **Age:** 27. **Previous Tests:** 5. **First-class debut:** 1947/48. **Test debut:** 1952/53.

King was the closest thing in the early 1950s to the stereotype of the West Indian fast bowler, a man of few words and many bouncers. He was not credited with much tactical acumen but had enough about him to become head groundsman and coach at Combermere College. There a young Wes Hall kept wicket to him, and took King's classical action as his model when he decided to become a fast bowler.

For Barbados, King made the MCC batsmen hop in 1948. But he had to wait another four seasons for his Test debut against India, a side still shell-shocked after their encounters with Trueman. He took 17 wickets in the series and fractured at least two Indian bones. There is a possibility that King had fallen out with the Barbados selectors in 1954: some reports suggest that he was not 'rested' against MCC but dropped because Goddard's local panel preferred Teddy Griffith and Carl Mullins. Nonetheless, Stollmeyer placed a premium on real pace and always wanted King in the Test side provided he was fit.

....

CLIFF McWATT (British Guiana)
Birthplace: Georgetown. **Age:** 31. **Previous Tests:** 0. **First-class debut:** 1943/44.

Once Walcott gave up the gloves, the position of West Indies wicketkeeper was wide open: Alfie Binns (Jamaica), Ralph Legall (Trinidad) and Clairmonte 'Leaning Tower' Depeiza (Barbados) all received partisan support on their own islands. Cliff McWatt, from Demerara CC, the same club as Christiani, appeared to have missed the boat. He had been to India as Walcott's understudy in 1948/49, without playing a Test. He then briefly lost his place in the BG side, after asking to be considered solely as a batsman due to a loss of form behind the stumps.

But McWatt's performances in the autumn trial games of 1953 were difficult to ignore: he kept well to the spinners and scored a century and two fifties. Like many left-handers, he was flamboyant, if sometimes fragile, outside off stump. McWatt, who served with the Royal Air Force in England for some of the war, was a popular figure with teammates, opponents and crowds. He developed a close friendship with another debutant, Holt, during the 1953/54 series.

....

BRUCE PAIRAUDEAU (British Guiana)
Birthplace: Georgetown. **Age:** 22. **Previous Tests:** 5. **First-class debut:** 1946/47. **Test debut:** 1952/53.

From a family of the Portuguese merchant class who were members of the elite Georgetown Cricket Club, Pairaudeau was still a Queen's College schoolboy when he scored his first century for British Guiana. Interviewed for this book, he remembered ruefully that, even as he compiled 161 in one of the 1950 tour trials, he sensed he would miss out because of the runs and reputations of other candidates. He went to England anyway for two successful seasons as an amateur with Burnley in the Lancashire League, but again failed to make the West Indies party to Australia.

Pairaudeau's weight of runs for BG finally forced him into the Test side against India. He scored a century on debut, one of three consecutive first-class hundreds. Although his form tailed off when he was promoted to open in place of Rae, he was still a likely starter against England. Given his background and elegant off-side play, Pairaudeau was considered long-term leadership material by the Board of Control.

....

SONNY RAMADHIN (Trinidad)
Birthplace: Esperance Village. **Age:** 23. **Previous Tests:** 15. **First-class debut:** 1949/50. **Test debut:** 1950.

Orphaned at an early age, Ramadhin's was a fairytale story. Within a year of being 'discovered' in a public park by former Barbados player Clarence Skinner, he was bamboozling England's batsmen at Lord's. His secret was what would now be called the 'doosra'. At a Canadian Mission school, he had learnt to spin his off-break and his leg-break with no obvious change in action (although some English players and journalists were quick to discern a jerk).

Initially, he cut a gauche figure, bowling with his cap on and sleeves rolled down, not sure where square leg fielded, who Len Hutton was or how to use a knife and fork. Worrell was one of the figures who helped a shy boy from the sticks come to terms with the spotlight, but Ramadhin's temperament began to be questioned after he limped off the pitch in tears during a close finish at the MCG in 1951/52. He was usually an uncomplaining dynamo, delivering nearly 20,000 first-class balls between 1949 and 1953 on top of his summer workload for Crompton in Lancashire. And he was still adored by Caribbean fans, especially those of Indian heritage in Trinidad and BG.

....

GARFIELD SOBERS (Barbados)
Birthplace: Bridgetown (Bayland). **Age:** 17. **Previous Tests:** 0. **First-class debut:** 1952/53.

The tragic event of Sobers' childhood was the death of his merchant-seaman father, Shamont, torpedoed by a U-boat in the Atlantic in 1942. The more curious event was his being born with five fingers on both hands – he was to remove one of the extra digits himself. Sobers was a natural and versatile athlete, going on to represent Barbados at golf, football and basketball. By the age of 13 he was playing in the Barbados Cricket League, starting out like Worrell as an orthodox left-arm spinner.

It took a special talent in those days to break out of the BCL into the more refined league of the Barbados Cricket Association. It was even more remarkable that Sobers was appearing, on Denis Atkinson's recommendation, for the BCA Police team within another year, and that he was selected for Barbados against the Indians at the age of 16. Polly Umrigar hit his second ball in first-class cricket for six but Sobers ended with commendable debut match figures of 89-40-142-7. Although Barbados had no other first-class games before MCC's visit, Sobers topped the BCA batting and bowling averages in 1953.

....

ALF VALENTINE (Jamaica)
Birthplace: Kingston. **Age:** 23. **Previous Tests:** 16. **First-class debut:** 1949/50. **Test debut:** 1950.

Gangly, gap-toothed, thick-lensed and bent-kneed, Valentine was an unlikely-looking left-arm spinner. His short, jerky run-up reminded the Australian journalist Ray Robinson of 'Groucho Marx getting into a lift before the door closes'. But the point was 'he'd chunter up to the wicket and rip it'. This was the verdict of Doug Insole, who had his first – all too brief – look at Valentine in 1950. On debut at Old Trafford, Valentine made history by taking the first eight wickets to fall and his remarkable series figures read 422.3-197-674-33.

Unusually for a West Indian outside the elite school system, Valentine had received expert coaching, from George Mudie (the Jamaican left-armer) and Jack Mercer (the ex-Glamorgan seamer). His impact had been less dramatic in subsequent series, given less helpful surfaces and injuries to his shoulder and spinning finger. But he still maintained a strike-rate of five wickets a Test and emerged in credit from the Australian tour. Valentine, a man with a beautifully rich voice whose only extravagances seem to have been snazzy shoes and jazz records, was by now a national hero in Jamaica.

....

CLYDE WALCOTT (Barbados)
Birthplace: Bridgetown (New Orleans). **Age:** 27. **Previous Tests:** 23. **First-class debut:** 1941/42. **Test debut:** 1947/48.

Educated first at Combermere and then the even more respectable Harrison College, Walcott is one of only two players, along with P.H. Tarilton, to have appeared in the BCA League as an 11-year-old. He took more time to find his feet in first-class cricket, but announced himself domestically with 314* against Trinidad in 1945/46 (breaking Tarilton's island record) and internationally with a superb tour of India in 1948/49 (452 runs at 64.57). Contemporary accounts of his batting invariably refer to his 'immense power': he was renowned for his straight-driving, off either foot, but this was not to say his hooking and cutting were less ferocious.

Walcott combined all this with reliable wicketkeeping, despite being 6ft 2in. But he decided to abdicate this role after a mediocre tour of Australia, where he endured a slipped disc, broken nose and harsh lessons taking on the short ball. Scores of 125 and 118 in the last two Tests at home against India gave warning that Walcott might become an even better batsman spared the intensity of keeping to Ram and Val. His lively off-cutters, honed in the Lancashire League with Enfield, were an added bonus.

....

EVERTON WEEKES (Barbados)
Birthplace: Bridgetown (Pickwick Gap). **Age:** 28. **Previous Tests:** 25. **First-class debut:** 1943/44. **Test debut:** 1947/48.

If Worrell was the most elegant of the Three Ws and Walcott the most powerful, Weekes was the most lethal: 'His eye was certain, his hand fatal, his presence of mind complete.' Weekes was one of the first players from the BCL to play international cricket. He made an ordinary start against England, perhaps lucky to retain his place for the final Test in Jamaica, where J.K. Holt was made twelfth man. Transport problems delayed his arrival, and he was roundly booed by the Sabina crowd when he replaced Holt on the field. Two days later they carried him off it in triumph. Dropped by Evans on nought, Weekes made 141.

His next Test scores, in India the following winter, were 128, 194, 162, 101 and 90 (run out by an umpiring error). His league experience with Bacup proved invaluable in 1950, when he averaged nearly 80 on the tour of England. In Australia, he had problems with a thigh injury and Ray Lindwall, but at home in 1952/53 he had been in masterful form, scoring 969 runs against the Indians (including 253 for Barbados) at an average of 121.

WEST INDIAN WITNESSES

In 1950, Jimmy Cozier was sent to cover the tour to England in what he called the one great 'cooperative effort' of the Caribbean Press Association. Cozier's reports, syndicated across nine regional newspapers, proudly championed the team in the face of English condescension, and he opened his own bottle of Goddard's Gold Braid Rum to celebrate the victory at Lord's. The Press Association was never as united again. It seems the only local correspondent to be physically present for all the Tests in 1953/54 was Stollmeyer's friend **Philip Thomson**, and he was engaged by *The Cricketer* to write dispatches for English consumption. Instead, the newspapers in each colony often had to rely on a syndicated report from an English journalist. Part II therefore draws on the testimony of other witnesses as well as the reporters who attended Tests on their home islands.

JAMAICA
Jamaican journalists boycotted MCC's first tour match, in protest at preferential treatment given to the English press. The established cricket writers for *The Daily Gleaner* were **Jack Anderson** and **L. D. 'Strebor' Roberts**, who wrote detailed accounts of the Tests played in Jamaica to supplement the syndicated report carried on the

front page. Although Roberts was a consistent advocate of Worrell throughout the 1950s, more polemical views were provided in the PNP weekly *Public Opinion*, from **Ken Jones**, its irascible sports editor, and **Michael Manley**, son of the party leader, whose opinion column was sometimes more devoted to cricket than politics. The Jamaican poet and academic **John Figueroa** attended both Sabina Park Tests in 1953/54 and recorded some of his memories in 1991.

BARBADOS

Jimmy Cozier was off the island and his son **Tony Cozier** was 13 years old (although he did later give an account of the series in his *Fifty Years of Test Cricket*). The most respected local journalist was **O.S. 'Santa Claus' Coppin**, a Combermere old boy who was a good enough player to turn out for Empire's second XI. Coppin was sports editor of the *Barbados Advocate* and also hosted a Saturday-night Barbados Rediffusion segment on local club cricket.

BRITISH GUIANA

The *Daily Argosy* provided long anonymous reports throughout the series, which seem to have been pieced together from radio broadcasts. By far the most outspoken leader articles touching on the cricket were by **Jake Crocker** of the *Daily Chronicle*. The literary critic and cricket historian **Frank Birbalsingh** was present for several days of the Test, and **Robin Wishart**, son of the secretary of Georgetown CC and the local Cricket Association, watched both the colony game and the Test match from the junior members' section in the pavilion.

TRINIDAD

Trinidadians would have to wait until the next MCC tour to read C.L.R. James's columns on cricket in *The Nation*. That paper – and the PNM, the party it represented – had not yet been formed. In 1953/54, the play was still covered in depth by the two main newspapers on the island, the *Trinidad Guardian* and *Port of Spain Gazette*. They commissioned special pieces from English pressmen and produced their own output. The lead reporters on the home Test were **George de Govia**, the *Gazette*'s sports editor, and **J.S. (Jack) Barker**, an expatriate playwright who was the *Guardian*'s cricket correspondent. *The Guardian* also ran columns by **Dick Murray**, **Albert 'Bootins' Alkins** and sports editor **Brunell Jones**, who recorded some further memories of the series in 1974. The Trinidad papers sent out individual correspondents to BG and Barbados, and to Jamaica for the fifth Test (although it is conceivable they were just listening to the radio in the last case).

MCC

LEN HUTTON (Yorkshire, captain)
Birthplace: Fulneck, near Pudsey. **Age:** 37. **Previous Tests:** 65.
Previous tours: 5. **First-class debut:** 1934. **Test debut:** 1937.

'You should have seen him before the war' was the unanimous verdict of Hutton's Yorkshire teammates from that era. The man himself agreed he was at his absolute peak in 1939, before his wartime injury: 'I knew I wasn't the player I could have become.' A wistfulness about what might have been was no less deeply felt for being only occasionally articulated.

And yet, judged in terms of runs, Hutton was as masterful as ever. In seven consecutive domestic seasons between 1947 and 1953, he maintained an aggregate of more than 2,000. He had topped the England averages in both the series he had captained. For Hutton's style of leadership on tour, the verdict of John Woodcock after the 1954/55 series in Australia also applied in the West Indies: 'He was full of paradoxes: self-contained yet vulnerable, reserved yet quizzical, shrewd yet enigmatic, gentle yet tenacious.'

....

CHARLES PALMER (Leicestershire, player-manager)
Birthplace: Old Hill, Staffordshire. **Age:** 34. **Previous Tests:** 0.
Previous tours: 1. **First-class debut:** 1938.

Bailey thought Palmer looked 'a natural for the role of hen-pecked bank clerk in a farce'. Appearances could be deceptive. Diminutive, bespectacled and balding, Palmer was capable of wristily powerful hitting. In 1948, while still at his first county Worcestershire, a dashing 85 against Bradman's Invincibles earned him a place on that winter's tour of South Africa. With the ball, Palmer's little dobbers looked innocuous but could break partnerships and take wickets in clusters (in 1955 he took eight against Surrey without conceding a run).

Palmer was not a high-caste amateur, and embarked on a career as a schoolmaster at Bromsgrove Grammar School after the war. But MCC always seemed to have a soft spot for him. They gave him a special registration to help keep him in the game as captain-secretary at Leicestershire, whom he soon took to unparalleled heights. However, Palmer's one previous encounter with the West Indians, in 1950, was hardly auspicious. The tourists' score at the end of the first day at Grace Road was 651 for two.

....

TREVOR BAILEY (Essex, vice-captain)
Birthplace: Westcliff-on-Sea. **Age:** 30. **Previous Tests:** 19. **Previous tours:** 1. **First-class debut:** 1945. **Test debut** 1949.

Woodcock seemed to specialise in balanced assessments, judging that Bailey was 'kind yet intolerant, thoughtful yet outspoken, cautious yet successful, precise yet amusing, aloof yet companionable'. The indomitable all-rounder could attract more severe adjectives, which David Foot once collected: 'boring, cussed ... pompous and mercenary'. But if Bailey was on your side, as he proved in the Coronation Ashes, he was a priceless asset. Keith Miller, who responded to Bailey's time-wasting at Headingley by trying to take his head off with a beamer, acknowledged that he played cricket 'in a way the toughest Australian could understand even if not always approve'.

From a lower middle-class background, Bailey became the protégé of his prep-school master Denys Wilcox, a former captain of Essex, who helped procure him a scholarship at Dulwich College. While an undergraduate at Cambridge, Bailey turned down a berth on Allen's boat to the West Indies. But he took six for 118 on debut against New Zealand, before a promising tour of Australia under Brown in 1950/51. After a short period out of favour, during which he won the FA Amateur Cup with Walthamstow Avenue, Bailey had re-established himself as England's man for any crisis.

....

DENIS COMPTON (Middlesex)
Birthplace: Hendon. **Age:** 35. **Previous Tests:** 54. **Previous tours:** 3. **First-class debut:** 1936. **Test debut:** 1937.

Alan Gibson wished 'that it had been Compton's arm and Hutton's knee to suffer, instead of the other way round'. This was too pat: Hutton pointed out that one of Compton's great assets was being 'a natural left hander' and Compton thought Hutton 'the most beautifully balanced player I ever saw'. But there was a clear division in Compton's career between the debonair years of dancing strokeplay and a more tortured second phase, when the infamous 'Compton knee' was a constant subject of press discussion.

The turning point was his *annus mirabilis* of 1947, when he scored a record 3,816 runs and 18 centuries but also felt the first signs of crippling synovitis (the legacy of a collision with a goalkeeper playing for Arsenal). After still proving brilliant and valiant against the Invincibles, Compton was forced to miss Tests in three home series running and hobbled through the Coronation Ashes. But, at the start of the West Indies tour, he was telling English journalists he had 'not felt fitter for a long time', having shed six pounds by following a strict fruit diet.

·················

GODFREY EVANS (Kent)
Birthplace: Finchley. **Age:** 33. **Previous Tests:** 49. **Previous tours:** 4. **First-class debut:** 1939. **Test debut:** 1946.

Evans forms the middle panel of the great triptych of Kent and England wicketkeepers between Les Ames and Alan Knott. He was the worst batsman of the three and the best gloveman, particularly brilliant when standing up to Doug Wright or Alec Bedser. Always bubbly, sometimes bristling, Evans was described by Arlott as 'the most unquenchable man in cricket'. The *Daily Mail* columnist Ian Wooldridge once painted a lively image of him notching a certain kind of century, when still a bachelor, on the boat-trip to Australia in 1946/47.

Behind the stumps, Evans was a perfectionist as well as an exhibitionist, admitting to a 'real stinker' when Australia chased down 404 at Leeds in 1948. He was haunted by the chances he dropped and took being dropped by England equally badly, an experience he endured briefly three times between 1949 and 1951.

But by the time of the Ashes triumph at The Oval, which Evans described as 'the most memorable day – and night – of my life', he was considered irreplaceable.

....

TOM GRAVENEY (Gloucestershire)
Birthplace: Riding Mill. **Age:** 26. **Previous Tests:** 14. **Previous tours:** 1. **First-class debut:** 1948. **Test debut:** 1951.

Northumbrian by birth but Bristolian by upbringing, Graveney often drew comparisons with his county forbear Hammond. He was the best professional batsman of his generation, and at the same time its most classical stylist. A high Edwardian back-lift and flourishing golfer's follow-through made his front-foot play especially easy on the eye. Graveney's early career progressed as serenely. He was selected for the Players at Lord's in his second season and made his Test debut the next summer. On the 1951/52 tour of India, Graveney scored his maiden Test century, easily England's best batsman in an understrength side. He was one of *Wisden*'s Cricketers of the Year in 1953.

But 1953 also marked the moment when his 'killer instinct' began to be questioned. He averaged only 24 against Australia. After playing superbly on the second evening of the Lord's Test in partnership with Hutton, he was yorked by Lindwall the next morning. Although they continued to respect each other's technique, Hutton never forgot Graveney's lapse of concentration, and Graveney never forgave his skipper for restraining his strokeplay against a tiring attack the evening before.

....

JIM LAKER (Surrey)
Birthplace: Bradford. **Age:** 31. **Previous Tests:** 18. **Previous tours:** 1. **First-class debut:** 1946. **Test debut:** 1947/48.

Known more as a batsman in the Bradford League, Laker developed his off-breaks on matting wickets in Egypt, where he was stationed for most of the war. Choosing to sign for Surrey on his return, he was selected for Allen's tour of the West Indies after just one full first-class season, taking nine wickets on debut in Barbados. He was already considered lethal on rain-affected wickets, registering first-innings figures of 14-12-2-8 in the 1950 Test trial. Hutton was on Laker's side in that match and admired both his control and his subtle variations: 'He makes you think.'

But Hutton had also played in two matches against the Invincibles when Laker was smashed out of the attack. From that point, he and the selectors seemed to doubt whether the off-spinner had a big-match temperament. Between 1948 and 1953, despite taking more than 100 wickets each season, Laker played in only 12 of 22 home Tests and was not taken on any of MCC's tours. Perhaps Lord's also doubted, like Alan Ross, whether Laker was 'always the easiest of men to deal with, in the employer-employee situation'.

....

TONY LOCK (Surrey)
Birthplace: Limpsfield. **Age:** 24. **Previous Tests:** 4. **Previous tours:** 0. **First-class debut:** 1946. **Test debut:** 1952.

Lock made a slow start in county cricket until two winters' intensive training at Allders indoor school in Croydon. He went in relying on flight more than turn in the Wilfred Rhodes tradition; he came out bowling medium-paced darts in a manner which anticipated Derek Underwood. This change in style brought him to the attention of both selectors and umpires. A week after his Test debut against India, he was no-balled three times in two overs for throwing his quicker ball. Lock later attributed these problems to a low beam in the Croydon nets which had caused him to drop his bowling arm.

But he still had two important advocates in Allen and Hutton, whose faith was vindicated by a five-for at The Oval in 1953. Hutton was not alone in observing that Lock 'is a slow bowler with a fast bowler's temperament'. Spine-chilling appeals, spine-bending celebrations and a thoroughly aggressive approach saw him often described as a 'stormy petrel'. He could certainly catch anything that moved – his first touch of the ball in Test cricket was a typically brilliant effort at short-leg.

....

PETER MAY (Surrey)
Birthplace: Reading. **Age:** 23. **Previous Tests:** 8. **Previous tours:** 0. **First-class debut:** 1948. **Test debut:** 1951.

Wisden thought 1953 had been a 'critical summer' for May. Targeted by the Australians – he scored 37 in his first five innings against them – his weight of runs for Surrey and a touch of steel in his character saw him successfully recalled for the victory at The Oval. May had already scored 30 first-class centuries, averaging nearly 2,500 runs a season between 1951 and 1953. A superb rackets player, he was arguably England's best-ever batsman, off either foot, through mid-on.

May had been a prodigy at Charterhouse, topping the first XI averages at the age of 14 under the coaching of the ex-Leicestershire and England pro George Geary. At Cambridge, he thrived on the featherbed of Fenner's and became the first undergraduate to score a Test century since the Hon. F.S. Jackson. He remembered that Hutton's only words from the other end on that occasion were 'Are you all right?' But the two men, buttoned up in their different ways, developed a strong relationship in the West Indies.

....

ALAN MOSS (Middlesex)
Birthplace: Tottenham. **Age:** 23. **Previous Tests:** 0. **Previous tours:** 0. **First-class debut:** 1950.

Alan Moss heard of his selection for the tour from his county colleague Don Bennett. He admitted to being 'surprised' after going wicketless in the Gentlemen v Players trial. But he had bowled well against the Australians, for MCC and Middlesex, and bagged 90 wickets in 1953 (to add to a haul of 95 the previous season). He also seemed to have added a yard of pace, perhaps the result of a winter spent felling trees on Stuart Surridge's willow plantations.

A policeman's son, Moss had come late to cricket, owing his entrée to a London Colts scheme run by the *Evening News*. But he was already becoming a Middlesex stalwart. Another, Angus Fraser, later paid him tribute: 'We were two grumpy, fastish bowlers that didn't care much for batsmen. I loved his honesty, his strength, and his mischievous sense of humour.' Hutton found Moss 'likeable and enthusiastic', and was making more of a point about social trends than personal character when noting that 'he talks a little too much for a young man of 23'.

....

DICK SPOONER (Warwickshire)
Birthplace: Stockton-on-Tees. **Age:** 33. **Previous Tests:** 5. **Previous tours:** 1. **First-class debut:** 1948. **Test debut:** 1951/52.

Birmingham's *Sports Argus* may not have been entirely impartial when it argued in 1951 that Spooner's 'infinitely greater ability as a batsman' should see him preferred to Evans. Spooner topped the Warwickshire batting averages that year in the all-professional side which won the Championship. When Evans took the winter off, Spooner's previous experience as a Commonwealth tourist in India may have helped win him a place on MCC's tour there. He averaged 35 in the Tests, promoted to opener for the last three games, and scored three centuries for Warwickshire in 1953. His left-handedness was another plus in the eyes of the tour selection committee.

Because of the war, Spooner did not play Minor Counties cricket for Durham until the age of 26. He had not even attended a County Championship match until his own debut for Warwickshire two years later. Voluble on the field and self-effacing off it, he was a popular tourist. He reckoned he had clocked up 22,000 miles travelling with MCC in India, where he had plenty of time to indulge his penchants for curries and crosswords.

....

BRIAN STATHAM (Lancashire)
Birthplace: Manchester. **Age:** 23. **Previous Tests:** 9. **Previous tours:** 2. **First-class debut:** 1950. **Test debut:** 1950/51.

Although Statham was a late developer – he preferred football and tennis on a scholarship at Manchester Grammar School – he made his Test debut in New Zealand on his 20th birthday in only his 20th first-class match, seeming to Cardus as if he had 'escaped from a Lowry canvas, lean and hungry'. The next winter, in India, *Wisden* saw 'signs that he might develop into a really first-class bowler'. Statham's opportunities in home Tests were more restricted but in the three domestic seasons before the West Indies tour he had taken 308 wickets.

Statham worked on the old principle of 'If you miss, I hit' – only Lindwall of the great Test fast bowlers had a higher percentage of victims clean bowled. At the same time, he was famously loose-jointed and full of what would now be called 'natural variation'. Unassuming, undemonstrative, uncomplaining, Statham was the antithesis of Trueman. Later in their careers, they roomed together overseas but they were not particularly close on the 1953/54 tour. After a long day's toil, Statham's bloodied feet and tobacco-stained fingers were the emblems of the dedicated artisan. Hutton thought 'Brian was always a grand lad'.

....

KEN SUTTLE (Sussex)
Birthplace: Kensington. **Age:** 25. **Previous Tests:** 0. **Previous tours**: 0. **First-class debut:** 1949.

As a promoter of youth, Warner was on the look-out for an English Neil Harvey, and he proved susceptible to Suttle's 'most refreshing' footwork against the spinners and his brilliant fielding. Suttle had also been coached briefly by one of Warner's favourite cricketers, Patsy Hendren. However, Suttle was not just a Warner project. Charles Bray of the *Herald* described him as the 'most improved player in the country' when suggesting him for the deciding Ashes Test in 1953. In his first full season of county cricket, Suttle had scored six centuries, three of which came in the fortnight before the final selection meeting for the West Indies.

Suttle had brief spells at Chelsea and Brighton & Hove Albion; he continued to play non-League football, appearing for Chelmsford City on his wedding day. But he had decided to concentrate on cricket and would go on to make 423 consecutive appearances for Sussex, a record for the County Championship. Known as 'Shuffler' for his neurotic movements in the crease, he was a chatterer on the field and a bundle of energy in the dressing room. According to Lock, Suttle 'thoroughly enjoyed' the tour of the West Indies, his first ever trip abroad.

FRED TRUEMAN (Yorkshire)
Birthplace: Stainton. **Age:** 22. **Previous Tests:** 5. **Previous tours:** 0.
First-class debut: 1949. **Test debut:** 1952.

Arlott believed it would be 'difficult for later generations to appreciate quite what Fred Trueman meant in 1952, not simply as a performer but as a symbol … constituted exactly to the demand of the day'. England had been demanding a second Larwood for 20 years. Here was a prodigy with no unhappy medium about him, an archetypal Yorkshireman from the coalfields and a prototype of the floppy-haired angry young man.

Brought along carefully by his county, Trueman burst onto the international scene in 1952, reducing India to 0 for four on debut at Headingley and taking eight for 31 in the first innings at Old Trafford. In the Coronation Ashes, he was held back until the final Test for various reasons, including his national service. The Oval crowd cheered wildly for his long run, nasty bouncers, six slips and four wickets: at last it was pay-back time for Lindwall and Miller blitzing the English batsmen with impunity. Hutton, who still considered Trueman a 'young colt', wanted to see more of the same in the West Indies in the hope he would develop into the leader of the attack in Australia in 1954/55.

....

JOHNNY WARDLE (Yorkshire)
Birthplace: Ardsley. **Age:** 30. **Previous Tests**: 7. **Previous tours:** 1. **First-class debut:** 1946. **Test debut:** 1947/48.

Also from South Yorkshire mining stock, Wardle deviated from the great tradition of Yorkshire left-arm spinners – Peel, Rhodes, Verity – in that he could bowl from the back of the hand as well. There was a native suspicion of wrist-spin but, in his more orthodox style, Wardle became the county's main weapon on wet pitches and their stock option on better ones. He bowled a record 810 maidens in 1952 and his first-class wicket tallies in the six seasons before the 1953/54 tour were 150, 103, 174, 127, 177, 146. Despite taking the scalp of Stollmeyer with his first ball in home Tests, his international career was embittered by his rivalry with Lock, whom Allen always preferred despite otherwise frowning on suspect actions.

Intelligent but obstreperous, Wardle divided opinion in the Yorkshire dressing room. Brian Close rated him 'an exceptionally deep thinker about the game', whereas Ray Illingworth found him 'an insecure and difficult man' who bullied the younger pros. Spectators in the West Indies did not see this side of Wardle. He was dubbed the 'Duke of Antigua' for his clowning in the field and his breezy batting in the Leeward Islands.

·················

WILLIE WATSON (Yorkshire)
Birthplace: Bolton-on-Dearne. **Age:** 33. **Previous Tests:** 9. **Previous tours:** 0. **First-class debut:** 1939. **Test debut:** 1951.

Watson was 'Willie' to the London press, 'Billy' in Yorkshire – after his father who was a distinguished wing-half for Huddersfield Town – and nicknamed 'William the Silent' by Peter May on tour: 'He seldom had much to say but was a great thinker about the game and, as befitted one of the last to play both cricket and football for England, a beautiful mover on his feet.' Watson, also a wing-half, was a non-playing squad member for the 1950 World Cup in Brazil, but decided to retire from soccer to take up his engagement with MCC in the West Indies.

Watson shares characteristics with David Gower: both were brilliant outfielders (with suspect throwing arms), both were left-handers who stayed classically still and both tended to make everything look so easy that their appetite for harder graft was sometimes questioned by selectors. Even though Watson's stock was high in 1953, after his match-saving century at Lord's in his first game against Australia, he was still dropped for the decider at The Oval.

THE ENGLISH PRESS CORPS

Three of the eight English journalists covering the tour – Alex Bannister, Charles Bray and Peter Ditton – travelled out by ship from Liverpool to cover the games in Bermuda in December. Most of the others made their way to the Caribbean before the new year, although Swanton did not arrive until the middle of MCC's second game in Jamaica. The eight-man press party are important to our story for three reasons. They were the main formers of opinion back in England, in the days before satellite television and ball-by-ball radio coverage of overseas tours (in 1953/54 the BBC's Light Programme did carry 15-minute close-of-play summaries broadcast live from the Caribbean by Swanton). Because their columns were often syndicated or summarised in Caribbean newspapers, they provoked immediate reactions in the West Indies. And, in the absence of any professionally shot film footage, archived sound commentary or consistent local press coverage, they provide the main day-to-day record. Despite the variety of journalistic styles and outlooks, the voices of those who were not on this tour but went out to Australia the next winter – Arlott, Bowes, Kilburn, Ross, Woodcock – are much missed.

Alex Bannister *(Daily Mail)* was fresh from the coup of persuading Bradman to come over for the Coronation Ashes and then ghosting his columns. Bannister had a reputation for being dyspeptic with sub-editors, a leg-puller with colleagues and tactful with his contacts in the game. He developed a good relationship with Hutton, collaborating on his final autobiography in 1984, even if he was sometimes prepared to criticise the captain's tactics. Bannister's Test reports were syndicated in Trinidad and therefore remained measured, but his colour pieces for the *Mail* always took the side of the beleaguered English cricketer.

Charles Bray *(Daily Herald)* was not the only correspondent with first-class experience – Swanton had played three games for Middlesex – but he appeared in 95 matches as an amateur for Essex between the wars. As a journalist, he cultivated the persona of a strongly opinionated expert. According to Doug Insole, MCC vice-captain in South Africa in 1956/57, he 'doesn't believe in wasting words, and … does not shrink from mention of the social side of touring'. Because of his paper's working-class readership, Bray generally supported Hutton and had canvassed for his captaincy as early as 1950. But he was also well connected with the MCC establishment and shared their distaste for negative play.

Peter Ditton *(Express Syndications)* was the youngest of the English journalists but under the onerous burden of being syndicated to *The Daily Gleaner* in Jamaica (the closest equivalent in the Caribbean to the London *Times*) as well as regional newspapers in England. His reporting was therefore generally restrained, even if he let slip the odd provocative opinion. Disparaging remarks about Headley caused Michael Manley to describe Ditton as a 'mewling schoolboy'.

Ross Hall *(Daily Mirror)*, as Bannister tartly pointed out, was 'on his first cricket tour'. His was the most 'tabloid' style in the press corps, made even more frenzied by his sub-editors' headlines. Hall was also most liable to sensational reporting of off-field activities, although he was essentially a Hutton loyalist in keeping with the *Mirror*'s editorial line.

Reg Hayter *(Reuters)* was generally well liked by cricketers for his discretion and commercial sense. He was reputed to have introduced Compton to his agent, Bagenal Harvey. Hayter's reports were syndicated to *The Times* and he therefore subordinated himself to that paper's house style. However, his strong patriotism – he was a founder member of the St George's Day Club – sometimes seeped through the sobriety. Hayter ghosted Hutton's retirement memoirs in 1956.

Frank Rostron *(Daily Express)* was more of a career journalist than a cricket enthusiast. He tended to treat sporting triumphs and disasters as a matter of national prestige, although he was at the same time an outspoken critic of the Lord's establishment. Insole felt he 'seldom allows himself to become too occupied by events on the field, preferring to look unashamedly about him for a "story"'. The story for Rostron on this tour was Hutton's fitness for captaincy, and he also agitated for Compton to be dropped.

E.W. Swanton *(The Daily Telegraph)* was generally viewed as pompous by touring cricketers, one of whom memorably described him as too much of a snob to be seen in the same car as his chauffeur. Swanton's reporting, if sometimes delivered from the pulpit, was crisper than any other correspondent. His attitudes were innately pro-amateur but he was not explicitly hostile to Hutton on this tour. He was also a genuine enthusiast for West Indies cricket and sympathetic to the local crowds. Rostron, with whom Swanton had a running feud, took the more cynical view that he was merely 'anxious to avoid stinks of any kind'.

Crawford White *(News Chronicle)* struck a young John Woodcock as 'this tall, slim matinée idol, with wavy hair and a David Niven moustache'. White admitted he 'hunted as a pair' with his close friend Bray on foreign tours, especially on the golf course. A good Central Lancashire League cricketer, White was called up as an emergency replacement along with Swanton at the end of Allen's 1947/48 tour. He was always on the look-out for a scoop, although he rarely betrayed his sources in the dressing room. White was yet another English advocate of brighter cricket, but he did dissent from the general opinion of the press box by advocating Palmer's qualities as a player.

PART II

THE TOUR

CHAPTER 7

BERMUDA

There were a number of informal conventions when MCC touring parties assembled before their outward journey. It was traditional for them to be guests of honour at a farewell dinner held in the Tavern at Lord's. It was traditional for their wives to complain about not being invited to the dinner, given that most of them would not see their husbands again for four months. And it was traditional for an MCC figure to offer some words of wisdom after the toasts.

An inadequate briefing

Given the political sensitivities in the Caribbean, MCC had arranged for a member of the government to lecture the cricketers. Sir Walter Monckton, the Minister for Labour, had recently served a term as Surrey president and would go on to fill the same post at MCC in 1956, despite once describing the club's main committee as making the Tory cabinet look like a 'band of pinkos'. He may have been invited by his friend Warner because of his considerable experience of foreign affairs. Unfortunately, most of it was East of Suez.

Monckton is also unlikely to have been fully focused on briefing the team, as he was in the midst of dealing with the threat of a Christmas rail strike. He put himself under so much pressure during the dispute – 'he wore himself out by giving way' according to Churchill – that he was admitted to hospital in January suffering from nervous exhaustion.

Judging from the reactions of his audience, his speech did not show many signs of advance preparation. Moss remembers some high-level remarks about 'black/white issues' which he confesses went over his head and did not contain any specific advice. There is a trace of sarcasm in Compton's recollection:

> It was pointed out that the political situation was in
> some places a delicate one, and our attention was
> directed to that more intangible and more explosive

thing, the difference in the colour of men's faces and the sudden sensitivities to which it might give rise. We were asked very courteously not to provoke any incidents. We listened as intelligently and attentively as we could.

For Hutton, the guidance was 'excellent as far as it went, but it did not tell us how sensitive the situation could be'. Trueman found all the abstract talk about treading carefully fairly rich, given that the professionals were being paid only £500 (pre-tax) plus a £50 good-conduct bonus for the tour: 'So I upped and said, with all due respect, that if I was expected to be a member of Her Majesty's Diplomatic Service, I should like to be paid like one and also receive the privileges associated with such a position.' He claimed he received a 'blustering' answer telling him not to take things so literally, although it is hard to know how literally we should take his story.

However, it is clear that Palmer was disappointed that the 'conditions' on the ground in each colony were not set out in more detail. British Guiana was the most obvious tinderbox, with British troops patrolling the streets after the suspension of the constitution. Trinidad was absorbing the return of Uriah Butler, the key figure in violent disturbances of 1937, who had gone back there from London just before the cricketers set out. In Barbados, a serious rift in the main nationalist party became public while MCC were on the island. In the run-up to the fifth Test, Jamaica's executive council would consider emergency-powers legislation to deal with labour unrest. Perhaps only the tour to Pakistan in 1968/69, eventually aborted in light of the events in what was to become Bangladesh, pitched English cricketers into a more difficult political situation.

Palmer felt that his team were 'not adequately briefed' on all this 'either by the government or by MCC'. He was also worried, with some justification, that the revised travel arrangements – a flight to Bermuda rather than a long sea passage – would remove a valuable preparatory 'breathing space' conducive to the building of team spirit. Another practical concern was that the roles of scorer and baggageman, usually combined on MCC tours by 'Mr Cricket' Bill Ferguson, were being outsourced, for budgetary reasons, to locals on each island.

LEICESTERSHIRE COUNTY CRICKET CLUB

President : **S. H. B. LIVINGSTON, Esq.**

Secretary : **C. H. PALMER**
SPENCER CHAMBERS, MARKET PLACE, LEICESTER
Phone : **5196**

L.Hutton, Esq.,
C/o Yorkshire County Cricket Club,
Old Bank Chambers,Leeds 1.   11th November, 1953

Dear Len,

~~temporarily~~ I have succeeded in scrounging this book
~~tentatively~~ from Miss Rait Kerr at Lord's. I don't think
it is really what we want but you might like to browse
through it. Perhaps you could let me have it back a little
later when you have finished with it.
        When at Lord's yesterday I learnt from
Billy Griffith that Cyril Merry, at present Secretary
of the West Indian Board of Control, is now in England,
and I am just waiting word from Billy so that I can go
down and meet him to get a bit of a preview on what to
expect. I do think this flying over to the West Indies
is a snag in many ways because it means that we are
catapulted into the activity of the tour without that
valuable breathing space when we can get among the side and
sort out one or two preliminary matters. I have written
to Billy Griffith suggesting that if you think it not a
bad idea, he writes to all the players and asks them to
come along to Lord's about an hour earlier than the
farewell dinner on Sunday, December 13th. That would then
give you and me the opportunity of having a few words
with them in private before we leave. If there is
anything you would like me to do on your behalf before
the 14th December, please let me know.
        With all good wishes,

                        Yours ever,

                        Charley

                        Secretary.

Hutton never got round to returning the book Palmer had borrowed
from the Lord's librarian, Diana Rait-Kerr, but he may have shared
the concerns the manager expressed in this covering letter.

An eventful flight

When the team assembled at Heathrow the next day, the first surprises were that Compton had not only arrived early but also remembered to bring some kit for the two communal bags MCC were taking with them to Bermuda (the players' heavier individual cricket cases were being shipped directly to Jamaica). Some in the party were reasonably seasoned air travellers – Hutton had made four long plane journeys on MCC duty – but others were making their maiden flights. Two of the younger tourists, from different backgrounds, found the prospect equally exciting. May had been on European tours with his school and university teams but air travel was 'something entirely new'. Moss had been a lowly aircraftman on national service in the RAF. He was exhilarated by the prospect of a journey on a luxury BOAC Stratocruiser, James Bond's airliner of choice.

Moss remembers that the two main attractions were the well-stocked lounge bar, in the belly of the aircraft, and the cockpit: 'Everyone was going up to the front of the plane and laughing and joking with the crew.' But, rather suddenly, one of the pilots started pushing and pulling at the controls in something of a panic: 'That wiped the smile off everyone's faces, I can tell you.' Palmer tried to remain calm during 'quite a to-do'. Trueman's recall of the pilot's message over the intercom gives some sense of the situation: 'Though there is no cause for alarm, I have to inform you we are past the point of no return and are experiencing electrical trouble.'

Earlier in 1953 there had been a fatal accident on the same route over the Atlantic; in 1954 there would be a fatal accident involving the same model of plane. Thankfully, MCC's Stratocruiser made it safely to Gander in Newfoundland, where the electrical fault was rectified. The players, many of whom had changed into what Lock called 'light summer suitings', made a mad rush through deep snow for the coffee-stall in the spartan airport lounge. Trueman found himself standing next to the Duke of Gloucester in the queue. The hastily arranged stopover also led to some interesting overnight pairings in twin-berth log cabins. Palmer roomed with Trueman, Hutton with Moss – 'Len barely said anything to me'. One tourist, possibly Wardle, became inconsolable when he realised he had forgotten to post his pools coupon. Then the players were woken in the middle of the night to get back on the plane, as a blizzard was set to hit Gander in the morning. After all this, the tour party arrived in one piece in Bermuda on 15 December, a day behind schedule.

A colour bar

The preliminary leg in Bermuda had been first proposed by Lord Cornwallis, who told the MCC Committee in March 1953 that the island's Governor was 'most anxious' for the team to play matches there 'en route to the West Indies'. The proposal was seconded by Robins, who had played on Julian Cahn's tour to Bermuda in 1933, and Wilfred Hill-Wood. Both men may have had connections to Stanhope Joel, the Anglo-South African diamond magnate who sponsored country-house cricket between the wars. Joel had agreed to underwrite MCC's expenses in Bermuda should a detour be made there.

Perhaps the anxiety of the Governor, Alexander Hood, sprang from the fact that he was supervising the wind-down of the naval dockyard and the removal of the army garrison. Bermuda was given several prestige events in 1953, as if in recognition that its status as an important British military base was diminishing. In November, it had been the first stopover on the Queen's six-month Coronation tour. Early in December, it hosted a conference of the three main allied powers, where Eisenhower privately told Churchill he was prepared to use nuclear weapons in Indochina.

Monckton's pre-tour lecture does not seem to have extended to social conventions in Bermuda, which had been modelled on the southern states of America rather than the British West Indies. Palmer was immediately taken aback when he suggested his contact from the local cricket board accompany him from the airport to discuss the playing arrangements: 'And then people started semaphoring "Not allowed to fraternise…Black and white…Not at the hotel." We had to arrange a special meeting elsewhere.'

The island's Hotel Keepers' Act of 1930 gave proprietors the right to deny entry to Negroes, Catholics and Jews. Presumably Joel, who fell into the last category, was granted some leeway by 1954. But the colour bar in Bermudan hotels had inspired a recent controversy. Frank McDavid, the brown president of the State Council of British Guiana, had to make an unscheduled stop in Bermuda in July on his way to be knighted by the Queen in London. He and his wife were not allowed entry to the St George Hotel and were instead offered lodging at the Imperial Hotel reserved for 'non-whites'. They protested by going back to the airport and sleeping on benches.

The discomfort of the McDavids may have been a cause of wry amusement back home for the many Guyanese who saw Sir Frank as a 'local white' and an arch collaborator with British rule. But it gave rise to a protest by the black members of Bermuda's parliament and questions – the week before MCC set off – in the House of Commons. The Colonial Secretary, Oliver Lyttleton, was forced to confirm that the government had reluctantly allowed the colour bar to remain in place 'at certain hotels' in Bermuda because it was essential to the island's tourist trade, 95% of which came from America. This provoked an understandably heated response elsewhere in the Caribbean, the Jamaican Evon Blake suggesting that such pandering to the Yankee dollar 'threatened the undoing of the British Empire'. The left-wing press in Britain was similarly exercised, the *Daily Herald* having already taken Governor Hood to task for a gross insult to 'coloured' people when not one of them was invited to the state reception during the Queen's visit.

The colour bar prevailed, more or less, in cricket. Even though the local Board of Control was by now ostensibly multiracial, the all-rounder Calvin Symonds remembers that the white Bermuda Cricket Association would not allow players like him from the black Somers Isles League onto its grounds. By far the most important event of the season for Symonds was the two-day Cup Match between the parishes of St George's and Somerset. 'Cup Match' had its roots as a carnival marking the anniversary of Emancipation and was described by the teacher and activist Eva Hodgson as 'the one truly spontaneous holiday' of the year for Bermuda's black majority. The three games with MCC would be played on Somerset's ground. Having lost the argument about the venue, the Cricket Association appears to have lost interest in the project, even if it supplied six players to a 'Pick of the Leagues' side for the first match. The Bermuda XI for the last two would largely be drawn from the Cup Match teams.

The embarrassingly low attendances at all the MCC matches were ascribed to a variety of factors: the games were taking place in the middle of the island's football season and in the run-up to Christmas; there was bad weather; transport links between the capital Hamilton and the venue in Somerset were poor. But the black president of Bermuda's Board of Control hinted that 'discrimination' was an underlying issue. Compton later put it more bluntly, remembering 'a total boycott of play by 99 per cent of the Europeans in the place'. The tourists found themselves playing cricket with teams which were predominantly black, while their social engagements off the field were almost entirely with whites.

Evans spent more time on the local golf courses than the local politics: 'Of course there is some kind of colour bar in Bermuda, although it was not too serious, so far as we could see. However, that was none of our business, and we had a very good time.' MCC were invited for a Sunday's golf at the exclusive Mid Ocean Club, where the Churchill-Eisenhower summit had been held. Wardle and Spooner had difficulty with the amount of water on the course; Compton and Palmer with the amount of alcohol they were offered by their hosts on the way round. Governor Hood had won the premier amateur matchplay tournament at St Andrews earlier that year. He played in a fourball against Hutton and Graveney, the best golfer in the party, who was another to remember having 'a whale of a time' on the island.

Another important social event was a party at Joel's mansion. For Statham, the spread was an upgrade on the curled-up sandwiches he was used to on the county circuit: 'Our menu that night included *pâté de foie gras*, caviare, and casseroled chicken and turkey which were served in a huge silver tureen, about six times the size of the FA Cup.' This was presumably also the occasion where Bailey was met with 'the astonishing sight of Errol Flynn consuming, of all things, iced cherry brandy out of a pint silver tankard'. While several MCC players seem to have taken similar advantage of the amenities provided by Joel, they were less impressed by the cricketing facilities.

A cricketing damp squib
Hutton faced the opening delivery of the tour. He edged it behind. This failure on his first appearance as captain overseas, albeit in a practice match not deemed first-class, added to a list of ducks on debut – for Yorkshire seconds, Yorkshire and England. Hutton had even failed to score in his first game as wartime captain of Pudsey St Lawrence.

131

He did make some runs in the next two matches against All-Bermuda. But in any case, despite these games being billed as 'Tests' in the local press, they were played in front of a few hundred people and proved of limited preparatory value. The matting wicket generated particularly high bounce, rendering the batting practice largely irrelevant even before the long interruptions for rain. Graveney, who scored a fifty in the first game, thought the Bermudan excursion 'pointless' from a cricketing point of view. Bailey felt the diversion justifiable 'for the benefit of spreading the gospel, but certainly not for the benefit of a team tackling the West Indies'.

The bowlers had to adjust their lengths to have any chance of hitting the wickets. It was at least useful for them to practice their run-ups, given that the pitches in Trinidad would also be artificial. While Lock was virtually unplayable on the bouncy surface in Bermuda, he had a pronounced drag for a slow bowler and found it difficult to keep his balance on the concrete underlay. Trueman was also a heavy dragger but found his main issue was the painful impact of his front foot on the concrete. He was reduced to bowling wide of the strip and felt this adjustment, however temporary, affected his rhythm for the rest of the tour. Judging from a report in the magazine *Bermuda Sports*, he took out some of his frustration on the officials: 'The spectacle of seeing a star England bowler indulging in what from the sidelines looked like an argument with an umpire was as unnecessary as it was futile.'

The experiment of the warm-up in Bermuda was somehow summed up by the revision of the schedule, which originally envisaged MCC playing their last day's cricket on the island on Christmas Day. A rest day was inserted, only for it to pour down on Boxing Day. At least Lock and most of the other players enjoyed the 'homely seasonal atmosphere' at the Christmas parties laid on for them by local families. However, Bailey remembered a 'dreadful Christmas Day dinner at Government House', where the post-prandial game of charades went on for two hours and one member of the party was told off by a 'dragon straight out of Oscar Wilde' for putting his feet on a sofa during his mime.

Once MCC landed in Jamaica, the time for charades had ended.

CHAPTER 8

JAMAICA

Welcoming Hutton's men, *The Daily Gleaner* noted the enormous interest the series had aroused on the island. The Ashes had crowned Coronation year in the 'mother country' and now a full-strength side had come out to fight West Indies for the title of 'undisputed cricket champions of the world'.

Sabina Park was about to host the opening Test of the first Caribbean tour to be taken seriously by England. It had just hosted the main event on the first tour of the island by a reigning British monarch:

> This has been a great year for Jamaica, and it is fitting
> that cricket should follow so closely on the heels of the
> Royal visit for in the minds of humble folk there are
> no greater spiritual links between these Colonies and
> England than the Monarchy and the game of cricket.

The reference to a 'great year' also recognised the fact that 1953 was an important landmark on Jamaica's road to independence: local politicians had been granted extended, if still ultimately limited, ministerial powers. But for those who saw *The Gleaner* as a mouthpiece for colonial vested interests – its offices would be besieged in the 'Black Power' riots of 1968 – its leader article was placing more emphasis on events where the union jack was waved than those where nationalist aspirations were unfurled.

The loyalist view that the 'average' West Indian was immutably bound to Britain by 'Crown and cricket' was shared by E.W. Swanton. It was also propounded by another episcopal figure, the Archbishop of York. He happened to be touring the British West Indies on a fact-finding mission at the same time as MCC, and was presented to the teams on the opening day of the Test. Although the Archbishop recognised that the root cause of the emergency in British Guiana was inequality, he also blamed Communist agitation. He concluded that the colour problem had been 'practically solved' in all the other West Indian colonies, whose 'desire for self-government is combined with devoted loyalty to the Queen and with the wish to remain within the Commonwealth'.

Mindful of the situation in British Guiana, both of the main political parties in Jamaica seemed prepared to play the game of self-government according to British rules. But the sense of a divided island, as opposed to a united Commonwealth, was never far from the surface. Ken Jones, sports editor of the PNP newspaper *Public Opinion*, accepted that 'the man on the street has a love for cricket which is second only to his delirious adoration of Royalty'. He also pointed out acidly that the main reason for the huge crowds which attended MCC's practice sessions was widespread unemployment.

If *The Gleaner's* sense of cricket fostering Commonwealth amity was wishful thinking, so was its belief that the 'honour of the game' was more important than the result:

> Len Hutton and his men have come out not only to
> try and beat the West Indies, but to play the game as it
> should be played, in the gallant and sporting manner in
> which these masters have been taught.

The reality was that MCC's cricketing and diplomatic missions were always in tension. It would prove impossible to reconcile playing hard with playing fair.

Non-fraternisation off the field

Compton remembered the tourists' first formal interaction with the press, during a reception on the evening of their arrival at the South Bank Road Hotel, introducing a 'nervous tension and conflict' into the series. He felt that journalists on both sides seized upon the idea of a play-off for the unofficial world championship 'with startling exhilaration'. Hutton later reflected that the 'so-called world championship tag was a nuisance', a sentiment echoed in the memoirs of all his senior players. But it seems fair to suggest they found it convenient in retrospect to lay all the blame on the media for creating an atmosphere which their own attitude had helped to engender. Walcott, while accepting the series was being hyped up, felt from the outset the English players 'seemed to think that they were the big boys'.

Walcott's impression was formed in the early days of the tour as the West Indian squad assembled from its various outposts at the same hotel as MCC. Graveney remembered an awkward three-week period 'managing in our irritation at constantly falling over each other, to make the hackles rise on friend and foe alike'.

The English did not think much of the hotel. Hutton worried that preparations were being undermined by the lack of 'off-the-field comfort': several of the party had to share single rooms and the food was 'nowhere as good as we thought it might have been'. Another problem was the 'cacophony' of barking dogs which kept them awake at night until the cockerels took over at dawn. Perhaps standards had declined since 1950, when the travel writer Patrick Leigh Fermor found the South Bank breakfast excellent; perhaps MCC had been spoiled by their treatment in Bermuda; perhaps the day-trip arranged for them one Sunday to the Tower Isle Hotel on the millionaires' playground of the north coast made their quarters back in Kingston seem more spartan. But the frosty atmosphere was less the result of the tourists kicking their heels than marking their ground.

Trueman told various stories of exchanging pleasantries with the home side, only to be warned by his captain 'that I was not to fraternise with the opposition'. The West Indians certainly felt they were being deliberately cold-shouldered. Worrell arrived late after his Commonwealth tour expecting to find the two sets of players 'staying together and reminiscing in the way cricketers always do'. Instead, he was 'answered in monosyllables' and was told by Walcott and Weekes that they had received the same treatment over the previous week, despite all efforts to be hospitable. Ramadhin felt his memory was too unreliable to give an interview for this book, but his view of Hutton recorded in 1992 was coloured by the atmosphere in the hotel: 'It was terrible the way he stopped the England players fraternising with us.'

Weekes, with the tranquility of a nonagenarian, now plays down the seriousness of all this and says the two squads rubbed along without much incident. Statham also recollected that 'personally I found the West Indies players good types and easy to get along

135

with'. There were prior relationships from recent Tests, northern league cricket and Commonwealth tours. New ones were forged during the months of close proximity. As just one example, McWatt, playing in his first series, was often seen discussing the finer points of wicketkeeping with Evans.

In the build-up to the first Test, however, Worrell detected a 'definite policy' of non-fraternisation. His suspicions were confirmed by a welcoming dinner for Hutton and Bailey which he attended as vice-captain. In contrast to the first cocktail party on the previous tour in Barbados, when MCC socialised enthusiastically, Stollmeyer remembered an uncomfortable evening: 'Conversation and pleasantries did not flow as easily as I expected and it set me to wondering if anything was amiss.'

If Stollmeyer took the brusqueness of his opposite number in his elegant stride, Evans later gave an earthier version of the instructions Hutton issued to his players:

> He said to us, in effect: 'Well, we've got to do these
> people, haven't we? We've got to do 'em. You mustn't
> speak to 'em on or off the field. Keep right away from
> 'em, don't take any notice of what they say. Get stuck
> right into the job and beat 'em at all costs'.

Hutton grew accustomed to southerners taking liberties with his accent, and Evans had his own reasons for taking some liberties with what his captain may have actually said (note the phrase 'in effect'). But there can be little doubt that what several of Hutton's men called his 'win-at-all-costs' attitude included the direction to remain aloof from the opposition.

Hutton's mindset was partly a function of his own introversion. He also claimed, having had previous experience of West Indian hospitality, that he was seeking merely to protect his younger players from interminable engagements and 'potent drinks'. The internal divisions caused by this policy came to a head in Barbados; as for the impression made on his hosts in Jamaica, Hutton expected them to take it as a compliment to the strength of their cricket as well as the strength of their rum. He would also have remembered what Laker called the 'defeatist attitude' of the previous tour under Allen, and took pride in the fact that 'the people of the West Indies quickly realised that we meant "business"'.

Primarily, though, on his first tour as captain, Hutton's approach was an act of homage to the 'intensity of purpose' which he felt the Australians brought to the international game. It was a West Indian, Constantine, who had pithily and admiringly encapsulated the attitude of Bradman: 'He pities none.' Such ruthlessness was already a Yorkshire trait but it was the Australians who taught Hutton that 'one side cannot afford to be magnanimous in Test cricket if their opponents are not prepared to be the same'. This lesson stayed with him always. Mike Brearley remembered Hutton's advice before MCC left for the subcontinent in 1976: 'Don't take pity on them Indian bowlers.'

It is one of the marks of a good captain to redeploy the tactics that have most unsettled him. Hutton thought the Australians were 'out to do me' and believed a significant aspect of the battering he and his opening partner received was that 'fraternisation between the rival combinations, Lindwall-Miller on the one hand, and Washbrook-Hutton on the other, was strictly limited'. He had formed the view that 'Lindwall-Miller', at Bradman's bidding, behaved in a calculatedly intimidating way to instil an inferiority complex in the opposition. Given that West Indies had buckled against the same combination the previous winter, Hutton seems to have encouraged his own bowlers to make them uncomfortable on both sides of the boundary.

Intimidation on the field
Hutton also took a leaf from the Australian playbook for the three warm-up games in Jamaica. He drummed into his players the importance of reaching the first Test at concert pitch and the benefit of scoring psychological points that might resonate throughout the series. Statham remembered a determination 'to establish an ascendancy over our rivals'. May, targeted by the Australians in 1953 with what his captain called 'typical thoroughness', understood that 'the days of missionary work and of Caribbean semi-holidays were over'.

Apart from their catching, where they struggled to adjust to the light and the atmospheric conditions, MCC played some very good cricket. Lock was particularly impressive in a useful two-day run-out against Combined Parishes on a sugar estate near Spanish Town. In the opening 'colony' game at Sabina Park, Jamaica were crushed by an innings and 21 runs, the first victory by an official MCC team over the island's representative side. In the second at Melbourne Park, the hosts escaped with a draw probably because MCC's emphasis was more on practice for the batsmen and rest for key bowlers.

A feature of the batting in the first colony game was a calculated effort to put Valentine off stride. Swanton arrived in time to see Watson and Graveney 'simply lacing' into the local hero, who was hit for 37 off three overs and ended with figures of 18-1-99-0. Even *Public Opinion* admitted that Valentine had been 'whipped like a schoolboy'. He was rested for the second game on the pretext of a sore spinning finger. Compton happened to be sitting close to Ramadhin in the pavilion as they watched his little pal come under attack. The English batsman indulged in some mild sledging, promising that this was 'the shape of things to come'.

A feature of the bowling was the sustained hostility of MCC's opening pair. Rae had been exposed by Lindwall and Miller in Australia and was immediately targeted by Statham and Trueman. He ran himself out in the first innings, apparently keen to get off strike, and had his off stump knocked out early in the second by Trueman, described as in 'full fury' by *The Gleaner*. Jamaicans were hoping Alfie Binns could press his Test claims as a wicketkeeper/batsman ahead of McWatt. Trueman hit him painfully on the hand in the first innings and under the heart in the second, forcing him out of the next game. A combination of these poor showings, failures by the Guyanese Pairaudeau in internal practice matches and Worrell's finger dislocation catapulted Michael Frederick into the Test squad. In six successive innings against MCC, he had dealt with the short ball better than anyone else.

If the Jamaican batting had been blown away, so were the Jamaican media. Jones thought the colony side had 'crumpled ... like shredded wheat' and that its lower order looked 'petrified'. *The Gleaner* could not remember seeing faster bowling on the island since Manny Martindale in 1935 and confessed Jamaica had been steamrollered by MCC's 'penetrating power'. Michael Manley wrote off the Test prospects of all the local quicks, reserving his grudging praise for the tourists:

Trueman is truly a fast bowler because he seems
to suffer a permanent sense of grievance against all
batsmen. He looks and acts as though he hates them ...
One test of his efficacy is that by the end of the game
I found myself disliking him thoroughly. Home team
spectators always dislike a real touring fast bowler.

Indeed, the aggressive intent demonstrated by the whole side
made Manley realise immediately that England would not be the
pushovers of 1947/48 and 1950: 'Psychologically, it is a team with
what I call "bite."'

Hutton would have been pleased to hear this – and pleased to
see that the West Indian captain and the Three Ws were present
when Trueman and Statham bounced Jamaica out. From a first look
at Trueman, Walcott thought he shaped like 'another Lindwall' and
should prove 'a real menace'. The psychological effect on Stollmeyer
became evident at a captains' meeting shortly before the Test.

This had been convened to clear up confusion about certain
playing conditions, including clarification that the new ball would
be taken after 65 overs not 200 runs. In Hutton's version of events,
Stollmeyer asked for a limit on bouncers of two-per-over and he
refused, ostensibly because the relevant section of Law 46 on
persistent short-pitched bowling was best left to the umpires.

An informal bumper-limit had been agreed on South Africa's
1952/53 tour to Australia. Stollmeyer later denied he made such a
request. But he did confess to having been anxious about how his
team would fare on the quickest track in the Caribbean. Hutton
also had an important piece of extra information by the time of the
meeting. Frank King, the only really quick bowler in the West Indian
squad, had injured his back in practice and would miss the first Test.
The England captain could therefore instruct his fast men to 'do 'em'
without fear of retaliation.

For Worrell, it became obvious that 'Trueman's fiery nature
was being used to carry out the MCC's plan of win-at-all costs'.
Several English players bear witness to Hutton telling Trueman to
concentrate on being a batsman-hater and not to worry about the
crowds making him 'Public Target Number One', nor about Rostron
of the *Express* finding fault with his 'dramatics'.

Trueman hardly needed encouragement. According to Arlott, he was 'young, feeling his oats, glorying in the violence of being a fast bowler'. On the eve of the tour, he was reported as saying, in an Associated Press article which found its way to Caribbean newspapers, 'if the batsman gets hit that's his fault, if he hits me that is my fault'. Laker felt the way 'Freddie was given the impression that a fast bowler should be fearsome and aggressive at all times ... both on the field and off it' was being taken to absurd lengths. He had wider reservations about Hutton's intense mindset. The warm-up games had proved 'up to a point that was a right approach'. They had also shown what could happen when 'some of the younger players carried it too far'.

The most symbolic confrontation was between young colt and old master. The MCC captain admitted, in retrospect, that his 'first mistake' of the tour was to give Trueman his head in the minor warm-up game where Headley captained the home side. Hutton, who had spent long hours in the field to Headley in 1939, remembered him to be 'one of the finest hookers I have seen in all my years of cricket'. But the veteran's reactions, quickly tested by Trueman, had clearly slowed. Opinions differ as to the length of the ball which injured Headley's arm but there is no doubt that, in Trueman's own words, 'George went down and the crowd went up'.

As he strained to live up to the stereotype, Trueman inflamed matters by returning to his mark rather than enquiring as to the batsman's health. He remembered his captain coming up to him and asking 'What have you done? What have you done?' But Hutton is also reported to have complained about a doctor being allowed onto the field to inspect Headley. This hardly defused the situation and MCC were given a police escort at close of play.

The nerve-endings in Headley's elbow had been badly damaged. He missed the first colony game and, had it not been for the size of the public subscription, would almost certainly have sat out the second. Manley, trying to put the best spin on his efforts in that match, claimed that 'fielding with one hand he was still brilliant'. When Mas George came out to bat at No.5, Bailey – captaining MCC as Hutton watched on from the pavilion – immediately brought Trueman into the attack. Headley played an instinctive hook shot which was well caught by Suttle on the boundary. Trueman told the story as follows:

'They ain't gonna like that, man,' said George as he made his way past me to the pavilion.

'Not here. I'll give you that. But back home it'll go down a storm,' I replied. A remark which brought a broad grin to George's face.

'Yeah, guess so, 'specially round Sheffield way, Fred', he said.

One reason this seems like a classic Trueman confection is the incredible detail of Headley smiling after getting out. But, even if the phrasing is invented, it helps convey the insularity of the English cricketers, wanting to do well for their people 'back home' but apparently not too bothered about the effect they were having on the people 'here'.

As it turned out, the Jamaica second innings proved an anticlimax. Headley joined J.K. Holt junior for a watchful partnership which ensured a draw. Hutton later revealed that in this innings 'we deliberately treated George as gently as we dare, without making our generosity obvious to the crowd'. One sign of largesse as the game wound down was a spell of 15-11-14-0 from Palmer, whose friendly medium pace Headley patted back in a non-aggression pact. Bailey and Hutton may well have been trying, in their canny way, to play Headley into the Test side and to hold back Trueman now that he had made his mark.

However, it was impossible to keep Trueman out of the spotlight. He threw his cap to the floor in frustration after a series of controversial umpiring decisions. In fairness, the senior players Evans and Compton also showed dissent after Holt was given a number of lives which allowed him to complete a century and secure his Test place. Karl Nunes, still president of the Jamaica Cricket Association, made an informal complaint to Palmer and a formal written complaint to Lord's about the standards of MCC behaviour.

Bannister's reports made coded reference to one bowler who 'appealed with such frightening vigour that many felt he threatened to become too belligerent' and another who 'frequently scowled and muttered at the batsman'. Compton, writing his autobiography four years later, felt he could be more explicit about the two players who had a particularly 'bad effect' on the crowds: 'Tony Lock's natural enthusiasm and expectancy as he bowled didn't exactly please them; but Trueman roused them and incensed them regularly.'

After the formal complaint about MCC tantrums, Bannister noted 'the two young offenders were given some friendly but pointed advice by manager Charles Palmer in his best ex-schoolmaster manner'. The suspicion that this manner was not severe is confirmed by the way Palmer defended his players in public: 'I must say it was a terribly difficult problem not to betray astonishment momentarily when incomprehensible decisions were given.' Trueman and Lock do not seem to have taken much notice of the manager. Neither did the captain. Moss suspects Hutton deliberately put Trueman and Lock in a room together to get their competitive juices flowing. In hindsight, most judges agreed with Laker that this was a grievous 'managerial blunder'.

According to his captain, Trueman 'retained a good deal of his Service spirit', implying that his mutterings to the batsmen were unprintable. Compton remembered 'language which was both unusual and colourful' – even Evans came 'within the scope of vigorous expletive' if he dropped a catch. As for Lock, Brian Johnston thought he was known at the start of his Surrey career for a 'spot of swearing and an aggressive approach'; at the end of his career, with Western Australia, he was described by Dennis Lillee as a 'master' of sledging. The roommates were probably the MCC players Walcott had in mind when he complained of on-field language which was 'appalling and would not be tolerated today'.

Off the field, Palmer had a great deal of sympathy for the way Trueman was 'catapulted into a society of which he had no experience whatsoever'. But the manager had to admit that 'he spoke as a Yorkshireman would speak in Yorkshire'. Trueman's demand for condiments at one function, when he found himself sitting next to a high-ranking official of Indian heritage, has gone into folklore – 'Pass t' salt, Gunga Din'. Derek Birley, from the same mining background, positioned this anecdote during the 1953/54 tour and noted that it 'clung to him throughout his career, for it seemed the sort of thing he might have said'.

Hutton was probably right to conclude that this story was pure 'invention'. But it is fair to assume that some players approached evening functions in the same way a shocked Worrell saw them reacting to cross-examination in the members' pavilions: 'The courtesy of our visitors' replies seemed to be based on the complexion of the questioner's skin.'

MCC preconceptions

Partly because he got on well with several West Indian players and partly because – even at this stage of his career – he liked to soften up his targets verbally, Trueman strongly disagreed with the policy not to fraternise. But he insisted that 'colour prejudice' was 'never in Len's mind when he issued the instruction'.

Many in the Caribbean drew a different conclusion after Hutton's account of the tour was serialised in their newspapers two years later. His pronouncement that 'the gradual exclusion of white folk is a bad thing for the future of West Indies' cricket' was found both laughable and insulting. As Michael Manley was to point out, leadership roles on and off the pitch were still reserved for 'the white upper-class stream of Caribbean society'. At the same time, Walcott was offended by the 'subtle implication' that West Indians from other streams were incapable of keeping up the traditions of the game.

Hutton paid generous tribute to black and brown players, including Walcott himself. But the overall picture he painted of the region, implying that it was too backward and too volatile to accommodate English cricketers, reflected what the Jamaican cultural theorist Stuart Hall characterised as 'that absolutely innate, unspoken, taken-for-granted assumption of natural superiority which went along with empire'.

Richard Hoggart came from the same respectable working-class stock as Hutton and coined the phrase 'sub-Kiplingesque' to describe the attitudes towards empire and race of the older generations of his own family. An elementary schoolboy from Yorkshire was bound to absorb stereotypes from lower-brow culture: black-face minstrels were still an integral feature of seaside towns like Scarborough where the Huttons went on annual holidays. Nor would any exposure to middle-brow culture undermine colonial assumptions: there was a thriving Gilbert and Sullivan society in Fulneck. By 1953, Kipling's notorious concepts of the 'white man's burden' and 'lesser breeds without the law' would already have bordered on unacceptable.

143

But traces remained in Hutton's description of West Indians as a 'temperamental race of people', an example of what Hall calls 'sedimented' racial attitudes.

Amateurs like May and Bailey might also have carried sediments of what the novelist John Fowles, who played cricket against both, called 'the thoughtless colour prejudice ubiquitous in public schoolboys in those days'. Bailey seems in fact to have been one of the most open-minded and adventurous in the party. In his cine film collection, there is some footage of him and Wardle, on what looks like a piece of waste-ground in Jamaica, enjoying an impromptu game of cricket with a group of youngsters. Bailey also visited record shops in Kingston to build up his calypso collection. Trueman, perhaps feeling himself closer to the pulse, became a student of the 'tougher sound' of the 'ghettos'. He professed a love for the 'Jamaican people' because, even in the hostility of their crowds, he sensed respect for his aggressive approach to the game.

Generally though, the atmosphere on the island reinforced what Evans called MCC's 'siege mentality'. Another novelist, Graham Greene, had recently predicted that Jamaica was a fertile ground for a 'second Mau-Mau', referring to the Kenyan guerrillas whose dreadlocks, some suggested, had been adopted in homage by the Rastafarian community in Kingston. The grave situation in Kenya, where news of killings by both sides was reported in Caribbean papers almost every day of the tour, may have coalesced in the MCC psyche with British propaganda about 'native' insurgencies. There was, for instance, a burgeoning genre of films depicting white settlers in danger of their lives. *The Planter's Wife*, a popular anti-Communist picture about the emergency in Malaya, had been released in the previous year.

Meanwhile, there was already a sense not just of two Jamaicas but of two Kingstons, the affluent uptown and the dangerous downtown. Trueman, like many British visitors to the city in the 1950s, remembered being 'briefed not to go out after dark, after 6.30, unless we were in a motor car because it wasn't the best place in the world for white people to be'. Downtown was probably not yet as dangerous as uptown made out. Keith Thomas did his national service in Jamaica, in the two years immediately preceding the MCC tour, and considered himself lucky to have been posted there rather than Kenya or Malaya. He spent much of his leisure time playing cricket. When he patrolled downtown Kingston he held it to be relatively safe, even though he held its inhabitants in disdain:

> I wrote home regularly and my mother kept my
> letters. Reading them sixty years later, I feel intense
> embarrassment. The writer's views on politics and
> race are callow and distasteful. Repelled by Kingston's
> crowded and filthy conditions, this bigoted youth
> attributed the poverty that surrounded him to the
> inherent idleness and fecklessness of the black
> Jamaicans. He was equally scornful about their desire
> for self-government.

If a conscript who went on to become a liberal Oxford don admits to harbouring these views, it seems safe to assume that professional cricketers, almost all of whom had spent time in the armed services, were as unenlightened. Graveney's first ghosted autobiography certainly recorded a similar sense of disorientation:

> Their world is strange, exotic, violent, a bewildering
> place in which to dump a group of cricketers snatched
> from the greyness of England in December. This
> is the world of silver beaches and lilting calypsos,
> of rum and gambling, of politics and knife fights,
> of couples producing half a dozen children before
> they marry, claiming to be in the exalted state of
> 'living independently'. This then is the West Indies,
> not perhaps as a sociologist would see it, but as an
> England cricketer saw it.

As it happened, studies of Jamaica by the sociologists Madeline Kerr and Fernando Henriques had been published in 1952 and 1953. Kerr made the point that most Jamaicans were also left 'bewildered and insecure' by the complex legacy of slavery and the want of economic development. But the England cricketers, who could barely hear themselves above the din of firecrackers at Sabina Park and saw members of the crowd toting guns, retreated further into their mental barracks.

145

Jamaican sensibilities

Bailey later acknowledged that 'like so many England teams we were slightly arrogant and distinctly intolerant of the accommodation provided and some of the arrangements'. Rumours quickly circulated that the tourists were refusing requests from autograph-hunters and arguing with officials about tickets for players' guests. Gatemen at cricket grounds are notorious jobsworths the world over, and local journalists had similar issues with the bureaucracy of Kingston Cricket Club. But gossip about the incidents added to the growing impression that the players were adopting a superior attitude. As a professed anglophile, Worrell looked to the tourists to provide exemplary models of conduct, but he was disappointed to find them acting like 'masters' in a different sense to that envisaged by *The Gleaner*: 'It was assumed by our fellow countrymen from the supercilious behaviour of this MCC team that the English considered that West Indians were still a bunch of savages.'

In the specifically Jamaican context, a feature of Norman Manley's speeches was the argument that colonial rule rested 'on a carefully nurtured sense of inferiority in the governed'. Especially symbolic was the contrast produced by Anglo-Saxon tourists in shorts flying into the island's stockaded resorts while black islanders in their Sunday best crowded into boats to emigrate to Britain. Given that a typical day's hotel charges exceeded the average Jamaican's monthly earnings, the burgeoning tourist industry was, as V.S. Naipaul later put it, a 'standing provocation'. Against this background, MCC's complaints about the noise near their hotel and the poor food will have had more significance than they may have appreciated.

The patterns of celebrity migration had a similar resonance. For example, into Jamaica came those tropical voluptuaries Errol Flynn, Ian Fleming and Noël Coward; out had gone Marcus Garvey, Harry Belafonte and George Headley, all later decorated as national heroes. There was still a sense that the only way for black people to get on in Jamaican society was to get out of it. The new jet set who wintered on the island were felt to be perpetuating Jamaica's ingrained white bias. What Compton called Hutton's determination to be a 'non-mixer' could therefore be misunderstood in particularly unfortunate ways.

Any policy of non-fraternisation had immediate connotations of 'Jim Crow', the period shorthand for segregation in the USA which Michael Manley suggested to his *Public Opinion* readers was operating nearly as actively, if more surreptitiously, in both Jamaica and Britain in 1954. Headley may also have remembered his pre-war experience in Lancashire when a South African international had refused to shake his hand: 'I am a great admirer of your cricket but where I come from we do not fraternise with you fellows.'

While Hutton's emphasis on intimidation through pace was mostly a function of his obsession with the Australians, it had something to do with the stereotype of West Indians collapsing under pressure. This theory was not yet expressed in Tony Greig's terms of making them 'grovel'. But it was shared by Compton who, like Hutton, had been a member of England sides which had first thrashed and then been thrashed by West Indies either side of the war. He supposed that the exuberance they had shown in 1950 was the flip side of the fragility they exhibited in 1939: 'The West Indies were on top most of the time, and when they are on top they are right on top. Contrariwise, if they are down, they are down at the bottom. The one is perhaps the corollary of the other.'

Bailey felt that the frequent attempts of MCC bowlers to make 'life physically unpleasant' for the West Indies batsmen 'was undoubtedly resented by the opposition and their supporters'. In fact, although bouncers invariably stoked up the crowds, the West Indian media made fewer complaints than the English in the 1980s, when the boot was on the other foot. There was, however, underlying sensitivity to the history of plantation cruelty. It was not MCC's fault that Headley's powers were waning. But they do not seem to have considered the full implications of targeting him physically. Mas George was being put back in his place by the Old Massa.

Local white prejudices

Hutton quickly realised that the atmosphere in Jamaica was 'having its effect on the players'. This was certainly because of hostility from nationalists. Swanton thought the phrase 'These black beggars don't like us' encapsulated the attitude of the touring cricketers. But their more frequent encounters with the island's white minority became equally problematic.

'MCC had hardly set foot in Jamaica,' according to the captain, before some local whites 'were drilling it into the players how important it was for them to win.' Palmer seems to have borne the brunt of entreaties to uphold British pride but other tourists remembered being similarly accosted. May was 'embarrassed to hear European residents impressing on members of the MCC team the vital importance of beating West Indies'. Bailey observed that 'matters were not helped' by a section of whites calling on MCC to win at all costs 'and so uphold the so-called racial supremacy'.

Bailey drew a distinction between 'white West Indians' and 'Englishmen who were in residence there and believed, somewhat illogically, that they were a major asset'. He quickly tired of expatriates approaching him to point out that 'England simply had to win' so as not to 'make the natives uppity', finding their protestations that 'their life would not be worth living' faintly ridiculous given that they 'seemed to be doing reasonably well, certainly better than most of their darker-skinned brothers'. The whites with more established roots in Jamaica were not such a homogenous group, and many of them would have passed the notorious Tebbit Test which requires allegiance to the sporting teams of the adopted nation rather than the ancestral home.

One thing, however, tended to unite ex-pat and Jamaican whites: their snobbery. Bannister had an early experience of this:

> The first day I was at the bar with one or two of the other boys. One of the locals came up and asked each of us which school we'd been to. He came up to me and said, 'Where did you go to school?' I said 'Watford Grammar School'. So he said, 'I can tell by your accent that you're a grammar school boy'.

These locals would not have been impressed by the background of the MCC leadership. The previous tour had brought them Allen (Eton & Cambridge) and Griffith (Dulwich & Cambridge). Now they had been given Palmer (Halesowen Grammar & Birmingham) and Hutton (Littlemoor Council & Pudsey Grammar Technical Drawing). Any Midlands trace to Palmer's received pronunciation was difficult to detect. However, Hutton's accent, softened but not strenuously elocuted, branded him on the tongue as an unsuitable skipper.

May (Charterhouse & Cambridge) was already a Hutton loyalist and 'amazed' to hear that 'MCC were considered to have slighted West Indies by sending a team under a professional captain'. Meanwhile, Palmer remembered being 'totally ignored' by one senior Jamaican cricket official for the duration of MCC's stay.

In addition to the class divide, there was usually a generation gap. The Archbishop of York concluded that 'older whites' were the ones to blame for 'holding aloof from the coloured people'. On the next tour in 1960, Swanton upbraided 'the intransigent attitude of those rare planter-types, venerable for the most part, who apparently suppose themselves still to be basking in the blessed aura of Queen Victoria' – and who were still saying they hoped England 'beat these black fellows'.

Many white Jamaicans sent their children for university education in England; few colonial officials brought younger family members out with them. They were not accustomed to fielding so many cocktail-party guests in their twenties. Here, again, Trueman's presence was especially provocative. The prototype of cocksure northern young men like Alan Sillitoe's Arthur Seaton or David Storey's Frank Machin, he was not going to show the deference which the local social circuit demanded.

Bannister remembered sharing a car with the fast bowler during the first warm-up game. They drove past a sugar plantation:

> Across the entrance was strung a banner exhorting
> the employees on the virtues of WORK, OBEDIENCE,
> DISCIPLINE. Trueman ... looked with disgust at the
> banner and exploded: 'I bloody wouldn't work here!'

Trueman had worked at Maltby Main Colliery as a teenager – although never underground – and may have been empathising with the conditions of another regimented workforce. He was certainly demonstrating the qualities that Michael Parkinson felt made him an emblematic figure in Yorkshire – 'outspoken, bloody-minded, Jack-as-good-as-his-master'. But what went down a storm in Sheffield did not go down so well in the white enclaves of Kingston.

The complaint lodged by Nunes about MCC's tantrums in the second colony game perhaps best explains the sensitivity of white cricket administrators:

English players have an added responsibility on a tour
like this where there is a mixed population, and we
are constantly holding up England, and the MCC in
particular, as a pattern of sporting behaviour.

The Jamaican historian Arnold Bertram discerned 'an instinctive
genuflection to imperial practice' in Nunes, who fondly remembered
his schooldays at Dulwich College. When Nunes worried about the
messages being sent to a 'mixed population', he was genuflecting
to the imperial theory that 'the indigenous population' of British
colonies relied for their conception of 'fair play and self-control'
on the example shown both by the 'white men who live among
them' and by the 'passing visitor' from the 'mother country'. These
views had been expressed by Stanley Baldwin, Prime Minister when
Nunes returned to Britain as West Indies captain in 1928. 'The day
that we cease to be worthy of respect,' Baldwin predicted, 'that
day the foundations of the Colonial Empire crack.' Even in 1953,
when those foundations had obviously cracked, some colonial civil
servants were not expecting to hand over control in the immediate
future, and the leaders of the 'boss' cricket clubs assumed they
would be setting the tone for some time to come. Nunes was not
the official who cold-shouldered Palmer, but he may have been the
man who took Hutton aside to say that 'West Indies cricket would
be doomed if ever a black captain was appointed'.

On the one hand, the English players were being told by local
whites to 'beat these black fellows' and not let their side down. On
the other, they were being told they were already letting their side
down because of a win-at-all costs attitude. Such was their dilemma
when the first Test began.

CHAPTER 9

FIRST TEST (SABINA PARK)

'Len was sitting in some kind of rocking chair, in his whites with his cricket cap on, rocking himself almost into a trance.' This is Alan Moss's recollection of the scene in the Sabina Park dressing room an hour before play began. Hutton was never unaware of his importance to the English batting. He seemed to be preparing himself, in the Moravian manner, for opening the innings should he win the toss.

Perhaps he was also revolving in his mind the possibility that he might insert the opposition. He had done so in the colony game at Sabina to excellent effect; on the eve of the Test the curator was quoted as saying that 'the wicket will be fast, very lively in the first hour or so'. Hutton's already strong suspicion that West Indies did not like it very lively had been confirmed by the captains' meeting held two days previously.

Stollmeyer won the toss and batted, so we shall never know Hutton's intentions had he called correctly. But the England teamsheet suggested that he might have bowled, as he did in the first Ashes Test the following winter. Moss was amazed to discover that he was in the starting eleven – in an attack of four pacemen and only one spinner. He heard this news not from Hutton, still swaying silently in his chair, but from the vice-captain Bailey. There was no ceremonial award of a first cap. Instead, Wardle rushed up to Moss, not to offer congratulations but his opinion, expressed in colourful language, that he should be playing instead.

Peter May reflected on the make-up of the team years later. He came to a different, if equally blunt, conclusion – 'No Laker'. Laker had hardly been overbowled in the warm-up games but nor had he overimpressed. Hutton wanted to protect him, and Wardle for that matter, from being 'put out of business for the tour' on an unhelpful surface against attacking batsmen.

The captain was predisposed towards pace but the pitch did seem to have what Michael Holding calls 'that old Sabina gloss'. Bannister thought it 'shone like the polished floor of a house-proud wife'. Moss retains the image of the barefooted groundstaff shuffling down the square on their backsides and shaving off any remaining grass with sharp glass. He swears that when play began he could see the reflection of Stollmeyer's immaculately white pads on the wicket.

The gamble on speed also lengthened the England tail. Lock would be batting at No.8, two places higher than for his county. The form of Evans, at No.7, would therefore be of particular concern, given that he was the only player in the Test team not to come off in the warm-up games.

For West Indies, Frederick was preferred to Pairaudeau. This decision may have been driven by the anxiety of Nunes to have a 'white Jamaican' in the Test team (even if Frederick was really Barbadian). Perhaps in return, Nethersole, the official Jamaican selector, got his way on Headley (even if this inspired another round of fierce criticism from the other colonies). Stollmeyer, who seemed nearly as enthusiastic about Headley's bit-part off-spin as his vast acumen, thought he was 'just the man for the job'. Walcott agreed his inclusion at No.6 was a 'good move' in a side with two batting debutants and only four front-line bowlers. In the absence of King, the all-rounder Gomez would take the new ball with the local medium-pacer Kentish.

DAY 1

A large and noisy crowd packed into the claustrophobic Sabina Park, with many others taking up vantage points on trees and rooftops overlooking the ground. Given the interest in the series, it is fair to assume the press box was equally crammed – on the next tour Alan Ross likened it to 'an overcrowded raft'.

England began with the intensity of the first colony game. Runs were hard to come by while the shine was still on the ball. The tourists were heartened by a breakthrough in the fifth over when Frederick, growing impatient to get off the mark on debut, gloved a hook off Statham. Graveney, running backwards from slip, made a difficult catch look easy.

But already disheartening was the behaviour of the pitch, which was not playing as fast as it looked, nor as fast as the pitch next to it had played in the tour match. Moss replaced Trueman for his

152

first bowl in Test cricket. Swanton, writing in 1966, remembered the scene:

> Moss duly appeared second change with instructions to keep them quiet if he could. In his first over he bowled something a little over a good length to Walcott.
> As Moss was still following through the ball came whistling past his head like a bullet, hit the concrete wall that forms the screen and flew back more or less at the bowler's feet!

Here we are immediately reminded, and should continue to bear in mind, that accounts of the cricket by players and spectators, especially if they are recollected in anecdotal tranquility, may not always be reliable. Swanton's daily reports for the *Telegraph* were models of brisk reportage. But, straining for a good yarn 12 years later, he gets almost every detail wrong. Moss came on first not second change. Walcott was not at the crease: the first Jamaican debutant, Frederick, had been replaced by the other, Holt. Swanton was presumably embellishing the daunting circumstances of Moss's first spell with a detail from a different passage of play: Statham and Trueman both told the tale of the prodigious rebound as if it were off their own bowling, so it obviously became a staple bar-stool story. And, on the first morning, the batsmen were keeping themselves quiet, conscious of the importance of building a platform in a six-day Test.

One thing that does ring true is the abrasive nature of the pitch surrounds. Only two boundaries, both off Moss, were scored in the first 15 overs: a controlled edge by Holt and a more authentic cover drive by Stollmeyer. But Moss remembers the ball becoming tattered very quickly. He tossed it to his captain, who had approached him as if to consult about the field, and facetiously asked something along the lines of 'How do you expect me to swing this?' Hutton was not amused. He threw the ball back without further comment and marched back to his position in the slips. No doubt he was already regretting his decision to play four quicks.

Lunch: West Indies 41-1 (Stollmeyer 29*, Holt 11*)

In sweltering afternoon heat, both captains seemed equally determined to give nothing away. Hutton continued to rotate his fast bowlers in short spells. He kept the over-rate slow and the fields defensive. Stollmeyer kept his head down. He did play the shot of the day when he pivoted on a Trueman long hop, but otherwise largely restricted himself to elegant deflections. Crawford White admired the composure of Holt, who was also batting with 'the patience of Job'. Worryingly for England, Lock was the most threatening bowler.

Tea: West Indies 114-1 (Stollmeyer 54*, Holt 54*)

The early exchanges of the final session were if anything even dourer, as both sides dug in before the second new ball. Only six runs were scored in the first six overs. The crowd became restless, although the atmosphere was lightened by two moments of horseplay. Lock threw up a bump ball as if he had completed a return catch and Stollmeyer made to walk off. Then a female admirer came out of the crowd at long-off to offer Compton an umbrella for protection against the sun.

The opening bowlers summoned up a last effort with the new ball. Statham struck almost immediately by pinning Stollmeyer on the back foot. Weekes, arguably the best batsman in the world on current form, came out to a deafening reception. He rode his luck to play a few shots, making most of the 27 runs added before the close.

Close: West Indies 168-2 (Holt 76*, Weekes 21*)

DAY 2

On the Saturday there was a record crowd of 15,000, several thousand above the ground's official capacity. Weekes set off at over a run-a-minute in the first half-hour. A feature of his innings was the dismissive short-arm pull. He also played some magnificent drives on the rare occasions the ball was pitched up.

On 48, he offered a chance to square leg off a Trueman bumper which Lock would have expected to take and England would have expected to rue, especially after Weekes lathered Trueman's next short ball for four to complete his half-century. According to Swanton, the crowd was now in 'a positive ferment of excitement'.

Lock went some way to redeeming himself when he and Moss were brought on to replace Trueman and Statham. England regained a modicum of control. After playing out four consecutive maidens from the spinner, Weekes nearly ran himself out to get to the other end. He then cut at a ball a little too close to him for the shot. The off stump came out of the ground. Moss recalls his first Test wicket with a twinkle in his eye – 'It was unplayable'.

A few minutes later Holt, virtually strokeless as his century and the lunch interval approached, got into a tangle anticipating a short ball from Statham which skidded through low. He was adjudged lbw taking evasive action. Predictably enough, all the England players and journalists who have written about his dismissal are adamant he was plumb, whereas most West Indian accounts suggest that he might – to use a local idiom – have been 'jooked'.

Those with the best view had no doubts. Evans felt the ball would have hit 'a foot up from the base of the stumps'; Statham thought it was taking out 'middle peg'. From the press box, Swanton and Bannister corroborated both length and line: Holt was struck 'on the back of the calf' and had 'palpably misjudged a straight ball'. But Michael Manley insisted there 'was a very real question whether Statham's delivery was lifting over the height of the stumps'.

In the 2007 memoir produced from his conversations with Hilary Beckles, Weekes also remembered the Jamaican crowd becoming mutinous because 'in their opinion' Holt was struck high up on the pad. Interviewed for this book in 2018, he could not recall seeing the incident himself. His considered view is that 'for a Jamaican umpire to give a Jamaican batsman out on 94 it must have been pretty close'.

In the words of Compton, or his ghostwriter, those in the popular stands immediately 'expressed their dislike with multitudinous vociferation'. They booed loudly again when the umpires came out after lunch. *The Gleaner* believed the crowd's outburst was already without precedent in the history of Jamaican cricket but the full extent of their anger did not become clear until the following day.

At this crucial juncture, Headley walked to the wicket. According to Ditton, the wonderful reception the old master received from his home crowd was matched by a 'wonderful gesture' by Hutton. At their team meeting, the England players had agreed to give

Headley one off the mark in affectionate recognition of his services to cricket – and also, Hutton later admitted, as an attempt to pre-empt any 'incidents'.

The field was duly spread and Statham bowled a leg-side full-toss. English correspondents did not notice this favour causing much ill-will at the time, claiming that it was appreciated by the crowd and the batsman. Headley reportedly raised his cap as he ambled the single with which he had been presented.

From the West Indian perspective, however, the setting back of the field was interpreted as at best patronising and at worst cynical. By giving Headley a single off the last ball from Statham, Hutton would get in an over of Trueman before lunch against a player who had been dismissed cheaply in three warm-up innings by the short ball.

Walcott, who was at the other end, seems to have been especially angered. He was unable to believe that a captain 'so dour and ruthless' as Hutton would give away even one run for purely sentimental reasons. He pointed out that singles were also offered to him after the interval, with less fanfare, in order to engineer further opportunities for Trueman to target Headley. The crowd had been jeering Trueman's bouncers and did not take kindly to the three that welcomed their hero. The bowler, not always a reliable witness, claimed Headley turned to him as they walked in for lunch and said: 'Man, this ain't cricket any more. This is war!'

Headley kept his counsel until 1956, when he registered three points in response to a serialisation of Hutton's retirement memoirs in *The Gleaner*. First, the England captain was accused of exaggerating the hostility of the crowds in order to exonerate his own failure to act as an 'ambassador of goodwill'. Second, Headley was unimpressed by Hutton's implication that he was over the hill and needed to be managed to avoid any unpleasantness. Third, he agreed with Walcott that the story of the single being 'generous' and 'given' – the sarcastic inverted commas are Headley's own – was concocted in retrospect to distract attention from a 'commonsense' plan to get him to Trueman's end.

On balance it seems fair to conclude that England *had* chivalrously decided to help Headley off the mark whatever the context of the game. Unfortunately, the context of the game when Headley came in meant that the setting back of the field, once England reverted immediately to hard cricket, was open to misunderstanding. Whereas Hutton thought he was making an agreeable 'little gesture', Walcott concluded that the gifted single 'probably caused more bad feeling than any other incident on the whole tour'.

Lunch: West Indies 235-4 (Walcott 13*, Headley 1*)

For an hour after lunch, Headley gave quiet support to Walcott, who handled a full ration of short balls from Trueman with élan. Swanton counted a dozen bouncers, both batsmen hooking 'anything they could reach without a step-ladder'. The crowd reserved its loudest cheers for the frequent occasions Headley shouldered arms.

Strebor Roberts of *The Gleaner* thought Headley's play was reassuringly 'safe'. Swanton agreed the local hero 'scarcely looked likely to get out'. This was until Graveney was placed at leg slip to Lock and Headley swept a ball bowled for the purpose straight into the trap. It was an astute piece of captaincy, but one which he may not have fallen for in his pomp.

Lock made another crucial breakthrough when Walcott, quick on his feet for a big man, advanced down the pitch once too often and yorked himself. Having reined West Indies back from 216 for two to 316 for six on a good wicket, England must have fancied their chances of a first-innings lead. Furthermore, another new ball was due immediately after tea against the last two recognised batsmen: Gomez, already living up to his reputation as a nervous starter, and McWatt, entitled to be nervous on debut.

Tea: West Indies 331-6 (Gomez 14*, McWatt 8*)

As sometimes happens, the faster Trueman and Statham bowled with the third new ball, the faster it travelled to the boundary. McWatt took a calculated gamble to go for his shots, most of which flew through the slip and gully area.

Swanton felt Hutton left his new-ball bowlers on far too long: 'One groaned for Lock and for Bailey.' 'The situation shrieked aloud,' concurred Charles Bray, 'for Lock or of course Jim Laker.' Hutton was also criticised for leaving third man vacant as McWatt flashed at

157

anything short outside off stump. But he may have judged it made sense to encourage the batsman in his favourite area, given the number of chances being offered.

On 14, McWatt spliced a short ball from Trueman into the gully: Watson dropped it. On 19, he edged Statham to second slip: Hutton juggled and dropped it. On 31, he nicked Statham hard to first slip, who dropped it. On 46, he flashed Statham to third slip: Bailey dropped it. The last two chances looked difficult; the first two were made harder by Watson staring into the setting sun and Hutton moving to his weaker left side. While all this was going on, Evans and first slip failed to react to an edge from Gomez which went between them – yet again off Statham, who noted wryly that 'none of us was pleased'.

Trueman was more forthright about what he thought was 'appalling fielding' for an international side. His arithmetic seems to be out when he claims that McWatt was dropped 'twice off the bowling of Brian Statham and, to my intense disappointment, three times off my bowling'. He also omits to mention that he was the man at first slip to Statham.

In fairness, as *The Gleaner* records, Trueman had been 'given a lot of stick in this hectic half-hour', in more ways than one. He had to leave the field, ostensibly to replace a damaged boot but also to get treatment for an injured heel. The crowd, noting how close he was to attaining an unwanted century, chanted 'We want Trueman'. Hutton, perhaps insensitively, gave them their wish when the bowler returned. Trueman's figures at the end of the day were 32-8-100-0. He remembered being 'cheesed off'. His words were probably saltier at the time.

The surreal partnership between McWatt and Gomez shattered more than the confidence of England's strike bowler. For the first time in the game, the tourists looked ragged in the field as the batsmen's luck, and two days of sun, took their toll. Compton also became most upset, after being hampered by an encroaching peanut-vendor, when the umpires did not take his word that he had pulled up the ball inside the boundary.

Lock was at last recalled and spreadeagled McWatt's stumps with one of his quicker balls in the final over of the session. One can almost hear another groan from Swanton.

Going into the rest day, most English journalists thought West Indies had accomplished their objective of ensuring a draw; a few hoped there was still time for the visitors to post a 200-run lead and exert some pressure. But Bray went out to inspect the pitch after the close and promised he would eat his hat if Ramadhin and Valentine did not extract turn from the surface.

Close: West Indies 408-7 (Gomez 41*, Ramadhin 4*)

DAY 3

It is hard to think of many series in the age before neutral officials where the away side did not register some sort of complaint about the home umpiring. West Indies had certainly done so on all of their post-war tours, to India in 1948/49, England in 1950 and Australia in 1951/52. But there may have been an extra edge to the attitudes of the England players.

For a start, several of them had been raised in the northern leagues where paranoia about home bias tended to run high. Next there was an ingrained assumption that English officials were, as Hutton later put it, 'in a class of their own'. England was after all the only country where umpires were professional, usually with long careers behind them as players. The flip-side caricature of the bumbling or biased overseas part-timer was operating before Idrees Baig and Shakoor Rana.

At Sabina Park, Perry Burke was standing in his first Test, Tom Ewart in his third. Neither had played first-class cricket. Palmer consistently held the official line that the issue was one of inexperience rather than partiality. In Hutton's less official view, 'English cricketers have a tendency to be put off their game and poise if they are convinced something wrong and irregular is going on'. The pivotal episode which Hutton remembered causing his players to become 'anxious and inclined to be rattled' in Jamaica was the aftermath of Burke's lbw decision against Holt. On the rest day, they would have read the first reports about the revenge taken against the umpire.

In its own way, Holt's dismissal was a cricketing tragedy. He had been out for exactly the same score in his first representative game for Jamaica. His famous father, who came to the ground each day in one of his colourful calypso shirts, is reported to have broken down in tears. Some of his countrymen will have had bets on the century; many will have been fired up not only by rum but by the perceived injustice of Holt junior having to wait until the age of 30 for selection; most will also have recalled that Holt senior never received a West Indies cap. Insular pride was at least as important a generator of controversy as any sense of solidarity with the Test team as a whole.

Hutton remembered only a 'stream of abuse' being directed at Burke's family watching in the grandstand, and the umpire saying he felt so frightened that he wanted to retire forthwith. But a Reg Hayter article, widely syndicated across the Commonwealth by Reuters, seems to have cemented the notion of 'brutal attacks' on the umpire's relatives. According to this account, Burke's wife was slapped in the face on her way home from the ground, his eldest son was beaten up on his way home from school and his longshoreman father, also a Test umpire, was threatened with being pushed into the wharf.

Some of these reports may have been confused or embellished in the telling. Evans, perhaps mixing up generations of the family, talked in 1956 of Burke's son being pushed into a river, but by 1960 he was remembering the boy being 'thrown into stinging nettles'. Graveney's version has Burke's father actually 'dropped in the docks', while a debate continued as to whether the umpire's wife was assaulted verbally or physically. In his *Gleaner* letter of 1956, Headley thought the whole affair had been 'overplayed' by English journalists. But Gladstone Mills, a proud Jamaican usually alert to English exaggeration, remembered Burke having to be provided with police protection. The facts remain unclear, although it is noteworthy that the Jamaica Umpires' Association asked for a pay rise the week after the Test.

What we can say is that reports of the intimidation allowed both sides to dig themselves into entrenched positions. Some English players and journalists were predisposed to conclude that the allegedly violent propensities of the crowd were, in Compton's words, 'not exactly an aid to impartial umpiring'. The West Indies press was quick to take offence at the contemptuous assumption that the umpires were so easily influenced and the supporters so out of control.

The English emphasis on impartiality also seemed hypocritical given it had become rather a cliché in Jamaica that colonial officials were not living up to their billing as independent constitutional arbiters. Just before MCC arrived, *Public Opinion* had attacked the British Governor for alleged bias towards the JLP in an article entitled 'How's that, umpire?'

At least the morning session went well for England. The West Indies tail was quickly clipped, the last three wickets adding only nine. Trueman gave his figures a semblance of respectability by dismissing Ramadhin and Valentine in successive overs, leaving Gomez stranded short of his half-century.

Innings close: West Indies 417 (Gomez 47*)

England lost an early wicket. Watson was bowled through the gate by a delivery from Gomez described by *The Gleaner* as a 'beauty of an inswinger' and by the batsman himself as a 'perfectly straight one'. As with his dropped catch the previous day, Watson felt the brightness of the Jamaican sun contributed to his being defeated by 'the sort of ball I am sure I would never have missed under normal circumstances'.

On a still docile pitch, Stollmeyer probably regarded Watson's wicket as a bonus before he turned to the spinners. When Ramadhin and Valentine came on, they were up against the two batsmen probably least scarred by the events of 1950. Hutton's last encounter with them had been at The Oval, where he had scored an unbeaten double century. May's only previous meaningful experience had been at Fenner's, on a wicket even flatter than Sabina, where he had scored a quickfire 44 before the University declared on 594 for four. Both batsmen looked assured in the first exchanges.

Lunch: England 29-1 (Hutton 15*, May 10*), 388 behind

After the interval, the spinners changed ends. Perhaps Ramadhin was trying to exploit the prevailing breeze or perhaps Stollmeyer was simply trying something different. Facing Valentine, Hutton may have been looking to drop a wide delivery down for a single when he succeeded only in playing the ball onto his stumps via his foot.

161

The Jamaican crowd, known for its exuberance, also knew its cricket. Frank Rostron saw Hutton pause in disappointment for a moment 'amid the loudest uproar of rejoicing ... I can recall on a cricket field'. Crawford White reported fans throwing parasols in the air and dancing on their seats as a 'Hampden-like roar hit Kingston'. According to Swanton, 'the noise went on and on so that Compton and May batted to a constant deafening din'.

However, these two appeared to have steadied the ship. As May recalled, 'I thought that we were playing rather well'. Then Compton – 'down the pitch' according to his partner – was adjudged lbw to Valentine. Already annoyed by the slur on his integrity in the field, Compton felt the umpires were trying to even things up after the Holt decision.

The crowd scented a wicket every ball now: May spooned Valentine tamely to Headley at midwicket; Graveney was another adjudged leg-before playing forward to Ramadhin; Evans, perhaps inadvisably in the last over before tea, attempted to disperse Valentine's close-catchers. His agricultural hoick against the spin lobbed sadly to deep mid-on. England had lost five of their best wickets for 56 runs.

Tea: England 106-6 (Bailey 6*, Lock 0*), 311 behind

With the follow-on seeming inevitable, the only question of the last session was whether England would have to start their second innings that evening. Bailey thrived on such rearguard actions. He managed the tail and the clock, appealing against the light in bright sunshine to force the umpires to confer just before the close. This trademark Bailey ruse failed. There was still time for McWatt, continuing his fine debut, to take a brilliant diving catch which did for Trueman, Bailey's last-but-one partner.

Both sets of journalists agreed that Ramadhin and Valentine had bowled with the same control and guile which had mystified England in 1950. Yet it was also agreed that the visitors had played some shots unworthy of a Test side. In the tabloid versions, England's performance was 'shocking ... inexcusable, almost beyond belief' (Hall in the *Mirror*) and 'miserable ... appalling ... pathetic ... awful' (Bray in the *Herald*).

Close: England 168-9 (Bailey 26*, Moss 0*), 249 behind

DAY 4

After a quarter of an hour and the addition of two runs, Gomez bowled Moss with a creeper. This hardly augured well for the future behaviour of the pitch and England clearly expected to follow on.

Innings close: England 170 all out (Bailey 28*), 247 behind

Stollmeyer duly came to the English dressing room. But this was to tell Hutton that West Indies would bat again. According to Bannister, 'a discreet silence greeted his announcement, but as soon as the door closed behind him a cheer of relief went up'. Bannister also recorded that the English players thought Stollmeyer had blundered, that they were now confident of saving the game and that Hutton, despite his native caution, was always a proponent of enforcing the follow-on for the 'definite psychological advantage' it drove home.

Stollmeyer had good reasons for his decision, stemming from established local precedent and immediate circumstances. The Lord's mandarins Allen and Robins, both with experience of local conditions, pointed out on BBC radio that non-enforcement, unusual on uncovered wickets in England, was perfectly normal in the West Indies. The chances of weather truncating the hours of play rarely arose. Sides therefore often chose to bat again rather than risk facing a fourth-innings target on a wearing pitch. West Indies had won their first Test against England, in British Guiana in 1929/30, after pursuing this policy.

Without Worrell and King, Stollmeyer had gone into the first innings happy to play for a draw; if he went in again he would expect to bat England properly out of the game. He had noted the cracks in the pitch which caused the occasional ball to squat and worried about facing Lock with anything above 150 to chase. He was conscious his own spinners had bowled more than 30 overs each in the first innings. He could also score a point against Goddard, who had been accused of overbowling them in Australia. Perhaps most importantly, Ramadhin had burst a blister on his spinning finger.

Walcott says the whole team agreed with the decision but also records that the 'cricket-mad' Jamaican public 'had other ideas'. As the captain walked out with Frederick, the crowd vented their considerable fury. Hutton had never heard anything like it: 'He was booed all the way to the wicket – a spontaneous outburst all round the ground.'

The simple fact of Stollmeyer being light-skinned made him a lightning rod for the wrath of the fans. Weekes's theory is that Stollmeyer was 'so elegant in everything that he did' that he was automatically connected in the popular mind with elite privilege.

There was also probably an element of protest about the grip Trinidad seemed to have on the West Indies team. Sir Errol dos Santos, the new Board of Control president, already had a reputation for his dictatorial style. The captain and vice-captain, with Gomez standing in for Worrell, were also white Trinidadians. Jamaicans could argue with justification that Headley was more qualified for either role. The ironies are that Stollmeyer claimed his strong support for Headley's selection caused 'the first of many disagreements' with dos Santos, and that Headley was the first person the captain consulted when nine English wickets were down, finding him 'in complete agreement' with the decision not to enforce.

But the main cause of the crowd's anger was their sense that Stollmeyer was collaborating with the British. Swanton overheard someone in the pavilion remark 'he's flattering the England batsmen'; less polite versions in the bleachers would have pilloried him for taking his foot off their throat. Walcott reported that arguments about the merits of the follow-on decision caused 'several street-corner fights' in Kingston, but there seems to have been a general desire to see England humiliated.

British observers had certainly noticed an evolving assertiveness on those streets. The father of the banker Peter Stormonth-Darling remembered black Jamaicans taking up more of the pavement if their cricket team was doing well. Mona Macmillan, who arrived on the island to write a book in 1954, noticed some of them hurling menaces at motorists as if 'in revenge for the time when rich whites and coloureds took pleasure in making black pedestrians jump'. What most Jamaicans wanted to see was the colonial master being kicked when he was down – rather than being helped to his feet by a white man from Trinidad.

Michael Manley, reflecting years later on the hostility to umpire Burke, noted that Jamaica in 1954 'was still at a point of social evolution in which class and national tensions rub like exposed nerves against objective events'. At the time, in *Public Opinion*, he condemned the treatment of Burke and Stollmeyer. But his journal's sports editor, Jones, went so far as to draw an analogy between the captain's failure to pursue an enemy 'on the run' and Hitler's prevarication about invading Britain after Dunkirk.

As the West Indies innings began, Stollmeyer acknowledged the loud heckling with a Hutton mannerism: a little touch of his cap. After Trueman leaked early runs bowling too short, Bailey was brought into the attack to make the cricket as mind-numbing as possible. Reprising his tactics from the previous Ashes summer, he bowled his first over so far outside leg stump that Stollmeyer could not connect at all. When the West Indian captain did manage to make contact in Bailey's next over, he succeeded only in glancing straight to Evans. He returned to the pavilion to another chorus of jeers. West Indies also lost Holt before lunch, leg-before to Moss.

Lunch: West Indies 33-2 (Frederick 21*, Weekes 2*), 280 ahead

Early in the afternoon session, Statham won another lbw verdict against Frederick. According to the Guyanese *Argosy*, 'the crowd continued to voice their disapproval at the decision of Stollmeyer to bat again as Walcott strolled out to join his countryman'. 'Countryman' here means Barbadian rather than West Indian: the two Ws playing in the Test were now together for the first time. They combated the negative leg-side lines of Bailey and Moss intelligently. However, despite some bonus overthrows, it was harder to counter an over-rate which hovered between 13 and 14 an hour. This was extraordinarily slow by the standards of the period. West Indies often got through 20 overs per hour, sometimes more when the spinners were in tandem.

The introduction of Lock saw no perceptible increase in the rate but presented Weekes with a different set of problems. John Figueroa remembered a wonderful duel: 'You could see him go forward to drive only to find the ball not quite there. Then he would think of a square-cut, only to find the ball too close to him. Then he would go back to late-cut, and decide against it.' Nevertheless, Weekes hit Lock for boundaries in three successive overs. In the end it was Walcott who mistimed the England spinner. He was brilliantly caught in the covers by the indomitable Bailey.

Headley got off the mark, without any assistance this time. But he was bowled second ball. Perhaps he could be forgiven for being late on the shot. Walcott described the delivery from Lock as 'the most flagrantly obvious throw I have ever seen'. Few England players seem to have disagreed. In the lively account of Evans, 'he didn't bowl it, he threw it, threw it like a rocket: it hit George's off-stump, uprooted it and sent it cartwheeling behind my legs, the bails whizzing past my nose to the boundary.' Hutton admitted 'a faster ball from an alleged slow bowler would be hard to imagine'. Graveney simply called it an 'old-fashioned chuck'. If Headley's dismissal in the first innings was met with shocked silence, Evans thought his castling in the second 'really did something to the crowd'.

The 'boos and jeers and yells of derision' remembered by the wicketkeeper were probably still ringing out during Lock's next over, during which he was no-balled. The signal came from Burke, standing at square leg, which indicated immediately that the no-ball was for throwing not overstepping even before the umpire, rather provocatively, made a bent-arm gesture. This was only the second time – and the first time in the 20th century – that such a call had been made in a Test match.

Swanton described the decision as 'a regrettable happening but not, I think, to be classed absolutely as a surprise'. As we have seen, several England players accepted that Lock's faster ball was not legitimate. However, there were a variety of factors, large and small, which explain why Laker thought they were justified in 'building up a feeling that the umpires had a "down" on them'.

First, as Hall noted, the crowd had been 'vigorously telling the umpires to no-ball Lock' from the first morning. Second, Lock had not been warned before being called, as convention demanded even if the laws did not. Third, England had grave doubts about Ramadhin's action. Fourth, they had complained about the Trinidad spinner's habit of scuffing up the wicket with his studs but the umpires had done nothing. Fifth, they may have read reports that Burke went to the cinema with Holt on the evening after he had given him out. Sixth, Burke awarded four leg byes in the over after his no-ball call when Weekes kicked one away without attempting to play a stroke. It was this incident, minor in itself, that caused both Hutton and Bailey to take out their pent-up frustration on the umpire.

Yet England could hardly complain about the lbw count – they got another decision against Gomez just before tea. Amid all the controversy, West Indies had not made the game safe.

Tea: West Indies 121-6 (Weekes 46*, McWatt 1*), 368 ahead

Weekes sought to combat Bailey's leg-theory by moving back from the stumps and hitting through the less protected off side, a duel both are reported to have enjoyed. After tea, he found an able ally in McWatt, who batted in a more orthodox fashion than in the first innings. Mixing brisk singles with crisp shots, Weekes and McWatt got properly on top for the first time in the West Indies second innings. England's demeanour prompted comments from Swanton in his best headmasterly tone:

> As the day wore on England's appearance in the field deteriorated sharply. There was much impetuous throwing by the younger brigade, one or two of whom are rather too demonstrative and to outward appearance lacking in self-discipline. Much of the throwing about of hands is merely the outcome of keenness no doubt, but one felt not for the first time that Hutton has a difficult task to curb the histrionics without sapping genuine and proper enthusiasm.

The 'one or two' youngsters Swanton has in mind are fairly obviously Trueman and Lock. For their aggression against Headley they were christened 'Mr Bumper Man' and 'Shylock' respectively. The managerial problem facing Hutton was one thing. The cricketing problem was that the two bowlers he considered his most potent weapons had been thoroughly demoralised.

Close: West Indies 203-6 (Weekes 86*, McWatt 34*), 450 ahead

DAY 5

Many were puzzled by the first mini-session. West Indies batted on for 20 minutes. It was understood that the main idea was to allow Stollmeyer use of the heavy roller in an attempt to break up the pitch. This was a common enough practice, although Stollmeyer himself said that he had never seen a heavy roller achieve this, 'nor have I met the man who has'.

Weekes and McWatt showed no urgency before the declaration, adding only six runs. England again employed negative tactics. The implication in Weekes's memoir is that he was upset about being left ten short of a century for no good 'cricketing reason'. But in his interview for this book he made it clear that Stollmeyer told him how long he had to bat, and that he concurred with his captain's emphasis on batting time.

Innings close: West Indies 209-6 declared (Weekes 90*, McWatt 36*), 456 ahead

When Hutton and Watson walked out on the stroke of noon, the target for safety was nine-and-a-half hours and the target for triumph was 457 runs. Of the two men it was natural for Hutton to have his eye on the draw and Watson on the win. But it should also be borne in mind that Watson had batted against type in the famous rearguard action at Lord's the year before, and that Hutton had scored the fastest fifty of the 1938/39 'Timeless' Test at Durban, where England would almost certainly have knocked off an enormous target but for rain and the boat timetable.

In fact, both men were keeping their options open, mixing what Swanton called 'good, phlegmatic Yorkshire stuff' with 'agreeable briskness'. Watson remembered 'the outfield was fast so that we felt we had a chance' and Hutton looked to exploit the short boundaries, especially straight of the wicket. The only alarm against the new ball was an edge by Watson which flew chest-high between two leg slips. It was little surprise to see the spin twins back on within the half-hour. A confident appeal against Watson for a stumping off Valentine was turned down.

Lunch England 42-0 (Watson 27*, Hutton 14*), 415 to win

Stollmeyer could perhaps be forgiven for having too much on his mind to give his fielding maximum concentration. He had been the leg slip closest to Watson's edge before lunch; almost immediately afterwards, the same batsman offered him a hard, low chance at mid-off. Stollmeyer remembered the ball bouncing out of his hands as he hit the floor. *The Gleaner*, perhaps pandering to local opinion, described the chance as a 'sitter'. The Sabina crowd again jeered the captain but as the session wore on became increasingly subdued. Watson was increasingly comfortable:

> You can usually feel it in your bones when things are going right, and I had that feeling. Len was batting excellently, and I felt brimful of confidence. I could see the ball and I was hitting it with the middle of the bat. In fact everything was so different from the first innings.

Watson timed his drives with nonchalant ease and swept the spinners to distraction. His fifty was the fastest of the match. Hutton was not far behind, reaching his half-century with two regal off-drives off Valentine. Excellent running kept the scoreboard ticking.

Stollmeyer turned to his closest comrade, Gomez, who managed to sneak an off-cutter into Hutton's pads. The ball had kept rather low but Hutton felt he was well forward: 'Gerry was always a fair appealer but when a batsman has played as long as I had he has a fair idea when he is out, and I was surprised not to be given the benefit of the doubt.'

If Hutton was not palpably lbw, he was palpably upset. He must have felt in his bones that England could win if he batted through and let disappointment get the better of him, making a remark to Stollmeyer as he dragged himself off. *The Gleaner* thought it a pity 'that such a sterling innings was marred by the skipper's obvious displeasure over the decision'. Ross Hall, the English pressman most prone to the sensational, also noted the captain's 'obvious shock' but left his readers in no doubt that Hutton had been the victim of an umpiring howler. Hall's strong implication that England were playing against 13 men was reprinted next day in *The Gleaner*. This unsurprisingly provoked more home indignation about 'biased and offensive' English reporting.

May began in extraordinary fashion. He got off the mark against Gomez with a streaky edge through the slips. His next scoring shot was a vast six straight out of the ground. He hit two more boundaries before tea while Watson carried on in his phlegmatic but fluid way. Another partnership was developing to give Stollmeyer cause for concern.

Tea: England 168-1 (Watson 93*, May 18*), 289 to win

Shortly after tea, Watson duly reached his second century in Tests – and his second century at Sabina after his 161 in the tour match. Stollmeyer took the new ball as soon as it became available with an hour's play remaining. Kentish extracted some variable bounce and the run-rate slowed, although May stroked him for two elegant fours.

As the shadows lengthened, Stollmeyer put himself on, to yet another cry of derision. The captain's unerringly inaccurate leg-spinners could be read as a sign of desperation – he had already tried Headley's off-breaks – but it was a canny enough move given both batsmen now had their eye on getting through to stumps. Watson propped at a googly, rather than sweeping as had been his wont, and offered a simple return catch off a leading edge. How the crowd would have reacted had Stollmeyer dropped it does not bear thinking about. Graveney, coming out instead of Compton, joined May to play out time.

Close: England 227-2 (May 50*, Graveney 1*), 230 to win

DAY 6

A match already full of incident was set up for an absorbing last day. It was not surprising that players on both sides were in for restless nights if, as it turned out, for rather different reasons.

Evans was playing in his fiftieth Test but Swanton was one of several to remark that he had not been his usual 'gay self', mainly because of a painful cyst on his shoulder. This did not imply that he was flagging outside of playing hours. Hayter remembered, as a motif of the tour, the wicketkeeper 'sprinting from the field at the end of a long hot day, as if already late for a prior engagement'. Evans did indeed have a prior engagement lined up on the eve of Day 6. He had been invited to a private party at the Blue Mountain Inn which he would be 'unhappy to miss'. But Hutton had imposed a 10pm curfew on the entire side. Evans felt such an injunction unnecessary for a player of his experience, and remembered being so upset that he 'couldn't sleep for hours'. His mood was not improved at breakfast when he learned that Hutton had attended the party as guest of honour.

Stollmeyer was rooming with his opening partner in the South Camp Road Hotel. He admitted to having a sleepless night. This was partly because of Frederick's tickly cough. But the main reasons for the captain's insomnia were the worrying state of both the game and the Jamaican public's mood.

In contrast to all previous days, the ground was practically empty when play commenced. Ditton noticed that 'for the first time the number of tree dwellers could be counted on the fingers of both hands'. The no-show was interpreted by the local newspapers as an impromptu boycott against the follow-on decision. Four women did turn up, but dressed for a funeral to make a protest: 'We are in mourning for West Indian cricket killed by Jeff Stollmeyer.' Others may simply have been unable to face the prospect of seeing West Indies snatch defeat from the jaws of victory. In his weekly column for *Public Opinion*, written at the end of Day 5, Manley conceded 'it seems that England is going to achieve the impossible'.

Manley was worried about 'May and Graveney in full flight'. They proved him correct in the first half-hour, proceeding at well above the required run-rate against the spinners.

Stollmeyer then recalled his quicks. He also recalled the tactics of Hutton. Swanton noticed several unhurried 'confabulations' between captain and bowlers in an attempt to slow the over-rate. Stollmeyer also set out to slow the scoring rate with negative lines of attack. From the Cathedral End, Kentish bowled the same kind of leg-theory as Bailey to a 2-7 field. From the Northern End, Gomez concentrated on an area outside the off stump to a 7-2 field.

Stollmeyer's switch to outright defence had the desired effect. May remembered 'a feeling that we were getting nowhere and that something had to be done'. Against Kentish, he began trying strokes he would 'not otherwise have played', sometimes copying the approach of Weekes by giving himself room, sometimes taking on the leg-trap. In the penultimate over before lunch, he looked to tickle a ball drifting past him to the fine-leg boundary.

Graveney at the other end was incandescent when May was given out caught behind: 'This decision was nothing less than terrible. At no time was May's bat within a foot of the ball.' Walcott, fielding at leg slip, did not appeal. He thought the ball had come off May's pad, but was eventually persuaded that McWatt was 'probably right' in thinking bat was involved. May reportedly hung his head before wending his way back to the pavilion. But he did not linger over the incident in his memoirs, saying he simply 'glanced a wide ball too fine'.

Compton watched his first five deliveries from Kentish land outside his leg stump. Stollmeyer's tactics had pushed up the asking rate to fifty-per-hour, a tall order. England could still entertain faint hopes of a spectacular triumph with two of their finest strokemakers at the wicket.

Lunch: England 277-3 (Graveney 31*, Compton 0*), 180 to win

After lunch, Stollmeyer persisted with Kentish's leg-theory at one end but brought Ramadhin back at the other. Ram soon got an off-break to turn a long way. There was also a long way between Compton's bat and pad. He was bowled for two. Back in the dressing room, the batsman is reported to have sat inconsolably, and uncharacteristically, with his head in his hands for the next hour. From the attacking point of view, Compton, held back the night before, must have been backing himself to take England close to victory if he had got set. From the defensive point of view, West Indies were now two breakthroughs away from England's long tail.

Two American academics took up posts at The University of the West Indies in the Mona district of Kingston in the early 1960s. They initially thought that the number of people they saw with earpieces on campus indicated some kind of widespread hearing disability. Then the penny dropped that everyone was listening to the cricket.

In 1954, the citizens of Kingston began flocking back to Sabina Park once they heard the clatter of English wickets on their radios.

With Bailey coming to the crease, it was natural to predict an attritional afternoon during which Stollmeyer would try to prise out batsmen with spin. But the veteran Kentish was keeping an accurate, if negative, line and getting the ball to lift off a length. Graveney was tempted into an uppish leg-glance. Weekes scooped it up right-handed inches off the ground at backward short-leg. He remembered the catch in his interview for this book, rating it one of his best.

Out strode Godfrey Evans. At Old Trafford in 1950 he had joined Bailey in similarly dire straits and scored his maiden century in a match-winning partnership. This was admittedly in the first innings not the last but the sixth-day pitch at Sabina was playing better than the first-day pitch in Manchester. As he walked out this time, Hutton's instructions were: 'Play yourself in. Don't do anything rash.'

Evans played himself in. For one ball. His eyes then lit up at a leg-stump half-volley from Kentish. Going for an expansive on-drive, he was utterly bowled. Evans might have argued that his best chance of survival was to play his natural game. But he would confess that his irresponsible shot contained an element of 'anger and resentment' at being grounded the night before. One imagines, as the ever-growing crowd summoned a mighty roar, that Hutton joined Compton with his head in his hands. Words were reportedly exchanged when Evans returned to the pavilion.

Lock was wise to Kentish's tactics and tried to keep his bat out of the way. Unfortunately, he succeeded only in padding a wide leg-side delivery into his stumps. Statham was pinned on the back foot by Ramadhin. Kentish, reverting to an orthodox line, produced one too good for Trueman. During England's collapse from 277 for two to 285 for nine, five wickets had fallen for a single run.

Even Bailey knew the game was up. To that point a model of defence, he got off the mark by lofting Ramadhin for six. Celebrations were in full flow as the final pair slogged 31 irrelevant runs. Perhaps fittingly, the game ended when Moss was run out after a misfield by Valentine. Hutton's nine-match unbeaten run as England captain had ended with a whimper.

Innings close: England, 316 all out
(Bailey 15*), lost by 140 runs

Hutton expected the first Test to be a 'holding operation'. Stollmeyer believed only a 'super-optimist' could have entertained thoughts of a West Indian victory. A particularly intense game left both captains with much to reflect upon.

Stollmeyer may have savoured the irony that the detachment of 150 policemen, sent to the ground to preserve order on the last day, found that their only duty was to form a protective cordon during the festive pitch invasion. One supporter broke through their ranks and raised the captain's hand in token of victory.

As another token of victory, a local businessman had ordered 25 quarts of champagne for consumption back in the pavilion. A smiling Stollmeyer was photographed sharing a drink with the new Jamaican hero Kentish and a crowd of local dignitaries which included the Chief Minister Bustamante.

But the captain never forgot the hostility of the Sabina Park crowd. According to one rumour, he asked for a helicopter to be ready to whisk him away from potential danger in the event of defeat. Such a precaution had looked advisable when England reached 277 for two. It was also alleged that Stollmeyer vowed he would never play in Jamaica again. He might have been forgiven for issuing such a threat at the airport, where his plane back to Trinidad was searched for bombs.

Hutton called this 'a chilling little example of the fanaticism of West Indies cricket', and also reported that he and Palmer were involved in meetings with Board of Control officials who wanted to move the final Test from Jamaica to Barbados. Stollmeyer wrote a letter to *The Cricketer* in 1956 denying all the rumours and expressing 'keen disappointment' with Hutton's 'mistaken' insinuations. However, the first Test had put paid to the West Indian captain's efforts to lance the boil of parochialism. The Trinidad newspapers, already incensed that Jamaica had bagged two Tests and won selection for five of its own players, leapt to his defence. A feedback loop developed in the press of the Big Four colonies which only increased their mutual distrust. After Headley's selection, *The Gleaner* had reprinted Guyanese protests about 'vulgar insularity' and Bajan jibes about the selectors caving in to local opinion. This inevitably provoked a stream of Jamaican invective in return.

We have already heard the first reverberations of the other feedback loop which would bedevil the series. The English journalists generally wrote their columns for home consumption. But their observations on the partisan umpiring and crowds were cabled back within 24 hours and sometimes reprinted in local newspapers. These newspapers would in turn take umbrage at the patronising tone of the English press, who would in turn re-quote their protests as examples of hysterical anti-British feeling. And so on.

Both these loops are active in the verdict of the *Port of Spain Gazette* on the first Test. Its leader article berated the English for whingeing about the umpires and presuming to leave Bedser at home. But it also berated the Jamaicans for their 'intemperate condemnations' of Stollmeyer.

Hutton admitted that the heavy defeat was 'both a surprise and a bitter blow' given that West Indies were without two of their key players, and given how strongly his team had performed in the warm-ups. Although the contributions of Statham, Watson and May were encouraging, the captain had misread the pitch, his batsmen had let him down in the first innings, Trueman admitted getting carried away with the bouncers and Lock was getting into trouble for his thunderbolts. Graveney felt that the tactics employed in the West Indies second innings had a 'great deal of bearing on the feeling between the teams'. Worse still, Hutton had been hoist with his own petard of leg-theory and slow over-rates.

Both these negative tactics happened to be hobby-horses of Allen. Here we see the beginnings of another feedback loop which also persisted throughout the tour, as the cricketing establishment in England reacted to reports on the action – or lack of action – in the West Indies.

Bailey noted that leg-theory was rarely used again because both sets of players acknowledged that it risked killing the game. They may have had some help from Lord's in reaching this conclusion. Although the telegram itself appears to be lost, minutes show that the Cricket Sub-Committee sent Hutton a message after the first Test 'promising him the support of MCC should he decide to discontinue wide, leg-side, defensive bowling'. If, as is likely, Allen helped draft the communiqué, he appears to have conveniently forgotten his own tactics in 1936/37, when Verity sometimes bowled outside leg stump to keep Bradman quiet.

MCC instructed Altham to convey the same message about leg-theory in his forthcoming meeting with county secretaries. Another agenda item was no doubt inspired by the lamentable pace of play in Jamaica: 'The number of overs per hour bowled by each County in both innings of a County match should be recorded and sent to Lord's.' Allen was probably again at work here. He, or Robins, may even have encouraged Bradman to enter the leg-theory debate with a newspaper article syndicated across the Commonwealth.

Bradman's piece began with praise for MCC giving West Indies cricket a 'shot in the arm' by sending a full-strength team. It also deplored the excess of home fervour which had led to 'basher' tactics against the umpires. But Bradman's main subject was negative leg-theory, a tactic which he warned 'will insidiously destroy the best features of cricket, and could be the means of ruining it altogether'. He noted that both sides had been guilty but it was fairly clear where he laid the blame. He assumed, as the West Indians were usually so entertaining, they had adopted leg-theory only as a 'reprisal'.

Hutton would have been distinctly unimpressed by Bradman, of all people, lecturing him that 'one team can't expect to have a monopoly of tactics'. He thought the Don had tried every trick in the book in 1948, including blatantly negative leg-side bowling by Ernie Toshack and Bill Johnston when Lindwall and Miller were resting. However, as MCC moved on to prepare for the next Test in Barbados, Hutton was probably less concerned about the moral high ground than the mountain his team now had to climb.

CHAPTER 10

BARBADOS

It is hard to think of any other nation in the world where the inauguration of its first home-grown members of government would be brought forward to an early hour so that everybody could then get to a sporting event. But this is what happened on the third day of MCC's game with Barbados in 1954, when Grantley Adams was invested as the island's first Prime Minister in good time before the scheduled start of play.

The cliché that Barbados was cricket-mad was also evidenced by the fact most shops in Bridgetown closed early for every day of the colony game, as they would for the Test match. It was further embodied in Adams, leader of the nationalist Barbados Labour Party (BLP) and once wicketkeeper of Spartan CC. His childhood consisted 'mainly of cricket and reading'. After winning an island scholarship to Oxford he played in college cricket with undiminished zest, once hitting four sixes in an over. He returned home to have a highly successful season for Spartan, which culminated in his selection for one inter-colonial game against British Guiana.

Cricket played an important role in the relatively good relationship between Adams and the British Governor, Brigadier Sir Robert Arundell, who still had powers reserved to him under the revised constitution. Like Adams, Arundell did not get his Blue at Oxford. But, while still at Blundell's School, he had played for Devon in the Minor Counties Championship. In his speech at the inauguration ceremony, Arundell felt the 'loyalty and stability' of Barbados was reflected by the event being timed so as not to 'interfere with the cricket'. He also thought it a 'happy augury' that MCC were in town, given the love of cricket common to the islands of Britain and Barbados, and the qualities common to cricket and cabinet government. For the latter analogy, he had a quotation ready from Douglas Hogg, the first Lord Hailsham:

> The institution, like the game, depends as much for
> its efficient workings upon sentiments of honour and
> considerations of practical convenience, as upon formal
> rules and regulations, and has evolved slowly and
> naturally through the centuries, remaining still in a state
> of development to-day.

These fine words risked ringing hollow. Hailsham was MCC president in the year of Bodyline. The Hogg family made some of its fortune from the sugar plantations of British Guiana. Assembly members such as Errol Barrow, tired of 'sentiments of honour' and impatient with the gradualist and anglophile approach of Adams, were about to announce their split from the BLP. Despite the slow transfer of political power to the black majority, the economic power still resided with the 30 white families who owned 80% of the land. The tiny island was the oldest and least cosmopolitan 'monoculture' in the British West Indies: the vast majority of its exports were sugar-related yet it had to import its citrus fruit.

Although Adams was to introduce a Discrimination Act long before Harold Wilson in Britain, Barbados was still renowned for what Gordon Lewis called an 'entrenched system of racialist prejudice'. When Patrick Leigh Fermor visited in 1950, he found the whole atmosphere redolent of the 'prejudices of a Golf Club in Outer London' and was not surprised to find the island in thrall to 'those twin orbs of the Empire, the cricket ball and the blackball'. Swanton, who was to make a winter home near Sandy Lane Golf Club, observed a decade later: 'The Barbadian, the most moderate and mild-tempered of West Indians, seems in his social contacts, or lack of them, the most conscious of colour distinction, the more fiery and turbulent Jamaican the least so.'

This colour consciousness often shrouded itself in the robes of loyalty to empire. Warner, who had briefly gone to boarding school on the island, romanticised it as the cradle of imperial naval power – Barbadians put up a monument to Nelson before the British – and celebrated its staunch, stolid allegiance to the 'mother country', summed up in nicknames like 'Bimshire' and 'Little England'. Paule Marshall, in a novel published in 1959, provided a different perspective:

That's Bimshire. One crop … The white people treating
we like slaves still and we taking it. The rum shop
and the church join together to keep we pacify and in
ignorance.

And yet, as the historian Keith Sandiford has argued, 'what was
remarkable about Barbados', given its obvious inequalities, 'was the
universality of agreement about the social good of … elite education
and cricket'. Swanton's suggestion that the phenomenon of the Three
Ws arose as much from a pervasive British 'ethic' as a new national
consciousness was endorsed by C.L.R. James. Worrell and Walcott
had both been through the elite school system. This may explain
why they both became such outspoken critics of the bad example
sometimes set by Hutton's men.

Although Worrell was one of a long line of cricketers who felt
forced to leave Barbados, he never wavered from the belief that
'in the West Indies we have always looked upon the English as
perfect gentlemen'. Walcott was 'disgusted' by racial prejudice, but
in cricket he maintained traditional – some in the West Indies said
'conservative' – values, always remembering that 'England gave this
great game to the world'.

Even Weekes, who did not enjoy the same educational benefits,
understood that he would come under 'colonial tutelage' instead
by becoming a cricketer. With typical astuteness, he knew that if
he managed to fight through the prejudices of 'the old clubs and
the school tie' he would face a degree of resentment in his own
backyard. But he concluded that cricket was 'the game of the
people' in Barbados precisely because it combined communal
spirit with traditional values. The mastery of 'English methods and
techniques' was something he found ultimately 'liberating rather
than oppressive'.

When MCC arrived in Barbados in 1954, Swanton was therefore
not necessarily imposing his own worldview when he explained
why they would be under 'close and constant scrutiny' on the island:
'Every West Indian is conscious that it was Englishmen … who first
sowed the seed of cricket. In every way this MCC side has a great
deal to live up to both on the field and off.' In Barbados, more

than anywhere else, they were expected to play with freedom, and behave with restraint, by the whole population.

Stop them throwing

Hutton's men arrived after a short visit to Antigua, which had the dual benefits of spreading the MCC gospel there for the first time and boosting morale with a thumping win. A crowd of 10,000 packed into the St John's Recreation Ground; a portion of the gate receipts was donated to local clubs. This pleased Evans 'for, after all, we were really out there to encourage their cricket'. The fact MCC had included the Leewards in their itinerary was of symbolic importance, although it is questionable whether, on such a short visit, their contribution to technical development extended much further than Palmer teaching the wife of the local Colonial Secretary to wolf-whistle.

Meeting the press at an airport which would one day be named after Grantley Adams, Palmer and Hutton were reported as 'looking forward to their stay' on the island they considered an 'extension' of the 'mother country'. The MCC management probably wished the tour had started in Barbados, as it had in 1947/48 and as it would in 1959/60.

The English players got off on a much better footing than in Jamaica at a special screening of *The Final Test*. Bailey acted as master of ceremonies, Compton charmed the audience and Hutton made a well-judged speech trusting his cricket would be better than his acting. The evening ended with a chorus of 'For they are jolly good fellows'.

The MCC stayed at their traditional base in Bridgetown, the Marine Hotel, now in the ownership of the Goddard family. John Goddard took his unofficial role as the tourists' liaison officer seriously, no doubt trying to score a few points against the Board of Control. He helped make sure the players enjoyed the beaches on the leeward coast, even though the Barbados tourist industry was less developed than Jamaica's at that time. MCC's various recreational activities carried certain dangers. Suttle became something of a local hero when he saved a swimmer in distress. A game of beach football between the players and the press resulted in Wardle twisting his knee and Evans stubbing his toe. The environment still seemed much safer and more agreeable than in Kingston.

Hutton however found his team 'quickly ran into more trouble in the colony match at Bridgetown'. Wardle and Evans were ruled out for a game in which Barbados were defending an unbeaten record against MCC. The outstanding performances on the home team were by the captain Goddard and the all-rounder Denis Atkinson. Atkinson scored 151 in the first innings in about the same time it took Suttle to make 96 when MCC batted.

Those who could afford entrance to the popular areas of the Kensington Oval, or the makeshift stands outside the ground, were more excited by the second first-class appearance of Sobers. He became a focus of attention in the tour match given that one of the Three Ws was not playing and the other two were playing in subdued fashion. Worrell now owed allegiance to Jamaica, and was in any case resting his damaged finger. Weekes was struggling with a long-standing thigh problem, which he aggravated during the game. Walcott made more of an impact with his bowling than his batting, though some in the MCC party felt his influence may not have ended there.

Walcott's uncle, Harold, was one of the umpires: he and Cortez Jordan would also be standing in the Test. The potential for nepotism was a subject of dry humour for the veterans of Allen's tour. Laker predicted that the policy of buying the umpire drinks before the game might not be as effective as usual; Evans that 'it was a waste of time appealing' at Walcott's end. These remarks were made more than half in jest. Walcott had given his nephew out lbw on 98 in the previous year's Test at Bridgetown, and the English players considered him one of the best umpires in the Caribbean. But they were not amused when he called Lock for throwing three times during the Barbados first innings.

The instance that caused most controversy involved Sobers, who was 'bowled' by the second delivery deemed illegitimate. According to some English accounts, the call was so late that the young batsman was already 'half way back to the pavilion'. For the *Barbados Advocate*, O.S. Coppin noted this 'body of opinion' but asserted that Walcott could be heard quickly enough from the press box. A photograph shows the umpire's arm extended at square leg by the time the bails are hitting – or have just hit – the ground.

Bannister reported Lock was 'plainly put out by the incident'. The bowler himself recognised in hindsight that his reaction had been unacceptable:

> This made me so angry that I felt like giving the umpire a piece of my mind. But I managed to check myself. Even so I could not refrain from looking disgusted. It is easy after this passage of time to say that I should not have displayed any outward feelings of annoyance. But, unless you have actually experienced this sort of thing in another country where perhaps the temperature is over 100, you cannot fully realise how trying and exasperating such moments can be.

The prevailing trade winds at that time of year meant the temperature felt more like 80 than 100 degrees, but Lock can hardly be blamed for getting hot under the collar. As in Jamaica, he had not been given a warning. Hutton intervened, as much to keep his fuming bowler away from Walcott as to register a protest. Lock later changed ends but Jordan no-balled him in the final over the day. It was obvious that the local officials were not going to tolerate his faster ball.

The MCC players again privately conceded that Lock was breaking the law when he strove for a quicker and flatter trajectory. Palmer took some cine film of the game which he felt 'certainly' showed up Lock's bent arm. His fellow spinners did not come to Lock's aid, perhaps because he had been keeping them out of the side. Laker thought the problem with his faster delivery was 'glaring at Barbados'. Wardle, the other left-armer, is once reported to have said: 'Just watch that bastard throwing it out there.'

Peter Ditton conceded that Walcott and Jordan were probably 'correct' about Lock. But he chose to stir the pot, knowing full well his match report was being syndicated locally: 'What will be interesting will be to see how Ramadhin is regarded when he plays before these same umpires.'

Hutton, who thought the no-ball calls had been 'drastic', agreed Ramadhin was taking too many English wickets with the same kind of 'jerk'. Interviewed in 2009, Graveney remembered the Lock incident in the same context. He believed Ramadhin knew what he was doing – 'That's why he had his sleeves rolled down' – and thought the problem was not just with his variation but with the orthodox off-spinner: 'He threw both of them.' These views were not shared by many West Indians. However, Graveney had already developed the view that the home umpires were turning a blind eye to practices 'tantamount to cheating'.

After the drama on the first day, there was drama on the last as MCC tried to chase down 196 on a wearing pitch. Suttle made the second of his gritty, if stodgy, contributions but the innings subsided into what Crawford White called an 'undignified crawl'. The last pair of Trueman and Moss managed to scamper the leg byes which won the game.

MCC had pulled off an unprecedented victory. But the upshot of the Lock incident was doubly unpalatable for Hutton. From the tactical perspective, Lock had taken five wickets in the first Test at 22 apiece, conceding a fraction above two runs per over. The removal of the quicker ball from his armoury might make it difficult for him to replicate those figures. From the ambassadorial perspective, the furore caused what Clyde Walcott called 'quite unnecessary ill-feeling' which lingered for the rest of MCC's stay on the island.

Stop them drinking

Although Evans found the Barbadians 'more pleasant in many ways than the Jamaicans', he felt that that their cricket crowds were again being 'kept at boiling point' by the world-championship hype of 'local pressmen'. Meanwhile, the tourists' sense of being hemmed in between popular hostility and elite snobbery was, if anything, more pronounced in Little England.

On Hutton's advice, MCC sought to limit the number of functions. But plenty were still reported in the society columns of the local press. Two days before the Test, a grand reception was held for MCC at the residence of Sir Stephen Luke, Comptroller for Development and Welfare, with the Governor and Lady Arundell in attendance. The next day, the Arundells joined the players again at a cocktail party hosted by the officers of HMS *Triumph*, which had just dropped anchor in Bridgetown harbour (the lower ranks would be allowed on the outfield at the Test because there was no room in the stands). The *Barbados Advocate* records the presence at the party not only of Brigadier and Lady Arundell but 'many heads of Government departments, their wives and prominent citizens of the community'. The Governor found time to move on to yet another cocktail party hosted by the *Advocate* for the English press, where he was photographed in convivial conversation with Swanton.

Presumably Swanton was not one of the journalists Moss remembers occasionally 'hiding in the bushes' to check on what time players arrived back at the Marine Hotel. But Moss points out that most of the English pressmen were keeping the same hours and going to the same functions as the team. More camaraderie existed than tends to be the case today; journalists not only turned a blind eye, but turned on those who did not. It was in Barbados that Bannister complained 'many of the English and white residents of each colony are to blame for the piffle and gossip which is spread around'. Graveney had cause to agree:

> The Navy were in at the time, and we had a bit of a party at the Barbados Yacht Club, where this bloke walked up to me and said, 'You'll never be any good until you stop Bailey, Evans and Compton drinking'. I gave him a suitable reply.

Graveney initially thought little more of this spat, apart from 'an occasional choking feeling' as he remembered how he had 'enlarged upon the theme'. But, when he came down to breakfast the next morning, Penny Robins, Palmer's secretary, told him that manager and captain had been summoned to Government House and were making a desperate attempt to prevent him from being sent home forthwith.

It turned out 'an influential person' staying with the Arundells had overheard Graveney's enlarged vocabulary and formally reported it. Palmer recalled that 'the Governor-Generals were like gods in their own worlds' and the Brigadier had a reputation for precise views about the moral example the British should be setting. When Hutton and Palmer got back from the meeting, where Arundell made other observations about MCC conduct, they convened the whole team and told them 'to be extremely careful about everything they did and said'.

The mud had already stuck. The reported comments of one 'disgusted' ex-pat seem a fair reflection of their prevailing view: 'In the past we expected playboy MCC teams. But after the last tour every Britisher here had a right to expect this time a team who would fight every inch of the way for the old country.'

Stop them feuding

Graveney was aware of the irony that he got himself into such deep trouble by defending the conduct of others. He made a resolution never again to talk to 'strange men' at parties, a resolution he quickly broke in Trinidad by shielding Trueman from the accusations of 'some pompous idiot'. But it is significant that in the earlier incident he was standing up for the senior professionals. He seems to have blamed them for most of the problems: 'There were quite a few scoundrels on that tour – Godfrey, Denis and all that lot.'

On the previous tour, in 1947/48, Evans had been deprived of his habitual drinking partner Compton, required that winter by Arsenal. He still teased readers of his 1951 autobiography: 'There is much I could tell you of our social activities in Barbados.' Stollmeyer was similarly euphemistic when he remembered some of the England players attempting to create 'records of unparalleled social endurance'. One can imagine the wicketkeeper being involved in 'the consumption of rum punch on an epic scale' during one journey late in the tour. One can also imagine Hutton, who had by this time arrived as a replacement, asking for a cup of tea.

Hutton was not programmed to understand cricketers who failed to put cricket first. In Australia in 1954/55, on the eve of a crucial Test, fellow Yorkshireman Bob Appleyard recalled having an after-dinner coffee with his captain in the Windsor Hotel in Melbourne. Evans, Compton and Edrich 'came down the steps all dressed up' for a night on the town:

> Len said: 'Look at those three, they're going out and the excuse will be that they've got to relax before a match.' Then he said: 'This is the time to be thinking about the match', and he was.

185

On the 1953/54 tour, Evans usually roomed with May, who noted drily that 'our waking hours did not often coincide'. The allergic reaction which was to keep Evans out of the fourth Test was mischievously diagnosed by Graveney as the result of shock at being 'sent to bed early one night'. Hutton's delphic sentence in the captain's report to Lord's – 'I feel that you know all there is to know about him' – can be read as a comment on his attitude to life as much as his attitude to cricket.

Yet the image Evans cultivated of himself 'on the old toot with a gin and tonic' concealed a more sensitive soul. He was fortunate that Spooner, 'always a grand reserve and tourist' according to Bannister, tried to support him rather than usurp him. He still worried about his poor form, partly attributable to the knocks he picked up on the beach and behind the stumps. He also endured a variety of painful dermatological problems caused by the combination of the heat and his abundant body hair. Evans seems to have let himself go even more off the pitch because injuries were preventing him from letting himself go properly on it.

Bailey sometimes roomed with Compton: 'The resulting chaos was to me one of the outstanding features of an incident-crowded trip.' Compton's memoirs have much to say about the failures of the tour management but they eventually allude to the possibility that his own conduct may have been unhelpful: 'As everyone knows, we were lamentably bad ambassadors, and I don't attempt to acquit myself of blame in the matter.' Like Evans, Compton may have felt the need to relieve some personal pressure. After the Jamaica Test, the *Evening Standard* conducted a survey of readers as to whether he should be dropped. West Indian newspapers lost no time in reporting the result as 50/50. Rostron pointedly assumed Compton held onto his place in Barbados only because of his experience and occasional bowling.

The Middlesex batsman also had genuine, if complicated, differences with his Yorkshire captain. On the one hand, Compton thrived on excitement: 'I loved playing cricket in the West Indies. It was my first and last tour there. Part of the reason that I liked it so much was because it was so massively controversial.' He felt that an already difficult tour was made more difficult by Hutton withdrawing into a 'shell of reserve and aloofness' instead of rising more spontaneously to the challenge. On the other hand, Compton and Evans had old-fashioned views about cricketing etiquette, and felt the captain's handling of Trueman, in particular, was far too lenient.

If Trueman thought they were 'getting away with murder' off the pitch, they thought he was getting away with murder on it. Evans felt that the young fast bowler 'needed a firm hand'. Compton resented Hutton's whole approach: 'We were to leave him to Len, Yorkshireman to Yorkshireman.' Like Evans, he thought Trueman required a stern talking-to, 'giving perhaps an indication that there was a regular service of boats and aeroplanes going back to England'. He took the opportunity to do it himself in the Barbados game. Hutton had to go off because of a chill on his kidneys. Bailey and Palmer were not playing, so Compton assumed the captaincy. The next time Trueman swore, he called the team into a huddle and vowed to have him sent home on any repetition.

Trueman always hated being dressed down in front of teammates. He also thought it was rich for Compton and Evans to get involved, given that they were otherwise taking little interest in the development of the junior players. His roommate Lock made a similar complaint: 'Not all the senior members pulled their weight in helping the younger ones to feel completely at home.' Compton claimed he took the initiative again as acting captain by ordering Lock not to bowl his faster variation on the second day. The old rakes Compton and Evans and the angry young men Trueman and Lock were the most obvious of the 'little cliques' which Laker thought had been allowed to develop.

Compton and Evans must be the 'established stars' from the 'southern counties' Trueman did not name when he accused them of deliberately trying to undermine Hutton's leadership. He believed they tried to 'get' at him when they could not get at Hutton; then they blamed him for being disruptive when he had the effrontery to defend the greatest batsman from the greatest county. It is to Trueman's credit that he seems to have steadfastly championed his captain in front of other players, especially as they could see that his own relationship with Hutton was deteriorating.

First, a county colleague he had always known as 'Len' now had to be 'Sir'. During Trueman's apprenticeship, Hutton claimed to have 'devoted hours and hours talking to him, both on and off the field'. He certainly took more interest in Trueman than in some other Yorkshire colts, giving him advice from mid-off and over the snooker table – both men had a passion for the game which they indulged on the county circuit. On tour, Trueman found Hutton more distant, to the point that his skipper kept putting off a promised private catch-up.

Then, as Graveney remembered, some of the pressure the captain was under began to be vented 'in sarcasm towards younger players'. Trueman thought he could see double standards everywhere and came to believe Hutton was as guilty as anyone, especially when he found evidence that the captain had kept to himself a consignment of sponsored cigarettes intended for the whole team.

Trueman's tour never properly recovered from being hyped up in Jamaica – by Hutton more than anyone – as 'the new white bowling hope'. Laker thought the first Test 'had knocked the bottom out of that theory' and also knocked the bottom out of Trueman, who developed the grievance that Statham was being nursed for the Tests while he was expected to get through lots of work in the tour matches.

Lock remembered 'sharing' with Trueman the 'new experiences' of representing MCC abroad. After their wings had been clipped on the field, they veered between stewing in their own juices in their room and letting off steam in evenings out, sometimes with another maiden tourist, Ken Suttle. By 1972, Lock was the veteran of eight MCC tours and philosophical about the occupational hazard of cabin fever: 'We all get homesick sooner or later; we get hangovers; we get on each other's nerves; we develop private grievances.' But on his first tour he was grievously hurt by the lack of management support: 'Freddie and I were allowed to go our own way. Feeling somewhat out in the cold, we sought each other's company as a sort of protective shield.'

Lock's reference to 'one or two' experienced players who made 'needless remarks' and 'sarcastic asides' was probably for once not aimed at Compton and Evans, but at his fellow spinners. Wardle was everyone's favourite clown on the pitch. Off it, as Evans later remarked, 'not many people on tour have got on well with Johnny'. Laker was already regarded as an expert in the laconic put-down and had a complex relationship with his Surrey colleague Lock.

Moss still felt he was lucky on his first tour to share a room with Laker, saying he learnt a great deal about cricket and life. They tended to go out with Watson, a man Moss also admired: 'Not a typical Yorkie, very smooth.' Moss says he also socialised with Statham, noting that they were non-drinkers at this stage: 'I think Brian discovered lager in Fremantle on the next tour.'

This informal group were arguably MCC's best ambassadors. Watson felt his mantra of 'taking people as I find them and trying to understand their different temperaments' served him well in the West Indies. Laker had forged relationships with the home team on the previous tour, and Moss remembers him 'putting an arm' around Headley.

In his end-of-term report, Hutton praised Watson's conduct as consistently 'excellent' and was more scathing about Wardle, and his effect on morale, than any other player. However, he still retained a grudging respect for Wardle's big-match temperament, and indeed for Trueman's enthusiasm. Hutton's issue with the other two Yorkshiremen in the party was that they were not archetypal Yorkshiremen. He thought everything came 'too easily' to Watson and, as Evans put it, 'was inclined to think that Jim had no real heart as a bowler'.

Graveney was slightly more advanced in his career than his usual roommate Statham, not least because he believed that 'in a hot climate beer doesn't do any harm'. Despite his faux pas at the Yacht Club, Hutton thought he 'was an excellent chap to have'. When functions required a select delegation, Graveney, who had been a captain in the army, was taken along with the four senior figures who made up the tour selection committee (Hutton, Palmer, Bailey, Compton) and the young amateur May.

May later wrote an account of his first tour which makes perceptive observations on other players. His fellow tourists had less to say about him. It seems he was not yet ready to assert his personality, although he certainly did his duty at official functions. The captain's report described him as 'a most likeable and popular man' who was 'highly respected by all members of the team'. But Graveney, conceding that May had social 'charm', thought he remained even more aloof than Hutton.

The role of the vice-captain Bailey, nicknamed 'Old Fag-Ash' by Moss, is ambiguous. As a cricketer, he gave unstinting support to his captain both by his own selfless contributions and by the leading role he played in rallying the troops after setbacks. Hutton always thought him a great asset: 'He is the type of man with whom I get on extremely well because he is prepared to fight.'

Bailey formed a bridge club with characters as diverse as Wardle, Graveney and Watson. But he also seems to have ventured forth frequently with his sometime roommate Compton. Even if he tried to avoid cocktail-party bores, they clearly felt he was part of the set Graveney called 'all that lot'. According to his son Justyn, Bailey maintained close friendships in later life with Evans and especially Compton. Both men appear in the list of 'Ideal Tour Companions' Bailey compiled in 1959. Hutton does not.

Bailey did include himself in his criticism of the 1953/54 tour's management as 'naive'. Certainly, the expedition seemed to lurch from one issue to the next, such as the Graveney incident, without any formal mechanism to manage either the players' conduct or their cliques. Several tourists later commended Palmer, recalling it was hard to pull the wool over his eyes yet he treated them like adults. Perhaps this was the problem. Although he had experience as a schoolmaster, if Compton and Evans were called into his study he would be trying to exercise authority over direct contemporaries. Conversely, the coltish Trueman had already demonstrated in county matches that he considered Palmer something of an old fart, bridling at his request to go easy on a young batsman and swearing at the Leicester players when given out stumped.

Meanwhile, Hutton always sought to avoid confrontational situations. Palmer was not the first person to find him difficult to penetrate:

> But the more I knew him and the more we had to go through adversity together, the more I got to like him. In fact, I got to respect him and to like him, two very different things.

Hutton returned the compliment:

> Both Charles and I were in a no-win position, and as I shared his burden and understood his problems I know

that no manager could have tried harder, been more diplomatic, or done his onerous job better.

These two essentially decent men deserve their remarks to be taken at face value. But there were still nagging issues of structure and personality in the dynamic of their relationship. Allen proposed Palmer as manager believing he would be an influence for brighter cricket. There was not much talk of that once the aeroplane doors closed. Perhaps Palmer became convinced that the win-at-all-costs policy made cricketing sense. Perhaps he was trying to prove himself to Hutton, a man four years older with deeper experience of overseas cricket. It would not be until the next winter in Australia that Hutton had a management team prepared to tell him things he did not want to hear.

Palmer was not given much playing time early in the tour. This may always have been the intention – he was usually described in the West Indian press as the 'manager-player' not the player-manager. But, narrating the cine film he compiled on tour, Palmer complained that events off the field gave him less time on it than he had anticipated. Hutton, however subconsciously, may have been content that Palmer was not establishing a strong position in the starting eleven, just in case Lord's decided to take emergency action. The impression remains that Palmer never felt he had Hutton's full confidence, in either sense of the word, and that Hutton thought Palmer was neither one thing, a fully focused player, nor the other, a manager who could relieve him of all off-field burdens.

Stop them slogging

Hutton was at a low ebb in Barbados. His kidney complaint puzzled local medics, and he became more agitated when he learnt his wife had read newspaper reports that his condition might be serious. What he called the 'double responsibility' of being captain and premier batsman was also weighing heavily upon him. According to Compton, Hutton had been insisting on the 'desirability of defensive careful play' from an early stage of the tour. According to Evans, it was on the Barbados leg that 'Len's policy' was repeatedly expressed in four words: 'You mustn't get out.'

It was not that Hutton was incapable of 'the most astonishing stream of beautiful strokes'. These were the terms Palmer used for

191

the captain's cameo of 59 not out in the colony game, when he had batted down the order because of his illness. Palmer remembered Hutton's 'risky' assault on Sobers through the less protected leg-side as one of the most brilliant pieces of improvisation he had seen. Hutton may have responded that it was a typical piece of application. Despite feeling under the weather, he had taken a long net in the morning where he carefully practised the tactics he was going to employ.

In the Tests, however, Hutton almost never left his shell and almost never left his crease. Richard Hutton felt his father always preferred to 'make the pitch as long as possible'. An additional reason for Hutton's caution may have been the memory of his uncharacteristic attempt to disrupt Valentine at Lord's in 1950. He was stumped by yards. It was only the second time he had been dismissed in this fashion in Tests – and the last.

In Bermuda, Evans hit his first ball of the tour for six. He then got out for several ducks when he could have been getting time in the middle before the Tests. He accepted his own approach in Jamaica had been 'madness' and could see where Hutton was coming from: 'He didn't throw his wicket away and he didn't like to see others throw theirs away.'

Nevertheless, he thought the safety-first policy was 'disastrously inhibiting' for the rest of the batting line-up, Bailey excepted. Graveney was resigned to the fact that 'Yorkies have a different approach to cricket from most of us' but agreed Hutton's tactics were counter-productive: 'I do not think it ever occurred to him that while the plan suited his own talents, it was alien to those of some members of his side.' The attacking players in the middle order were being placed under the psychological constraint of not using their initiative and the technical constraint of not using their feet.

Although Evans and Hutton had apologised to each other about the Blue Mountain Inn incident, the wicketkeeper still got the feeling that 'you mustn't get out' was his captain's indirect way of saying 'you mustn't go out'. Scyld Berry knew Hutton and Compton in their retirement and noticed that one of the few things they had in common was a trait of 'chatting to hotel porters and doormen'. He put this down to the fact that in their playing careers they wanted never to be 'caught unawares, as professionals in the society of amateurs'. Another possibility is that Hutton liked to prepare the ground for catching people out too late and Compton to prepare the ground for not getting caught. Evans certainly felt he was under surveillance by Hutton. After each low score, his captain would remark: 'Not in very good form at the moment, go and get some practice.'

The strained relationship between Hutton and Evans, who normally got along well despite their contrasting characters, is indicative of how the touring party had ended up in a bad place in Barbados. The captain was exasperated by the senior professional's loose shots and late hours; the senior professional found the captain's restrictions on his strokeplay as constraining as the restrictions on his nightlife.

CHAPTER 11

SECOND TEST (KENSINGTON OVAL)

Hutton declared himself fit to play in a match he said 'must be won if we are to win the series'. The dilemma for the tour selection committee was how to introduce, at the same time, variety into the bowling and sinew into the batting: numbers seven to eleven had averaged 5.8 in the first Test.

The first obvious move was to replace Moss with a second spinner, particularly as Laker and Wardle were both useful lower-order batsmen. Laker was preferred, partly because he had taken nine wickets in Barbados on debut in 1947/48, partly because Wardle was still hampered by his beach-football injury. The next obvious move, given Trueman's attitude and form, was to sacrifice another fast bowler for Suttle, who had top-scored in both innings of the tour match. This would mean Bailey taking the new ball with Statham, and England going into the game with six specialist batsmen and a four-man attack of two seamers and two spinners. As the selectors mulled this over, Palmer was asked to leave the room: 'When I came back in, they told me that I was included in the side.'

The English journalists were puzzled. They could see Palmer offered Hutton another bowling option but asked why, if he was under consideration for the Test, he had not been selected for the tour match. The 'manager-player' had gone nearly a month without meaningful cricket.

The younger English players were upset. Trueman claimed that the squad was 'gobsmacked' by the team announcement, believing Palmer's inclusion to be 'completely inconsistent' with his role as manager and a 'rank injustice' to Suttle. No doubt Trueman was letting off some steam about his own deselection. But, with less of an axe to grind, Graveney found the decision 'illogical' and Moss thought that the introduction of Palmer was 'simply not right'. He explained in his interview for this book that he fully understood why he was going to be dropped and that he was 'enjoying' the tour too much to feel aggrieved. He also thought Palmer was a 'lovely man' and a shrewder manager than Swanton and other journalists assumed. That Moss remembers the treatment of Suttle causing controversy suggests Hutton's determination to ignore Warner's protégé risked further damage to team spirit. Palmer himself confessed to the feeling he was 'filling in' rather than getting in 'on merit'. Back in London, Warner sourly observed in *The Cricketer* that 'surely the selectors were at fault in ... the art of choosing a team'.

For West Indies, two of the five Jamaicans who appeared in the first Test were not asked to travel to Barbados. There would have been outrage in his home island had Headley not played at Sabina; there would have been outrage in the other islands had he played anywhere else. The fact that Frederick's first Test was his last first-class game also says something about the structure of West Indian cricket in the 1950s.

Holt was moved up to open instead of Frederick, freeing up a place in the middle order for Atkinson, who had starred in the colony game. Worrell had a fitness test on his damaged finger and was given the all-clear to come into the side for Headley. With King now also recovered from his back injury, Barbadians would be hoping to achieve the same five-man 'quota' for their home Test as the Jamaicans, should King be preferred to Kentish.

However, another local favourite failed his fitness test. After playing 19 consecutive Tests, Weekes had to stand down because of his thigh problem. This brought Pairaudeau, twelfth man at Sabina, into the team and may have sealed the fate of Kentish, considered a 'certainty' for selection by the Jamaican press after his heroics in the first Test. Kentish had been asked to fly to Barbados, so the usual pretext for insular selection – travel expense – was not available. Stollmeyer later expressed regret that room could not be found for him. But King had the virtues of being faster and being Bajan, even if a rumour later circulated in Jamaica that Kentish had been overlooked for protesting about a social function to which only the white members of the squad were invited.

The straw-coloured Kensington pitch looked a belter. Swanton was stating the obvious when he said it would again be a 'mighty fine toss to win'. Hutton lost it, for the seventh consecutive time in Tests.

DAY 1

The first day was scheduled on Saturday, which guaranteed a capacity crowd of 10,000. They were rewarded for their patience, after a sharp shower delayed the start, by an exhilarating morning of cricket which contrasted with the dour first session at Sabina Park.

Statham was steadily rising to the challenge of filling Bedser's shoes with the new ball. Hutton gave him an attacking field, with eight close catchers in a thick crescent stretching either side of the wicket between gully and short-leg. The crescent failed the bowler twice in the first over: Holt was dropped by Hutton chest-high at third slip and then by Evans diving low to his right.

England could ill afford a continuation of the lapses which had marred their out-cricket in Jamaica. A comical run-out came to their aid. Holt pushed into the vacant leg-side and called for a single just as his captain called for two. Amid the tumult of the crowd, neither batsman could hear the other and Stollmeyer, who had turned blind, found himself standing next to Holt. Watson threw to the wrong end but Statham had time to relay the ball to Evans.

Worrell came to the crease for the first time in the series. He had a right to be nervous because of his lack of match practice, because of his preference for the No.4 position and because he was not universally popular on the island of his birth. Beaten for pace by Statham, Worrell played on second ball. It was his first duck in Test cricket. When Holt sparred once too often outside off stump, the catch this time accepted by Graveney at first slip off Bailey, West Indies had been reduced to 25 for three on a pitch Wardle thought 'looked good for 1,000 runs'.

Walcott, batting a place higher than usual at No.4, had marched out with a brand-new bat and told Lock, who dismissed him for a duck in the colony game, that he was going to give the bowlers 'some stick' with it. Swanton used a different register: 'Walcott came in and made several light-hearted strokes as though it were a Sunday school match.' When the spinners came on, Hutton kept the close-catchers up and Walcott kept going for his shots, blasting anything full or short for four.

Pairaudeau was happy to play second fiddle, given the circumstances of the game and the fact he was trying to cement his place. Apart from one leg-glance for four off Lock, which had some

English correspondents complaining about the field placement, he was scoreless before lunch. Walcott had already hit nine boundaries.

Lunch: West Indies 58-3 (Walcott 43*, Pairaudeau 4*)

Walcott's exhibition of power continued unabated in the second session. Typically, Bailey seems to have been the English bowler who rose best to the challenge of trying to keep him quiet. Many of the English fielders remembered a remarkable maiden he bowled early in the afternoon session. This is Evans:

> One of Trevor's overs was the best cricket over I have ever seen bowled in my lifetime. Trevor was bowling to Clyde and each delivery he sent down was different, each ball delivered from a different spot at a different pace, on a perfect length, and each one doing something different off the pitch: a classic example of Trevor's highly intelligent craftsmanship. Clyde Walcott hit each one of them like a rocket, hooking, square-cutting, on-driving, at the top of his magnificent form before the spectators of his native island. And each one was brilliantly fielded and not a single run conceded. Every aspect of the game was perfectly played.

Evans perhaps exaggerates the range of Walcott's strokeplay in this particular over. Other witnesses corroborate the superb fielding but say the stops were made in an arc between extra cover and the bowler. Bailey, credited with several of them, reflected that on another day his maiden could quite easily have 'cost 24 runs'. Perhaps it was during this passage of play that he broke his right ring finger. He certainly had cause to remember Walcott's 'thunderous' driving as the finger proved to be bent out of shape permanently.

Many of Bailey's colleagues testified to the hardness of the hitting. May, fielding at mid-off, said his own fingers 'were extremely sore from the battering they received in trying to stop some of his drives'; Statham described Walcott's shots as 'always hard enough to make our hands tingle'; Hutton noted that fielding in the silly positions, 'no place for the faint-hearted at the best of times', called for 'extra nerve with Clyde'. Watson was perhaps one of the luckier fielders, posted out in the deep and chasing 'around the field trying to cut off some of his flashing strokes'. Palmer was stationed at cover point: 'Oh boy, you really didn't want to field the ball.'

Some of those unimpressed by Palmer's selection suggested he did not field it very often. Ross Hall, never a fan of the manager, attributed five boundaries to his inability to get behind Walcott's drives. Moss retains the image of Palmer diving as if in slow motion while the ball flashed underneath him. The contrast with Suttle, arguably MCC's best outfielder, was stark.

Pairaudeau was running well for Walcott and also getting into his own considerable stride. As he progressed to his half-century, 24 of the last 28 runs came in sweetly timed drives. Statham's hostility, Bailey's tenacity and Laker's accuracy provided Hutton with a semblance of control. His main problem was Lock.

Being asked to bowl into the wind did not help but Lock seemed neutered without his faster ball, kept shifting from over to round the wicket (ten times in four overs) and kept dropping short. By mid-afternoon, Hutton gave him a break to change ends. English correspondents were puzzled by the captain turning to the part-time wrist-spin of Compton rather than Palmer, supposedly in the side as the fifth bowler. Swanton noted that the partnership was proceeding at more than a run a minute 'without risk or palaver'.

Walcott did offer two chances late in the session, one very hard and one fairly easy. Lock, perhaps the best catcher in world cricket, spilled the easy one off his own bowling. It rather summed up his afternoon.

Tea: West Indies 173-3 (Walcott 95*, Pairaudeau 67*)

Shortly after the interval, Walcott reached his century by pulling one of Lock's many long hops for four. Pairaudeau played himself in again carefully. But, just when Ditton thought 'the pair would go on for ever', he drove too early at Laker and Hutton took a good catch low down at mid-off.

Even with the second new ball, England were reduced to offering Walcott singles. Statham pinned Gomez lbw, but not before

Walcott had begun thrashing the harder ball to all parts. Apparently concerned about how the spinners might be treated, Hutton kept his pacemen on for almost the whole of the last hour. Again, Palmer was left to graze in the field. The game was delicately poised but England had recently seen enough of Walcott and Atkinson to know their partnership would have to be broken early after the rest day.

Close: West Indies 258-5 (Walcott 147*, Atkinson 18*)

The touring party had other matters on their immediate agenda. In Bailey's case, this involved a visit to hospital for an X-ray and, once the fracture to his finger was confirmed, the application of a splint. Back at the Marine Hotel, Saturday was the traditional 'club night' when the whole squad met up to administer leg-pulling fines, no doubt meted out in beer or rum. It was also Trueman's 23rd birthday.

Early the next morning Hutton came to the room Trueman shared with Lock to report a 'serious complaint' made against them by the wife of an MCC member. She had apparently been insulted and jostled, after remonstrating with two players who had been inebriatedly pushing a food trolley up and down a corridor, and then into the lift where she was standing. Swanton was called on to provide 'moral support' at the ensuing summit meeting:

> I arrived on the Marine balcony to find captain, manager, Messrs Trueman and Lock, all sitting nervously on the edge of their chairs, and two English ladies, the larger of whom, whose rank in the ATS could not possibly have been lower than brigadier, holding forth rather in the manner of Bertie Wooster's Aunt Agatha. The theme, of course, was what was expected of English teams abroad in the way of behaviour and example, and I found myself applauding the lady's sentiments, expressed, as I recall, in a fine, manly baritone, more in sorrow than in anger, and at the same time feeling intensely sorry for poor Len.

As Arlott points out of poor Len, 'complaints like this horrified him: they were the very stuff of danger to his position', an example of a professional captain not being able to keep fellow professionals under control. It was also the stuff of danger to the future of the players involved. An incident in a lift, admittedly with Pelham Warner rather than a member of the public, had finished Charlie Parker's Test career.

This may explain how nervous Trueman and Lock appeared during their dressing-down. The two accused players thought it prudent to take their medicine and there are several witnesses to the exchange between captain and fast bowler once their apology had been accepted:

> Hutton: I thought you took that pretty well.
> Trueman: So did I, since it weren't us.

Lock 'strenuously' denied the charges. Trueman said he was nonplussed by the whole business, as they had retired straight to their room 'at a reasonable hour' after a few drinks. He also claimed 'it later transpired that the culprits were Denis Compton and Godfrey Evans'. These two had 'previous' as partners-in-crime with Edrich on Hammond's tour to Australia. They had also featured prominently in the high spirits of Mann's tour to South Africa, where several pieces of horseplay in hotels included the amateur captain rugby-tackling a night porter.

On the other hand, while Moss stresses he was not present in the corridor nor in the lift, other players told him that Trueman and Lock were definitely involved and probably to blame. Furthermore, while he associates Compton and Evans with exuberant behaviour, he does not associate them with the 'robustness of phrase' which Swanton deduced was at the heart of the lady's complaint. Moss says that 'if he was there, Denis was more likely to have given her a hug than have sworn at her'.

But the possibility of mistaken identity, and the possibility of junior professionals, in Lock's words, having to 'carry the can' for their seniors, cannot be ruled out. It was certainly unfortunate timing, on the very day rumours of the incident broke, for the *Daily Express* to demand that Edrich be flown out immediately to bolster England's batting.

DAY 2

Rain again delayed the start, this time by nearly an hour. In the 40 minutes of play possible, West Indies scored quickly without taking undue risks against Statham, characteristically dogged, or Lock, still uncharacteristically muted.

The left-armer was perhaps not helped by the tactic of all nine outfielders being placed 35 yards from the bat to save the single. Swanton lamented that in modern field-setting 'the principle of the inner and outer ring has gone completely by the board'. Crawford White was more baffled by Hutton's stubborn persistence with Lock: 'I estimate that the delay in bringing Laker into operation cost us a good 50 runs.'

Lunch: West Indies 288-5 (Walcott 159*, Atkinson 36*)

Laker was at last called into the attack after lunch and given the kind of long spell he always preferred. He had Atkinson caught behind, although not before the all-rounder had registered his first Test fifty.

England reverted to feeding Walcott singles and chipping away at the open end. Lock finally got a wicket when McWatt was lbw sweeping. Once Walcott reached his double century, with a boundary off Laker, he really let himself go – and Lock let slip another return catch. Statham returned to remove Ramadhin with a slower-ball yorker. He remembered executing an even better yorker, at top pace, only to see Walcott dig it out with such force that the ball raced for four. Walcott then lifted Laker for six with what Swanton called 'lordly ease' but was stumped playing a less dignified shot to the next ball. The last pair added five runs.

As Walcott had walked off, Hutton patted him on the back, one of the few such gestures recorded in the series. Statham rated his 220 'comfortably the best innings ever played against me'. For his own part, Walcott thought it among his finest, 'quite apart from its size'. He sensed its importance in the context of the game and felt he had managed his innings well once England tried to manoeuvre him off strike.

Innings close and tea: West Indies 383 all out (Valentine 0*)

Stollmeyer gave all four of his faster bowlers a turn with the new ball. Hutton found them easy to score off, driving Worrell sweetly for ten in one over. The spinners came on within the hour. To Ramadhin's very first ball, Watson overbalanced trying to smother the turn and was neatly stumped by McWatt.

May, perhaps wary of a similar fate, remained rooted to the crease. When Ramadhin tempted him with a delivery flighted so high it almost amounted to a donkey drop, he played a fast-footed drive and holed out to cover point. Compton seemed glad merely to exist until bad light brought an early close.

Close: England 53-2 (Hutton 34*, Compton 5*), 330 behind

DAY 3

Swanton described the morning's play as 'at once the grimmest, the tensest and the slowest imaginable'. The spin twins immediately settled into suffocating lengths, to which Stollmeyer set suffocating fields. Ramadhin began with five consecutive maidens. The crowd was not as large as on the first two days but soon expressed its displeasure. Hutton offered his bat to the spectators, reportedly more in irritation than supplication.

Compton, perhaps surprised to get a loose ball from Valentine, launched it straight to King at backward square leg. According to Ditton, Graveney 'began as if he meant to push the score along a bit' but withdrew into his shell after making 'one or two strokes with more good intent than execution'. The batsman's own account gave himself more credit and his captain more blame:

> Ram was bowling when I came in and I hit the first
> two like a rocket: one at mid-off, one at mid-on. A yard
> either side, and I would have had eight runs. And Len
> walked down the wicket. 'We don't want any of that,'
> he said.

Graveney tried his best to comply with instructions. In just under an hour before lunch, he scored four. Hutton ground out 14 runs over the whole session. By the interval, Ramadhin's figures for the innings were 27-17-25-2; Valentine's 27-16-17-1. This was on a

202

good pitch and fast outfield where Walcott had made his first 50 in an hour.

Lunch: England 80-3 (Hutton 48*, Graveney 4*), 303 behind

Somewhat surprisingly, Stollmeyer took the new ball. This had the effect of increasing the scoring rate dramatically – above one per over. King got a few deliveries to lift but both batsmen were in control of the situation, if not of their timing. Endless forward defensives against the spinners seemed to have sapped their rhythm against the quicks. Inevitably, Ramadhin and Valentine came back on and, almost as inevitably, their first overs were maidens.

The crowd gave a sarcastic cheer when Graveney achieved double figures. They lost all patience after the score had been stuck on 97 for more than half an hour. A slow hand-clap reverberated around the ground.

Hutton moved away from the stumps and refused to continue until the noise abated. The fielders sat down. After at least a minute, he resumed his guard despite the cat-calls and whistles still emanating from the schoolboys' enclosure. The local youth seem to have had a low tolerance for defensive play – Swanton records even Sobers being 'humorously slow-clapped by the irrepressible Barbadian schoolboys' on the next MCC tour. But their cries of 'Hutton can't bat' and 'We want our money back' were perhaps justified by the fact that the Barbados Cricket Association had increased their usual admission charge. Now they were being asked to watch a day's play which, according to the *News Chronicle*'s statistician Roy Webber, broke several Test records for slow scoring.

Graveney had not registered a boundary in more than two hours when, as so often happens in such circumstances, one of the few poor balls on offer got him out. Ramadhin reportedly slipped in his delivery stride and bowled a high full toss. Graveney could have hit it anywhere. He tried to go over mid-on and lobbed a leading edge back to the bowler. As the ball dollied up, Hutton slumped incredulously on the handle of his bat. Graveney was haunted by this image of his captain, 'sheer disbelief and despair written in every line of his body', squatting on his haunches 'looking like a man betrayed'.

By the next over, something in Hutton seemed to snap. After nearly four and a half hours of painstaking defence, he suddenly went 'wild' (Ditton), 'beserk' (Bray), 'crazy' (Hall). He slogged Valentine's first ball to leg. He missed the next trying another enormous heave. Third ball, he careered down the wicket to launch over extra-cover. He came out again to the fourth delivery and tried to hit it, against the spin, over mid-on. Initially, it looked as though Hutton had got away with a terrific skier but Stollmeyer had shrewdly moved Ramadhin back a few yards after the previous boundary, and the ball held up in the prevailing wind. The series to date was somehow encapsulated by England's captain getting out caught Ramadhin bowled Valentine.

To attempt an immediate repeat of a successful piece of risk-taking, to take on a spinner plumb into the breeze, to throw caution literally to the wind with recognised batsmen still remaining – all these were things Hutton would normally consider poor cricket. Why did he lose it?

He had a right to be very tired, physically after his recent illness and mentally after all the recent problems on and off the field. Perhaps Graveney's tame dismissal was the straw that broke the camel's back. Perhaps the barracking of the schoolboys did get under Hutton's skin, although he must have heard worse things in the Bradford League. Or perhaps the sight of Palmer coming out to bat as high as No.6 broke his resolve.

Palmer freely admitted he could not read Ramadhin from the hand; Wardle may at some point on tour have reminded Hutton of how he once 'diddled' the manager in a county game at Harrogate by showing him the chinaman and then bowling him with a googly. To his first ball in Test cricket, Palmer was beaten playing for a leg-break when the ball turned the other way. To his second, he hit an extravagant cover drive for four. The way Palmer started, with only an injured Bailey and an out-of-form Evans left before the tail, may have made Hutton feel the innings was on borrowed time.

As it transpired, Palmer and Bailey put what had gone before into some kind of perspective. They batted sensibly and brightly, accumulating 28 in 40 minutes before tea and seeing off the spinners, however temporarily.

Tea: England 147-5 (Palmer 18*, Bailey 13*), 236 behind

Palmer added one more boundary before he followed a big leg-spinner from Ramadhin and was brilliantly caught at slip by Walcott. Gomez and Atkinson were then recalled. Stollmeyer had generously allowed Bailey to strap his broken finger, despite this breaching the playing conditions. But perhaps he was not above trying to ginger Bailey up.

Evans, cheered for a lofted drive off Gomez, then played as bad a cross-batted mow as in the first innings in Jamaica. Bailey was caught behind. Laker pushed a half-volley to short-leg. As was becoming all too familiar, England's lower order subsided under the pressure Stollmeyer was expertly exerting. He did not seem in a hurry to capture the last wicket, either wishing to avoid an over or two's batting or wanting the evening to consider whether to enforce the follow-on.

Close: England 181-9 (Lock 0*, Statham 3*), 202 behind

There is no clearer indication of the woeful run-rate on Day 3 than Bailey's observation: 'I scored more quickly than any of my colleagues.' England had mustered 128 runs in 114 overs. Swanton reported that the reaction in Barbados was 'one of complete bewilderment'. His reaction, and that of his fellow English journalists, was one of complete embarrassment. They cabled back various – and furious – accounts of England's 'humiliation'.

BOWLER.	BOWLING ANALYSIS. RUNS FOR EACH OVER.																		Overs.	Maiden Overs.	Runs.
UMPIRES :—Messrs.						RESULT OF MATCH														LENGTH O	
	1	2	3	4	5	6	7	8	9	10	11	12	13	14	15	16	17	18			
1																					
2																					
3																					
4																					
5 K. J. Ramadhin	M	M	M	M	M		M	M		M	M	M									
6 a. Valentine	M		M		M	M	M	M	M		M	M	M	M							
7 a. Valentine	M	M	M	M			M	M	M		M	M			M						
8 K. J. Ramadhin				M	M	M		M		W	M			W	M	M	M				

An excerpt from the official scorebook for England's first innings:
more than 400 balls of spin and 33 scoring strokes.

(Reproduced by kind permission of the Marylebone Cricket Club Archive, ref: MCC/CRI/4/3/7)

It was at this point that Hall decided to break the prevailing convention confining reports to events on the field. He filed a shrill piece for the *Mirror* on the 'real story' behind the debacle. Hall asserted that Hutton was being let down by senior players who 'ought to know better'. Late-night parties were understandable as a relaxation between Tests, but not during them: 'Players get jaded, inevitably – and they look it on the field.'

Hall's first coded reference to individual MCC players was to Compton and Evans: 'Two of them do not always act as if the sole reason for their being out here is to win for England.' His second was probably to Wardle, possibly to Laker: 'We should not have one veteran tourist openly criticising the captain when talking to younger players, because he considers that he has not been given a fair chance by Hutton.' Hall felt that England would not recover from such a crippling blow to their prestige without 'stronger discipline'. He laid the blame squarely on Palmer, who, in his opinion, was not shouldering his responsibilities and needed to show toughness as well as charm.

Hutton usually presented a poker face to the media just as he presented the maker's name to the bowler. But, after excerpts from Hall's *Mirror* article were helpfully reprinted by West Indian newspapers, he decided to give an interview to White in the *Chronicle*, saying he would take notice of constructive criticism but not of wild rumours about 'drunkards and playboys'.

The tensions within the MCC party were now out in the open. Some players consoled themselves that they had reached 'rock bottom' and that things could not get any worse. Perhaps they were a day out in that calculation.

DAY 4

England did not add to their overnight total. Stollmeyer once more declined to enforce the follow-on. Although there were dissenting voices, the decision had fewer critics this time. The spinners had bowled more than 100 overs between them and the Bridgetown pitch, its cracks already opening, was expected to deteriorate more than the surface at Kingston.

Innings close: England 181 all out (Lock 0*), 202 behind

Stollmeyer and Holt put on a fifty partnership in under an hour with what Swanton described as 'the minimum trouble'. They were still having maximum trouble between the wickets. Stollmeyer became the first captain to be run out in both innings of a Test.

Worrell had to face one delivery before lunch, which happened to be one of the few in the game Lock spun and landed in the right spot. But the turn took the ball past both bat and stumps.

Lunch: West Indies 51-1 (Holt 23*, Worrell 0*), 253 ahead

The afternoon belonged to Holt. He launched an all-out assault on Lock. First, he slog-swept an enormous six over square leg which, according to Ditton, 'only just missed entering the car park wherein some of the latest British and American models were packed tight'. He then took five fours off Lock in three overs, a burst of hitting which included drives, pulls and late cuts.

The bowler may by this point have been questioning the wisdom of Hutton's reluctance to post a sweeper on the off-side boundary, as well as the placement at short third man of the handicapped Bailey, past whom the ball seemed to keep going. Nor would Lock's mood have been improved when, halfway through Holt's barrage, a difficult chance was dropped by Graveney at slip. As Swanton noted, Lock was never a cricketer whose body language was hard to read:

> There is nothing of the patient philosophy about him
> that one associates with the great left-arm bowlers
> – the Rhodes, the Veritys and the Blythes. He seems
> perpetually angry, either with himself, with the batsman
> or with the world in general.

The perpetually cheerful Palmer was finally tossed the ball – after nearly 200 overs in the field. Almost immediately, and he confessed quite accidentally, he produced a leg-break which Worrell charged at and missed completely.

Unfortunately, so did Evans. He was having a poor game. His keeping had probably never been described as 'staid and elderly' before, but the contrast with McWatt's glovework prompted Bannister to make this observation. Hall, who was campaigning against out-of-hours behaviour, may have had his own reasons for counting seven missed chances. However, there was little doubt that Evans had not recovered properly from his various ailments and was not in the right place mentally.

Worrell was playfully barracked by the Kensington crowd for his comparatively slow scoring. But he had taken it upon himself, with frequent pep-talks and generous running, to nurse Holt towards the hundred denied so painfully in the first Test. His partner duly reached the landmark with a single taken after an overthrow by Watson. It is much easier to score quickly without scoreboard pressure when the fielding side is waiting for a declaration. But the comparative rates of scoring were lost on no one. Holt's effervescent century, including six more boundaries than the England team put together, had taken only 48 minutes longer than Graveney's stagnant 15. West Indies needed 400 fewer balls to make the same number of runs as England had crawled to the day before.

Tea: West Indies 168-1 (Holt 106*, Worrell 31*), 370 ahead

The one thing Hutton felt he could not do to staunch the flow was employ leg-theory. But he held off taking the new ball, perhaps wisely given that there had already been two occasions when it increased the rate of scoring. A more facetious suggestion recorded by Ditton was that 'England did not want to get Walcott in'. The runs still came quickly. Worrell stroked Bailey through the covers for consecutive boundaries; Holt hit Lock wristily for three fours in three balls.

Philip Thomson, who reported on several post-war series as *The Cricketer*'s West Indian correspondent, described Holt's innings as 'one of the best Test hundreds I have seen'. He remembered Statham being 'reduced' to bowling with a man on the cover boundary when the new ball was finally taken. Other journalists suggested Hutton had been far too slow in posting what the locals called a 'minesweeper', given that no English bowler managed to take a wicket the whole day long. Hall summed things up, perhaps with another veiled reference to evening exertions: 'Boundaries flowed like the spirit out of England, and it was a pretty dehydrated English team that walked off.'

Close: West Indies 272-1 (Holt 166*, Worrell 74*), 474 ahead

As the English players braced themselves for another rearguard action, Trueman remembered a 'whiff of rebellion' in the air. Even Statham, a Hutton loyalist who liked to see the opposition ground down for a chance to put his feet up, felt that his captain's determination to 'cut out the gay stuff' was becoming 'ridiculous'.

There are differing accounts as to exactly when and exactly how Hutton was told something had to give. Compton's story, corroborated by Evans and Graveney, is that he led a deputation to the captain's hotel room on the evening of the first-innings debacle:

> It was time we did something, and some of us went
> to see Len Hutton about it. It was time, I pointed out,
> to throw away our chains and to allow the stroke
> players to play the game their own way. Watson, May,
> Graveney and myself must be encouraged to attack,
> otherwise we were, quite obviously, very hopelessly
> in the cart. Len said then that he wouldn't interfere
> with such a policy, and so a new plan went into
> operation. We were to attack, and attack we did.

Bailey placed more emphasis on a dinner he arranged after the Test for the senior players to discuss matters between themselves before approaching Hutton. It seems Bailey came out in favour of Compton's demand for more positive cricket but exhorted him to adopt a more positive attitude to the captain and to the youngsters. Perhaps both interventions were required to clear the air and get the tactics clear.

Hutton was, in Arlott's words, 'never a man voluntarily to share his troubles'. But he seems to have quickly accepted that what his players were telling him made cricketing sense. At about the same time, he pragmatically relaxed his attitude to off-field relaxation. Evans remembered this quiet change of policy as an example of how, as a captain, Hutton was 'very clever at putting things right without appearing to do anything'. Certainly, the collective reaction to what the tourists called their 'Black Tuesday' was pivotal to an improvement in team spirit. There was a clear quid pro quo: the players rallied round on condition the captain loosened up.

DAY 5

Stollmeyer batted on for 25 minutes. This again allowed him use of the heavy roller, but also allowed Holt and Worrell the chance to get the six runs they needed to break the record second-wicket partnership of Headley and Nunes. Statham put paid to that by catching Holt second ball off his own bowling. Walcott came out to do most of the scoring before the declaration. The equation this time was 495 runs in 565 minutes (compared with 457 in 570 at Sabina Park).

Innings close: West Indies 292-2 dec
(Worrell 76*, Walcott 17*), 494 ahead

Watson failed to survive King's first over, feathering a high-kicking, late outswinger through to McWatt. May later admitted he was also in difficulty against King. After he played a loose drive, his skipper came down the pitch for a quiet word. Graveney must have feared Hutton, perhaps not as profanely as Arthur Mitchell, was telling May that was no use. But the captain was reported to have said: 'If you want to crack these chaps get to it and hit 'em hard.'

Suitably emboldened, the young amateur immediately proved to Bray that 'Englishmen can still play cricket strokes'. Having hit the shine off the new ball, May says he was also 'determined not to be dominated by Ramadhin and Valentine and things began to go rather well'. He chasséd down the wicket, first to launch the ball over mid-on and then to caress it through extra cover. Ramadhin conceded 14 in his first two overs, whereas his first 14 overs had gone for only 11 in the first innings.

Hutton was also entering into the spirit of things. Rostron reported him waving cheerily to the fans, 'a man transformed from the scowling, dour figure who was irritated by the same crowd'. He stroked two beautiful fours either side of the wicket off Valentine. When Stollmeyer brought in three close-catchers just before lunch, Hutton played for the interval by lofting the ball over them. The developing partnership had certainly refreshed a press box thirsting for some vintage play. For Swanton it was 'a long deep draught of fresh air'; for Rostron a 'first draught of champagne'.

Lunch: England 56-1 (Hutton 25*, May 31*), 439 to win

May continued to hit the ball as though he were getting something poisonous out of his system. The spinners had at last been knocked off their lengths, and Stollmeyer was forced to turn to his faster bowlers. May welcomed King with one of the shots of the match, a back-foot drive which bounced back yards off the boundary boards. The hundred was raised in only 97 minutes, well ahead of the required rate. But May then tried to force Gomez once too often, and Walcott took a fine one-handed slip catch.

Compton's average for the series stood at 9. Rostron was probably not exaggerating when describing his walk to the crease as that of a 'former Test idol, struggling desperately to save the crumbling edifice of his whole Test career'. Compton's nerves were evident in running which was even more haphazard than usual. But he also put the new plan into operation, hitting some powerful boundaries off the back foot.

Tea: England 149-2 (Hutton 60*, Compton 26*), 346 to win

With the second new ball, King again worked up a fair pace. He hit Hutton successively on the hand, the buttock and the toe, sending the schoolboy stand into a frenzy. The bombardment, or the schoolboys, provoked one strange lapse from circumspection in Hutton, who inside-edged a wild pull down to fine leg. The captain then recomposed himself to play two classical on-drives.

Compton was shaping much more like his old self. In one Worrell over, he played a square cut which screamed to the boundary, a hook off his eyebrows and a sumptuous cover drive.

A sign that the partnership was becoming genuinely dangerous was Ramadhin's decision to go around the wicket for the first time in the game, usually a sign that he was looking to contain rather than attack. But the change in angle induced Hutton to sweep, not a stroke in the Pudsey repertoire. He got hold of the ball almost too well and picked out the one man saving the single on the leg side. Worrell took a good catch at backward square leg.

In the 40 minutes remaining, Compton celebrated only his second fifty in his past ten Test innings with a sweep, a shot certainly in his repertoire. One of his drives split Pairaudeau's thumb, an injury that turned out to be more serious than it first appeared. But the size of England's task on the final day was suggested just before the close by an unplayable ball from Valentine, which pitched six inches outside leg stump and turned past McWatt for four byes. Journalists inspecting the pitch described it as a giant crossword puzzle and noticed that the surface had disintegrated on a good length at one end. Compton still bet Charles Bray ten dollars that England would not lose.

Close: England 214-3 (Compton 65*, Graveney 5*), 281 to win

DAY 6

The start was again delayed by rain. The loss of 50 minutes all but extinguished England's faint chance of victory yet gave them stout hope of a draw. Graveney survived a chance to silly mid-off in the first over but he and Compton still reckoned that the best way of saving the Test was to play their natural games.

There was a pleasant rhythm to the English batting, both men looking stylish off their legs. The spin twins got the odd ball to turn prodigiously, but White thought they were made to look 'very ordinary indeed'. The only other alarm in the truncated first session was a sharp shoelace chance offered to Walcott at first slip by Compton off Atkinson.

Lunch: England 251-3 (Compton 86*, Graveney 19*), 244 to win

Ten minutes after the resumption and seven short of his century, Compton pushed well forward to a googly from Stollmeyer, who was trying his arm in a degree of panic. Statham remembered the sense of English disappointment when Compton was adjudged lbw: 'Frankly to all of us on the players' stand it looked to be a bad decision.' From that vantage point, May was 'not sure that the bowler appealed', while at the non-striker's end Graveney thought Stollmeyer merely 'made a noise in his throat' to register the moral victory of beating the bat.

As with May's dismissal in the first Test, Graveney felt he was in 'a particularly good position' to form a judgement. He thought the ball 'could never possibly have hit the wicket' on height grounds alone. He also claimed 'there was considerable embarrassment in the middle' after the finger was raised. Compton himself, described by Ditton as 'normally the most expressionless of characters concerning a decision', was patently 'not satisfied'. He was still seeking satisfaction in 1980, when he reminded Stollmeyer of the incident during the Centenary Test at Lord's. Stollmeyer recorded his own reply: 'Never mind, you were illiterate anyway and deserved to be out.' This seemed to concede that the umpire had misread the googly as badly as the batsman.

Hope remained for England. Graveney did not look like getting out, it looked like it might rain again, there were three hours to survive and the next three batsmen boasted 35 first-class centuries between them.

Palmer was first. He drove a half-volley from Atkinson straight to silly mid-on. Next was Bailey, England's defensive (if now disabled) pillar. He steered a high full-toss from Stollmeyer into the hands of square leg. Then Evans, who tried to apply himself for the first time in the series, played back to Ramadhin and was bowled.

Graveney farmed the strike and treated the crowd to the array of strokes he had been forbidden to use in the first innings. But his last three partners were all dismissed for what the local papers liked to call 'globes'. The last six English batsmen had managed nine runs between them.

Within 90 minutes of Stollmeyer winning the decision against Compton, the game was over. West Indies had now defeated England five times in a row.

Innings close: England, 313 all out
(Graveney 64*), lost by 181 runs

Crawford White noted that England's 'humiliation' inspired 'undisguised glee' amongst the 'coloured' population of Barbados and provoked 'horrified talk' amongst the white community. 'Of course, it put the whites right on the back foot,' recalled Palmer, 'so they didn't like us at all.' If anything, England's brighter display in the second innings merely served to bring the ignominy of their first innings effort into sharper relief. Hall recorded the comments of a retired army officer: 'I do not mind England losing. It is the method of losing that angers us. And we feel ashamed when we hear them called upon to "play cricket."' Palmer, who bore the brunt of these strictures, remembered that 'after a while it ate into our souls'. According to Statham, the endless criticism of the whites in Barbados was the main reason 'we were all glad to get into the aeroplane which took us to British Guiana'.

Back in 1950, an English businessman was overheard on an aeroplane discussing West Indies' victory at Lord's: 'It's like when your son beats you at squash for the first time, isn't it? You regret it and try harder next time, but there it is: it was bound to happen.' This reaction combined typically British condescension with typically British equanimity. In 1954, some ex-pats in the Challenor Stand, still reserved in practice for local whites, may have been as philosophical. But the hard core, who had barracked Headley on points of etiquette when he captained West Indies in 1948, were still unreconciled to England being outmanoeuvred by a team of mostly 'coloured' cricketers.

The English players probably took more notice of the reaction back home, easy to monitor when it was reprinted in West Indian newspapers. Bailey was contemptuous of the excerpts he read: 'We were written off by the popular press ... and also by Jim Swanton ... because we had failed to lose with the apologetic grace and false smile of a civil servant from a minor public school.'

This was unfair to Swanton. His observations on the second Test were scrupulously balanced. Indeed, cricketing balance was at the heart of his verdict that there was no disgrace in losing to West Indies. The home side bristled with world-class batsmen, the 'inimitable' spin twins and three genuine all-rounders; Stollmeyer's leadership was 'welding all this talent into a coherent whole'. By contrast, Bailey and Evans, the only tourists who could really do two jobs for Hutton, were struggling with injury.

Nor could Swanton's criticisms of England's 'exaggeratedly defensive mentality' in the field and at the crease be easily dismissed. The local journalist Coppin thought West Indies had 'dictated the tempo' from start to finish. The toss was a crucial factor but Hutton was too wise a man to deny he had been out-captained by Stollmeyer. It is telling that he could not bring himself to discuss details of the actual cricket in the second Test in anything he subsequently said or wrote.

Bailey may also have been surprised by the way Swanton's *Daily Telegraph* readers mostly sprang to Hutton's defence after the Barbados defeat, in reaction to a critical letter sent in by the journalist Colm Brogan. Brogan was a provocative and paradoxical figure, a Glasgow Celtic fan of humble origins who became a staunch defender of empire. He conceded that Hutton was 'perhaps a better diplomat than Mr. Jardine' but was in no doubt that Jardine 'would have gone through the West Indies like Sherman marching through Georgia'. The need for stronger generalship was now urgent: 'That and no less is what is required of Mr. Hutton – or of somebody else.'

England's failures also became a subject for discussion in the correspondence pages of *The Times*. The most cutting intervention was made by no less a figure than Field Marshal Montgomery. Monty came from the other Scots-Irish tradition, Ulster-Protestant, but he was essentially saying the same thing as Brogan. In cricket, as in war or politics, 'once a general begins to lose his battles he must expect to be replaced in command'. And the extra edge implicit in his criticism was that a leader taken from the lower ranks was incapable of inspiring 'the infectious optimism and offensive eagerness' essential to the success of any unit.

What Bailey called the 'popular press' promoted the MCC values he tended to deride – brighter cricket and good ambassadorship – even more actively in its post-mortem on Barbados. Rostron of the *Express*, whose newspaper was now proposing amateur reinforcements, tried to sum up the essence of the problem: 'With his added authority as captain, Hutton has been imprinting his methods on the whole team.'

In the same issue of the *Mirror* in which Hall rounded on the playboys, the self-styled 'Man They Can't Gag', Peter Wilson, rounded on Hutton. Wilson was as interesting a character as Brogan in reverse, an Old Harrovian who voted Labour. He had never wanted Hutton, a man without 'personal magnetism', as captain even at home. But he now echoed a view held by some in the inner circle that a professional was simply not equipped for the 'very different' challenge of leading an MCC tour. Wilson correctly predicted a 'Court of Inquiry' at Lord's. By referring to rumours that the captain was at 'the end of his tether', he seemed to be inviting Hutton to fall on his sword before that.

Norman Preston, the editor of *Wisden*, was by no means a mouthpiece for inner-circle opinions. But his notes to the 1954 edition, written after the second Test to meet his spring deadline, could have been dictated by Warner, Allen or Robins. Significantly, Preston endorsed Bradman's comments on leg-theory and strongly implied a linkage between the safety-first attitude of the England team and a decline in the popularity of the County Championship. Like Brown, whose diatribe against over-defensive play was the very next article in the 1954 Almanack, Preston acknowledged the part played by Bailey and Hutton in the Coronation Ashes before making a pointed reference to the modern batsmen who left 'the impression they are shouldering the burdens and troubles of the whole world'. The tenor of the editor's notes seemed to be provoked by Hutton's reversion to 'ultra-cautious' tactics in Barbados, which were lambasted in Preston's opening paragraph: 'I hope the MCC players who went to the West Indies realise they caused all cricket-lovers at home to seethe with indignation at the negative methods which were adopted at Kensington Oval.'

CHAPTER 12

BRITISH GUIANA

Guyana translates as 'land of many waters'. It is a country of high rainfall, hostile ocean and mighty rivers. Mike Atherton has described its barely inhabited interior as 'a vast, largely uncharted wilderness … of infinite beauty, hardship and endless possibilities'. In the 1950s, most of the population was confined to the territory's thin coastal strip, a classic 'monoculture' of very limited possibilities. The ranges where sugar workers lived, often in deplorable conditions, were still sometimes called 'nigger yards' but were now mostly occupied by Indian 'coolies', the persistence of the opprobrious epithets indicating ethnic tensions, but also the innate contempt of the ruling elite.

For English cricketers, British Guiana had long held the reputation of being the least salubrious leg of West Indies tours. On the first official MCC visit, in 1925/26, Hammond picked up something mysterious there which nearly killed him and put him out of cricket for a year. In 1934/35, fast bowler Ken Farnes concluded that the colony was 'the worst place in the world'. Two veterans of the 1947/48 tour had happier memories of local hospitality, yet Wardle recalled it was difficult to adjust from the 'golden beaches' of Barbados to the 'oozy, squelching mud' of the Demerara estuary, and Evans found the humidity below sea-level caused him unbearable prickly heat. May, Hutton's successor as captain on the 1959/60 tour, had a miserable time convalescing from a serious injury: 'Georgetown is an interesting old place built by the Dutch but it is no holiday resort.'

As well as the oppressive climatic conditions, the English players were being pitched into a repressive political situation. They immediately noticed the Argyll and Sutherland Highlanders, sometimes in kilts and sometimes in shorts, patrolling the streets of the capital.

A state of emergency
Hutton fretted about the accommodation – which Graveney thought 'awful' – and about how to keep 'young men happy in Georgetown'.

MCC's main recreational outlet became the cinema, which they soon sensed had become a political outlet for the Guyanese.

When a newsreel of an old Joe Louis fight was shown, Hutton was fascinated by the way 'almost the entire audience leaped to its feet cheering and gripped with excitement'. Although the captain had been warned BG was a 'hotbed', he may not have fully appreciated how 'The Brown Bomber' provided a focal point for opponents of white supremacy. Bannister was shocked by 'the bulk of a cinema audience remaining seated during the playing of the National Anthem'. This brought alive a point Constantine made to British readers that year in *Colour Bar*. He argued that the situation in BG was caused less by Communist agitation than the deep-seated antipathy to the British of 'most of the coloured population', given literal expression by the way they had long 'refused' to stand for the anthem.

Hutton also noticed the crowd for the tour match was louder than on his previous visit in 1948, and that wire fencing had been erected in some parts of the ground. Mounted police patrolled the boundary. Flares were visible in the distance from military exercises being conducted by the Argylls. And, on the first day, the nationalist leaders Cheddi Jagan and Forbes Burnham returned home after a world tour trying to garner support for their cause. The crowds lining the route to welcome them back made a mockery of emergency powers prohibiting unlicensed assemblies of more than five people, and indicated the popular resentment simmering under the uneasy calm.

The circumstances leading up to the suspension of the constitution were complex. Jagan later admitted to political immaturity and tactical mistakes during the 133 days he was allowed to exercise limited ministerial power. But the British intervention uncannily prefigures their better known operation against Nasser in Egypt three years later. Put in the simplest terms, they were not prepared to parley with a charismatic leader who looked more towards Moscow than London.

Jagan, an MI5 agent wrote in 1951, represented 'something new in British Guiana politics'. He was possessed of the common touch and, despite himself being of lower caste, a brahminic purity of mission. After the shooting of five sugar workers at Enmore in 1948, he launched a movement, later renamed the People's Progressive

Party (PPP), to campaign against capitalist 'imperialism' worldwide and the monopolistic power of the British company Booker in BG.

Jagan's crusade to usurp 'King Sugar' was perhaps energised by personal experiences. He had trained in America as a dentist and his father, a plantation 'coolie', had become diabetic. His main political aim was to mobilise impoverished rural Indian communities, especially in his home county of Berbice, to grow rice for themselves not sugar for the British. The spirit of Jagan was shortly to find cricketing expression in Rohan Kanhai, who also hailed from Port Mourant, the village dubbed by some as 'Little Moscow'. Whether Kanhai sought the comparison with Jagan or not, they became the symbols of a new confidence and panache in the Indian-Guyanese community.

The PPP phenomenon undoubtedly accelerated a programme of conspicuous welfare which the progressive chairman of Booker, Jock Campbell, was already minded to undertake. But the party's greatest achievement in its early years was its multiracialism. Jagan had formed a crucial alliance with Burnham, whose power base as leader of the African-Guyanese was Georgetown and the other towns of Demerara county. Although Burnham responded to the charge of Communism more pragmatically than Jagan, he had returned home from his legal studies fired by radical ideas and anger about the discrimination he had suffered in London. For the Jagan-Burnham coalition, the significance of Enmore was not that the victims were all Indian and the police all African, but that the real culprit was the vested interests of Booker and the British.

After it was turfed out of office in 1953, the PPP slowly unravelled, to the satisfaction of MI5 and CIA agents operating in the colony. Jagan and Burnham may have parted ways in any case because of the competition of their egos and the deep structural resentments of the communities they represented. But, on their return from their world tour in March 1954, the leaders of the PPP still presented a united front. The leaders of the MCC team were working hard to do the same.

A state of urgency
The state of emergency seems to have impinged hardly at all on the state of the tourists' minds. This may have been because

the authorities relied on cricket to convey the impression of business as usual or, as nationalists insisted, because there had been no emergency until the authorities had intervened. On the day British troops arrived to help enforce the suspension of the constitution, the Governor allowed British Guiana's inter-colonial Test trial with Trinidad to go ahead. There was not a hint of trouble. Now that the situation had become edgier, the great interest in the Test series proved a distraction, even if there were half-hearted attempts to boycott the MCC matches under the slogan 'No Constitution No Cricket'.

The main explanation for the players not paying much attention to the political crisis was that they were focused on their own cricketing crisis. Georgetown, despite its discomforts and tensions, provided a better environment for them to do so than the supposedly calmer waters of Barbados. For whatever reason, social functions proved less of an ordeal. Several players remembered British Guiana as the place where the better team spirit that had been hammered out after 'Black Tuesday' became fully forged.

Moss may have complained of being kept awake by tropical storms battering the corrugated-iron roof of his room. Bailey may have indulged in the old joke that BG had little to recommend it 'apart from the airport when you are about to depart'. But they bonded on an excursion through the forbidding interior to visit a mining settlement managed by one of Evans's business contacts. May says he and Evans attached such 'particular significance' to the high morale in the hotel room they shared that it became their codeword: 'In Test Matches, whenever England's position may be grim, we will say to each other "Room 45, B.G." – and will gather fresh heart.'

Swanton, sounding rather like Monty, still bemoaned the lack of 'drill' in the field in the colony game. But Bannister noted a new energy in the party and frequent 'pep talks' about the challenge ahead. These would have found motivation from the feedback loops between English and local newspapers – Watson remembered that 'we knew all about the things that were being said of us'. Before the tour match, Hutton had to deny rumours that an 'SOS' had been sent out for Bedser, currently supervising the winter training of Redoubtables Ladies CC and the construction of his new house.

The captain's response may have acted as another boost to team spirit: 'We have a very good side and we have to sink or swim with what we have got.' He certainly saw signs of 'a far more united side, maybe drawn together by the constant criticism and a sense that many were "agin us"'.

The tourists also detected a hint of complacency in their hosts. A couple of newspaper interviews could have given the impression the home players felt they just had to turn up to win. Statham took note of the local 'wide boys' offering short odds on a West Indies victory to clinch the series. Caribbean leader-writers were worrying that interest would evaporate if West Indies went 3-0 up.

Even the extra humidity of BG was welcome in one sense because it offered the bowlers a rare chance to exploit their native aptitude for swing. Ditton observed that Trueman, cutting down his pace in net practice, 'moved the ball considerably in the air'. Statham normally got most of his movement off the pitch but he remembered Bourda was one of the few places he could get the new ball to really wobble. The tour match provided evidence of the potential for early swing when Hutton and May fell on the first morning to the fast-medium Richard Hector. Compton then provided Lance Gibbs with his first wicket in first-class cricket.

This proved to be the only session in which the home side was ahead of the game. Graveney cited as an example of Hutton's 'tremendous shrewdness' his coming back to the pavilion, after his duck, to tell the padded-up batsmen they would get 'a bucketful of runs'. It was Graveney, with Watson, who embarked on a record-breaking partnership of 402. Watson then threw his wicket away to give others batting practice. The scoring rate of well over a run-a-minute reflected MCC's new attitude, but also the benign pitch, small playing area and sub-standard attack. Only Suttle, perhaps affected by the pressure of being under consideration to replace Palmer, was becalmed.

In the field, the two bowlers obviously on trial were Trueman and Wardle, now recovering from his knee injury even if prone to headaches in the humidity. The fact that Wardle, often turning to his 'allsorts', and Compton bowled 99 overs between them suggests that Hutton felt he would need wrist-spin to take 20 wickets in the Test. The BG side was evidently weak: Kanhai, Basil Butcher and Joe

Solomon had not yet broken through. But MCC's crushing innings victory contrasted with the streaky one-wicket win against Barbados and provided what Ditton called a 'tonic' before the Test. Further disputes about the umpiring had also livened up the atmosphere.

'Black bastards' in the colony game

The two locally appointed officials, slated to stand in the Test as well, were Cecil Kippins and Alwyn 'Toby' Rollox. Kippins was an average club cricketer whose only previous first-class experience had come in the inter-colonial games against Trinidad allowed to go ahead four months earlier. Rollox had officiated in the previous Bourda Test, had played inter-colonial cricket and, as a decent left-arm spinner, might have been expected to understand the nuances of the lbw laws. But English players and journalists were unanimous, even if there were varying degrees of circumlocution, that the officials were not up to the mark.

Ditton's syndicated reports referred mildly to 'one or two umpiring decisions which gave the batsmen perhaps more of the benefit of the doubt than they were entitled to'. Bannister limited himself to observing that 'a lot of private indignation was aroused by the refusal of almost every leg-before appeal'. With the passage of time, Bailey allowed himself a reference to 'some of the most peculiar umpiring ever seen'. Hutton's own recollection for public consumption was that Kippins and Rollox 'were not quite of Test standard'. His private view, in his end-of-tour report, was that they were responsible for 'the worst umpiring I have seen in first-class cricket'.

An ill-tempered match gave rise to formal and reciprocal protests. MCC objected to the standards of the umpires and one of the umpires objected to the standards of MCC's behaviour. The only detail of the complaint lodged by Kippins which came into the public domain at the time was that it had been made against Trueman. Bannister had little difficulty locating it to a moment late on the third day when it 'was only too clear' Trueman had 'said something which he should not' to Kippins. Hutton came out of the slip cordon and swapped places with mid-off, variously reported to be either Wardle or Suttle, for the rest of the over.

The incident was one of several on his maiden tour which Trueman brooded over for years. He refers to it in four of his autobiographies,

222

adamantly denying he insulted the umpire, complaining about Hutton hauling him over the coals in front of other players and stating that he asked to be sent home forthwith if tour management still believed he was the guilty party. In 2011, Trueman's biographer Chris Waters tracked down Kippins, now living in America, who supported the fast bowler's assertions that he was not the fielder responsible for any aggravated language:

> It wasn't Freddie, it was Johnny Wardle. I mistook one
> for the other … and I managed to get their names
> mixed up when I complained to Hutton. Freddie didn't
> call me a black 'b'. It was Wardle who made an abusive
> remark. That Wardle, I didn't like him. He was my
> problem, not Freddie. I completely absolve Freddie of
> any blame and I'm sorry it never happened at the time.

Wardle was certainly unimpressed by the umpiring. He cited an instance involving Christiani, who shuffled across to a ball of full length 'which was bound, or so I thought, to have hit the middle stump'. The immediate rejection of the appeal prompted Wardle to follow the (unnamed) umpire to square leg at the end of the over for an explanation – 'I wasn't bothered; I just wanted to know'. The reply, Wardle claimed, was that the batsman had to be given the benefit of the doubt because he was obscuring the umpire's view of the stumps.

It is therefore easy to imagine Wardle following up at some point with an off-hand remark, especially as it was an observed feature of northern discourse to qualify the word 'bastard' with the most gratuitously offensive adjective available. Sellers, Wardle's first Yorkshire captain, once introduced himself to Tony Lewis with an apparently good-natured greeting of 'Na then you little Welsh bastard'. There is the same sense of casual insult in one version of the Bourda incident recounted by Arlott, where Trueman is supposed to have backed up the words 'cheating black bastard' with the clarification 'And there's nowt o' colour prejudice in it – if you weren't black I'd have called you a cheating white bastard'.

But 'black bastard' is one of the specific taunts frequently recorded – into the 1980s and beyond – in the lists of abuse emanating from the

Western Terrace at Headingley and from the terraces of rugby-league and football grounds in Yorkshire. The comedian Charlie Williams, born six miles away from Wardle and 20 from Trueman, played for Doncaster Rovers in the 1950s: 'They used to chant, used to try and hurt me. And naturally, they tried to get at me through my colour. They used to shout "You big black bastard."' It would have been a natural, if inexcusable, way for either Wardle or Trueman to 'get at' Kippins.

If Wardle was standing at mid-off, Hutton could have swapped places with him as much to move him away from the umpire as to intervene with Trueman. The captain's priority in allocating guilt at the time could also have had something to do with the better balance Wardle would bring to the Test team. But in Hutton's report to Lord's, which had nothing good to say about Wardle's conduct, he remained adamant that Trueman was responsible.

And something does not quite ring true about Kippins absolving Trueman of 'any blame'. There was a rapprochement between the two men on the next tour, when they sometimes clowned together for the crowd, and this may have rose-tinted the recollections of the incident six years earlier.

First, there is a discrepancy in their final version of events. Trueman repeated in his last autobiography that he brought Kippins into the dressing room the next day to confirm that the racial abuse came from 'another of the Yorkshiremen on the field', and 'made Len listen to what the umpire had to say'. Kippins told Waters that he never spoke to Hutton again after the various words exchanged during the incident itself, because the captain's refusal to address his complaint 'broke down all communication as far as I was concerned'. According to Kippins, the only question Hutton asked him was 'Why aren't you giving these batsmen out lbw?'

Second, a chain of circumstances will have wound up Trueman in the mini-session where the altercation took place. Hutton wanted early inroads as BG began their follow-on with 20 minutes of play left. Trueman, wicketless in the first innings, must also have felt that this was his last chance to press for a Test place. Kippins rejected an lbw appeal off Trueman's first ball – Bannister says Spooner behind the stumps found it 'hard to contain himself' – and no-balled him twice later in the over. Then Trueman induced an edge from Glendon Gibbs, which Moss put down at leg slip. Trueman's drag tended to become more pronounced when he was striving for pace and/or losing his temper: Kippins no-balled him again. Next Kippins rejected another confident lbw shout against Gibbs. The bowler clearly thought this was a home-town decision, whether or not he knew that umpire and batsman hailed from the same club in Georgetown. To cap things off, Trueman had to watch Moss, who had dropped the man he had softened up, clean bowl Gibbs.

Third, there are other witnesses to support the captain's report that his fast bowler stepped over more than the no-ball line during this passage of play. Robin Wishart was watching from the junior members' section. He distinctly remembers Trueman spitting 'if not at the umpire, certainly in his general direction'. Wardle could still have been responsible for the verbal abuse. But in the end the question of who offended Kippins became less of a talking point than the question of who would be umpiring in the Test.

'Indian' and 'Chinese' replacements

Hutton's request to change the officials was perfectly understandable in cricketing terms given England now had to bowl West Indies out six times on flat or matting wickets to win the series. In Australia in 1946/47, he had seen Hammond hesitate about asking for replacement umpires, and then get accused of being a sore loser when making an unsuccessful attempt to do so later in the series.

The tourists' grievance was also perfectly human, even if Palmer continued to stress in public that the issue was one of competence not bias. Any cricketer who has played in a match where he or she believes the umpires are systematically favouring the opposition knows how soul-destroying the experience can be. It was one West Indies themselves felt they endured several times in the 1950s, especially at Edgbaston in 1957 when the English umpires Elliott and Davies persistently denied Ramadhin's lbw appeals against the pad-play of May and Cowdrey. Wardle reportedly greeted the intransigence of the Guyanese umpires with sarcastic laughter but, as twelfth man at Edgbaston, he responded with the empathy of a fellow spinner: 'I could have cried for Sonny ... I reckon a good proportion of them were absolutely plumb.'

MCC's formal complaint led to a meeting with local administrators the day after the colony game. It was held in a corner of the

Bourda pavilion to the incongruous backdrop of a large pre-Test cocktail party. Stollmeyer was also in attendance. He was reportedly sympathetic to the English view, perhaps because he had developed a jaundiced opinion of Guyanese officials on tours with Trinidad cricket and football teams. According to Bailey, the English proposed that Burke, who had given Holt out in Jamaica, and Walcott, whom they rated despite his calls against Lock in Barbados, should be flown to BG to stand in the Test match. Other accounts suggest that either pair of umpires from the first two Tests was acceptable to MCC.

They were not acceptable to the BG Cricket Association nor the Board of Control, for whom Nethersole issued a clarifying statement from Jamaica. It was granted that the MCC captain was at liberty to request replacement umpires from the Board but 'surely he cannot dictate to them as to where these umpires should be taken from'. The statement did not even bother with the usual niceties about travel expense. The West Indies cricket establishment clearly felt that MCC had trespassed on its jurisdiction improperly.

Hutton believed he had learnt from Hammond's experience by making his protest after an innings victory. But, at 2-0 down in the series, he came across to some West Indians as a moaning Englishman. Previewing the third Test from Jamaica, Jack Anderson cited the example of 1946/47 specifically when he noted that MCC always 'made the same fuss' over the umpires when they were losing. Clyde Walcott's understanding of the incident in the colony game was second-hand but he registered the general feeling in the Caribbean that MCC were acting in an arrogant manner: 'It was a matter of wide discussion that Hutton's approach to the situation suggested strongly at the time that he didn't much mind what Trueman said.'

The president of the BG Cricket Association, Stanley Jones, was an empire loyalist who had lost his son in the war. He was determined to show no 'sign of weakness and appeasement' to the PPP. Jones accompanied the British Governor, Alfred Savage, when he was presented to the teams during the Test and no doubt agreed with the Governor's radio broadcast at the time of the suspension, which portrayed the PPP as Communist plotters who had 'no intention of making the constitution work'.

Jones was therefore in an awkward position. An early issue of Warner's *Cricketer* had gone so far as to describe the umpire as a 'symbol of constitutional government' – the symbolism of locally appointed umpires being replaced at the behest of MCC, shortly after a locally elected government had been replaced with direct rule by the Governor, was obvious. Savage's broadcast had emphasised that allegiance to the Throne and protection by it were 'reciprocal' and that the subjects of the colony were best served by putting their faith in British institutions to provide a secure path towards self-government. Jones could hardly allow one of those institutions to parachute in Jamaicans or Barbadians on the grounds that Guyanese umpiring was not sufficiently self-developed.

The compromise reached was that the nominated officials, Kippins and Rollox, would be replaced by two different local umpires, 'Badge' Menzies and 'Wing' Gillette. Palmer was quoted as saying that he realised MCC were 'taking a risk in having someone they had never seen'. But, having already seen the alternative, it was a risk they were prepared to take.

Hutton was told Menzies was the best umpire in BG cricket. The conflict of interest with his role as Georgetown CC groundsman was cited as the reason he had never stood in a first-class game at Bourda. Bailey was told Gillette had announced his retirement after the 'unfortunate incidents' of the previous season's Test against India, when he had been heckled by the crowd during a long rain delay. Robin Wishart thinks Gillette, whose mixed ethnicity included some Chinese, was the direct superior of Rollox, the man he replaced, at a firm of commission agents in which the Pairaudeau family, GCC members, had an interest. Although Gillette was not a GCC member, he seems to have been considered part of the Georgetown cricket establishment, described as a 'dignitary' at a function for the Pakistani tourists in 1958. The involvement of the 'boss' club in the choice of new umpires could therefore be interpreted as an attempt by local whites to assert their traditional prerogatives.

Bailey chanced upon another potential sensitivity when a guest at the Bourda cocktail party explained to him that Guyanese cricket was in decline because of colour prejudice: 'It was at least twenty minutes before I realised that he was not complaining about whites being unfair to blacks, but blacks being unfair to Indians.' The only

Indian player in the colony side against MCC was Sonny Basdeo, who batted at No.11 and bowled five overs. The dominance of GCC and other Demeraran clubs had become a cause of both regional and ethnic tension.

Bourda had experienced a demonstration of self-assertiveness from the heartland of Jagan's support at the previous season's Test, when a large contingent from the sugar plantations of coastal Berbice had made the arduous journey into the capital to see their heroes from India. Professor Hubert Devonish has argued that 'the attitude of African Guyanese to this outpouring of support for the Indian team was one of tolerant amusement'. But the attitude of the Africans, by far the majority in Georgetown, may not have been so relaxed in 1954 – the very moment the PPP's racial unity was beginning to split asunder – about the black umpires Kippins and Rollox being replaced by an Indian (Menzies) and a Chinese (Gillette), especially as a commentator sympathetic to Burnham, Peter Simms, observed that the instincts of the Chinese in BG 'probably incline more towards the Indian than the Negro'.

It is important not to overplay these factors. The tensions in Guyanese cricket at that time were as much regional as racial – Berbice against Demerara, rural against urban – and there was arguably less of an animus against the Chinese community in Georgetown than in some other Caribbean capitals. But Hutton, who realised his objection to the original umpires 'entered sensitive local territory', would soon find out just how sensitive that territory was.

CHAPTER 13

THIRD TEST (BOURDA)

As generally anticipated, England brought in Wardle as an extra bowler. Swanton and Rostron, for once in agreement, wondered whether the 'hot-headed' Lock should have been dropped to accommodate Palmer or Suttle. But the selection committee clearly felt, at 2-0 down, it was now a case of sink or swim.

The first issue for the West Indies selectors was the traditional one of ensuring sufficient local representation. Their task was further complicated by the otherwise pleasant headache of how to accommodate Weekes, sufficiently recovered from his thigh problem, in a winning side. The BG press clamoured for the inclusion of Christiani, who had scored two attractive half-centuries in the colony game.

How could Christiani be fitted in? Holt could hardly be dropped after his 166 in Barbados. Pairaudeau had played a crucial innings there in support of Walcott. Worrell was out of form but his overall record spoke for itself and he was vice-captain.

The problem was partly solved by the fact that Pairaudeau had suffered an allergic reaction to the finger injury he sustained in Barbados. Rostron noted that Pairaudeau 'is officially announced as having a skin rash', taking the cynical view that he was encouraged to stand down for 'local political reasons'. Pairaudeau says he was genuinely ill and had been desperate to play in his home Test. It was nevertheless potentially helpful, in the context of the suspension of the constitution, that a privileged GCC player had made way for a popular hero.

One of the remaining 12 still had to be stood down for Weekes. Atkinson had scored a fifty in the second Test, with match figures of 32-17-40-3. Gomez had been struggling with a damaged hand and had failed in his last two innings. But his series figures were 66-23-117-7 and Stollmeyer would have wanted his closest comrade beside him. Almost by a process of elimination, the only bowler of genuine pace, King, was left out. This meant the new ball would be shared by three batting all-rounders. It also meant McWatt would be coming in at No.9. Hutton 'wryly guessed what would have been said of me had England been two ahead and packed their side with batting'.

At least – and at last – he won the toss: 'I was never more determined, as W.G. Grace used to say, "to take what the gods offered."'

DAY 1

Because of a tropical storm, the cricket gods had not quite offered the batsman-friendly conditions which usually prevailed at Bourda. The outfield was slow, the square had a tinge of green, the new ball swung a lot, the old ball turned a bit and there were signs that the pitch was two-paced. Swanton felt the first morning's cricket was also 'conditioned by some admirable West Indian bowling and fielding'. There was some brilliant work in the covers by Atkinson and Walcott, who was patrolling there to allow Weekes to rest his thigh in the slips.

Hutton still had the luxury of playing himself in against Gomez and Worrell, new-ball bowlers of gentle pace by Test standards. Off the latter he allowed himself a couple of boundaries, but otherwise batted with extreme caution.

Watson was scoring about six times more slowly than in the tour match. He had survived a chance off Gomez, juggled and eventually dropped by Stollmeyer (who injured his shoulder in the process). Watson also struggled with his timing when the spinners came on. Ten minutes before lunch, he was bamboozled by Ramadhin. Frank Birbalsingh was sitting almost directly behind the bowler's arm. He still remembers Watson's reaction to being bowled: 'His face registered a suspicion of mystery, as if the delivery had somehow confounded scientific laws.'

Lunch: England 40-1 (Hutton 28*, May 0*)

May started nervously and seemed unable to reproduce the dynamic form of his second innings in Barbados. Indeed, with Hutton ignoring every tempter the spinners tossed up outside off stump, the whole England effort was resembling their first innings there, down to the significant detail of loud barracking.

Perhaps May was provoked by the noisy reaction to his caution into aiming an ugly-looking pull at one of Atkinson's off-cutters. Correspondents from both camps agreed he was 'plumb' lbw.

Compton was welcomed by cheers and by the immediate reintroduction of Ramadhin. This move probably reflected Stollmeyer's view that Compton was having difficulty picking him. But one important development was the growing confidence of the two senior English batsmen against Ramadhin, even if they still took great care against him. They both admitted, after a rearguard partnership at The Oval in 1950, that they had played him off the pitch because they could not read him. By now, they had seen a lot more of him. They were also seeing him better: both remembered that as the series progressed they found it easier to distinguish his leg-break in the brighter Caribbean light.

Moreover, the turn Valentine extracted from the Bourda pitch was slow. Whenever Hutton and Compton had come across him before, he had proved something of a bogey, taking their wicket in more than half the innings where they faced him. Whether because of his sore spinning finger or their familiarity, he now rarely looked like getting them out.

Even so, after one delicious late cut, Compton repressed his attacking instincts. Despite his differences with Hutton about team strategy, he seems to have appreciated the importance of helping his captain establish a platform. Hutton himself, despite recent concessions to Compton in the interests of team spirit, was doing things his way and grinding the bowlers down.

Tea: England 107-2 (Hutton 62*, Compton 17*)

After tea, the attritional battle continued between an attack which looked very accurate but not very dangerous, and a pair of great batsmen who were never really in trouble but never really on top. The second new ball was greeted by a superb shot through the covers from Compton and a classical on-drive from Hutton. But Stollmeyer then reverted to leg-theory and England withdrew into their shells, ending the day in watchful defence against the spinners with men surrounding the bat. At least, from England's point of view, a long day in the field had put Holt out of action with a reportedly serious thigh strain.

Apart from the wickets column, a return for the day of 153 for two from 106 overs was hardly better than the 128 for eight off 114 which had brought such opprobrium upon England on Day 3 in Barbados. Rostron, a persistent critic of the tourists' negativity, felt their approach 'lacked all the spark of enterprise'. White found the batting 'shattering' in quite the wrong sense and feared the good name of English cricket 'will be killed stone dead in these parts of the Empire'. Likewise, Swanton damned Hutton's modern 'system' of batsmanship with faint praise: 'If it be marvelled that anyone so magnificently equipped with strokes can wilfully deny himself as he did, at least the captain must be credited with the courage of his convictions.' With the platform established, the next day would prove whether Hutton's convictions were correct.

Close: England 153-2 (Hutton 84*, Compton 37*)

DAY 2

Hutton and Compton took two maidens against the spinners to play themselves back in, but then began looking for runs in a more confident manner. Hutton unveiled his peerless cover drive, Compton his famous sweep to reach fifty.

The captain had a sticky patch in the 90s, and Valentine turned one past him for only the second time in the match. But, once he reached his hundred, he immediately sought to disrupt the left-armer's tactic of bowling well outside off stump to a 7-2 field. Reprising his tactics against Sobers in the Barbados tour match, Hutton looked to mow Valentine over midwicket. He missed his first heave against the tide but then connected twice for boundaries. Soon he was scoring off nearly every ball, his eye now utterly in. Compton was happy to give Hutton most of the strike.

Stollmeyer brought himself up to the bat at short-leg for the final overs of the session – Compton dabbed the ball straight to him. The batsman thought he 'perhaps' lost concentration trying to play for lunch. But Compton had contributed 64 to a round 150 partnership with his skipper.

Lunch: England 227-3 (Hutton 129*, Graveney 0*)

Like Watson, Graveney's form in the colony game did not carry over to the Test. He was bowled by Ramadhin for a duck. Some English journalists thought he should have played forward but Walcott rated the delivery 'the best leg-spinner I have ever seen Ram produce on a West Indies wicket'. Bailey was due in next. Instead Wardle walked out.

Hutton, in typical fashion, had come in for lunch, vaguely asked Wardle whether he fancied batting at No.6 and wandered off. Towards the end of the interval, the captain told him to get padded up without any further instructions. Hutton probably calculated that he and Bailey would gum up the innings batting together; a change in the order might also arrest the alarming collapses of previous Tests.

Wardle immediately began lofting drives, one of which dollied up to Stollmeyer at deep mid-off. The batsman remembered the West Indies captain 'even had time to cast a cheerful grin in my direction' as the ball was coming down. Stollmeyer was in fact squinting into the sun, his excuse for dropping what he acknowledged was a 'sitter'. Wardle made the most of his reprieve, mixing beefy hitting with cheeky running. He also injected Hutton with some of his freedom, probably as the captain intended. Hutton lifted Atkinson for four and then six as the partnership raced past fifty. Given all the criticism of England's run-rates, he may have enjoyed landing the six straight into the press box.

Hutton eventually succumbed to tiredness and, as in Barbados, a rare sweep shot off Ramadhin. His 169 off 499 balls was a perfectly constructed innings, of which he remained quietly proud. Swanton found it fascinating how the 'alibis' for slow scoring dissolved on the second day, implying that England could have accelerated much earlier. Hutton could have responded that mastery over such tight bowling had to be earned not assumed. Wardle soon played on to Ramadhin. His job, less crucial but extremely useful, had also been done.

Tea: England 327-6 (Bailey 6*, Evans 6*)

After Evans fell to Atkinson, Laker provided some further impetus. The over in which he was bowled by Valentine went dot-6-4-2-dot-wicket.

233

Valentine's meagre returns contrasted with what Watson called Ramadhin's 'brilliant marathon of bowling'. But his one scalp at least provided him with his hundredth Test wicket. He became the player quickest to that milestone, achieved within four years and five series, often on unhelpful pitches. Swanton found the crowd's wild celebrations 'an amusing demonstration of West Indian exuberance'. The mounted police had to restore order when some of the fans, whom Rostron observed 'gaily dancing calypsos and mambos', encroached on the outfield. Nobody could prevent the pitch invasion of a stray dog, which held up the final deliveries of the day.

Close: England 401-8 (Bailey 40*, Lock 0*)

DAY 3

England batted on – 34 useful runs were added in even time. Bailey showed uncharacteristic enterprise and characteristic unselfishness, turning down several singles on 49 before edging a cut off Ramadhin to Weekes at slip. Ram then bowled a scything Lock to register the notable figures of 67-34-113-6.

Innings close: England 435 (Statham 10*)

West Indies had 50 minutes to bat before lunch. Worrell, acting as emergency opener for Holt, took strike because his captain had a superstition about not facing the first ball. Statham started inauspiciously with an outrageous wide which ended up at third slip, about the only wide anybody can remember him bowling. If there were shades of Steve Harmison at the Gabba in 2006, the bowler explained that the misdirection was caused less by nerves than the fact he slipped in his delivery stride.

The next ball was rather better. A perfect outswinger drew Worrell forward and he was caught behind. Statham had learnt from observation the virtue of pitching the new ball well up in the heavy atmosphere. Stollmeyer admitted he hardly saw the 'beauty' which swung into him and then cut away after pitching to take his off stump. Hutton and Evans both compared it to the famous ball they had seen close-up in Adelaide in 1947, when Bedser bowled Bradman neck and crop. Statham modestly suggested he felt his fingers move across the seam half by accident. But he did savour the delivery nearly 50 years later in an interview with Frank Keating:

> The best ball he ever bowled? You have to drag it out of him. Okay, Jeff Stollmeyer, good bat, Guyana Test one time. Flat track. Pitched fractionally outside leg stump. He went to glance – and it just popped off the top of the off bail. Beautiful, eh?

Statham's two early wickets set up a moment of high drama. Walcott strode to the wicket in a similar situation to Bridgetown and, by his own admission, with the same counter-attacking intent. Hutton recalled taking the 'calculated risk' of placing himself and Bailey as joint silly mid-offs at 'dangerously short range'.

The field-setting was partly designed to force Walcott onto the back foot against the swinging ball, a plan Statham abetted with a well-directed bouncer which struck the batsman on the hand as he tried to hook. It was also designed to get Walcott's 'beans' going. He crashed one boundary through the covers. Trying to repeat the shot, he inside-edged a fast, full inswinger. White noticed the mess twice made of the stumps: 'Only the leg wicket was left standing. The angry Walcott knocked it down as he began to trudge back.'

If Walcott was guilty of a rare fit of pique at having risen to the bait – White is the only journalist to record it – he had calmed down when he talked to Rostron: 'I tried to blast Statham, but he beat me with sheer pace of ball. It was a gamble, and this time I lost.' Hutton recounted the dismissal with the dry satisfaction of a Yorkshireman who had worked someone out.

Swanton was greatly enthused by the sight of England's strike bowler continuing to race in from the Northern End, 'his drenched shirt sticking to his body, his neckerchief flying'. Statham had Christiani in all sorts of trouble, shaving his off stump, inducing a hook that just cleared the infield and then finding an edge which dropped short of Watson at second slip. Although Statham failed to take the fourth wicket he deserved, his penetrating spell made the omission of King, as Stollmeyer later admitted, look like 'an error of judgment'.

With Walcott out, Weekes limping and Holt injured, Hutton must have started to think victory was possible. But he spent the rest of the day watching what Statham called 'the mother and father of all tropical storms'. Statham remembered the sight of Badge Menzies having a busy afternoon in his day job:

> We spent our time in the pavilion laughing our heads off as the groundsmen indiscriminately scattered tarpaulins all over the field. They anchored them by laying a few old railway sleepers across them … and the rain kept teeming down. We were quite certain we had got the West Indies now, because there were bound to be wet patches on the pitch where the rain had seeped through.

The captain went out to prod the playing surface. He noted the pitch was sweating under its improvised covers and started thinking about how to exploit the sticky wicket Statham anticipated. But Hutton also confessed to a sleepless night under his mosquito net, worrying that Demerara's rainy season might render England's hard work in vain.

Lunch and close: West Indies 31-3 (Weekes 21*, Christiani 3*), 404 behind

DAY 4

To England's amazement and disappointment, the pitch was bone dry the next morning and play started on time. They would have swapped a delay for a gluepot. Hutton told Bannister he would be placing an order for raincoats made out of the same material as the tarpaulins.

The West Indies batsmen chose to play their way out of trouble. Weekes took the majority of a short spell from Statham and then hammered the spinners. Christiani lived dangerously, taking 14 from his first 14 balls, before a loose shot to Laker was scooped up by Watson at midwicket.

The fielder rolled over after the catch and was asked to confirm that the ball had carried. West Indian correspondents suggested Christiani should have been given the benefit of the doubt; Bannister begged to differ and thought the batsman's long hesitation 'a poor compliment to the sportsmanship of Watson'.

Lunch: West Indies 118-4 (Weekes 79*, Gomez 7*), 317 behind

The discriminating Weekes continued to dead-bat the good balls and dismiss the bad ones. Gomez supported him intelligently, contributing just one run after lunch to the fifty partnership. There was nearly a run-out after a direct hit from May. His fielding in the deep had been so impressive that Frank Birbalsingh started focusing on him from the stands:

> In between overs he looked with a curious mixture of incomprehension and wonder at us in the crowd. It was not disdain or even hostility. I suppose May was trying to smile to suppress something like fear, but couldn't make it very convincing.

Statham forced another important breakthrough when Gomez chopped a ball on to his stumps. Weekes unselfishly tried to take most of the bowling until his new partner Atkinson was acclimatised. But he became bogged down himself in the 90s against Lock, the bowler who had caused him most trouble so far in the series.

When England raised an appeal against Weekes, there was confusion at first as to what had happened. Umpire Gillette, apparently unsighted, went to confer with Menzies at square leg, who seemed in no doubt the batsman was out. Evans explained that Lock's delivery 'just flicked the outside of the leg stump and very quietly dislodged only one bail'. The press box thought the off bail had been disturbed, but in any event Evans told the batsman to be on his way. According to Bannister, Weekes apologised to the England manager at the next interval for tarrying at the crease and Palmer told him he was quite within his rights to do so.

Interviewed in 2018, Weekes insisted he did not hear a tell-tale 'rattle'. He found it strange the stump had moved slightly forward not back, and believed the bail may have been dislodged by Evans, whom the admittedly partisan Jake Crocker reported diving 'half swallow' to the ball. One possible explanation for the batsman's confusion is that the stumps were loose because of the custom of Caribbean groundsmen to water the wicket-holes, so that the crowd could see the stumps come out of the ground if a fast bowler was on target.

Lock had been uncharacteristically subdued and error-prone in the field during the previous Test at the Kensington Oval. Bannister was delighted to see 'Tony Lock of Kennington Oval' come back to life when the bowler adjusted in his follow-through to take a brilliant left-handed return catch offered by Atkinson. Atkinson stayed on the field, not because there was any question this time about the dismissal. He was going to act as runner for Holt, who limped out at No.9.

England considered Holt and McWatt to be their most streaky opponents, a mindset which may have contributed to their difficulties in getting them out. Statham recalled being 'on his knees' with exhaustion but asked his captain for one last over against McWatt. He got the edge he was after but not the result – Compton dropped it at second slip.

Statham, normally the most equable of great fast bowlers, admitted to losing it completely with the fielder. There were a number of reasons he could be forgiven. McWatt had been dropped off his bowling three times in Jamaica. Compton, who claimed he simply did not pick up the flight, seemed to have made a lackadaisical effort with one hand when he could have used two. The incident may also indicate that Trueman was not the only young tourist to find Compton an unhelpfully laid-back teammate.

McWatt then made hay against the left-arm spinners before the second new ball. Some exasperating byes and overthrows leaked through. Holt continued to try English patience, not least because some fielders were sceptical about the seriousness of his injury. He also stayed put after a confident appeal for caught behind off Lock.

Tea: West Indies 201-7 (McWatt 40*, Holt 19*), 234 behind

After another hour of resistance, the McWatt-Holt stand had reached 98. The crowd began slow-handclapping in anticipation of the 100 partnership. May, at deep square leg, was alert to the batsmen looking for a second run once McWatt had dabbed the ball towards him: 'I raced in, picked up and threw in to Godfrey Evans as fast as I ever did in my life.' 'It came with a bang,' confirmed Evans, 'right

238

into my gloves over the wicket.' Watching his first Test from a good position in the North Stand with his parents, Shan Razack was left awestruck by May's 'feline' piece of fielding.

McWatt was reported to have carried on running back towards the pavilion, and no witness from either side contests the fact he was out. But the range of estimates as to how far suggested McWatt was not so 'hopelessly short' as Hutton remembered. Compton thought the batsman was 'half-way down the wicket' when the bails were removed, but the distance then reduces from 'four or five yards' (Evans), to 'three' yards (Statham), to 'perhaps a couple of yards' (Swanton) to 'a yard and a half' (Graveney), to 'a yard' (Bailey).

In the surviving photograph, the danger-end is furthest away from the camera and McWatt's momentum is taking him well past the popping crease: it is possible to see how partisan supporters might have been able to convince themselves that the decision was tight. Crocker, who claimed to have taken the testimony of spectators in a variety of vantage points, suggested another reason for disquiet: 'Umpire Menzies's finger lifted skywards before the ball had been returned to the wicketkeeper.'

There was a moment's eerie silence as Ramadhin walked out. Then, according to Compton, 'someone yelled disapproval and threw a bottle on to the pitch; then someone else, and someone else and someone else'; then wooden packing cases and all manner of other missiles began to be hurled in the general direction of Menzies; then 'the mood of the crowd developed quickly into a kind of frenzy and it spread like a bush fire round the ground'. Robin Wishart, watching from the comparative safety of the pavilion, says 'the whole thing just took off from nothing'.

The genre of films about the Second World War was in full flow in 1954. *The Cruel Sea*, starring Jack Hawkins, and *Malta Story*, starring Alec Guinness, were both playing in Caribbean cinemas during MCC's visit. English accounts of the riot veered between proud celebrations of the officer's stiff upper lip and the light relief of comedy in the ranks. Lock appreciated the 'timely wit' of Laker's instructions: 'Married men to field close to the wicket and the single men out on the boundary.' Graveney told Ramadhin, as everyone sheltered in the infield, 'if you hit the ball down there, Sonny, you can bloody well get it yourself'. Wardle, the self-appointed on-field clown of the party, helped diffuse the situation considerably by pretending to drink from the bottles and then staggering around in mock drunkenness.

But it was Hutton, perhaps improbably, who was credited with taking the Jack Hawkins role. For Compton, not otherwise a devotee of his captaincy, 'Len never had a greater moment' than when he refused to leave the field against the recommendation of local officials:

> He was cool, nerveless, courageous, quite
> unconcerned about the demonstrating crowds which
> surrounded him in angry thousands.
>   'No,' Len answered, 'I'm not leaving the field … I
> want another couple of wickets before the close of
> play tonight.'
>   It was superbly defiant. It was, if you like, the
> saying of the century. It was characteristic Len.

Bannister, arguably Hutton's closest journalistic confidant on this tour, also found his response 'magnificent' and worked himself up into a rare purple passage:

> The simple action of the dour strong-minded
> England captain in turning his back on the mob and
> concentrating on the job on hand was a symbol of
> English character and, as such, more eloquent than
> a thousand speeches, more forceful than a volley of
> bullets. I have never felt prouder of 'our Len'.

Bailey cast some doubt on what he called this 'delightful story' and suggested that the captain was as bemused as the rest of the team. Whether 'a determination not to allow the crowd to control the situation' was as clear a motivation as Hutton later remembered, Wardle probably had it right that 'one corner of his astute cricket brain' quickly whirred into action so that England did not lose their grip on the game. Hutton made sure Watson intercepted umpire Menzies before he could run off, and promised not to place any fielders on the boundary if play could be resumed.

After a delay of about ten minutes he got his reward. Graveney thought Ramadhin 'showed little interest in staying'. He was out to Laker's first straight ball.

Close: West Indies 241-9 (Holt 38*, Valentine 0*), 194 behind

DAY 5

Palmer had overnight discussions with the Commanding Officer, Major Troup, as to whether the Argylls, some of whom had been watching the game as spectators, should attend in a more formal capacity after the rest day. Perhaps wisely, it was decided that the presence of British soldiers might inflame the situation. Instead, Palmer rang Government House to ask for the number of police at the ground to be doubled. Ditton sensed there was still 'considerable tension in the atmosphere' when the Test resumed.

It took ten minutes and ten runs for England to close the West Indies first innings. When Menzies gave another run-out decision against Valentine, Hall was relieved to hear 'complete silence' from what was now known as the 'bottle-throwing' section. Given the state of the weather and the state of the series, Hutton did not hesitate to enforce the follow-on.

Innings close: West Indies 251 all out (Holt 48*), 184 behind

It was perfectly normal practice for a batsman with his eye in to continue as opener in a follow-on. But the English fielders felt Holt's continuing use of a runner was taking a liberty. The English reporters also detected the first sign of Menzies trying to even things up. Bray thought Stollmeyer 'more than a little lucky' to survive an lbw shout from Statham. No West Indian correspondent found the appeal worthy of mention. As in the first innings, Stollmeyer had a novocaine injection in his shoulder before going out to bat. But the West Indies captain looked comfortable enough once the shine was off the new ball.

**Lunch: West Indies 41-0 (Holt 16*,
Stollmeyer 25*), 143 behind**

The openers made further progress in the first 40 minutes of the afternoon, Holt strong off the back foot and Stollmeyer off the front. They brought up the highest West Indies opening stand of the series.

Then Laker built up some pressure and Stollmeyer got a thick inside-edge to one of his off-breaks. Compton dived full-length and grabbed it one-handed inches from the ground. It was a catch to write home about, particularly as Compton's fielding so far on tour had certainly not been.

Worrell seemed understandably nervous given his recent failures, nearly running himself out to get off a pair. Facing Statham, he almost played on and then edged through to Evans for the second time in the match. Worrell was fast becoming Statham's 'bunny', dismissed by him three times in the space of seven balls.

Statham thought he had another caught behind in his next over. The appeal against Holt was extremely confident. The English suggested that the batsman had begun to walk off, and that his runner had taken his gloves off, before Menzies shook his head. Evans made his disgust obvious. Beside him at slip, Graveney was probably also fuming, as he later condemned 'compensatory' umpiring decisions as 'dishonest and intolerable'. But no great harm was done as Lock turned one past Holt to bowl him half an hour later.

The pitch was beginning to show signs of wear and the Surrey spinners, arguably for the first time in the series, looked dangerous bowling into the rough. Nevertheless, after the time lost on the third day, England's margin for error was small. Weekes and Walcott saw West Indies quietly through to tea. On the basis of their current form, the home side would end the day with a meaningful lead if they were not separated in the final session.

Tea: West Indies 135-3 (Weekes 23*, Walcott 2*), 49 behind

Laker and Lock continued to threaten for eight overs after the interval. Hutton, always prone to revert to pace, still took the second new ball. He may have been relying on Statham to break the back of the innings. But it was Bailey, cutting down his pace with Evans standing up, who made the crucial breakthrough. Weekes, having just driven Statham brutally for four, edged a leg-cutter and Graveney took an excellent ankle-high catch at slip.

Christiani responded to Statham's attempts to sucker him on the hook-shot with a six and a four. A huge cheer greeted his wiping off the arrears. But Bailey, this time with an off-cutter, bowled him. It was then the home side's turn to complain about a decision when Walcott was adjudged lbw to Laker. According to the batsman, 'Jim admitted to me afterwards that he only "asked" because he knew he was so near his target' (his thousandth first-class wicket). Gomez and Atkinson survived to the close by what Swanton called 'the grace of a beneficent Providence'.

Close: West Indies 205-6 (Gomez 13*, Atkinson 0*), 21 ahead

DAY 6

Both sides must have known the crucial importance of the Atkinson-Gomez partnership. If the two all-rounders could bat into the afternoon and build a lead, time would begin to come into the equation. As the first hour wore on, Hutton's field changes and bowling changes, even by his standards, were frequent. Having started with Laker downwind and Bailey into the wind, he swapped them for Lock and Statham, and then quickly brought Laker back for Lock and Wardle for Statham.

Hutton told Wardle not to be frightened of bowling wrist-spin and not to be frightened of giving the ball air. He repeated this advice after Atkinson had smashed Wardle's first chinaman for four through midwicket. The bowler remembered a rare display of emotion when he bowled Atkinson through the gate with his next one: 'Len isn't one for showing his feelings, but, to my amazement, he dashed across and flung his arms round me.'

In Barbados, the captain had been widely criticised for his field-settings – now his every move seemed to come off. He brought in Wardle's field to tempt Gomez into an indiscretion: the batsman duly flashed at a wide, short ball and Graveney took another good slip catch in front of his face. Next Hutton brought back Statham, downwind this time, because of Ramadhin's nervousness against pace: the yorker did the trick second ball. Wardle then picked up his third scalp of the morning when Valentine, who was to notch only two more runs than wickets in Test cricket, made the mow of a natural No.11.

Lunch: West Indies 256 all out (McWatt 9*), 72 ahead

Hutton sent in May and Graveney. Perhaps he wanted to give them match practice after their failures in the first innings. Perhaps he wanted to see how they fared against the new ball should he decide to end the experiment of Watson opening. The two youngsters started with some cavalier drives and took 18 off the first two overs, more than England had sometimes scored in an hour's play.

This prompted an immediate change in tactics from Stollmeyer. Gomez bowled an over of blatant leg-theory and Graveney refused to make any stroke. Next Atkinson, who had taken the new ball in preference to Worrell, rubbed it into the dusty patches on the pitch to remove the sheen. If the leg-theory seemed a waste of goodwill given the match situation, the ball-roughing reaped immediate rewards when Atkinson bowled May with a shooter.

Swanton was pleased to see Watson come in with 'no intention of puddling about'. Stollmeyer eventually acceded to the crowd's demands to see Christiani and Weekes have a bowl, and Weekes acceded to their wish to see the game end with a six. He served up a 'lollipop' which Watson planted over the square-leg boundary. After the events of Day 4, journalists on both sides made a point of noting that the crowd cheered the England batsmen and greeted the result 'with admirable sportsmanship and good humour'.

England 75-1 (Graveney 33*, Watson 27*) won by nine wickets

The third Test had seen a marked improvement by England in all departments. As Bannister noted, it also proved a personal triumph 'for the much criticised Len Hutton'. He had captained his side with great shrewdness. He had played the match-winning innings. And it could be argued he had stopped the match being abandoned. All this was quickly recognised in a telegram he received from Headquarters:

> Best congratulations to you all on a well-deserved
> victory, and to you on your personal contribution and
> fine example in difficult circumstances. MCC.

The irony was probably not lost on Hutton that it took a riot for Lord's to provide him, for about the only time on tour, with its unequivocal support.

Swanton thought that the Georgetown riot of 1954 'quite paled' into insignificance compared to the Port of Spain riot of 1960, a crowd disturbance with which it otherwise had many similarities. The trouble in Trinidad on the next MCC tour was again sparked off by a local batsman (this time Charran Singh) being adjudged run out by a 'Chinese' umpire (this time Eric Lee Kow) in a Test West Indies were losing (this time 284 behind on first innings).

Moss, although admitting that the two incidents sometimes merge into one in his fading memory, concurs with Swanton that the second was more frightening. Statham, another to go on the next trip, felt the same way because at least the bottles 'remained intact' at Bourda before they were thrown. The Georgetown police did not use tear gas, a feature of crowd control during the BG political crisis and in later riots at Caribbean grounds. Photographic evidence suggests that the players taking refuge on the square at Bourda were out of immediate danger and it seems that the playing area was cleared quickly. This was partly through the efforts of enterprising schoolboys, one of whom got a further pelting for his trouble and returned fire with what Graveney thought was a decent left-arm throw.

But it would be wrong to underplay the gravity of the situation. Hutton said he would 'never forget' the look on May's face as he ran for cover with Menzies from square leg; Watson remembered the umpire 'shaking with fright' when he stopped him running off into the pavilion; Trueman thought the situation was 'really dangerous'; Wardle 'truly nasty'. Graveney chuckled about Ramadhin being 'terrified' but quickly added that 'everybody was'. Lock recalled the moment when a few of the rioters surged onto the field: 'I thought we'd had our chips.' Asked in 2018 whether press accounts had exaggerated the incident, Weekes gave a clear answer: 'No, it was really bad.'

Certainly, the reverberations of the disturbance were felt for years. Tony Cozier pointed out it was 'the first demonstration of its kind in the West Indies and received major, and adverse, publicity'. Any discussions of Caribbean cricket for the rest of the decade seemed to include an obligatory reference to the shame brought upon the region by what Christopher Nicole called the 'unfortunate bottle throwing incident'. From the English perspective, Palmer stressed that the trouble occurred long before football hooliganism had inured press and public to crowd violence: 'In those days it was quite outstanding to have something like that happen.' May added that riots at cricket grounds were 'unknown in modern times' and that the impact of the disturbance was therefore 'immense'.

When the Australians toured in 1954/55, the Senior Superintendent of Police, A.H. Jenkins, gave Ray Robinson a fairly uncomplicated account of the previous year's trouble: 'We think it was an instance of mob psychology. One stupid man, probably drunk, threw the first bottle, followed by a lot of other stupid people.' The explanation was good enough for Board president dos Santos, who blamed a single idiot 'high in his cups'.

Guyanese rum, some of the best in the world, seemed to permeate all echelons of society. European immigrants were renowned for their hard drinking; a liberal Christian missionary found strong liquor 'almost universal' in the black communities of Demerara; the historian Clem Seecharan grew up in an Indian village in Berbice, where he remembered a 'rum-consuming culture'. On the day of the riot, it took young Shan Razack the whole lunch break to get his drinks – soft in his case – such was the 'big crowd at the booth'. This suggests that the booth was doing good trade, and the effects of the sun in the uncovered popular areas of the ground will have exacerbated the effects of the rum.

If they felt drinking may have fanned the flames, most English witnesses settled on gambling as the main cause of the disturbance. Throughout the tour, starting with the Jamaican practice of betting on which of the two drinks waiters would come out of the pavilion first, Palmer thought 'it was extraordinary what some of those boys would bet on if they'd had a rum or two; they'd bet a fortnight's wages'. In Georgetown, the MCC party had seen the enthusiasm for horse racing at the Demerara Turf Club and goat racing at the British Guiana Cricket Club. During the Test, Bannister noticed a three-card-trick stall doing brisk trade outside the ground; inside, from his interactions with the crowd, Wardle realised that many of them had backed him to take more wickets in the match than Valentine.

Compton, with the innate understanding of a keen gambler, observed that the McWatt-Holt partnership was 'a nice situation for a man who had doubled up on his betting'. His theory was that the most popular wager that afternoon involved an accumulator on the record stand (already achieved), the century stand (which would have been achieved if McWatt had made his ground) and the saving of the follow-on (47 runs away with three wickets in hand at the time). These accumulators will all have gone down when McWatt was out and the middle leg was lost: 'There must have been quite a number of people in that crowd who stood to win quite a lot of money, and who, if the later evidence of bottles meant anything, may have been celebrating a little in advance, with a natural, and added, exhilaration.'

However, while the long association of cricket, drink and gambling has sometimes contributed to crowd trouble, it is hard to see why it would by itself have led to rioting at Bourda. Indeed, the explanation could be considered grossly offensive in the wider social context. One of the sugar interest's depositions to the 1938 Moyne Commission is particularly astonishing to a 21st-century sensibility and attracted widespread ridicule at the time. This was the assertion that the main aspirations of the 'Negro labourer' were 'a little spare money for rum or gambling and the opportunity for easy love-making'. Even the last of these pieces of caricature entered the Superintendent of Police's profile of the bottle-throwers: 'Some of these men have no fixed address and just as likely will be living at the other end of town with some other woman tomorrow.'

It is therefore understandable that Worrell, conscious of his role as a disperser of such stereotyping, sought to dismiss suggestions that the crowd was out of control because it had succumbed to its supposedly traditional vices. He sought to put the 'now famous' bottle-throwing 'in its right perspective', claiming that 'no incident in international cricket has ever been more exaggerated' and that play restarted with 'no more than the ordinary delay'. Alcohol and gambling had no part in his explanation, which rested on the fact that it was common practice, at Bourda and other Caribbean grounds, for empty mineral water bottles to be tossed just inside the boundary.

According to Worrell, the trouble started when an English player 'misunderstood this local custom', throwing a bottle back at the spectators. That Compton did this at some point is uncontested – something Compton does not mention in his own memoirs but which even his friend Evans realised could have inflamed the situation greatly had the bottle not 'fortunately' fallen short of the enclosures. But Worrell and Christiani are the only witnesses to suggest Compton incited the riot rather than reacting to it; everybody else thinks he hurled a bottle back angrily after it landed too close to May for comfort.

While Worrell placed the incident in the context of the tourists not having made themselves 'the most popular of characters', he still took care to emphasise, as did the equally anglophile Thomson in his report for *The Cricketer*, that no missiles were deliberately aimed *at* any of the English players. Walcott still felt the crowd's anger had been fuelled by MCC's reputation for bad sportsmanship, Hutton's objection to the original umpires and Trueman's 'little speech' to them in the colony game. The more specific background was the fact that Menzies had been 'involved in two other decisions that would doubtless be referred to the third umpire today'.

May noted drily that Christiani's reluctance to walk 'may have been unwise' in the light of subsequent events; Walcott thought Watson's catch 'had been low enough to justify his hesitation'. And while Walcott believed Evans 'as good a sportsman as one could wish to meet', he did not blame the spectators for harbouring 'thoughts' about Weekes's dismissal: 'An appeal for "bowled" is, after all, not a very common thing.' Walcott felt that drink and gambling were only contributory factors, found a political explanation 'wildly improbable' and implied that the Bourda crowd thought Hutton had Menzies in his pocket on the fourth day.

These points had been made even more strongly in the immediate aftermath by the local journalist Jake Crocker. Crocker referred to the 'spitting' incident in the colony game without naming individuals. But he did name Hutton when making his most startling allegation: that the disturbance was the direct result of the England captain waving 'the "shut up" sign' behind his back to the people booing him in the College Stand as Ramadhin was taking strike. This explanation cannot be ruled out. It would account for the delay between the run-out and the bottle-throwing and Hutton definitely made gestures to the crowd in Barbados. But Crocker's piece is so strident in its denunciation of the 'foreign Press' for explaining the riot in political terms that there is a sense of his protesting too much.

The BG press, which was arguably controlled by the sugar industry, reacted to the riot either apolitically or very politically. The *Daily Argosy*, sounding rather Swantonian, simply bemoaned a 'flagrant breach of good manners' and hoped that 'this same crowd will strive its best in an effort to regain some lost decorum for this hospitable and friendly land of Guiana'. The *Sunday Chronicle* regretted that the 'vulgar expression of discontent' had damaged the reputation of West Indian cricketers, previously acclaimed (or caricatured) as 'jolly sporting fellows, who took defeat with a broad, wide-toothed grin'.

Although the *Chronicle* noted in passing that the disturbance added to the colony's 'worldwide unwelcome notoriety in other fields of endeavour', it was the *Guiana Graphic* which put the bottle-throwing squarely in the context of a campaign by 'foreign-trained propagandists' to stir up 'a spirit of hostility to the old ideas of order and discipline'. The *Graphic*'s leader-writer therefore opined it might be a blessing in disguise that the Constitutional Commission sent by London was still in the colony 'to witness for itself the pitch of lawlessness to which the masses of our people are being egged on'. The Commission would reach the inevitable conclusion from the bottle-throwing that British Guiana was not ready for self-government, and that 'a spirit of disloyalty to the Throne to which we all owe Allegiance' risked leaving the colony unprotected against 'foreign enemies'.

It is hard to believe that the authorities had any evidence that the Bourda disturbance was a premeditated political act. This is for the simple reason that they were busy publishing – and indeed fabricating – any shred of evidence which supported their view that PPP activities were part of an international Communist conspiracy. For example, the Governor's allegation that the PPP was planning a coordinated arson campaign, based on information from informers and unusually high sales of kerosene, proved grossly exaggerated.

The Right Hon. Alan Knight (Archbishop of West Indies and Bishop of British Guiana) had telephoned Bill Cooper (editor of the *Argosy*) 'reporting that he had heard from various sources that trouble would be raised by the crowd during the Test'. But the Archbishop had a particular motive for spreading alarm because Burnham, as the PPP's first Minister of Education, had immediately tried to break the church's institutionalised control of Guyanese schools. That Knight's prognostication came to pass does not necessarily mean his 'sources' were reliable: they also predicted incorrectly that his house would be burnt down in the purported arson campaign.

Bourda Green was a traditional venue for political speeches and demonstrations. However, no evidence has emerged that anyone in the PPP encouraged their supporters to cause trouble at the Test. The Guyanese interviewed for this book thought it unlikely that the riot was pre-planned. None ruled out a political explanation completely, perhaps because of their experience of Burnham's methods after independence. It would take many years, and rigged elections which marginalised Jagan, before Burnham indulged in 'the ridiculous practice of laying personal claim to the West Indian cricket team'. The activist Walter Rodney wrote these words shortly before he was assassinated by a car-bomb in Georgetown in 1980.

In 1954, Watson seems to have been the only England player to be 'convinced that the demonstration was caused by political rather than sporting agitation'. But this was on the grounds that he believed cricket fans incapable of throwing bottles rather than a detailed analysis of the local situation.

That situation was so complex it is impossible to reach a firm conclusion. Perhaps we can surmise that the particular circumstances of the day's cricket released a pressure valve at a time when organised political demonstrations were proscribed. And perhaps the most important antipathy was not Guyanese against British or African against Indian or Demeraran against Berbician, even if all these issues were in play, but crowd against pavilion.

The England players took understandable pride in their steadfastness during what must have been a frightening experience, also symbolic of the way they had regrouped as a team. When, on his return, Lock bought a new house in Warlingham, he named it *Bourda* after the ground where he fondly remembered the 'old lion' roaring back and his own bounce-back from Barbados. Hutton recalled that at close of play after the disturbance, while the two umpires hurried off the field, his players 'strolled off with studied nonchalance', surrounded by a 'protective wall' of 'pavilion officials and English residents'.

Many in the Bourda crowd no doubt drew a connection between the nonchalance of the English team and the arrogance of the British governors. But the few hundred supporters who reportedly massed in front of the pavilion at the end of Day 4 may really have been after the officials inside it. C.L.R. James certainly believed that the protective wall of what he called 'rich whites and their retainers' was the true target of riots at West Indian grounds. He argued that the common factor in all such incidents was the popular conviction that 'as usual, local anti-nationalist people were doing their best to help the Englishmen defeat and disgrace the local players'.

It is impossible not to feel sympathy for Badge Menzies. In difficult weather conditions, he had crafted a pitch which produced an excellent Test match. Under even more difficult circumstances, he had found himself at the end where nearly all the tricky decisions were required. And he had probably filled in as umpire under duress. Hutton was surprised when one of the local officials told him: 'If I say he's got to stand, he *will* stand.' While Menzies' Indian heritage may have been provocative to some Georgetown blacks, he was also a symbol of GCC, not only its groundsman but its tenant – he lived in a shed under the pavilion which was now under police guard. The missiles thrown at him were perhaps really being aimed at his employers.

Out of the pavilion, when the bottles were thrown, came Stanley Jones, who rushed onto the field to advise Hutton that he should come off. Jones was not only president of the Cricket Association but a managing director of Booker. Robin Wishart remembers he was known as one of the 'poker millionaires' who played cards every cocktail-hour in the GCC pavilion or other citadels of privilege. To anybody growing up in Georgetown in the 1950s, like the schoolteacher Seegobin Ragbeer, GCC 'was the domain of the Whites … It was their watering hole. It was their almost exclusive club.' Wishart also remembers Burnham later making political capital out of this, threatening GCC with eviction from Bourda and refusing to enter the pavilion on a visit to the ground – instead he sat ostentatiously drinking rum in one of the popular sections under the scoreboard.

Brown and black cricket administrators in BG, like Wishart's father Ken (who supported Worrell at Board of Control level) and Berkeley Gaskin (mentor of Lance Gibbs and Clive Lloyd) could not avoid connections with Booker, such was the company's grip on the island. Booker investment into facilities and coaching was probably the crucial factor in several Guyanese becoming international cricketers in the late 1950s. But, as the sociologist Raymond Smith astutely observed, 'the very paternalism of these efforts arouses more antagonism than it allays'. The antagonism was rooted in a suspicion that the vested interests who seemed to dominate cricket might still be dominating the country long after it became 'free'. In the disturbance of 1954, elements of the Bourda crowd were venting their feelings about an old joke that had become a PPP slogan: BG stood not for British Guiana but Booker's Guiana.

14 December 1953: The MCC party about to board their BOAC Stratocruiser to Bermuda. First column (in ascending order): Hutton, Palmer, Bailey, Watson, Spooner, Suttle, Graveney. Second column: Compton, Evans, Moss, Wardle, Trueman, Statham, May, Lock, Laker.

Alexander Bustamante of the JLP (pictured above electioneering in Kingston in 1946) and Norman Manley of the PNP (pictured below celebrating independence in 1962) bestrode Jamaican politics for three decades. Although nationalist movements developed in different ways across the West Indies, after the war the popular yearning for full self-government was obvious, however much the British dragged their feet.

Yet the loyalist belief in 'Crown and cricket' as indissoluble links with the 'mother country' was not entirely fanciful. 35,000 children turned out at Sabina Park to see the Queen during her Coronation tour. The photograph of Hutton practising in Jamaica was taken in 1948, but the crowds attending MCC's net sessions in 1953/54 were even larger.

First Test, Sabina: Not entirely for cricketing reasons, West Indies included five Jamaicans. Standing: Frederick, Holt, Kentish, Valentine, McWatt, Pairaudeau (twelfth man), Ramadhin. Sitting: Weekes, Gomez, Stollmeyer, Headley, Walcott. In a fitting finale to an incident-packed game, England collapsed to Kentish's leg-theory: Weekes pulled off a brilliant catch to dismiss Graveney.

Barbados: At first, 'Little England' seemed friendlier than Jamaica, MCC enjoying the hospitality of locals such as John Goddard, who was the bowler (off-camera) in a beach cricket match enjoyed by Compton, May and Reg Hayter of Reuters. But off-field behaviour quickly became an issue again: some of the juniors lost the plot at official functions; some of the seniors kept up the social pace they had set in Jamaica (where Bailey and Compton had been photographed in the bar of the Tower Isle Hotel).

Barbados tour match: Harold Walcott repeatedly no-balled Lock for throwing – in the most controversial instance Sobers had been 'bowled' (Spooner and Trueman look on). Second Test: Harold's nephew Clyde scored a power-packed double century to help West Indies take a 2-0 lead (Evans behind the stumps).

British Guiana: MCC arrived in the colony to find British troops helping enforce a state of emergency. During the tour match, the PPP leaders Forbes Burnham (waving from the first car) and Cheddi Jagan (leaning out of the second) returned home to a reception which made a mockery of restrictions on public assembly.

Third Test, Bourda: McWatt is run out, sparking off a serious disturbance in which bottles and crates were hurled onto the playing area. Hutton, standing with hands on hips to the immediate left of umpire Menzies, refused to leave the field against the advice of local officials.

CHAPTER 14

TRINIDAD

After a bumpy time in British Guiana, MCC endured a bumpy flight out. They arrived in Trinidad looking nauseous, fatigued and sunburnt. Hutton mouthed bromides about Trinidad seeming 'a nice country' and wanting to provide the brand of cricket 'people here like to see'. But he appeared to cut short his interview at the airport: 'I'm very tired, so I think I'll take a rest.'

Any rest was short-lived as MCC were soon on another plane for a goodwill trip to Grenada. By this stage, strong differences about the conduct of the tour had emerged among the journalists, with Bannister and Swanton clearly at odds in their interpretation of events.

Bannister had written an opinion piece for the *Daily Mail*, defending the players from 'stunt stories' about their ill-discipline and their captain from criticism by the 'anti-professional' lobby. Both lines of attack represented a 'stab in the back' by armchair critics uninformed about the 'almost impossible umpiring' and the 'childlike demonstrations' of West Indian crowds. Bannister insisted the players' mood had darkened only because 'the colour question, with its political background, has followed them around like an evil shadow'. They were all 'shocked at the intensity of anti-British feeling here', to the point that future tours must now be in question.

Bannister did not, however, pick up the intensity of the political background in Grenada, where the nationalist leader Eric Gairy had tried to organise a general strike two months before MCC's visit. The Governor declared the inevitable national holiday for the cricket but, as in BG, measures were otherwise in force against public gatherings.

For Bannister, the Grenada leg was primarily an example of a schedule that was, by the standards of the day, far too taxing. He noted that Palmer had tried, without success, to have the Trinidad tour match reduced from five days to four in recognition of MCC's island-hopping. Bannister also felt Hutton's men were still trying their best to be ambassadors of goodwill. They had put up with the jockeys' dressing room at the racetrack-cum-cricket ground at St George's; Wardle had clowned for the crowd, hiding the bat of the best Windward Islands player under the matting wicket; the whole squad had entered into the 'homely atmosphere' of the two-day game, tucking into 'cakes baked by the wives of the committee-men'.

Swanton, on the other hand, finding it easier to socialise with the wives, found evidence of 'shocking manners'. He discovered it was hard to find volunteers for the second-day tea in Grenada, given the surly behaviour of MCC on the first: 'Please don't bring any more English sides out here unless you bring nicer men.' Swanton did bring his own English (and Commonwealth) side out to the southern Caribbean two winters later, a goodwill tour welcomed by many West Indians and described by his captain Cowdrey as a way of 'making amends for an awful lot in spite of the fact they will never forgive MCC for 1953/54'.

Back then, Swanton had little time for the argument that the English players had been thrown into a hostile environment, and no time for the way West Indian supporters were being 'stigmatised'. He believed 'there is no better-informed crowd than that of Barbados' – Lord's of course excepted – and 'no more generous-minded crowd than that of Trinidad'. Even in the more 'noisily ebullient' venues of Jamaica and BG – which Swanton's team did not find time to visit in 1955/56 – the spectators had been 'perfectly fair to the efforts of the English side'. Swanton made his observations on Grenada retrospectively, in a private letter to MCC president Viscount Cobham. He never seriously questioned MCC's off-field conduct in his *Telegraph* columns. But whereas Bannister ascribed the tour's difficulties to trouble on the ground, Swanton was developing the view that the trouble was at the top – with Palmer and Hutton.

Fire in the Queen's Park stand
Significant work had been conducted at the Queen's Park Oval in anticipation of MCC's visit to Trinidad. The stands were renovated and augmented to increase the official capacity to 25,000, a figure which possibly overestimated how many people could be crammed into what was still a small stadium. A new press box was built at the south-eastern end which, some journalists may have been pleased to

learn, came 'complete with a bar and other conveniences'. However, on the same weekend as the Georgetown riot, news came through that the Oval's main stand had burnt down.

Thrice in the 19th century Port of Spain had nearly been destroyed by fire, the damage on the last occasion going more unchecked because most of the town had been on a half-day holiday attending a cricket match at the Oval between All Trinidad and R.S. Lucas's English touring side. In the 1950s accidental fires still seem to have been common in Trinidad, largely because of the use of kerosene for domestic cooking and lighting. In the week of MCC's arrival, the local press reported a number of house fires, with other causes ranging from an electrical fault to a bungled attempt to resurface a wooden floor after a police party. Given the recent construction work, it was possible the stand had burnt down accidentally.

However, the emergency services suspected a calculated act of arson, claiming to have found the remains of a device designed to pour fire accelerant through the taps of the men's toilets. Trinidad did not yet have a seriously organised political movement ready for self-government like the PPP in BG (or indeed the JLP/PNP in Jamaica and the BLP in Barbados). Dr Williams, who was about to fill the vacuum with the PNM, ascribed this to 'the well-known jealousy and individualism of Trinidadians'. Such individualism fed into the pattern of arson on the island, which was often caused by 'fire bugs' with a grievance acting on their own devices. One story doing the rounds was that 'loafers', who had been sleeping under the stand with semi-official sanction, set fire to it in revenge for the club secretary turfing them out.

The police ascribed the incident to the 'sheer wickedness' of vandals, although arson – especially the torching of cane fields – had long been associated with political resistance in the Caribbean. The history of Port of Spain provided another relevant precedent: in 1903 rioters protesting about fixed water rates burnt down the 'Red House', the most symbolic colonial edifice.

Arson was also a feature of recent anti-colonial activity. During disturbances in 1952, the Egyptians had set alight various British institutions, ranging from the Cairo Turf Club to the bookshop managed by Warner's son Esmond. Because the last voyage of the *Empire Windrush* started at Port Said, there were rumours of sabotage when it sank after an explosion in its engine-room the week after the Trinidad Test. As Wardle noted, 'some people ... thought it more than a coincidence' that the Queen's Park fire 'started on the evening of the bottle-party in British Guiana'.

Swanton still trusted there would be a 'less explosive' atmosphere in Trinidad. On MCC's next visit he observed that 'as the island gives the example of many races living together in amity – more or less – so do the cricketers'. He gave a long list of them, suggesting that names like dos Santos, Grant, Gomez, Stollmeyer, Constantine, Achong, Lee Kow, Asgarali, Ganteaume and Jones illustrated 'that Trinidad is the most cosmopolitan cricket community in the world'. This was probably true, and it was arguably true that what Albert Gomes called Trinidad's 'crazyquilt' of races knitted together more peaceably than in other colonies.

That said, the absence of a mature nationalist movement may have increased the level of violence when pent-up emotions were unleashed, as in the serious disturbances in the oil fields of Fyzabad in southern Trinidad in 1937. The island's atmosphere of 'expatriate snobbery' caused some to find in cricket not the spirit of amity but a prime example of the 'diabolical astuteness of the English ruling class'. This was the verdict of the novelist Alfred Mendes, another contributor to Gomes's *Beacon* along with C.L.R. James and Hugh Stollmeyer. Mendes could certainly see West Indians were making their own 'magic' out of cricket, which helps explain the 'enduring fascination' the game holds for his grandson, the film director Sam. But Alfred believed it was designed to exercise 'a restraining influence over the colonial masses' as well as being the 'public relations officer' of empire.

Just as Mendes thought Trinidad's government was 'still *very* Crown Colony', its cricket was still ruled by the private, predominately white club that owned the Queen's Park Oval. QPCC's charismatic chairman was the first man on Swanton's list. Sir Errol dos Santos, like Gomes and Mendes, was another prominent figure of Madeiran-Portuguese descent, but as an ex-Colonial Secretary of Trinidad he was devoted to the status quo.

Dos Santos is reputed to have started making plans for the reconstruction of the stand at his beloved Oval at four o'clock in the morning after the fire. He brought in the British construction firm Ash

& Watson to supervise the work. The *Trinidad Guardian* celebrated the way 'the Queen's Park authorities acted with a swiftness and sureness of purpose that equalled any military junta'. This may have raised a wry smile from Ganteaume, not selected for Trinidad in 1954, who called dos Santos 'the Dictator'. The rebuilding project also suffered a delay when the workforce downed tools for the sacrosanct Trinidad Carnival. If the Carnival embodied a spirit of 'al o' we is one', QPCC embodied elite privilege, which was the most plausible reason for its stand being burnt down.

Dos Santos wanted the Oval back in pristine condition for the visit of MCC and was prominent in the round of social events in honour of the tourists. He held what was described as a 'stag party' for them at his own residence. He attended functions at the Yacht Club and the Union Club, venues where many local cricketers still struggled to gain admittance. As in BG, MCC's associations with the 'boss' club may have increased the hostility of the rest of the population. Two British expatriates, arriving late on the second day of the Test, remembered having to find seats in one of the public areas of the ground, where they 'endured with fixed smiles an endless teasing, which had a sharp edge to it'. But it transpired that the Queen's Park members became some of the loudest critics of the English tourists. Yet again, MCC would be caught between the growing frustrations of the people and the intransigent attitudes of the local whites.

Less fire in the Queen's Park mat

The tour match against Trinidad seemed initially to represent 'a very welcome change indeed' for MCC. So wrote the *Trinidad Guardian*'s cricket correspondent J.S. Barker, who felt the first day played before the Governor was as 'pleasant and good-tempered … as one could wish to see'. Barker reported that the 6,000 crowd enjoyed Trueman's 'vigorous encouragement' of the home batsmen to take on his bumpers, which he served up with his 'usual generosity'. MCC's liberal use of the short ball was less well received as the game progressed.

Bailey, captaining the side as Hutton rested, later attributed much of the tour's bad atmosphere to the way the English bowlers 'tended to target the bodies' of the home sides. He, Moss and Trueman, faced with a placid matting wicket, resolved on a plan of attack based on bouncers. Nyron Asgarali, whom many Trinidadians were touting as an opening partner for Stollmeyer, made runs in both innings but got himself out playing a tennis smash to a short ball from Bailey. The veteran Rupert Tang Choon was still on some wishlists for a Test debut should Trinidad be allowed to adopt what a local journalist sarcastically called 'the Jamaica pattern' of packing the side with home players. In the first innings he was seen backing away from Moss before nicking a leg-side bouncer to Spooner; in the second, he seemed so nervous he ran himself out for a duck.

Tailenders were not exempted, especially as MCC pressed for victory in the second innings. The popular leg-spinner Ferguson, a more serious candidate for Test selection, could certainly hold a bat: he had scored 75 at No.9 in the fourth Test against Allen's men on the previous tour. He may therefore have been considered a legitimate target, even before he said something to Trueman. Moss vaguely remembers giggling in the slips as some of the MCC players encouraged 'Fergie' to wind 'Freddie' up some more. But Trueman was playing for his Test place and did not see the funny side. He was no-balled for a bouncer – Moss thinks he overstepped by a wide margin – which hit Ferguson in the face.

All the fielders came to the batsman's aid, except Trueman. He went back to his mark and rolled up his sleeves another notch. Bannister was left with the 'sad but unmistakable impression that he saw himself as the victorious gladiator'. Palmer, not the on-field captain Bailey, eventually persuaded him to apologise. The next delivery was a very fast full toss. Perhaps mercifully, it bowled Ferguson, who was treated by St John Ambulance-men on the field and eventually taken to hospital for X-rays on his swollen jaw. At the close of the innings, Trueman compounded his breaches of etiquette by running off in front of the last pair of batsmen. He was received in silence by the members, who then pointedly applauded the other MCC fielders who had waited at the pavilion gate.

Trueman's own various accounts of the incident are a self-consoling travesty. He recalled it occurring in a 'minor match' with 'nothing at stake', when in fact MCC were pressing for an unprecedented clean sweep in the colony games. He said he lost his temper only after Ferguson had twice called him a 'white English bastard', where the possibility escaped him that the batsman may have been riffing on the language he was alleged to have used against the umpires in BG.

Stollmeyer once joked that Ferguson was 'no Valentino' and the local joke now was that the blow to the face had improved his features. He recovered in time to be available for the Test. It should also be recorded that Trueman did eventually shake Ferguson's hand on the field and tried to contact him in hospital. But, again, the damage had been done. The Trinidad papers were full of bile about 'frightfully unsportsmanlike conduct' and scorn for Palmer's attempts to placate the crowd: 'The days when the British handed out pretty beads to the natives are long past.'

England required 231 in 300 minutes on the last day. Bailey opened the batting, a sign he might be under consideration for the role in the Test but also a signal that he was leading from the front. Swanton was aghast to see England's slowest batsman in charge of the run-chase and found Bailey's careful early progress 'agonising watching'. But Bailey knew what he was doing. The plan was to open up after lunch. He also had the satisfaction of instructing Compton, 'with a straight face', to concentrate on batting through the innings while he started flogging the bowling to all parts.

Aside from the Ferguson incident, the game against Trinidad was a triumph for Bailey. To cap things off, on the rest day he had beaten Swanton, a man he never particularly cared for, on the golf course. The victory on the cricket field marked a considerable achievement in itself. Trinidad had not been beaten at home in any representative game for nearly a quarter of a century. It had been twice as long since they had lost to an English touring team. The clean sweep of wins against the Big Four was something MCC – and England XIs once tour matches fell outside the club's auspices – have never came close to achieving before or since. Crawford White pointed out that the colony game was also a 'splendid stimulant' for the Test, noting that local warnings about the impossibility of bowling sides out on the Port of Spain mat had proved as false as equally confident predictions about the Bourda bowling green.

The difference between those surfaces was due to an environmental idiosyncrasy of Trinidad. The prevalence of the mole cricket, a voracious grass eater and burrower, made the preparation of turf pitches difficult. Since 1934, all representative matches at Queen's

Park Oval had been played on jute matting, laid over a base of hard-baked clay and softer sand. The pace of the wicket depended on the mixture of the underlay.

Grenada also had a matting wicket, which May remembered was 'as fast as we cared for'. Wardle, who claimed he was promoted in the order for laughing when the recognised batsmen hopped around against Frank Mason, was not 'madly keen' to face the new ball. The Trinidad surface was traditionally much slower. On the previous tour, its predictable bounce helped Griffith to his maiden century, as he conceded in an ironic telegram to Swanton: 'Trust you warn batsmen immense difficulties Trinidad wicket.' But in 1954 the pitch did seem to have something in it for bowlers prepared to bend their backs. In a practice game held at the Oval before MCC's arrival, between a Tang Choon XI and a Prior Jones XI, two batsmen had to retire hurt and four were hit. Then the English fast bowlers got most of their wickets with short balls.

MCC's strong performance under Bailey may have had one detrimental effect. Stollmeyer, celebrating his 33rd birthday on his home ground, was one of the few Trinidad batsmen comparatively at ease, scoring 89 and 48. He was talking a good game before the Test, ascribing the collapses in BG to injuries and Worrell's temporary loss of form. But he did observe that his batsmen had struggled with Statham's speed until the Bourda wicket flattened out later in the match.

While there is no direct evidence that Stollmeyer looked to make the Queen's Park pitch as placid as possible, one can imagine him telling his home groundsman not to stint on the sand. Barker, a correspondent with local knowledge, thought the Test surface played 'even easier' than the one for the tour match.

CHAPTER 15

FOURTH TEST (QUEEN'S PARK OVAL)

West Indies made three changes. Pairaudeau was restored ahead of Christiani (who had not been named in the squad) and Asgarali (who had). King's pace would be required on the mat and a place was freed up for him because Gomez had pulled a hamstring in the tour match. Valentine was reportedly still struggling with his sore spinning finger. One suspects he may have been fit to play, but he was passed over for Ferguson. The leg-spinner would get more turn on the mat, strengthen the batting slightly – and make up for the absence of Gomez by keeping the home colony's representation up at three.

Despite resting for the Trinidad game, Evans remained in too much discomfort from septic boils on his foot and wrist. Spooner came in for his sixth cap. Bailey was pencilled in to open, with Watson dropping down to No.5. The big decision was whether to stick with three spinners or bring back Trueman. According to Rostron, the fast bowler was called into the selection meeting and told he had been chosen on condition he maintained 'his on and off-field manners as well as his play'. Clearly the selectors had decided that his potential threat to West Indies on the mat was worth the risk of further incidents with the umpires.

Wardle was unlucky. There was some suggestion he was still struggling with his knee, although he had played against Trinidad and would act as a substitute fielder during the Test. The Surrey finger-spinners had bowled well at Bourda but it did seem conservative, at 2-1 down, to go into the game with only Compton as a wrist-spinning option.

The toss may have mattered less than usual on an artificial wicket not expected to deteriorate. Hutton lost it in any case. Swanton understood why West Indies would bat first, seeking to tire out the fielding side in gruelling conditions. He also tried to look on the bright side for England: 'At least they will not finish the game with wickets to get and a lot of runs frozen in the bank.'

261

DAY 1

The early exchanges suggested there were a lot of runs trapped in the mat. Both openers edged the new ball along the ground through the slips off Statham, but otherwise mixed watchful defence with authentic strokeplay. The most likely chance of a wicket, as so often with Holt at the crease, seemed to be a run-out. The spinners at least slowed the scoring rate slightly. Then the otherwise sedate first session exploded into life in its last quarter-hour.

Hutton brought back Trueman, presumably asking for an all-out burst in the two or three overs he would fit in before lunch. That Trueman gave his captain everything is suggested first by two no-ball calls and then by several well-directed bouncers. Stollmeyer tried not to show any pain after being hit on the back trying to duck under one of them. But he did look ostentatiously at the square-leg umpire, Ellis Achong, as if inviting him to intervene.

Achong took no action but Trueman was angry enough about the lack of leeway Ken Woods, the umpire at his end, was allowing his drag across the bowling crease. He is widely reported to have 'snatched' his cap from Woods once the eight-ball over was finally completed. This was not an unknown reaction by a fast bowler in the era of the back-foot no-ball law: Fingleton admitted Lindwall took his sweater 'rather brusquely' in similar circumstances during the 1953 tour to England. However, Trueman's show of temper, which Bray felt made him look like a 'petulant six-year-old', provoked a predictable reaction from the packed crowd.

At the other end, Hutton's hunch was to bring on Compton. Holt played out a respectful maiden. Trueman then continued to trouble Stollmeyer until the batsman escaped by taking a single. Umpire Woods, seeking to avoid a repeat of the previous over's kerfuffle, bowled Trueman his cap. Worrell later recorded the Yorkshireman's reaction:

> And what did Trueman do? He caught his cap, broke into that broad grin of his, walked up to the umpire and put his arm round his shoulder. Together they walked towards square leg like a couple of buddies.
>
> For that action Trueman received a greater cheer than was accorded to any MCC player throughout the whole tour.

When Worrell wrote up this account, in 1959, he was seeking to defend a man he now considered a good friend. But the clowning side of Trueman went underreported in 1954.

The *Trinidad Guardian*'s Dick Murray, familiar with Stollmeyer's reputation for paying 'a fair amount of attention to the clock', was surprised when he miscued a drive straight back to Compton. The bowler had gained some revenge for his controversial dismissal by Stollmeyer in Barbados. Hall, who credited Trueman with softening up the captain, described Stollmeyer walking off 'dazed, bruised and angry'; Bannister thought his face was more a 'picture of disappointment'.

Stollmeyer's slow trudge to the pavilion ensured Compton's over would be the last before lunch. Weekes survived the customary communication problems with Holt to take a single off his first ball. For the last delivery of the session, Compton tossed up a wide half-volley. Holt failed to read the googly and the ball came waist-high towards first slip. Graveney, relatively new to this position, always felt he had to be 'alert' when Holt was on strike given the batsman's propensity to flash hard outside off stump. There must have been a surge of adrenalin as he pouched the catch and excitement all round about making two breakthroughs so quickly after a morning's toil:

> I pocketed the ball gratefully and in the same
> movement started to walk to the pavilion for lunch.
> After a few paces, I realised that I was alone, so a
> little uncertainly I looked over my shoulder to see
> that Holt was still at the wicket. I could hardly believe
> my eyes. I called to him: 'Come on, then,' but still
> he stayed. Hutton walked in from mid-off, disbelief
> etched on his face, calling to umpire Achong: 'What
> about it, Ellis?' Compton joined in the dialogue,
> saying: 'Give him out, Ellis.'
>
> Then Achong made his important contribution. He
> said: 'No, not out.'

Compton gave a similar account, admitting that the language used as tempers unravelled was perhaps 'a little stronger' than transcribed. Statham remembered Hutton, 'not an easy man to shock', was so amazed that he appealed three times as all the while Graveney 'shouted his view on the matter'.

It was not just what Graveney might have said. He hurled the ball to the ground. And left it there. Barker appeared rather to relish the ensuing scene: 'Somebody then realised it was time for lunch and eleven Englishmen stalked towards the pavilion with faces red from causes other than the sun.' They were booed all the way there and then, according to Compton, 'the members stood up and jeered us all the way to our dressing-room ... It is the first and last time that I have ever been jeered by a crowd.'

Swanton reported the ground was still abuzz over lunch, 'with everyone airing his version of what occurred'. His was that the catch was good. It immediately reminded him of the infamous incident in 1946/47 – described by Hammond as 'a fine bloody way to start a series' – when Bradman was given not out after apparently edging straight to second slip. Even Barker accepted that Holt had 'turned to walk to the pavilion' before having second thoughts.

But if few doubted the validity of Graveney's catch, few could question the intemperance of his reaction. Bannister, perhaps more prepared to excuse English behaviour than any correspondent, described him hurling the ball to the turf 'as if it had suddenly become white hot or diseased'.

Lunch: West Indies 79-1 (Holt 34*, Weekes 1*)

The Holt incident did not cost England dearly if measured only in runs. After adding six to his lunchtime score, the opener flicked Trueman to backward square leg. The fielder happened to be Compton, who celebrated in a manner which was perhaps understandable but hardly calculated to diffuse the sulphurous atmosphere.

Out walked Worrell, Barker quietly alluding to his three recent failures by describing him as 'the dignified, the elegant, the graceful and the much-criticised'. Worrell caressed his first ball, a Trueman full toss, through mid-on for four. But he still had to face the challenge of his recent nemesis, Statham. The play was now as full of mettle as the mat would allow. The English quicks were looking altogether more dangerous than in the morning. The batsmen, while severe on anything short, were conscious that the bowlers were straining every sinew.

This became painfully clear when Statham pulled up in his delivery stride. He had felt something go just after lunch but had struggled on for a couple of 'do or die overs'. He was especially motivated by having the wood over Worrell, and indeed he still nearly dismissed the vice-captain despite his handicap. But Statham realised he had done something serious to his side. He hobbled off to be checked out in hospital. Swanton observed that it was to Trueman's credit that he 'kept up his pace and fire, heat or no heat', Statham or no Statham. The temperature of the match increased again when Hutton changed the bowling.

With his own score on 42, Weekes nearly played on to Lock. He came on strike to Bailey in the next over when, again according to Swanton, 'there was the sort of appeal for a catch behind the wicket that is less a question than a statement of fact'. Graveney, whom one imagines still red in the face, thought Bailey had induced 'the thickest under-edge you ever saw'. He claimed Weekes, before resuming his guard, even apologised to the keeper Spooner for not walking.

At the time, Weekes was reported by Barker to have 'gazed abstractedly over the distant hills' while the English protested. In 2018, he said he could not remember the specific incident, although he sounded fairly unimpressed with Graveney's account when reminded of it. He made the more general point that he had been brought up to walk, but his reward for doing so on his early overseas tours was to be repeatedly 'sawn off'. For example, Weekes thought he got an 'abysmal' lbw decision from Frank Chester at Old Trafford in 1950. Perhaps by 1954 he was tending to let the vagaries of umpiring even themselves out.

By this stage, some of the English players had become light-headed in their dissent. 'I heard it at extra cover,' Compton told umpire Woods, 'it must be a different game we are playing out here.' As the field changed ends, he, Spooner and Graveney were all observed cupping their ears to indicate their view of the umpires' powers of hearing. If Woods and Achong were alleged to have missed the sound of a thick edge, they proved capable of picking up some more coarse language. The umpires immediately had a word with Hutton. At the next interval, they made a formal complaint about England's swearing.

The batsmen kept their concentration commendably. They were focused on taking West Indies into the safety zone and their own scores into the record zone.

Tea: West Indies 188-2 (Weekes 70*, Worrell 31*)

Weekes had twice been denied a century in the series, first by Stollmeyer's declaration at Sabina, then by a controversial decision at Bourda. He was already in the 90s when the second new ball was taken and soon reached his hundred, off a Trueman bouncer, with a curious-looking overhead slash. Footage taken on Bailey's cine camera during the game shows that fielders on both sides were no longer in the habit of applauding the opposition's milestones. But Trueman sportingly came down the pitch to shake Weekes's hand.

Worrell, now finding his stride, reached his fifty by driving Trueman handsomely to the boundary. For most of the session he and Weekes were complete masters of the bowling. The scoring rate did fall below a run-a-minute when Bailey, observing the unofficial Lord's edict against leg-theory, instead bowled very wide of off stump to a packed field. England also indulged in some blatant time-wasting towards the close. But Weekes and Worrell had already equalled the record West Indies partnership for the third wicket.

Close: West Indies 294-2 (Weekes 130*, Worrell 76*)

Perhaps this was the 'bad day' on tour when Hutton remembered bumping into a squad member back at the hotel:

> 'What a terrible day,' he began. 'Well, you saw it,' was my tired response. 'Oh no,' he replied. 'I've been listening on the radio.'
>
> At that I blew my top. As a Yorkshireman I had automatically expected everyone to be at the ground, and the non-players to be in the dressing room to lend moral support.

The non-player may have been Evans, who said he listened to the fourth Test 'on the wireless' in the 'dreary' Queen's Hotel. He did have a reasonable excuse not to drag himself to the Oval as he was still spending most of his time in bed, pumped 'full of aureomycin and penicillin and goodness knows what' as treatment for the festering carbuncle on his foot.

It would not have taken much even for Hutton to let off steam. From the cricketing point of view, for all the drama before lunch, the two incidents in the afternoon when Statham was forced to leave the field, and Weekes was allowed to stay on it, greatly increased the odds of the England captain returning home a loser. From a diplomatic perspective, it was already clear to him that the fracas before lunch would provide his critics with a 'field day', even if the reactions of the local and English press would take time to filter through.

Looking back much later on 'a totally unnecessary incident', Hutton suggested the English took 'total' blame when there were in fact three links to the chain of events: 'The batsman shouldn't have stayed ... ; the umpire shouldn't have made such a whopping mistake; and Graveney shouldn't have lost his temper.'

Graveney's explosion was the most impetuous and the best remembered of all MCC's on-field tantrums during the 1953/54 tour. Worrell thought it 'foreign to his whole nature'. May agreed he was 'not normally demonstrative' but had to admit his outburst became a notorious instance of unsporting behaviour, still 'referred to as such in an age when, alas, countless more robust and offensive gestures are being made'. Graveney might have protested that the Australians were already known for similar actions: the previous summer Miller threw the ball down in disgust when Chester, an umpire revered in England but not elsewhere, failed to give a run-out at Leeds; the next winter, again in Trinidad, Ron Archer did the same thing when a decision went against him. But May is borne out by the way in which West Indians referred to Archer behaving 'à la Graveney'.

In later life Graveney was sheepish but not particularly sorry. He supposed he 'shouldn't have done it' but felt something had to be done. He had simply had enough of the man he called the 'inevitable' Holt. 'That's the fourth bloody time' is the toned-down version of what Graveney said as he lost control of his temper and of the ball. Holt had not walked for the first time in a Jamaica tour match, when the bowler Wardle claimed he had snicked 'hard enough for the sound to be heard all over the ground'. He stayed put for the second and third time in the Bourda Test, where Graveney had a good view at slip of caught-behinds England were convinced he had edged. In Graveney's book, that was both 'morally wrong' and also ill-advised given the 'electric' atmosphere of the series.

There is an age-old argument as to whether the spirit of the game is best upheld by the players self-policing the laws, or by their accepting that interpretation of the laws is always at the discretion of the umpires, right or wrong. An open letter to Hutton by Barker, published by the *Trinidad Guardian* on the second morning of the Test, took the latter view:

> The criticising of umpire's decisions, whatever your private opinions, the public arguments with, and even the brow-beating of those much-tried gentlemen is not the conduct to which we are accustomed, or which we expect from men dignified by the colours of the MCC.

Swanton pointed out that the West Indian players were almost never guilty of public arguments with the umpires. Hall and Bannister retorted that this was because the officials blatantly favoured the home side. But MCC could also be accused of double standards with respect to walking. Palmer played his best innings of the tour in the Trinidad colony game. When he had made 87, a confident shout went up for caught behind. Palmer remained rooted to the crease until the umpire raised his finger.

Ellis 'Puss' Achong's appointment to stand in that game and the Test match had caused local controversy. The Trinidad Umpires' Association made a formal complaint to Queen's Park CC because Achong was not an accredited official and was still playing league cricket for the Orange Grove club. With some irony, he had recently caused an umpire to walk off the field after protesting heatedly about being denied a stumping off his bowling.

The authorities appear to have brought in Achong, given the incidents in the first three Tests, on the grounds he would cope with big-match pressure. Although he had never stood as an umpire in a Test, he had played in six before the war, a left-armer who could bowl finger-spin and wrist-spin. According to legend, he had inadvertently helped name the very style of bowling which deceived Holt. At Old Trafford in 1933, Robins was stumped after failing to read a back-of-the-hand delivery from Achong and is supposed to have said: 'Fancy being done by a bloody Chinaman.'

This may be a tall story as the expression was already in cricket parlance. But Constantine remembered another incident in a home Test where he and Achong, who appears to have been a feisty competitor, provoked Patsy Hendren into 'one or two of the more redhot words of the parade-ground'. After his international Test career ended, Achong spent 15 years in the leagues of the north of England, where he will have seen all the tricks of the trade.

There were two reasons, neither in fairness raised by MCC at the time, why Achong could have been accused of bias, if not incompetence. He was a Trinidad selector in 1954, along with Ben Sealy and Harold Burnett (Stollmeyer and Gomez were co-opted to the committee to pick the side to play MCC). It was not unprecedented, and is in many ways sensible, for an umpire to provide input to a panel of selectors. But it does seem somewhat irregular for Achong to have stood in the tour match when he had helped choose one of the teams.

Achong's long stint in the leagues meant he was well known to some of the England players, especially Statham whom he coached as a youngster. Some of these relationships had an edge to them. Gerald Howat recounts a 'tale' from a Bradford League match between Pudsey St Lawrence and Windhill in 1944:

> Pudsey needed four to win and Hutton needed four
> for his 50. He was batting with his brother George to
> whom he indicated that he would get the four and they
> would go halves on the collection for Leonard which
> would follow. Ellis Achong, the bowler ... overheard
> the remark, resented the assumption of victory, and
> promptly bowled a ball which went for four byes,
> leaving Leonard stranded on 46 not out.

When Leonard shouted 'What about it, Ellis?' in Port of Spain, the memory of this incident must have added to the feeling between the two men.

DAY 2

The morning brought some more unpalatable, though not entirely unexpected, news for Hutton. Prognosis on Statham: torn intercostal muscle, pain-killing injection, unable to field, unlikely to take any further part in the match. Temperature: 88 degrees. Humidity: high. Pitch report: unnecessary.

The captain seems to have decided that a draw, and therefore a halved series at best, was all he had left to play for. Lock began with no close fielders; Bailey began with more 'off-theory' which caused some adverse reaction from another capacity crowd. The bowlers scored a few moral victories: Lock induced an edge from Weekes (though the slips were vacant); Bailey struck Worrell on the pads (though the appeal was rejected); in the first hour both bowlers kept a check on the scoring (though the batsmen took clever singles with the field back).

Graveney was alluding to the properties of the Trinidad mat, as well as the qualities of the Three Ws, when he recalled 'once they had played themselves in you had to reconcile yourself to the fact that they were not coming out until they got tired'.

In the supposedly nervous 90s, Worrell played what Barker rated the shot of the whole innings, a 'swift and tigerish' late cut off Lock. He then stroked a four through the covers to reach his century. It was his first in a Test in Trinidad, even if he had gorged himself on the mat in inter-colonial games in the 1940s. The vice-captain had made an important statement after his recent failures against Statham.

The only other bowler used in the morning was Trueman. He was taking five minutes to get through an over and Swanton noticed him firing many deliveries down the leg side, 'whether inadvertently or not one could hardly say'.

Lunch: West Indies 361-2 (Weekes 159*, Worrell 107*)

On and on the partnership went. Soon enough, Weekes and Worrell surpassed their record all-wicket stand for West Indies of 283 at Trent Bridge in 1950. Through quirks of injury and selection none of the current England team had endured that experience. They were chasing enough leather here – although Bray awarded them 'full marks' for some superb ground-fielding.

The next milestones were the 300-stand, the 320 all-wicket record against England (for a Test side other than Australia) and Weekes's second double century at the Queen's Park Oval. Two Test records set at The Oval in Kennington were also beginning to heave into view: the Bradman-Ponsford all-wicket stand of 451 and Hutton's individual mark of 364.

Weekes had by now scored a hundred in boundaries. On 206, he launched into yet another square cut off Lock which had many looking towards the ropes. But Bailey, diving to his left at point, took a brilliant catch – and all the skin off his elbow.

Gomez joined several Trinidad stars past and present in carrying a sheet, suitcases and cricket bags around the ground to make a collection for Weekes and Worrell. All the England bowlers received was a loud round of cheers when each of them reached their centuries of runs conceded.

Tea: West Indies 475-3 (Worrell 149*, Walcott 25*)

The new ball had been due for some time but Swanton presumed Hutton wanted to be 'humane' on his bowlers by giving them some refreshment beforehand. Then it went for five fours in the space of 12 balls. In fairness, Walcott was already in full cry and the two quicks had an extra right to be tired after their outstanding work in the field.

Hutton quickly reverted to the Surrey spinners. Lock at last got some reward for a day of sustained control when Worrell played on to an arm-ball. Padded up for the best part of two days, Pairaudeau was almost doomed to miss out. After 37 barren minutes, he was sold short by Walcott and run out by Trueman's good throw from the deep. He remembers that he was complimented by Weekes for one of the best ducks in history: 'I played all the shots – it's just they kept stopping them.' As poor Pairaudeau's zero was hoisted onto the scoreboard, Swanton thought it 'a grotesque contrast to the general orgy'. Wardle admitted that the 'slight disappointment' of being dropped was 'eased day by day as I saw the quite indecent scores being piled up'.

Close: West Indies 546-5 (Walcott 70*, Atkinson 5*)

'Even the infamous 1932 tour of Australia couldn't have been as bad as this.' Hutton is reported to have reached this conclusion by Ross Hall, who had probably told him that the 'sensation' of the umpires' complaint about English behaviour had made the front page of the *Mirror* back home – admittedly on a slow news day when the events in Port of Spain were assigned a small headline box beneath the burning debates as to whether working women should reveal their salaries to their husbands, and whether Princess Margaret smoked cheroots.

Cricket was always on the front page of the *Trinidad Guardian* during West Indies Tests. But on the second day it had also given a prominent position to the open letter in which Barker rebuked Hutton for 'the astonishing departures from all canons of good taste and good sportsmanship made by certain members of your team'. Barker's letter was one of the most wounding West Indian opinion pieces, not least because he was writing in a 'loyalist' newspaper and because – as he reminded Hutton – he was Yorkshire-born. Hall and Bannister tried to rally round the England captain by emphasising that there had been two appalling decisions, and that the umpires seemed to have far too much to say for themselves as they chatted to Queen's Park members after close of play. But there was no doubt whose side the members took.

On the fourth evening of the Test, MCC were required to attend a cocktail party at Government House. While May was assigned to make pleasantries with the Governor's wife, it seems other players, already exhausted, had to field complaints from Trinidad's white community about the bad example they were setting. This may have been the occasion Compton asked an expatriate Lancastrian to 'either shut up or step outside' after being accused of poor sportsmanship.

DAY 3

Walcott pulled the first ball from Trueman for four, a sign that he and Atkinson were under instructions to up the tempo. Some of their shots were literally devastating. Walcott raised his own hundred with a trademark straight drive and then the West Indies 600 by hitting Laker for six over long-off. The stroke broke the back off a wooden chair, the splinters reportedly salvaged by the crowd as if they were parts of the true cross. Three balls later, Atkinson broke

272

his bat smiting another six off Graveney, whose leg-breaks had been given a rare turn.

After 81 runs in the first hour, Laker took a smart return catch to dismiss Walcott and then bowled the slogging McWatt. But there was still no sign of a declaration. Atkinson hit perhaps the biggest six of the innings off the man Swanton was now calling 'the everlasting Lock'.

Lunch: West Indies 656-7 (Atkinson 54*, Ferguson 3*)

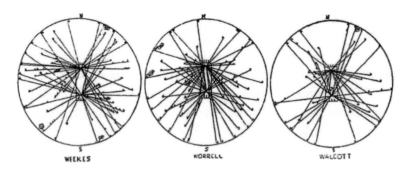

The wagon wheels of Weekes (206), Worrell (167) and Walcott (124).

Stollmeyer may have wanted to give Atkinson the chance to attain the fourth Barbadian century of the innings. England were finally put out of their misery when the all-rounder pulled Compton to midwicket.

The final total of 681 was a West Indies record, to be superseded in Jamaica four years later when Sobers broke Hutton's Test-record individual score. It was their highest home score against England, to be superseded in Antigua 50 years later when Lara reclaimed the individual record. It remains the highest Test total at the ground.

Innings close: West Indies 681-8 declared (Ferguson 8*)

When West Indies took the field, Bannister reported 'dead silence' from the crowd for about the first time in the series. Everyone, it seemed, was on tenterhooks as to whether the home bowlers could extract more from the mat than England.

Hutton snicked his first ball from King along the ground into the slips. But Swanton thought England's response was thenceforth 'notably serene and free from strain'. Bailey never enjoyed opening after a long spell in the field, although his captain had not asked him to bowl on the third day. He got his head down while Hutton allowed himself some strokes. Stollmeyer had tried six bowlers, including himself, by tea.

Tea: England 65-0 (Hutton 41*, Bailey 22*), 616 behind

Hutton's policy was to duck King's bouncers but he got a nasty throat-ball soon after the interval which he could only fend off one-handed, dollying up a simple catch to Ferguson at short leg. A terrific roar went round the ground. At 73 for one, the follow-on target of 532 seemed a long way off.

However, May looked in good touch and Bailey in dour mood. Ferguson dropped some teasing leg-spinners in a long spell but more than 50 runs were added without much alarm before the close.

Close: England 130-1 (Bailey 46*, May 38*), 551 behind

DAY 4

Play was delayed by 45 minutes because of problems with the surface under the mat. The official explanation was that the groundstaff had watered overzealously after repairing damage from King's studs. Swanton was pleased to report that 'the crowd, packed as they were and grilling under the sun, accepted the information with marvellous good humour'.

England were less amused. The usual practice was for the mat to be taken up each evening so that the base could be watered, rolled and repaired. It would then be left at the side of the wicket and replaced under the supervision of the umpires once the captains had inspected the underlay. But on the fourth morning it was already pegged in place. According to Statham, Hutton, 'a skipper you could scarcely accuse of being naive', promptly asked for the matting to be lifted again so that he could have a look underneath. There was a wet patch on a good length and he refused to start until it dried out.

Bailey, who accompanied Hutton on his inspection, suspected 'foul play'. Perhaps this was also because he was out to the first ball he received from Ferguson on the resumption. Ramadhin then produced a good leg-break which beat May's forward defensive. But he eventually took out his frustration with the surface by trying a bouncer, followed by a beamer which went for four byes.

Lunch: England 157-2 (May 50*, Compton 11*), 524 behind

Stollmeyer took the new ball directly after lunch and, as so often in the series, the rate of scoring increased. May successively cut, drove and glanced Worrell for three scintillating fours. King had the wind at his back but Murray complained that 'his imagination seemed to be limited to bouncers and full tosses'. While the bowler was indeed not renowned for much imagination, his tactics here were at least an attempt to circumvent the tyranny of the mat.

Compton dealt with the bouncers, reminding Swanton of the way 'he used to hook Lindwall and Miller'. Once King was seen off, May became 'fascinated' by his partner's expert handling of Ferguson, who was getting prodigious if predictable turn. Even Compton's running was impeccable. Stollmeyer resorted to Walcott's off-cutters, which proved harder to get away through a tight inner ring.

May reached his second Test century with a flowing cover drive. Compton swept Ramadhin for four and then ambled a single to post his fifty. One of his strokes had split the finger of Stollmeyer, who took no further part in the innings. Worrell was now on-field captain. He was following in the footsteps of Constantine and Headley by leading West Indies on the field. Like them, he knew there was little chance – even in 1954 – of the tenure becoming permanent in the near future.

Tea: England 291-2 (May 127*, Compton 63*), 390 behind

May had hit five boundaries in five overs either side of the interval but his fine innings ended when he drove King to cover. Tea and a wicket seemingly added yards to King's pace: he hit the new batsman Watson several times in a fiery spell. As in BG, despite scoring a hatful of runs in the tour match, Watson looked scratchy in the Test. He took 35 minutes to get off the mark. Then the first shot he properly middled, a pull off Walcott, was acrobatically caught by Atkinson at backward square leg.

Graveney survived a big lbw appeal second ball from King but he and Compton batted out the last 40 minutes. The well-travelled Crawford White opined in the *Chronicle* that 'King bowled more bouncers in one day's cricket than I have seen anywhere in the world'.

Close: England 332-4 (Compton 81*, Graveney 6*), 349 behind

DAY 5

With the new ball due after 20 minutes and King refreshed after the rest day, the bouncers kept coming. The English batsmen dealt with them well. Once King's bolt was shot, progress was pleasingly uneventful from their point of view. Worrell won plaudits for ringing changes in the field settings and the bowling attack. But Compton reached a chanceless hundred, his 15th in Tests.

**Lunch: England 403-4 (Compton 117*,
Graveney 37*), 278 behind**

Tiredness may have got the better of Compton when he propped a return catch to Ramadhin after six hours at the crease. His dismissal was the cue for Graveney to show some aggression, this time in a way which pleased the crowd. He hit nine fours and a six, dominating a partnership with Spooner which put on 69 in even time. Graveney fell eight short of his century to an agile caught-and-bowled by Walcott, who was again putting in accurate work. Perhaps it was a quirk of the mat that return catches had accounted for more than a quarter of wickets so far taken.

Walcott then found a gap between Spooner's bat and pad. Suddenly, after nearly five days of monotonous run-glut, there was some late drama as to whether England could save the follow-on.

Tea: England 497-7 (Laker 2*, Lock 0*), 184 behind

With another new ball four overs away, Laker and Lock biffed the follow-on target down to 25. King and Worrell then took over and the acting captain trapped Lock lbw with a well-disguised slower ball. The crowd was aroused by the entrance of Trueman. After the events of the tour match, would the fast bowlers' convention of not bowling bouncers at each other be observed?

The tale of what happened next was possibly embellished over the years in the after-dinner speeches of both batsmen. During a mid-pitch conference, Trueman is supposed to have said: 'Jim, lad, I've had a look at both of 'em and I reckon I can deal wi' Worrell if you take King.' We can turn to Laker for the punchline: 'It was a pretty fair assessment of the situation. In the next over from King I was helped off with blood pouring from a cut over the eye.'

Laker had tried to hook and edged the ball into his face. Bailey recalled that the stricken batsman's exit from the arena was so 'swerving' that he could not film it properly. Palmer did manage to take some footage where Laker, in an era before concussion protocols, looks half-unconscious as he is frogmarched off the field. The incident initially 'looked funny' to Statham but not when he got to the wicket (with damaged ribs and Lock as his runner) to see 'spatters of blood everywhere'. It was another grim example of the way the series had, in Tony Cozier's words, 'brought modern Test cricket to the West Indian public for the first time – and accentuated all its attendant faults'.

There were still 12 runs needed. Statham remembered Trueman being hit on the chest by another King bouncer: 'Freddie reacted to this unseemly treatment by standing at the batting crease with hands on hips, giving him the glare.' When Statham came on strike, he got a ball from King which, to borrow a phrase from Viv Richards, had the ingredients on it. Statham reckoned he was an 'inch' away from joining Laker in hospital: 'I played it one-handed with the handle of the bat just in front of my Adam's apple.'

There was a degree of clowning as well as glaring from Trueman as he tried to get England over the line. According to Rostron, he 'sloshed with the bat like a buccaneering pirate and alternately played the comedian as he took off his cap and bowed in response to the crowd's jeers and derisive laughter'. As in the Barbados tour match, Trueman got the serious business done, driving King for the runs which saved the follow-on.

Some West Indies players were unhappy about King, who was most unlikely to bat himself, being allowed free rein with his bouncers. The injured Gomez, watching from the radio commentary box, was quoted as saying 'the whole thing today was disgusting'. Walcott later reflected that the barrage against the tailenders was 'silly'. He was 'not keen that our tactics should be compared too closely with MCC's in the colony match just past, certainly as far as the Ferguson incident was concerned'. Stollmeyer had a word with King afterwards, but Walcott felt 'the damage had already been done'. For Worrell, who bowled a few bouncers himself with the new ball, the chance of enforcing the follow-on as acting captain seems to have become more important than sportsmanship towards tailenders.

Innings close: England 537 all out (Statham 6*), 144 behind

Stollmeyer was still nursing his split finger and Holt was in a nursing home with asthma. The choice of Ferguson as one of the makeshift openers delighted the crowd but indicated that the match was entering its village-green phase.

Close: West Indies 5-0 (Pairaudeau 1*, Ferguson 4*), 149 ahead

DAY 6

Bailey did not yet seem prepared to enter into the spirit of exhibition cricket. Perhaps seeking revenge for Laker, he peppered Pairaudeau with bouncers until the batsman ducked into one and hit his own wicket. Weekes soon departed, well taken by a diving Suttle at short leg. Had the other substitute Moss not misjudged a catch offered by Worrell, the game may have stirred into something approaching life. But, as Swanton observed, England were 'rather too tired to think in terms of the miraculous'.

**Lunch: West Indies 58-2 (Ferguson
38*, Worrell 14*), 202 ahead**

Ferguson's fun was ended when he played on to Bailey. Worrell let himself go with some big hits, sending a ball from Compton clear

278

out of the Oval before Moss redeemed himself by taking a running catch. For the rest of the afternoon, Walcott and Atkinson tucked into some buffet bowling. Compton retired to the boundary to chat with the crowd, Trueman twirled some slow stuff and Hutton turned his arm over. It was to be his penultimate bowl in Tests – he would dismiss Richie Benaud with the last ball of the drawn match in Sydney the next winter.

Tea: West Indies 212-4 (Walcott 51*, Atkinson 53*), 356 ahead

West Indies made a token declaration at tea. Weekes opened the bowling. Ferguson and McWatt swapped roles, the former pulling off two catches (quite smart ones, standing up) and the latter taking his only Test wicket (not a bad scalp in May). The crowd, understandably thin in the unreserved sections, stayed on to see Hutton bat out time. The match had certainly ended more quietly than it had started.

Close: England 98-3 (Hutton 30*, Graveney 0*) Match drawn

There were several repercussions from what Compton called 'an unhappy, unpleasant game'. The locals recognised that the mat risked killing international cricket on their island. It guaranteed high gate receipts but also high tedium in predestined draws. Immediately after the Test, Stollmeyer is said to have asked the Queen's Park authorities to dig up the pitch and accelerate their experiments with turf wickets. This was an easier thing to do now that the draw, which ensured West Indies could not lose the series, was safely in the bag. The expert entrusted to supervise the new Queen's Park square was the man last encountered scurrying off the Bourda ground. Badge Menzies, who looked after what was widely acknowledged to be the best turf pitch in the Caribbean, was brought in from British Guiana.

For the tourists, the draw in Trinidad probably did not come as a surprise but also came at considerable cost. Statham, easily their best bowler so far, was now doubtful for the fifth Test in Jamaica. So was Laker, arguably England's best spinning option back on grass.

As well as the boil on his foot, Evans would soon discover he had chipped a bone in a finger. Hutton clearly suspected the mat had been prepared to benefit the home side in Trinidad and will have expected another batsman's paradise at Sabina Park.

Finally, there was an attempt to repair diplomatic relations. Dos Santos hosted a farewell function for MCC. The Board of Control president announced that a written apology had been sent to Lord's for the disturbance in British Guiana. He commended Hutton for defusing that situation. He also appeared to blame the players and press of both sides for the 'modern "battlefield" atmosphere' which had caused such acrimony in Trinidad. Dos Santos planned to go to Jamaica as an 'observer' and trusted there would be fewer bumpers and a better spirit in the fifth Test. Palmer, making the final speech of the evening, welcomed the opportunity 'to resolve any troubles that may have beset us' and promised 'MCC will always work as it has done in the past to foster and develop the game'.

Before that Hutton had responded to dos Santos with a speech of drier humour but greater pique. He was no doubt preoccupied by the prospect of losing the series and irritated by opinion pieces on the Graveney incident. In the shrillest *Trinidad Guardian* columns, Brunell Jones complained of 'the mistake England made' in sending out a professional captain, and Dick Murray concluded that Lord Hawke had been proved right.

Although Hutton congratulated the Three Ws and trusted 'some good' would come out of the incessant criticism of MCC, he denounced the Queen's Park mat. He implied disapproval of the umpires by suggesting they should be paid by the Board of Control. He implied disapproval of the press when he advised the players 'to pay little attention to what they read in the papers'. Hutton also made no apology for his team playing hard to the finish: 'I know Jeff Stollmeyer thinks I am a strange sort of fellow, but at the end of the last Test we will all be the best of friends.'

CHAPTER 16

FIFTH TEST (SABINA PARK)

After a tiring game in Trinidad and a tiring flight back to Jamaica, with two transit stops at Caracas and Curaçao, there was only a week's interval before the final Test. But MCC did find time for some much-needed rest and recreation. The tour had already turned a profit for the Board of Control and the squad was put up in a luxury hotel in Montego Bay, one of the best tourist resorts in what remained of the 'Colonial Empire'. There was some golf, some sea-fishing in glass-bottomed boats, plenty of swimming and a gentle run-out against a Colts and Country XI, even if this two-day game became less lighthearted after rain made the pitch dangerous.

Three of the senior professionals who were stood down for that match enjoyed a particularly pleasant break. Dorothy Hutton and Jean Evans had flown out to meet their husbands, while Valerie Compton had been with the party since Trinidad. Richard Hutton recalled 'it was very unusual in those days for wives to go on tour'. But his father, and Evans, had been away from home for five winters out of eight since the war. MCC may have acquiesced in their case – albeit on a strictly no-expenses-paid basis – in recognition of this, and in Compton's case because he was playing on one knee. Evans found the Montego Bay interlude 'wonderfully refreshing'. Perhaps with a degree of jealousy, as his wife Lily was heavily pregnant back home, Laker later observed that the arrival of the wives 'coincided with good form shown by their husbands'.

The winding 100-mile road trip back to Kingston was enhanced by 'a sumptuous lunch at the famous Jamaica Inn', again paid for by Stanhope Joel, and a lavish tea with an English banana-planter. When MCC reached the capital, they were greeted by the American millionaire Henry Sayen, who could boast of playing first-class cricket in 1909 for both the Gentlemen of England and the Gentlemen of Pennsylvania. The tourists considered Sayen a lucky mascot (because he had attended the Ashes Test at The Oval) and a generous patron (because he offered prizes for their individual achievements).

All this was a world away from what the historian Obika Gray calls 'the poverty, abominable living conditions and chronic joblessness of the urban poor' in Kingston in the 1950s, conditions which were increasing the levels of emigration to Britain. The JLP and the PNP, when they were not squabbling about constituency boundaries for the 1955 election, were trying to appeal to the Jamaican masses while making sure to disassociate themselves from the 'Communist' agitation in British Guiana.

This was the context for a fiery opinion piece written by Ken Jones in the PNP's *Public Opinion* after the Trinidad Test. Jones believed 'a more biased set of typewriter punchers' than the English press corps 'could only be found in the offices of the late Dr. Goebbels'. He characterised the English cricketers as 'a bunch of sour sports who can't take it', asserting that their 'thorough misbehaviour' was 'unequalled in the history of representative cricket here'.

At the same time as being an agitator for change, Jones was the type of West Indian who was a stickler for protocol. He blamed Hutton for allowing conduct which could 'never, never happen' under the patrician captains who had led English tours to the Caribbean in the past. Jones also pointed to the 'immaculate conduct of Stollmeyer and his men'. He was inviting an analogy between the way West Indies had shown MCC how to play 'the gentleman's game' and the way the PNP could show the British how best to govern Jamaica.

The British Governor was Hugh Foot, the brother of the Labour politician Michael Foot. He seems to have intervened to deal with the anti-British feeling inspired by the cricket. Compton recalled that 'by then the goings-on had been the subject of concern and inquiry at Government House level' and that 'action and influence from there had had a calming effect'.

Lord's was possibly in communication with the Governor and certainly in communication with Swanton, who may already have been telling them that the tour had become 'a diplomatic and sporting disaster of the first magnitude'. Hutton was 'surprised' to receive telegrams from the MCC secretariat shortly before the deciding Test. One of them is preserved in the Lord's archives:

WRITTEN YOU TODAY SOUTH CAMP ROAD
HOTEL STRESSING IMPORTANCE NO RESENTMENT

282

SHOWN TO UMPIRES DECISIONS UNDER ANY
CIRCUMSTANCES IN FIFTH TEST AND NO COMMENT
MADE TO PRESS

Hutton dutifully passed on these instructions, although he was preoccupied by how many of his walking wounded would come through final practice. Bailey tried to give Laker, whose right eye was still three-quarters covered in plaster, as gentle a net as possible but it was obvious that the off-spinner was still experiencing problems with his vision. Moss and Suttle were put on standby. There was better news on Evans, who came through a fitness test of fierce throw-ins, and Watson, who was available for selection despite having six stitches inserted after hooking into his face during the Montego Bay game.

The most important fitness test had been left until the end of the session. Hutton and Bailey had wanted the Essex masseur Harold Dalton on tour with them, but because of the Board of Control budget this had not been permitted. Whether by accident or design, Dalton had turned up in Jamaica that winter and supervised Statham's recuperation on an unofficial basis. He sent his patient out to the nets 'strapped up from neck to navel'. But Statham 'knew it was hopeless' the moment he began trying to bowl. He still felt twinges of pain six weeks later when he reported to Old Trafford for the new season. At least Wardle could now be accommodated without lengthening the tail, but the loss of England's best fast bowler was a heavy blow.

For West Indies, Gomez had recovered from his hamstring injury and was set to play instead of Pairaudeau. Frederick (not Rae) had been called up as cover when Holt missed pre-match practice because of his asthma. Sobers, who at this point bowled only orthodox left-arm, had been flown in as standby for Valentine. Some of those who correctly predicted the young Bajan would make his debut felt that Valentine, whatever the official reasons given to manage local sensibilities, was making way more because of the weakness of his batting than the rawness of his finger. Stollmeyer still sounded positive in interviews but his emphasis had fallen increasingly on defence. Kentish's status as a batting rabbit was now more relevant than the rabbit he had pulled out of the hat in the first Test. From five representatives then, Jamaica was down to one. Headley had gone back to Dudley.

On the morning of the game, Holt was passed fit for West Indies and Laker for England, an important boost for their revised strategy without Statham. The groundsman told Hutton that the pitch was good for a first innings score of 700. 'Our only hope was to bat,' Bailey recalled, 'then bowl them out with spinners. And Len lost the toss.' Bailey never forgot the 'despairing look' on the skipper's face when he broke the news. According to Graveney, 'spirits in the England dressing-room plummeted'. 'My feelings,' Hutton said simply, 'can be imagined.'

DAY 1

The England captain thought 'everything was wrong' for Bailey's style of bowling, but gave his vice-captain choice of ends. There was a gentle breeze blowing diagonally across the ground. Bailey's cricket brain and team ethic both clicked in, as he opted for the southern end into the wind:

> The reason was obvious as Fred Trueman was not only yards faster, but, like me, relied very largely on the outswinger. Fred had to come down wind and I thought that after his initial burst I would replace him at that end.

To Bailey's fifth ball of the morning, Holt prodded forward. The ball took the inside edge and Lock scooped it up at short leg. After this early setback, Stollmeyer and Weekes batted with extreme care. There was only one scoring stroke in the first five overs, a flick by Stollmeyer off Trueman which just evaded the leg-trap.

Weekes was evidently growing impatient at not getting off the mark. Bailey bowled him an inswinger which, according to Evans behind the wicket, also then 'came back like a rocket' off the pitch. There was some debate as to whether the ball brushed Weekes's bat or pad but the only other question was how many yards his off stump came out of the ground – ten thought Crawford White.

In his next over, Bailey tempted Stollmeyer outside off stump. Perhaps playing for inswing as he tried to drive, the captain snicked behind. After his morning pitch inspection, Bailey said he would be happy with three for 100 as his first-innings figures. He had taken three for 3 in his first five overs.

According to Hall, 'the happily-noisy Jamaican crowd were struck dumb'. They were no doubt stunned by the crash of wickets but also surprised by the surreal nonchalance with which each one was greeted. Bannister, who was aware of the team's pre-match instructions, reported that 'the England players gathered slowly in small discussion groups as if no more thrilled than if a wicket had fallen in a charity match'.

Worrell may have been pleased to see Trueman instead of Statham – until he was bombarded by bouncers. Taking involuntary protective action against a ball speared into his chest, Worrell spliced into the leg-trap. Lock made a despairing attempt to catch the ball as it looped over his head. But the other leg slip Wardle, running behind him, took an awkward catch despite being momentarily unsighted. The score after 45 minutes play was a scarcely believable 13 for four. To use a period phrase, the molasses had fallen into the West Indian turbine.

Things could have got even worse for them had first slip Graveney held on to a relatively easy chance given by Atkinson off Wardle, on as first change for Trueman, or had second slip Watson been standing a touch closer when the same batsman edged a drive from the last ball of Bailey's eight-over spell.

Lunch: West Indies 38-4 (Walcott 12*, Atkinson 13*)

The fifth-wicket stand became slightly more expansive in the afternoon. Walcott off-drove Trueman for two fours, although this did not move the silly fielder that had become one of England's set plans against him. Atkinson raised the fifty partnership off Lock. Then Bailey came back for a second spell from the other end. He was still able to move the ball in against the breeze and trapped Atkinson lbw. The new batsman Gomez flicked Bailey off his toes for four but then gave catching practice to Watson as he tried to steer a ball to third man. 75 for six.

While Swanton thought McWatt 'lived from hand to mouth' as West Indies tried to rebuild, Rostron felt Walcott looked 'supremely safe'. But, after reaching his fifth half-century of the series, Walcott contrived to top-edge a long hop from Lock towards mid-on. Hearts must have been in England mouths because Laker was the man positioned there. So far in the field he had appeared hesitant, but he steadied himself and coolly pouched the chance. The three England spinners were making a significant contribution – by catching everything that moved.

Out came the debutant Sobers: 'Without being arrogant, I could not understand why we had lost so many wickets. The pitch was good and the light was perfect. Trevor was not a bowler who did a lot with the ball.' Sobers defended calmly for 15 minutes until a sudden shower forced the players in for an early tea.

Rain delay and tea: West Indies 111-7 (McWatt 22*, Sobers 0*)

Only 20 minutes of playing time were lost. Trueman and Bailey were faced with the problem of a slippery ball, which had to be dried after almost every delivery. But Bailey had an immediate stroke of luck when McWatt played an authentic leg-glance, only to see it caught at full stretch by Lock.

King came out at No.10. The Laker incident had not been forgotten by Trueman. 'He will tell you to this day,' wrote Statham in 1961, 'that he was savouring the thought of letting King have the fastest bouncer he had ever bowled.' However, the combination of the wet ball and his red mist caused him to lose direction. After King had played a few shots it was Bailey who knocked out his leg stump. Trueman refound his radar to pin Ramadhin leg-before. Sobers had run out of partners. This would happen to him only twice more in 93 Tests, despite the fact he usually batted at No.6 throughout the mid-1960s.

West Indies – whose team average in the first four Tests was 344 – had been dismissed for 139. Bailey's figures of seven for 34 were the best yet recorded by a pace bowler in Tests between the two sides and would remain the best of his Test career. The England fielders formed a lane for him to lead them into the pavilion. The Jamaican crowd, 'strangely quiet' all afternoon according to Swanton, gave him a generous ovation. In ten minutes he would be opening the batting.

Innings close: West Indies 139 all out (Sobers 14*)

John Figueroa rated King's burst in the last mini-session of the day as 'one of the greatest displays of attacking fast bowling I have ever seen'. He observed how Hutton was 'in all kinds of worries', often taking the bottom hand off the bat. It also became noticeable, especially to his opening partner, that Hutton seemed keen to get off strike. Bailey stood firm to round off a memorable day for him and for England.

Close: England 17-0 (Hutton 8*, Bailey 9*), 122 behind

Bailey went for a swim in the hotel pool and had dinner with Sayen, who was presumably picking up the tab. He remembered spending part of that night 'wandering about my hotel, a case of mental, rather than physical exhaustion'. In later years he would reflect that 'I simply experienced one of those dream days when everything went right' and nearly every catch went to hand.

There was definitely more swing than in any other game MCC played in Jamaica, and the pitch offered some assistance despite its rock-hard appearance. Even though Trueman found it 'as dry as old parchment', Wardle remembered there being a fair amount of moisture under the surface: 'Each ball left a slight dent in the pitch and suited Trevor's seam bowling admirably.' Evans still thought there was not much wrong with the wicket, and was so surprised by the lift Bailey extracted that he wondered whether 'perhaps there was something unusual' with the ball England had been given.

If Bailey could hardly believe what he had done, Bannister reported that West Indies 'could scarcely credit what had happened to them'. 'That's cricket,' McWatt told him, 'you just can't explain it.' Walcott did try to explain the events of the first day, agreeing that the Sabina pitch 'had more life in it than usual' and also paying tribute to the way Trueman had softened up the top order. Stollmeyer agreed Bailey was 'aided and abetted' by Trueman but felt another factor was 'some rather irresolute batting'. He would have rued his own shot, as would Gomez and Walcott, who suggested that the home side's long batting order, with Sobers at No.9, may have led to a false sense of security.

Swanton still thought it was less a case of the West Indians getting themselves out than Bailey thinking them out: 'He seems

287

to have summed them up just as he summed up the Australians on MCC's last tour.' The Australians had played their part in Bailey's development before that series in 1950/51. The most formative experiences of his career were his four encounters with Bradman's Invincibles in 1948, three lost by an innings (his aggregate figures 84-7-406-6). He realised a bowler of his type had to develop set plans for individual batsmen as well as variations of pace and angle. Weekes takes his hat off to Bailey: 'It was doing a bit and he made the very most of it.' West Indies would now have to bowl extremely well themselves to have any chance of winning the match and the series.

DAY 2

Rain delayed the start by 15 minutes and the pitch was lively after sweating under the covers. King was arguably even more of a handful than on the previous evening. Swanton rated his first spell 'the fastest I have seen in the West Indies'; White judged it 'as hostile as anything I have seen since Lindwall and Miller at their best'. King's field included two leg slips and a forward short leg. It was inevitable that his strategy would amount to not much more than a fusillade of short balls. Bailey found Hutton's strategy nearly as predictable: 'I ducked, dived and weaved, while Len smiled approvingly at me at the other end.'

If Bailey rather savoured telling the story in later years, Stollmeyer did not think the England vice-captain 'particularly enjoyed' seeing his skipper turn down singles to third man. In turn, Hutton did not care for the 'inference' in Stollmeyer's autobiography that he was scared of King's bouncers. He insisted Bailey had fully endorsed an approach which 'made good tactical sense'. The batsmen rotated the strike once in the opening overs, but quickly assessed the situation after seeing how much life King was getting at one end and how much movement Atkinson was getting at the other. They played out ten consecutive maidens.

Bailey's job was to deal with King. He was determined not to hook and either avoided or dead-batted the bouncers. Already wearing strapping because of a shoulder strained in his heroic bowling stint, he took several for the team. He was hit on the hand and the elbow by King before gloving a bouncer into his jaw. Bannister and Bray both thought Bailey would have been knocked out cold but for the deflection off his glove. The makeshift opener staggered, shook his head and carried on. Hutton may well have remembered this piece of stubbornness, among many others, when he opined that Bailey's 'service to England cannot be overestimated'.

Meanwhile, Hutton dealt with Atkinson, perhaps the nearest equivalent to Bailey in the West Indies attack. McWatt felt the England captain 'stopped' the best ball of the entire day when Atkinson made one cut back off the pitch. It was only right at the end of King's spell that the batsmen crossed. According to Bannister, Hutton got three bouncers in four balls but 'remained unshaken to the point of seeming indifference'. Weekes thinks Hutton's management of the strike, which he had seen before at The Oval in 1950, was a sign of intelligence rather than cowardice: 'It was very clever what he did. He knew it needed a long innings and he knew the best place to be early on.'

England scored just one run in the first half-hour, 13 off 19 overs in the first hour and 24 off 24 in the truncated session. The wickets column was all Hutton and Bailey had been worried about.

Lunch: England 41-0 (Hutton 18*, Bailey 23*), 98 behind

His job done against the new ball, Bailey started looking for runs when West Indies introduced their young left-arm spinner. The man who faced Sobers' first delivery in Test cricket would later write his biography:

> This was the first time I had played against Garry,
> and I was happy to see him come on as third change,
> because I have always preferred facing bowlers who
> aim to make the ball leave the bat. With the England
> total 43, Garry dropped one fractionally short outside
> my off stump. I could not resist the square cut, only
> to discover it was his arm-ball, with the result that I
> was too close and was snapped up behind the wicket.
> Bailey c. McWatt b. Sobers 24.

Over the years Bailey refined this anecdote to three deadpan words – 'Silly little cut'. Sobers had become the youngest wicket-taker in Test history.

May was grateful to Sobers for a half-volley first ball 'which went nicely through the covers'. He had much more trouble with King, back for another spell. But, as the afternoon progressed, he was 'becoming rather pleased with the speed with which we were approaching West Indies' score with only one wicket down'. Just after Hutton pulled Ramadhin for four to reach his fifty, May put Sobers over the sightscreen for six and then Walcott temporarily out of action, injured off his own bowling trying to stop a return drive.

When Ramadhin gave May some width, he laced yet another drive through the covers – 'or so I thought – but Bruce Pairaudeau, fielding for Walcott, dived and brought off a wonderful catch'. Swanton described it as 'hatefully good', the fielder throwing himself full length and 'covering his shirt and trousers with grass and earth in the process'. Pairaudeau can no longer remember the precise details but he does recall feeling rather pleased with himself.

Compton looked in prime form, almost immediately finding the boundary with a cover drive and a leg-glance. But he then shut up shop like his captain with an eye on tea and the crucial challenge of the second new ball. Bannister reported that Hutton's 'disinclination to hasten drew from a section of the crowd the slow hand-clap – surely the silliest invention of modern sports crowds'.

Tea: England 129-2 (Hutton 62*, Compton 14*), 10 behind

The anticipated duel between King and Compton duly materialised. Compton was too early on King's first bouncer, which hit him on the back of the glove. He got hold of the next one so well that it flew through the wire netting at long leg into the crowd. King responded with another bouncer described as 'colossal' by Charles Bray. Compton was caught in two minds, tried to back away, got his bat tangled up in his pads and cracked the back of his head on the hard wicket as he fell over.

When he came to his senses, he discovered he had been given out. A bail had been dislodged. Both batsmen seem to have argued strongly that Compton had not been playing at the ball and so should not have been adjudged hit wicket. Rostron later reported that Compton was more hurt by a 'controversial' decision than by his fall. But the other English correspondents, remembering his carbon-copy dismissal against Miller at Trent Bridge in 1948, all agreed the decision was correct and that umpires Burke and Ewart were having a good game.

King then fooled Watson with a slower ball. Graveney made a nervous start and played an indeterminate shot to a good in-ducker from Atkinson. From 152 for two England had subsided to 179 for five. The game was back in the balance.

Hutton carried on, outwardly unperturbed, and ended the day with a square cut off Atkinson which left the fielders standing. Despite the mini-collapse, there were two reasons he could take succour from the last exchanges of the session. First, after 21 overs of sustained aggression, King limped off holding his thigh. Stollmeyer might perhaps be excused for bowling him into the ground given the high stakes and the fact that his other main weapon, Ramadhin, had been economical but unthreatening. Second, Evans came to the crease not in typical biff-bash mode but looking more like the man who had batted against type at Adelaide in 1946/47. He had taken 90 minutes to get off the mark there, in support of Compton, and now blocked 23 balls for Hutton before the close. Still, England were only 55 ahead with five wickets left. They would have to bat last on a pitch which had been doing a bit more for all kinds of bowlers than in the first Test.

Close: England 194-5 (Hutton 93*, Evans 0*), 55 ahead

DAY 3

'King Will Play' was the headline in several Caribbean newspapers, whose sources suggested the fast bowler had responded to treatment. Hutton will therefore have been greatly relieved to see that King would not: he was sitting in the pavilion with heavy strapping around his thigh.

Evans played and missed frequently early on but, according to Hayter, 'disciplined himself well to defence'. It was the England captain, just after reaching his century, who suddenly lashed out at Ramadhin. His first lofted shot was miscued, Gomez getting fingertips to a very difficult chance at deep mid-on; off the next ball, he cleared Gomez more comfortably. This sudden spasm of hitting after six hours of mostly flawless circumspection was interpreted as a lapse of concentration or a rush of blood on the hottest day of a hot Test.

We have seen this feature of Hutton's batting several times during the series, most notably when Palmer came to the crease in Barbados. On the previous afternoon he had aimed two consecutive leg-side slogs at Sobers. Graveney could never quite get out of his head the image of his captain's batting in the 1953/54 series: 'this slight, pale, always silent man', playing defensively forward to someone like Atkinson 'ball after ball, each shot so like the one before that it might have been a photograph'. Graveney could not understand why he would pick particular balls for savage punishment and then go straight back into his shell: 'But he would have had a reason because I doubt if Len Hutton ever did anything without reason.'

The reasons may sometimes have been tactical but were also a combination of the mental, the physical and the technical. Hutton was 37 and under constant pressure. The hard Caribbean pitches exacerbated his sore shins, the legacy of bone grafts taken from both legs in the operations to reconstruct his left arm. At least, in the warmer climate, he enjoyed 'comparative freedom from pain' in the arm, but it still caused him problems in long innings.

Hutton had learnt from Hammond that 'the right hand is a sinner', a point he once made even more starkly to David Steele: 'The top hand is life and the bottom hand is death.' Mike Brearley observes that the word 'ascetic' was made for Hutton's batting, but even Hutton allowed himself a few shots on the bottom-handed dark side every so often.

What Swanton called 'a mere war of attrition' then resumed. Hutton would tend to take a single early in the over and Stollmeyer would then crowd Evans with close catchers. By the time of Sobers' last over before lunch, eight were counted round the England wicketkeeper. He maintained what Ditton described as 'a straight, almost motionless bat' which was 'not greatly appreciated by the Jamaican crowd'. What a contrast with the first Test on the same ground, when Evans had vainly tried to scatter the close field in the first innings, and got himself out to an awful shot in the second. With Compton he had been the most vocal critic of Hutton's grinding approach. But at the crucial moment, like Compton in BG, he had repressed all his instincts to help his captain secure a platform. The lead was now in three figures.

Lunch: England 244-5 (Hutton 133*, Evans 10*), 105 ahead

Stollmeyer decided to try his own leg-spinners immediately after the interval, which Hutton and Evans took as their cue to change their policy. Evans took eight off one Gomez over, nearly as many as he had scored during the previous two hours. He added further quick runs, reverting to his normal free style, before failing to keep down an off-drive off Ramadhin.

The new ball was due but Stollmeyer delayed taking it, perhaps in the faint hope King might come back after tea. A more likely explanation is that he feared the consequences if the incoming Wardle, likely to be in his element in this situation, came off. Wardle was therefore allowed to get his eye in by hitting Ramadhin for two humming fours and a six which went out of the ground. Hutton had already hit what Swanton described as a more 'princely' six off Atkinson to raise England's 300, the ball bouncing into a garden behind the sightscreen. Hall, once close to hysterical in his criticism of the tourists, was now becoming hyperbolic in his praise: 'None who saw it will ever forget it. What grace! What beauty! What power!'

Stollmeyer did now give Gomez and Worrell the new ball. But he had lost control and his team, for the first time in the series, seemed to be losing heart in temperatures of more than 90 degrees. Wardle's habit of pretending to head off to the pavilion when he played and missed caused great amusement in the bleachers, but was probably less appreciated by the fielders.

There was no sign of King to take the smirk off Wardle's face, which widened when Walcott dropped him on 50. True, it was a steeper, the sun was in Walcott's eyes and he was carrying a finger injury. But the sight of such an ultra-reliable fielder putting one down symbolised how down West Indies now were. Hutton reached 200 just before tea off Sobers with what Swanton called 'one of the best specimens of his cover drive'.

Hutton's beautifully paced double century at Sabina was not only his last great innings in Test cricket but also, given the match

293

situation, arguably a greater innings than his 364 at The Oval. On that occasion, his great friend Hedley Verity tended to him at every interval with tobacco, tea and counsel. Bailey remembered the same drill in Jamaica:

> We take his pads off, we smoke a cigarette for him.
> 'I'm so tired, I'm so tired,' he says. 'Come on Len, a few more runs,' we say. We drank a cup of tea for him.

After nearly nine hours at the crease, Hutton was no doubt looking forward to another of these pit-stops with his mind still on batting West Indies completely out of the game. On the way into tea he is reported to have ignored – or even brushed aside – a figure trying to congratulate him in the members' aisle which led to the sanctuary of the dressing rooms.

Tea: England 390-6 (Hutton 205*, Wardle 56*), 251 ahead

Within seconds that sanctuary was unceremoniously breached. Bailey recalled opening the door to a 'political lackey'. Palmer remembered this uninvited guest being a 'large man', a fact he was presumably able to confirm after being lifted off his feet by his lapels. Hutton recollected a good deal of shouting about a 'crowning insult'.

The person he had failed to acknowledge in the members' aisle turned out to be Alexander Bustamante, the Chief Minister of Jamaica. One of Bustamante's entourage was now taking fairly obvious exception to what he saw as a deliberate affront. Most of the interval was taken up by the England players dealing with what they called 'wild accusations'. Evans thought he could see the outlines of a gun-holster which 'bulged very significantly' under the intruder's armpit.

Hutton confessed he was in 'a mental whirl after the rumpus'. He was caught behind off Walcott directly after tea without adding to his score. Swanton, ever one for high standards, complained that 'the rest of the English batting was inevitably anti-climax but it need not have been quite such tedious anti-climax'. In mitigation, the England dressing room was probably still in a state of shock after the tea-time incident. Hutton's dismissal also injected some vim back into West Indies' effort in the field. And Sobers bowled very well after tea, even if his last victim Laker was attempting to slog him into downtown Kingston.

Innings close: England 414 (Trueman 0*), 275 ahead

In an awkward period before stumps, Holt survived a half-chance to the leg-trap and a full quota of bouncers from Trueman. But West Indies got through with all their wickets intact. If they could stretch out their innings into Day 6 – and they had batted across three days twice in the series – they would build a big enough lead to save or even win the game. Strebor Roberts felt the home side had a 'magnificent opportunity to show why … they are acclaimed the greatest batting machine of recent times'.

Close: West Indies 20-0 (Holt 7*, Stollmeyer 12*), 255 behind

Whether at Hutton's initiative (as he later remembered) or at Nethersole's (as local papers suggested), the England captain shared a cordial drink with the Chief Minister after close of play in the club bar. He said he was prepared to apologise for any offence caused and Bustamante was happy to assure him none was taken, even if he did add that Hutton's snub was 'hardly the conduct of an English gentleman'.

DAY 4

Throughout the series, *The Gleaner* had led its front page with Ditton's syndicated report of the previous day's play. On the fourth morning the match report was accompanied by a short column on the 'unpleasant incident'. According to *The Gleaner*'s sources, Bustamante had made very clear he wanted Hutton to pause to accept his congratulations. Hutton could not have failed to identify him because, before he re-entered the dressing room, the Kingston CC chairman, Monty DaCosta, had explained who Bustamante was. The words then exchanged were 'in dispute' but the fact DaCosta was 'sworn to silence' implied that Hutton had given him short shrift.

Hutton was disappointed to see this account 'prominently front-paged', having assumed his drink with Bustamante had cleared the air. The controversy was obviously going to rumble on and Palmer was seen making a trip into Kingston on diplomatic business during the day.

On the field, 20 minutes passed largely without incident. Then Holt, again looking uncomfortable against balls targeted back-of-a-length on his body, fended Trueman to Lock in the leg-trap. Bannister wearily reported that Holt 'stood uncertainly and had to be given out' despite 'as clean a catch as could be seen'. Albert Alkins, who as *Trinidad Guardian* correspondent may have been equally tired of English complaints, pointed out that Holt had taken his eye off the ball and had a right to wait for the umpire's finger.

Despite this early breakthrough, Hutton brought on his spinners. He was possibly bearing in mind the workload of the two fast bowlers on a day when the palm trees fringing Sabina Park stood motionless. But perhaps there was also a plan for Weekes. The square cut had yielded countless runs for him during the series. England now seemed to be offering him the shot but a little less room to play it. Trying to cut a ball from Laker, Weekes gave a difficult slip-chance to Graveney. He then dragged the ball onto his wicket playing a similar stroke to Wardle.

Stollmeyer and Worrell got their heads down, whilst still leaving Swanton with the impression that 'West Indian players are not constitutionally happy when the accent is on defence'.

Lunch: West Indies 54-2 (Stollmeyer 29*, Worrell 12*), 221 behind

Laker bowled accurately for most of the afternoon. When he came off for the second new ball, 15 of his 21 overs in the innings had been maidens. His roommate Moss had seen him try all kinds of remedy for his sore spinning finger – 'He even used to wee on it'. Because of his eye-wound Laker was the only spinner to miss the two-day game at Montego Bay, and a week's rest may have helped. His changes of pace made him a wicket-taking threat; his ability to cork an end allowed Hutton to rotate his other bowlers.

Stollmeyer was batting as if his life depended on it. While the Sabina crowd was much less hostile than in the first Test, he must have known this would be the only home series he would captain against England.

He would not want to be remembered for throwing away a 2-0 lead on three grounds where West Indies had lost only one Test against England in the past. He reached his fifty in just over three hours.

The second new ball was perhaps the moment Evans chose for some amateur psychology, instructing the close fielders to 'wildly applaud' Trueman's first poor delivery. But Trueman's blood was up in any case. He was trying hard to comply with the instructions from Lord's. Rostron noted that he behaved 'correctly' throughout the Test by immediately tending to any batsman he hit. He was trying even harder, as Hall recognised, to recapture the potency that had made him such a talking point before the series: 'It was the Trueman we have been waiting for, a fiery, bumper-bowling, aggressive win-or-bust Trueman.' He peppered Worrell with the new ball and induced the same kind of involuntary stroke as in the first innings, Graveney taking a deflection off the bat handle at slip.

There followed the same kind of duel between Trueman and Walcott as the crowd had enjoyed between King and Compton on the second day. Walcott remembered getting one half-volley from Trueman during his innings, and the bowler's response when he hit it through the covers: 'You won't get no _____ more!' He now received at least five bouncers in two overs. Walcott smacked the first magnificently for four – but nearly trod on his stumps in doing so – and miscued three other hook shots. Two fell safely into the outfield and one eluded May, staring into the sun at deep square leg.

Tea: West Indies 123-3 (Stollmeyer 64*, Walcott 16*), 152 behind

Perhaps surprised to get one in his own half during Trueman's first over after tea, the West Indies captain played round a fast straight ball and was adjudged lbw. The man who had stood at Stollmeyer's side throughout their careers, Gomez, knuckled down to play one of his better innings of the series. Apart from an indulgence against Bailey, when he helped himself to three boundaries in an over, he concentrated on defence, supporting Walcott through the 90 minutes of the session.

Close: West Indies 184-4 (Walcott 50*, Gomez 21*), 91 behind

DAY 5

There was a large fifth-day crowd, reflecting a belief that all was not lost for the home side. But Gomez looked typically scratchy restarting his innings. He was soon leg-before, beaten in the flight by Laker.

Atkinson came out to join Walcott. Not for the first time in the series they put up stern resistance. It was also in both their natures to put away the bad ball. According to Hayter, Atkinson was 'often at his wit's end solving Wardle's oriental problems', but he also hit full-blooded drives and pulls for four. Surviving a sharp chance behind off Lock, he and West Indies were still alive.

Lunch: West Indies 238-5 (Walcott 75*, Atkinson 27*), 37 behind

Trueman was given a preparatory over before the third new ball. Walcott hooked two bouncers for four and powered a back-foot straight drive for another. The crowd cheered every stroke, able to count down the deficit more quickly than before lunch. But, once the new ball was taken, Walcott was hit a nasty blow just above the glove by Bailey, who then tempted Atkinson into a fatal indiscretion outside off stump. Atkinson took some time to drag himself off, but the way he wrung his bat in anguish indicated disappointment not dissent.

McWatt obviously intended to end the series as he had begun it. He cut the fast bowlers for two rasping fours. Hutton brought back Laker. McWatt drove him off the middle of the blade. Wardle made incredibly quick ground and dived to pull off a catch hailed by the English journalists as 'magnificent' and 'phenomenal'. It won Sayen's £5 prize for England's most spectacular piece of cricket.

Wardle felt his effort was partly down to luck but partly down to his Yorkshire training: Sellers always had his outfielders walking in aggressively. The dismissal also encapsulated England's improvement in the second half of the series. The spinners were now exerting pressure, not soaking it up. Hutton was captaining pro-actively, not letting the game drift. His fielders were taking great catches, not dropping easy ones. And, it has to be admitted, the fortune which once favoured the brave McWatt had deserted him.

298

Walcott fought on. He had reached his century with two boundaries off Trueman and now posted the team's 300 off Laker with another of his famous back-drives. But he was clearly tired – he had done quite a lot of bowling in the past two Tests. He was also clearly in pain – play had to be stopped twice for his wrist to be bandaged. Laker bowled a slightly slower ball and Walcott edged to Graveney at slip. It had been a superb innings, nearly as good in the context of the game as his double century in Barbados.

Sobers again appeared unfazed by a close field that was almost in touching distance. He managed the strike like an old hand. Observers on both sides realised, without the benefit of hindsight, that they were watching a young cricketer with a future. As the minutes ticked on, Swanton felt 'all virtue seemed to depart from the England team'. Surely West Indies were not going to set a meaningful target after all the hard work had been done? Sobers got half an hour out of Ramadhin and half an hour out of King, but at last tickled one to Compton off Lock.

Innings close and tea: West Indies 346 all out (King 10*), 71 ahead

Hutton once more sent in Graveney and May to knock off the runs, and perhaps audition for an opener's role in Australia. In the first over, and in a final display of home pride, King made a spectacular mess of Graveney's stumps with a rapid yorker.

May looked in excellent touch and survived the opening barrage. He was clearly under instructions to get the job finished that night, especially as there were indications of a brewing tropical storm. England got home with ten minutes to spare. As in BG, Weekes came on to bowl as the last rites were administered. And, again as in BG, the English and West Indian press emphasised that the home crowd greeted the winning runs generously, and that play ended in a 'happy atmosphere' all round.

England 72-1 (May 40*, Watson 20*) won by 9 wickets

However, nobody was pretending that MCC's visit had been a diplomatic success. The Bustamante affair was still rumbling on.

On what proved to be the last day of the series, *The Gleaner* carried a letter written in Hutton's name and Palmer's style, expressing regret that 'an unfortunate impression' had been created and also 'the greatest respect and admiration for the Hon. Mr. Bustamante'. The letter emphasised that Hutton had been 'extremely tired' and completely focused on the cricket. It repeated he simply did not realise Bustamante was present among those congratulating him. Had the England captain been 'forewarned', he would have been 'delighted and honoured', but 'when returning to the pavilion through a mass of applauding spectators a batsman rarely singles out an individual and there is merely an undefined sound ringing pleasantly in his ears'.

The letter was designed to draw a line under the matter. But the English tour management and the English journalists were dissatisfied for several reasons. First, the captain's letter appeared on page eight whereas the report implying Hutton had deliberately snubbed Bustamante had appeared on page one. Second, its wording, the result of careful crafting reportedly approved by the Board of Control, had been sub-editorialised by *The Gleaner* so that it no longer made clear Bustamante had accepted Hutton's apology. Third, a statement from Bustamante was not inserted underneath Hutton's letter, as requested, but reported indirectly: rather than a public declaration from the Chief Minister that he had 'not been offended in any way', he was quoted merely as saying 'no affront was intended'. Instead, Bustamante gave another interview to Ditton which was widely syndicated after the match: 'This tour may not have done any harm. But it hasn't done any good.'

As they prepared to leave the Caribbean, Hutton and Palmer were in damage-limitation mode. They insisted that future tours had not been put in jeopardy by crowd behaviour, and that their recommendation for an umpires' panel was intended to raise standards rather than imply bias.

However, Robin Marlar, the off-spinner overlooked for the tour, was to claim that Hutton bore a lifelong grudge against West Indies over the Bustamante business. Characteristically, the captain's first reason for being annoyed was that it got him out. He could also complain with justification about having his privacy rudely invaded in the dressing room, having to apologise in such a formal way, having that apology manipulated and having it implied that the side he captained had been responsible for a long line of offences. If Jones had compared the English press to Goebbels, Hutton later compared Bustamante's entourage to 'the Gestapo'.

He would also be only human if he felt the 'blatant discourtesy' distracted attention from his almost chanceless double century and the remarkable achievement of coming back from 2-0 down. Hutton certainly rated his innings as one of his very best. Those who witnessed it describe it as 'truly remarkable' (Compton), 'astonishing' (Lock), 'a thing apart' (Swanton). Statham thought it the 'greatest innings' he ever saw, 'played in extreme heat and taxing circumstances'. Palmer remembered a 'tremendous test of character and technique' under the added pressure of a halved series being at stake: 'He knew damn well that unless he got a good score we couldn't do it.' Graveney agreed: 'Never have I seen a man so determined to win a match on his own if necessary.'

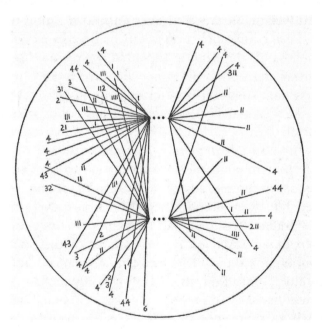

The wagon wheel for Hutton's 205, made off 489 balls in 534 minutes.

Hutton was reading very little about his innings and rather more about his manners. One Kingston CC official had reportedly described him as 'without any background' and the incident could be fitted into the argument of Jones's *Public Opinion* article that old-fashioned gentlemen were better equipped to lead MCC in the West Indies. The *Trinidad Guardian* also noted in its end-of-series review that 'the old bogey of a professional captaining an England touring eleven has reared its head again'. The *Guardian* concluded that Hutton had been the victim of his own press placing too much emphasis on national prestige. However, it published a letter pointing out that 'the vice-captain of the West Indies team is also professional, and yet he has taken charge of his team without the heavens falling in'. This may have overlooked Worrell's role as acting captain in the Laker incident but it reflected a general view in the region that Hutton had put results before sportsmanship.

As for the motivations of Bustamante, he was such a mercurial character that diametrically opposed theories cannot be discounted. Hutton's own local intelligence was that the whole episode was a 'put-up' job. This would tally with the considered view of colonial civil servants that Bustamante would usually choose 'the most flamboyant and exhibitionist' course of action to advance his personal standing. On the other hand, the author Lance Neita, whose home village hosted Saturday afternoon cricket matches which the Chief Minister enjoyed attending, suggests Bustamante's approach to Hutton was more likely the warm and spontaneous gesture of a genuine fan.

It also recalled an occasion in London the previous year. In his 1977 book *The New Elizabethans*, Churchill's private secretary Sir John Colville remembered the Coronation as 'an occasion of loyal Imperial solidarity unmarred by any sign or sound of dissent'. There were, however, some discordant notes. Nehru, the first leader of the Indian Republic, had to spend most of the ceremony in close proximity to Malan, the first leader of the South African Republic under apartheid. The Kenyan delegation stood out as unrepresentative: Jomo Kenyatta, who would be its first leader after independence, had just started a term of seven years' hard labour; his Kenya African Union was proscribed as a terrorist organisation a week after the Queen was crowned.

Bustamante certainly stood out in a group photograph taken with the Queen at a Buckingham Palace reception for Commonwealth Prime Ministers, held two days before the Coronation. He was wearing a grey morning suit between Nehru and Churchill, while everybody else was in black morning suit or national dress. The stranger thing was that he had talked himself into the photograph in the first place. He was the only representative of the colonies of the empire, rather than the independent Dominions of the Commonwealth, to make it into the shot. He looks rather pleased with himself. As well as the tweak to his vanity, he must have been proud of a symbolic coup which promised Jamaica was on the way to being an equal partner, not a loyal subordinate, of the 'mother country'.

Swanton promised to 'long retain' the image of Hutton marching off the field just before the Bustamante incident, with 'West Indies trailing wearily into their tea' behind him. No doubt he intended to treasure this tableau as a souvenir of Hutton's cricketing mastery rather than as an emblem of racial superiority. Nevertheless, Evans thought the comeback 'gave the Europeans in the islands a tremendous fillip', and some expressions of British pride bordered on chauvinism. The company of the flagship of the West Indies squadron, HMS *Sheffield*, and the garrison in Jamaica, the Duke of Cornwall's Light Infantry, are reported as giving England 'vociferous support' throughout the match.

This support will not have been universally welcome given the ongoing military operation in British Guiana. Jagan was arrested on the last day of the series for breaching restrictions on his movement outside Georgetown, and transported to a remote area in the interior for four months. In Jamaica, a campaign had begun for the permanent British military presence to be removed. A magnanimous handshake in this atmosphere, between the leader of an emerging nation and the captain of an imperial institution, had a potential for political symbolism which the English cricketers were not qualified to understand.

Laker was given dispensation to travel back to England by air because of his eye injury and his wife's pregnancy. The rest of the party came back on an old banana boat, the SS *Ariguani*. The same vessel had taken Freddie Calthorpe's MCC team home in 1926. As Bailey observed, the travel arrangements in 1954 were 'the wrong way round': three weeks of close proximity on board ship would have been helpful to team-bonding on the outward trip, but could have proved grating after a long tour.

However, team relations proved smoother than the sea conditions. Lock, whom Graveney recalled turning whiter than his dinner jacket on the first evening, was confined to the cabin he shared with Trueman for three days. Trueman himself did not emerge for a week. But they were up and about in time for a fancy-dress party, where they sprayed Suttle with tomato ketchup as the finishing touch to his prize-fighter outfit.

Moss remembers being popular when he returned home as he had managed to secure an enormous bunch of bananas, then still a luxury in Britain. Trueman was also laden with presents for his family and friends. When the *Ariguani* docked in Avonmouth, Hutton and Palmer had other baggage to attend to. The manager gave the same kind of speech as when he left Jamaica, at pains to make clear that the tour's 'incidents' – a word now held in the tongs of inverted commas – had been 'magnified out of all proportion'. As he and Hutton started writing up their reports of the tour for MCC, they must have worried that its many controversies would overshadow its many achievements.

PART III

THE AFTERMATH

CHAPTER 17

THE TRUEMAN AND BAILEY CONTROVERSIES

In 1964 Fred Trueman became the first bowler in Test history to take 300 wickets. But the autobiography he published the next year began in score-settling as much as celebratory vein: 'The repercussions of my first ill-fated tour to the West Indies in 1953 are still going on. I suppose they always will.' Trueman believed, with some justification, that the measures taken against him then had cost him a chance of taking 400 Test wickets. In his various memoirs, he aired the specific grievance that he was the victim of mistaken identity when accused of swearing, whether in the lift at the Marine Hotel or on the field at Bourda. He bore the deeper grudge that he had been made the 'scapegoat' for the bad behaviour of others and unofficially banned from touring for five years.

Trueman would never renounce his faith in Hutton as the greatest batsman he had seen. Equally, he would never forgive his captain for singling him out as the 'problem child' of the Caribbean tour. He remembered also, after his return home in 1954, hearing 'on good authority, that the big guns of the MCC – Freddie Brown and Gubby Allen, along with Brian Sellers, the Chairman of Yorkshire – decided they were going to sort me out and bring me to heel'.

Allen, now emerging from Warner's shadow as the most powerful figure in the inner circle, was too skilful an operator to leave a trail of incriminating evidence. But it is safe to assume he used his influence in committee, just as his good friend Swanton used his influence in print, to make an example of Trueman. It is also clear that the MCC 'big guns' had more established targets in their sights as they conducted their inquest into the tour. The vice-captain Bailey was unwise enough to provide them with a pretext to bring him to heel as well.

Trueman pursued Hutton on the subject of the West Indies for many years, surprising him in a 1964 television interview by talking about little else. One of the captain's responses was to direct him to the 'official papers at Lord's', fairly safe in the knowledge that they were incomplete. Conversely, one of the most crucial records – of the MCC Cricket Sub-Committee's post-mortem on 25 May 1954 – had been touched up. In the minute-book, an insertion has been pasted over the original entry discussing Hutton's tour report. The MCC secretariat, Aird and Griffith, already possessed a bureaucratic talent for converting the liveliest passages of meetings into the deadest passages of prose. But they covered up whatever they had originally written with the following terse paragraph:

> The reward of £50 for discipline during the tour
> should be given to all the professional cricketers of the
> team with the exception of F. Trueman. This was in
> accordance with the recommendation of the Captain
> [Hutton] and the Manager [Palmer] at the time of their
> interview [on 30 April] with the President [Rosebery]
> and the Treasurer [Altham].

The tour reports of captain and manager were presumably tabled at this earlier interview as well as the Cricket Sub-Committee. Hutton kept a copy of his own report, even if Lord's did not:

> Trueman gave me much concern and until a big
> improvement is made in his general conduct and
> cricket manners I do not think he is suitable for MCC
> Tours, particularly a tour such as the one to the West
> Indies. No captain could wish to have a better trier
> than Trueman. He is very keen and wanted to do
> well, and this was probably responsible for some of
> his aggressive actions on the field. Cricket today does
> require characters and, in Trueman, cricket has got a
> character and ultimately I think something can be done
> with him under capable leadership.

A more disciplinarian captain, such as Brown or Sellers, would have made a less even-handed assessment. Hutton went on to assert that there was 'no vice, envy or jealousy in Trueman'. He was tacitly inviting comparison with Wardle, criticised in the same report for having shown 'jealousy, bitterness and envy' to other members of the team.

However, Hutton made further reference to Trueman's 'aggressive manner', and he must have been aware that the word 'character' would have only negative connotations in an MCC committee room. Trueman was almost certainly right to believe that Hutton and Palmer offered his head on a platter to forestall criticisms of their own failures in man-management. The report's curious reference to Trueman possibly being tractable under 'capable leadership' may simply have been Hutton's understated way of saying he remained the man for the job. But there could be a concession to one of the classic objections to professional captains – that they were too close to the ranks to enforce discipline. As it was, until such distinctions fell away, Trueman never played for England under a professional captain again.

The tampering with the minutes still suggests that, when the Cricket Sub-Committee met, there was some debate, or some confusion, about the specific matter of the good-conduct bonus. As early as 1938, Allen had been arguing in MCC committees for this clause in professional contracts because 'he regarded the behaviour of individuals on tour as more important than their actual playing ability'. He registered the same point with greater vehemence ten years later, after he had led a tour to the West Indies where team spirit was nearly as bad as the team's results. As Allen had already given Palmer his opinion that Trueman was a cause of 'much of the trouble' this time, he was no doubt the strongest advocate in committee for the bonus to be withheld.

In an interview with Chris Waters, Trueman's friend Bob Platt recalled: 'Fred never got over being docked his bonus. He used to say, "some players on that tour were shagging the blacks and all I did was fucking swear."' This may have raised a laugh in the working men's clubs where Trueman would later perform stand-up comedy, but he underestimated the impact of his industrial language at a gentlemen's club in Marylebone.

Just after Trueman had blazed onto the Test scene in the summer of 1952, Colonel Rowan Rait-Kerr, Aird's predecessor as MCC secretary, felt compelled to send letters to the Yorkshire captain Yardley and an influential member of the Yorkshire committee, Clifford Hesketh:

> It was mentioned to me first by Admiral Norris, who is Chairman of the Combined Services Cricket Association at a luncheon party attended by the First Lord of the Admiralty, several Sea Lords and members of the Air Council and Army Council. Admiral Norris said that he had never thought that he would live to have a complaint lodged by one of the Indian Touring Team during the Combined Services match at Chatham to the effect that the Indian players felt perfectly disgusted with Trueman's language.

Rait-Kerr was one of the more avuncular members of the Lord's hierarchy and on the verge of retirement. But his initial reaction here was visceral for two reasons: disquiet was being registered in the most 'responsible circles' (in other words the very highest ranks) and those circles were experiencing the exquisite embarrassment of being dressed down by former colonial subalterns (Rait-Kerr once told a fellow administrator 'I can't stand educated Indians').

After Yorkshire gave Trueman what amounted to a verbal warning, the Colonel softened his tone in a second letter to Hesketh, accepting that 'the boy' was possibly not 'conscious of any undesirable adornment he might be giving to his conversation'. But he still felt Trueman was 'swollen-headed', precisely the term Allen had used for Voce and Larwood on the Bodyline tour.

Whether or not Allen took over Rait-Kerr's file, he took it upon himself to monitor Trueman's congenital swearing going forwards. In 1961, he embroiled Herbert Sutcliffe in a punctilious inquiry as to whether Trueman had said 'fucker' or 'bugger' to an opposing batsman. Five years earlier, Doug Insole witnessed an argument in which 'Fred was going "fucking Gubby Allen this and fucking Gubby Allen that"'. Trueman had exploded when Allen asked him to land the ball on a handkerchief in a public net session at Headingley. The relationship between the two men would always be strained by what Hutton called Allen's 'specially keen, almost paternal, interest in all fast bowlers'. It was also marked by a titanic clash of snobbery and bolshiness.

As a successful chairman of selectors later in the 1950s, Allen managed this clash effectively enough to accommodate Trueman, even though it was his general policy to 'eliminate' players he considered 'prima donnas'. But in 1954 he was convinced that the disaster in the West Indies might have been avoided 'had Trueman not been a member of the team'. Not coincidentally, Swanton concluded in *West Indian Adventure* that 'I would not be happy to see his name again in a touring team'. Both men were doing their best to eliminate him from the tour to Australia.

As early as 31 May, the main MCC Committee resolved that any consideration of Trueman's 'eligibility' for Australia should be delayed until further reports on him were received from Yardley. The selection sub-committee, on which Yardley still sat in any case, met the next week to draw up its primary list of players to be sent availability letters. This list included all those chosen in the first tranche of the previous year's party to the West Indies – except Trueman. After the next meeting, on 14 July, two more availability letters were sent to fast bowlers. The minutes include a rather perverse entry: 'It was decided ... that, at present, no letter on availability be sent to F. Trueman. This, however, would not exclude F. Trueman from consideration for selection.' The plot thickened at the last meeting of 25 July, where Hutton joined the committee to finalise the tour party: 'The Chairman [Altham] reported that he had informed the Yorkshire Committee to assume at their meeting that a letter of availability had been sent to F. Trueman.'

To borrow a Truemanism, it is difficult to know what was 'going off'. Perhaps there had been an about-turn – Hutton insists he argued in favour of his county colleague – and Trueman had been sent a letter, care of the Yorkshire secretary John Nash. Perhaps Sellers was colluding with MCC to convey the impression that Trueman had been treated as fairly as other candidates. The bowler's own recollection was that Nash 'came to me and confessed that the MCC had in fact asked if I was available for that tour, but that he had forgotten to tell me'. This does not quite square with the formal request Yorkshire made later in the summer that it should in future receive copies of any reports on its players by MCC captains or managers. Perhaps Lord's was simply trying to keep Headingley quiet by telling them to 'assume' Trueman's availability had been checked out.

In any event, Trueman's supporters had a fair idea that he was not going to make the boat. One Yorkshire correspondent made an obvious reference to his case when complaining that certain candidates for Australia had been 'smeared with gossip that they are not good tourists'. A week before the team announcement, Altham took the unusual step of denying that Trueman would be excluded for non-cricketing reasons: 'This is completely new to me. There is absolutely no foundation for such a suggestion.' He also dismissed as 'absolute and complete nonsense' rumours that other players would refuse to tour should Trueman be selected.

When Trueman was duly omitted, his supporters found these protestations impossible to believe. The Yorkshire papers, and the *Herald* and *Mirror* in London, launched a concerted campaign against the hypocrisy of MCC. E.M. Wellings of the *Evening News* – himself prone to emotional outbursts – felt this became 'hysterical'. But the semi-official account of the selection process which appeared in *The Cricketer* undermined Altham's categorical assurances:

> Statham and Loader, after the recent Gentlemen and
> Players match at Lord's, were obvious choices, and if
> the non-inclusion of Trueman has caused murmurings
> in some quarters it must be remembered that selectors
> have information and facts at their disposal which
> are not available to the general public, and though
> Selection Committees in the past have made mistakes –
> as they probably always will make – it is certain that on
> this occasion every avenue of form and temperament
> was closely examined and closely debated.

The piece is signed off 'VIATOR', a touch as pure Pelham Warner as the rest of it. The Latin for 'traveller' was appropriate for an article on an overseas tour but also sought to establish the credentials of an author who, from an early age, was able to argue that 'as I have played all over the world I think I am entitled to an opinion'.

It is characteristic that the Gentlemen v Players trial is treated as infallible, that strong objections to a decision Warner approved are portrayed as 'murmurings', that the selectors are praised for being impeccably thorough and unimpeachably fair-minded and that 'temperament' is considered just as important as form. Hutton would certainly have endorsed the last sentiment. But, in his lexicon, temperament simply meant the ability to win high-pressure matches, whereas in Warner's it also had the connotations of good breeding and bearing. Warner had in fact once been a great enthusiast for Trueman, repeatedly pestering Hutton to play him in the Ashes series at home: 'He has Fire in him & has a Lions heart.' But the fire had become a little too hot for Warner to handle given the 'information and facts' accumulating in the MCC dossiers on Trueman dating back to 1952.

If selection had been based solely on the national averages of 1954, Trueman would have gone. Statham, Loader, Jackson and Bedser were the only fast bowlers fractionally above him, and he took more wickets than any of them. Reports circulated that Hutton and Yardley had supported him, and that he had lost out in a vote of the selection committee by a margin of just one. On the other hand, Altham always insisted that if Hutton had really wanted Trueman in Australia he could have had him. Hutton was probably content to leave Trueman behind given the risks to his captaincy if the problems of the West Indies were repeated. But we can be certain which side Allen took if it came to a show of hands. When MCC was searching for a late replacement for the 'A' tour to Pakistan in 1955/56, the relevant selection committee decided, 'after very full discussion', to extend an invitation to Trueman. There was a lone dissenting voice: 'Mr G.O. Allen expressed his disagreement with this recommendation.'

Trueman was not the only controversial omission. The party for Australia was announced in a single tranche, apparently at the initiative of Robins, on the last day of a round of county matches in late July. Surrey were playing Kent at Blackheath. Lock was so upset to learn he was not included that he could not bear the commiserations of his teammates. He rushed to his car and drove home in desolation: 'I had so hoped to go that the news knocked all the stuffing out of me.'

Lock had been a *Wisden* Cricketer of the Year in 1954 with 'a career full of possibilities before him'. He no doubt suffered by association as Trueman's roommate in the West Indies, and was later at pains to point out that he had not been docked his good-conduct bonus 'in spite of the stories you might have heard to the contrary'. More immediately, Lock responded by taking 49 wickets in the last ten Championship matches to help Surrey to another title. His superb form after the tour party was announced prompted some London pressmen to hope he might receive a late call-up, even if this was as unrealistic as the Sheffield journalist Frank Stainton's suggestion that 'informed public opinion' might force the selectors into a U-turn on Trueman.

Hutton justified both decisions in his retirement memoirs by pointing out that Trueman had averaged 46 in the West Indies and Lock 51. In his eyes, both of them had fluffed their trial runs: 'Conditions in Australia were expected to be almost identical to those in the West Indies and the Selection Committee considered Trueman and Lock hardly likely to improve on these figures.' Wickets had been covered in the Caribbean and – for the first time – they would be covered in Australia. With no prospect of gluepots, Hutton wanted bowlers who could offer batsmen a challenge, when the pacemen were resting, without much assistance from the pitch. Both Wardle and Bob Appleyard, in their different ways, offered him two bowlers in one. Wardle reportedly practised three hours a day on-deck during the passage to Australia – bowling wrist-spin not finger-spin.

The Blackheath CC car park was a busy place after the announcement of the tour party. Cowdrey, highly surprised to learn he had been selected, chose to make a brisk getaway given that the atmosphere when he walked past the Surrey dressing room 'could have been cut into cubes and sold as solid fuel'. Laker had been left behind as well. His replacement, Glamorgan's Jim McConnon, is now remembered, when he is remembered at all, for not being Jim Laker. At the time, he had just bowled well against Pakistan and it seems some of the selectors felt he might be better suited to Australian conditions. Hutton later claimed to be 'very unhappy' about the decision, as he had argued for Laker's inclusion. But one of Graveney's favourite after-dinner anecdotes suggests he did not argue very hard:

313

On the West Indian tour of 1953/54 we were sitting round a table, Brian Statham, Jim Laker, myself and Len. Len asked Brian if he wanted to go to Australia the next year. 'Well, of course I do', he said. Then Len asked me the same thing. 'I've never been', I said, 'and it's the pinnacle of cricket to go on a tour of Australia. I'd love to go.' Then he turned to Jim and he said: 'Have a drink, Jim?'

If this story has not been overembellished it provides another example of Hutton's insensitive management of men he deemed surplus to requirements. His tour report described Laker as having an 'inferiority complex' and 'a tendency to be afraid' of certain batsmen, recommending that the off-spinner 'should be considered in committee before future selection for overseas tours'. In view of Laker's superb long spell in the heat of Jamaica, with a sore spinning finger and a plaster over his eye, this assessment seemed particularly unfair.

It seemed as unfair that Wardle would be on the boat, given that the captain's report had recommended his case should also be 'discussed in committee' because of his 'embarrassing' behaviour. Perhaps a sense of Hutton's priorities can be found in the list he drew up in 1956 of players with the right Test-match temperament, a list where Wardle is present and Laker is absent. Perhaps also, as several England players later suggested, Hutton had not been able to forgive Laker for moving to Surrey.

With some irony, the Surrey bowler who had been rested for the West Indies caused Hutton his biggest headache in Australia. Bedser never quite recovered from a debilitating attack of shingles early in the tour. But the decision not to bring him back for the crucial third Test at Melbourne, where he had enjoyed great success in the past, was as big a shock as Hutton's own omission in 1948. The captain's psychosomatic collapse on the morning of the game, when he sat in his hotel bed staring at the wall insisting he was too ill to play, may have resulted in part from the accumulated pressures of being a professional captain. But the main cause was his inability to break bad news to Bedser, lending some credence to the inner circle's belief that amateur leaders were innately better equipped for man-management.

Even after Hutton had been persuaded to come to the ground by a delegation of senior players, he still let Bedser inspect the MCG pitch. A yeoman servant of England, accustomed to being the first name on the teamsheet, was left to find out from the teamsheet itself that he was not playing. Arlott thought Bedser was 'too great a cricketer to be treated in this way'. Hutton might point out that his dilemma sprang precisely from his empathy with a comrade who had stood alongside him in so many losing battles against Australia. He could also point out that England won the match.

It remains astonishing that not one of the great quartet of bowlers who had brought home the Ashes at The Oval in 1953 – Bedser, Laker, Lock and Trueman – would play in the three Tests in Australia which were won to retain them in 1954/55.

The only constants in the English bowling attack on the tours of 1953/54 and 1954/55 were therefore Statham and Bailey. On his return from the West Indies, Bailey's place in the side had never been more secure. He may also have been forgiven for thinking that he was favourite to be next England captain when the time came – and that moment seemed to be drawing closer given Hutton's frequent absences through injury in the summer of 1954.

Indeed, when the need for a stand-in skipper against Pakistan became clear in July, *The Times* thought Bailey was 'most likely to be chosen' because he had proved a 'wise and successful counseller' to several previous captains. Bannister had described him as Hutton's 'able lieutenant' in the West Indies; Hutton's own end-of-term report had praised him as 'every captain's ideal – responsive, perceptive, a tactical move ahead'. In MCC's press statement after the series had been squared, Aird felt the vice-captain deserved 'particular mention'. Laker pointed out that Bailey had done 'an excellent job' as MCC skipper when Hutton was resting. Bailey led MCC again against the Pakistanis at Lord's in May and received good reviews. Relatively attacking declarations and sympathetic handling of the amateur spinner Marlar would normally have appealed to patrician taste.

However, during this very game Bailey felt compelled to write a five-page letter on Lord's headed paper to Aird. He was trying to explain an article which had recently appeared under his byline in *The People*, the first in a series of six to promote his autobiography, *Playing to Win*. The problem with the article was its references to 'incidents' in the Caribbean. There was a long-standing convention, enshrined in professional contracts, that members of MCC touring parties were not allowed to make any public comment on a series until 12 months had elapsed, unless prior permission had been granted by Lord's.

The edict had been framed, reasonably enough, in response to two amateurs on the 1920/21 tour of Australia cabling back controversial articles on games in which they had just played. It can also be likened to the Fourteen Day Rule (not removed until 1957) which prohibited any discussion on BBC airwaves of matters up for debate in Parliament. Bailey's letter marks the beginning of a disciplinary process which rumbled on for the first half of the summer. The Bailey controversy provides a study of a modern cricketer failing to juggle his outside interests very efficiently and an ancient club very efficiently prosecuting – even relishing – its prefectorial role.

Bailey's elaborate self-defence in his letter to Aird suggests that he already sensed the matter would go as far as the headmaster's study. The original title of his *People* piece was 'The Australians in the West Indies'. The intention had been to describe what the next tourists to the Caribbean 'might be expected to encounter'. Bailey insisted that he had taken 'a great deal of time' to ensure that any allusions to what MCC had recently endured 'did not offend against the clause in the contract of Professional players relating to not writing on a tour until a certain time had elapsed'. He had telephoned Robins 'to ask whether in his opinion a certain sentence was likely to offend anyone'. He also had the article checked over by his county captain Insole before he posted it off to the newspaper from Cambridge, where Essex had been playing the University.

To Bailey's 'surprise and indignation', when his agent phoned him on the Friday evening before publication and read out the galley proofs, the changes from his manuscript were so numerous, including a reference 'tantamount to calling a West Indian player illegitimate', that he felt the article had been 'fundamentally changed' without his consent. His initial reaction was to forbid publication. He then tried to correct proofs himself at Chalkwell Park, his local

316

ground in Westcliff-on-Sea, where Essex were convening for their next Championship match against Derbyshire. Finding this solution unsatisfactory, he then listened over the telephone to his agent's efforts to fashion a compromise text. Bailey finally decided to issue an ultimatum to the newspaper's editor stating that 'he must either print my original article or *nothing at all*'.

The next morning no such undertaking was received. Bailey contacted Lord's in order to give prior warning that an article would be appearing under his name that was 'not in fact entirely my own work'. He discussed various courses of action with his county secretary and chairman before they persuaded him to go out to bat against Derbyshire (c Dawkes b Gladwin 48). Griffith rang back from Lord's while Bailey was at the crease to suggest the intervention of the Press Council, although it was eventually decided that this course of action 'might do more harm than good'.

Aird's first response to Bailey is no longer on file but his next, taking the 'gravest view' of the article, shows that MCC never really believed Bailey's story, especially as he could not produce his original manuscript because it had been 'destroyed in the routine way' by his agent. Bailey may have had genuine grounds to complain about the embellishments of *The People*'s sports desk but, as he confessed years later, he had asked his journalist brother Basil to 'spice up' the text before he submitted it.

A copy of the published article survives in the Lord's archives. The mark-ups in blue ink (presumably made by Aird) of potentially offending passages total 107 lines out of 276, nearly two-fifths of the whole piece. This was an overreaction – the final text contained no controversial references to any individual – but the tabloid style and headline undeniably tended towards the melodramatic: 'DRAMA ON THE CRICKET FIELD BY THE IRON MAN OF THE TEST MATCHES: Black eyes, bottles and such excitement!'

Bailey was duly summoned for an 'interview' at Lord's with Warner and Altham. Aird, as always, was in attendance. At this meeting, held during the first Test against Pakistan, Bailey seems to have mounted the technical defence that he was not legally bound by the clause he was supposed to have breached. Amateurs were merely provided a copy of the contract the professionals signed, with the tacit understanding that they would also abide by its terms.

Bailey left the interview under the impression that it had 'cleared up the matter'. This may simply have been wishful thinking – Aird immediately closed any loophole by drafting 'a special form of Agreement' for amateurs. But it does seem that someone at MCC, perhaps Altham, decided to study Bailey's autobiography at more leisure after the meeting.

Bailey's comments on the West Indies tour in *Playing to Win* were not sensational and now seem remarkably prescient. On the subject of umpiring, he suggested 'neutral officials for all Tests, as is customary for international soccer'. On negative bowling, he proposed a 'limit to the number of fielders one can place on the leg side'. On the 'colour question', he stressed that the only cricketing criterion should be 'one's ability as a player', expressing the hope that Worrell might graduate from the vice-captaincy to become 'the first man of his race to be chosen for this difficult and exalted post'.

But for MCC the simple fact such issues had been discussed in the same year as the tour was a disciplinary matter. Furthermore, Aird was able to dig out correspondence proving that Bailey had twice explicitly promised to have proofs of *Playing to Win* cleared by Lord's before publication. All the player could produce in his defence was an apology from his brother, who 'forgot' to follow his instructions to do so in the 'rush' of finalising the text, and the argument that his reflections, restricted to 'cricket conditions', did not risk bringing the game into disrepute. Sir Hubert Ashton MP, president of Essex, had become involved in the controversy and best summarised why MCC felt it had an open and shut case:

> We found it a little difficult to get into Trevor Bailey's
> mind that he had given a categorical undertaking in
> two places to show what he wrote about the West
> Indies Tour before publication, entirely irrespective of
> what he might have written. In other words, even had
> there been no reference to cricket but only to bathing
> beauties he had this obligation.

The main MCC Committee met on 21 June. Aird wrote a letter the next day, addressed to 'Trevor' not 'Bailey' in recognition of amateur status, but in the tone the secretary usually reserved for errant professionals. The committee had found it 'difficult to reconcile' the story about *The People*'s interventions 'with the fact that much of the material contained in the article is also contained in the Chapter in your book on cricket in the West Indies'. Bailey was therefore in clear contravention of the relevant clause in the professional contract which he 'undertook to observe' when accepting the invitation to tour. Aird reminded Bailey that he had also undertaken, 'so that we might be quite sure your own interests were protected', to pre-clear his autobiography: 'Had you carried out your promise in this respect, I am quite sure that the MCC Committee would have asked you to delete several paragraphs.' Although he asked Bailey if 'there is anything further you wish me to tell the Committee', Aird made it reasonably clear what would happen at its next meeting: 'You will I am sure realise that there is no point laying down conditions for those who accept invitations to tour with MCC teams abroad unless those conditions are carried out and unless some action is taken if and when the conditions are not carried out.'

The moment Bailey read this letter, he must have known that he would never captain his country. Ashton, who had been copied in, enjoyed giving Aird an account of Bailey's angry reaction: 'I may say that in the course of our conversation at one time he said that if the MCC were anxious to see something really controversial he would be quite prepared to write it' (here Ashton adds an exclamation mark in lurid green biro to his typed text). Bailey was too proud a man to sign off on the grovelling apology which Ashton helped prepare for him. Instead, he confined himself to an admission that he should have pre-cleared the proofs of his book and that 'a difference of opinion' could arise as a result of its contents.

When Bailey lost his temper with Ashton he may already have heard the news, announced on the same day, that David Sheppard would stand in for Hutton as captain in the second Pakistan Test. Jack Bailey (county teammate but no relation) was in the Essex dressing room at this moment, and remembered it being immediately 'apparent' that the appointment of a man five years younger was 'a slap in the teeth' which 'would take him some time to absorb'. Trevor's immediate response was to skip an Essex game and take his wife on a long weekend to Paris. According to Jack, he was 'most reluctant' to talk about the matter again.

With a punctiliousness bordering on vindictiveness, Aird encouraged his superiors to take a further disciplinary measure by enquiring whether Bailey should be ruled out of consideration for the upcoming Gentlemen v Players match. In the event he was selected, even if he again had to play under Sheppard. Sheppard's special circumstances, described in the next chapter, meant he was prepared to serve as captain in Australia but not as vice-captain. Bailey may therefore have clung to the hope that he was still under consideration for that role.

But Ashton, in particular, was energetically canvassing against a candidate who 'does not seem to improve a great deal as he grows older'. He was most put out by Bailey's failure to thank him 'in any way' for his 'considerable trouble'. In a letter to Aird of 17 July, he asked the MCC Committee to consult him before making any decision about Bailey's suitability for the vice-captaincy in Australia. That body, in its meeting of 19 July, did not accept Bailey's explanations and formally stripped him of the vice-captaincy, instructing the selectors to 'bear in mind the claims of Youth and future requirements'. This directed the relevant sub-committees, meeting later the same day, straight to Peter May. It was only after the announcement of the tour party, with May as vice-captain, that Bailey saw fit to send a brief apology to Aird 'for any trouble which my actions may have occasioned'.

This last, curt letter from Bailey began by registering the fact he was 'most disappointed'. It must have been difficult for him to concentrate on his cricket for England that summer. The Test reports for *The Cricketer*, written by Bowes, noted that he continued to 'play the part of a first-rate team man'. Bowes praised Bailey's 'complete self-effacement' in giving the double-centurion Compton nearly all the strike in the second Test at Trent Bridge; then his unselfishness as a 'utility player' when he opened in place of the injured Simpson in the third Test at Old Trafford.

It would be fascinating to know what, if anything, Sheppard and Bailey said to each other as they walked out to bat at Manchester. Spin-friendly wickets may also help explain why Sheppard saw fit to give Bailey only three overs during the course of the two matches under his watch. But Bailey clearly sublimated some of his crushing disappointment into an active dislike of Sheppard, which seeped out in his final set of memoirs published in 1986. He claimed that Sheppard was a 'somewhat intolerant' captain 'who plainly believed in ruling by divine right'. He further asserted that the Cambridge side Sheppard led in 1952 was 'certainly the most unpopular since the war' because of the 'overliberal' use of bouncers and beamers which Sheppard allegedly encouraged. While accepting that Sheppard had 'much to offer the game', Bailey also lamented his inclusion on the 1962/63 tour to Australia, implying that he made himself available only for the 'extra publicity' it would garner: 'It must help in the ecclesiastical profession to be a bishop who is known to the general public.'

Bailey is one of the few people to say a recorded bad word about Sheppard. His sarcastic remarks about the prelate's infallibility may redirect his regret at his own folly. The captaincy had been within sight, but he had chosen to sail in dangerous water. Under the prevailing regulations, Aird was merely doing his job by pursuing the matter.

Yet by modern standards Bailey's comments on the tour were innocuous. MCC was wrong in its assertion that 'much of the material' in the article overlapped with the book, and even the article was much less controversial than the ghosted material which saw Wardle banished from the tour to Australia in 1958 and Laker stripped of his honorary MCC membership two years later.

MCC could be accused of hypocrisy as well as overreaction. For decades Warner had managed to combine a central role in the framing of laws and the selection of teams with contemporaneous output as a journalist for *The Morning Post* and *The Cricketer*. But he only came near a disciplinary committee as one of the disciplinarians. When Robins went on television during the 1953 Ashes series, to make the fanciful claim that Don Kenyon was solely Hutton's choice as opener, Griffith fielded complaints from Yorkshire by arguing that the former captain was appearing 'purely as a private individual' and not 'representing or speaking on behalf of MCC'.

There is an inescapable sense of an old-boy network using Bailey's indiscretion as a pretext to bring him down a peg. Aird may have involved Sir Hubert Ashton simply because he was Essex president. But the two men, both awarded the Military Cross, were also members of the same gentlemen's club, the Oriental, where it is possible to imagine them conspiring over a glass of port. It was natural for Ashton, a Winchester captain, to have what he called 'a word' with Altham, a Winchester master, about the Bailey affair as they watched the school's match against Eton together. Altham would later nominate Ashton as his successor as MCC president.

Ashton's caricature of Bailey as arrogant and ungrateful may have been coloured by the belief that he got to public school and Cambridge only as the result of helpful patronage and sports scholarships. Not even Griffith, who had been Bailey's housemaster at Dulwich College, came to his aid, stating in an autumn memo to Aird that the all-rounder 'never seems to be able to lose an opportunity to have a dig at somebody or something'.

A series of other associations reinforced the inner circle's sense of Bailey as 'not quite', none of which will have helped his cause given they wanted heads to roll for the conduct of the West Indies tour. First, while Dulwich had at least the same prestige as Sheppard's Sherborne, it was not quite in the first rank of great public schools. For the many golfers in the MCC hierarchy, Dulwich may have had connotations of P.G. Wodehouse but also of Henry Cotton (educated at Alleyn's, the sister school to the College). Cotton was not quite forgiven for making professionalism respectable in English golf.

Second, Essex was perhaps not quite one of the Home Counties. For Warner in particular, always an admirer of professionals who played like amateurs – Hobbs (Surrey), Woolley (Kent), Hendren (Middlesex) – the Essex connection will have reminded him of the dour and bruising J.W.H.T. Douglas, an amateur who certainly played like a professional. Douglas became England captain when Warner fell ill in 1911/12; once Warner recovered, he spent a good deal of energy seeking to undermine an all-rounder whose default stroke was a prototype of Bailey's famous forward defensive.

Third, as Jack Bailey relates, his namesake was perceived by many at MCC to have the 'faint shadow of Douglas Jardine' about him. Bailey was not fast enough to bowl Bodyline but he had become the most notorious English exponent of negative leg-theory. The very title of the book which had caused the trouble, *Playing to Win*, encapsulated an attitude which was not welcomed by an inner circle still wedded to the cult of the English gentleman.

Fourth, and here the analogy would be with another Surrey captain Percy Fender, Bailey had a reputation for using his fame as a cricketer to pursue every possible journalistic and commercial opportunity. Mostly this was for his own benefit – and Lord's never forgot Bailey's leading role in getting the amateur allowance increased for the 1950/51 tour of Australia. But Bailey had also carefully researched the football-pools scheme successfully introduced to county clubs by Worcestershire (an idea Palmer took with him when he left Worcester for Leicester). Ashton, a religious man opposed to anything approximating gambling, blocked all attempts to introduce such a scheme at Essex against Bailey's advice.

The final factor is that Allen and Bailey appear to have developed a strong mutual dislike. Bailey characterised the management set-up in the West Indies as a typical MCC arrangement: 'Gubby Allen at his absolute worst, and his best wasn't very good.' Ever competitive, Bailey may have first formed an aversion after fielding as an undergraduate to Allen's highest first-class score. He was finally awarded an lbw decision once Allen had made 180. But the main clash was of attitudes. Allen's relentless campaigns against defensive tactics, whether leg-theory, time-wasting or unenterprising batting, often seemed to have Bailey as their implicit target. As late as 1961, in a first-class captains' meeting, Bailey remained something of a lone voice: 'He felt we must face the fact that there were inherent weaknesses in the game and, on occasions, the game must inevitably be dull – in fact, it sometimes paid to play dull cricket.' It is not hard to decipher whom he was asking to face these facts. The role of Allen, as so often, is impossible to substantiate but also impossible to discount in the decision to send Bailey back to the ranks.

Some argued, as Bailey was already squeezing every last droplet out of his ability, that the additional burden of captaincy would have placed impossible pressures upon his individual form. But Bailey was such a redoubtable character that he would probably have found the challenge invigorating (like Illingworth or Greig) rather than inhibiting (like Botham or Flintoff). The sad fact is that we shall never know. Hutton certainly regretted the trivial reasons for which his vice-captain in the West Indies lost the opportunity to succeed him: 'It was a real pity Bailey dropped out in this way for he would have been a strong leader with many ideas.' As a very different character, Ted Dexter, put it: 'He remains the England captain manqué.'

CHAPTER 18

THE CONSPIRACY AGAINST HUTTON

The mandarins of Lord's had been in the habit of praising captains who had come home from MCC tours as gallant losers. Warner, for example, had commended Brown for returning 'with all the honours of war' in 1951 and went so far as to compare him to the Confederate General Robert Lee. The silence from the inner circle in 1954, after one of the greatest comebacks in Test history, was pointed. We have to turn to Alan Gibson, a mordant observer of what he called the 'Old Guard', for what they may have been saying in private: 'Precisely, said those still suspicious of professional captaincy. Told you so. Disaster. Lost a Dominion, near enough.'

The British territories in the West Indies were all still colonies, not yet sufficiently autonomous to be granted 'Dominion' status. But Gibson was alluding to the remark attributed to Rockley Wilson, Jardine's cricket master at Winchester, when he heard his erstwhile pupil had been made captain to Australia: 'We may well win the Ashes, but we may very well lose a Dominion.' Like Jardine before him, Hutton was felt to have brought the name of MCC into disrepute. In Swanton's assessment, his players 'did not manage to leave behind the sort of memories that a visiting side from the United Kingdom must be expected to leave'.

As we have seen, some of the most powerful members of the Lord's hierarchy were still haunted by the memories of Bodyline. Allen was convinced that 1953/54 would have been less reminiscent of 1932/33 'had Len been persuaded that a bloody battle did not necessarily involve a lack of courtesy'. Palmer recalled 'there were one or two people who made you feel that you had your head on the chopping block and they just wanted to see how the axe was going to be wielded'. There can be little doubt that Hutton's feeling 'run down, and rather dispirited' during the early summer of 1954 was attributable more to his sense of having his neck measured up than the fact that his back was playing up.

MCC fired its first shot across Hutton's bows the day before he took the banana boat home. Its main Committee approved in the playing conditions for 1954 measures discouraging leg-theory and slow over-rates. MCC was forever tinkering in search of the holy grail of 'brighter cricket' but it is not coincidental that these two blots on the modern game were pet hates of Allen, who was particularly exercised by their deployment in the West Indies. One dynamic of the campaigns against Hutton and Bailey was a projection of MCC's anxieties about the county game onto selection of the international team.

The other dynamic was the damage to cricket – and the embarrassment to MCC – caused by the tour's diplomatic incidents. Also on the MCC Committee's agenda was correspondence from dos Santos. This letter is missing from the archive, but it no doubt repeated the observations in the letter Lord's had previously received from Nunes. From MCC's perspective, having West Indians complain about English sportsmanship was rather like having Indians complain about Trueman's language. Swanton hit the nail on the head in a Home Service broadcast on his return from the Caribbean: 'The West Indians are sometimes considered rather temperamental customers on the cricket field, but in this series the temperament came from England.'

MCC decided that Hutton and Palmer, 'on their return', should be summoned to Lord's to discuss the 'contents' of the dos Santos letter with the Earl of Rosebery (MCC president), Altham (the newly installed chairman of selectors) and Aird. This debrief took place on 30 April, the eve of the season's curtain-raiser between MCC and Yorkshire. The only record of it is the recommendation that Trueman's good-conduct bonus be withheld. Although Hutton was reported to have met the selectors after his game finished on 4 May, it was apparently left to Palmer alone – for whatever reason – to face questioning from the main MCC Committee the next day. A letter from Allen to Palmer congratulating him on his performance confirms the impression that the knives were out:

> You had to take a section of the committee which was, and I know what I am talking about, very hostile to the events of last winter and were looking for any slip on

your part which would help their case. You were so very clear and forthright in your answers that they got absolutely nowhere.

'And I know what I am talking about' – Allen justifies his reputation as a consummate committee-man in the very act of playing up to it, because there is every reason to believe his sympathies lay with the hostile section. Palmer was something of a protégé and so Allen came to the self-serving conclusion that the problems of the tour had arisen not because the manager was the wrong man, but because he had been given the wrong remit – and possibly the wrong captain.

Yet there is something of a double meaning in Allen's private question to Palmer: 'Do you think a manager on a rather higher level is a solution and indeed a worthwhile proposition, especially if Len is to captain?' Here Allen was germinating the idea of managing Hutton himself in Australia, even if the precedent of Warner managing Jardine was inauspicious. As it turned out, on the premise that there were interesting investment opportunities in Australia, Allen did secure permission from his stockbroking firm to go out for some of that winter.

It did not take long for a trial balloon of the inner circle to be floated in public. On 10 May, Charles Bray reported 'a certain amount of witch-hunting going on at Lord's' with regard to the West Indies tour. He still felt Hutton was 'odds-on' for Australia but approved of the 'definite action' he heard Lord's was now determined to take. Bray's understanding was that MCC would appoint a 'Big Boss' as manager, to enforce discipline and relieve the captain of all off-field cares: 'G.O. Allen immediately comes to mind.' Is it too convenient to conclude that G.O. Allen was Bray's immediate source?

By that time, Hutton had been confirmed, on 6 May, as captain for the first Test against Pakistan. There was nothing necessarily sinister in his appointment for only one game. Such limitation of tenure was, as Ian Peebles put it, 'customary' for home Test matches. It is difficult to piece together every selectorial communiqué but C.B. Fry (in the special circumstances of the Triangular Tournament of 1912) may have been the only England captain so far that century to have secured a guarantee in advance that he would be in place for an entire summer. Hutton had been appointed on a Test-by-Test basis in both previous home seasons.

However, just a week after Bray reported the plan to appoint a high-powered manager, he produced a more sensational scoop: 'A behind the scenes campaign has been launched to persuade young David Sheppard to return to big-time cricket for a limited period.' Sheppard was presumed lost to the international game because of his decision to become a church minister. But, if prepared to change his mind, he was an obvious figure around whom the anti-Hutton faction could coalesce. When his captaincy credentials were appraised against those of the two amateurs guaranteed a place in the team, he was less uncompromising than Bailey and more experienced than May.

Sheppard was clear about the reason he was first sounded out: 'There had been some unhappy moments on the West Indies tour, and some blamed the captain Hutton for these.' According to Bray, 'very influential members of the MCC' were now supporting his candidature. Warner confided to Menzies that he 'told them' Hutton was no leader after the West Indies. It may have been entirely coincidental that *The Cricketer* ran several features on captaincy in the spring of 1954, including the serialisation of an earlier Warner essay opining that 'an eleven is the reflex of its leader, as is a company or a battalion, and even higher formations'. The same issue carried an article on leadership by Glamorgan's Wilf Wooller paying tribute to Robins as 'a great psychologist'.

In the rejig of the home selection committee which had seen Altham replace Brown as chairman, Robins, a natural antagonist of Hutton, replaced Wyatt, a natural supporter. Robins has often been seen as the ringleader of the attempt to depose Hutton, Gibson asserting that he 'seems to have acted, not for the first or last time, with an indiscretion that was almost light-headed'. He was certainly a Sheppard fan, taking great lengths as chairman of selectors in 1962 to tempt him back to Test cricket, just as Allen, when chairman in 1956, brought Sheppard back into the team for Laker's match at Old Trafford.

When Sheppard himself felt he could be more 'indiscreet' with the passage of time, he preferred to emphasise that 'Errol Holmes made much of the running'. For Sheppard, Holmes was 'one of the old brigade who thought that leadership should be a matter for the amateur, first, last and all the time'. Furthermore, Holmes was 'a natural backstairs intriguer' and had 'infected' Aird with the feeling that a change was immediately required. There was not much love lost between Holmes and Robins in the mid-1930s, given their rival claims to the England captaincy and some unsavoury incidents in Surrey v Middlesex games. But they may have become allies in the common cause of defending the principle of amateur leadership. They could also share anecdotes of being barracked by Yorkshire supporters.

'Who killed Cock Robin?' sang the Tykes who had come to The Oval in 1937, after Robins challenged Sellers to a one-off end-of-season game and lost by an innings, Hutton scoring a century. Holmes remembered the catcalls of the Bramall Lane crowd after Hutton had been dropped in 1948: ''Ere 'e cooms', 'Call thesel' a selector?' 'Where's 'Utton?' Then their delight when Ron Aspinall hit him on the backside second ball: '"How's thee feeling now?"' I heard, and something about turning the other cheek flashed across my mind.' And then 'pandemonium' breaking loose when he was dismissed for a pair, Hutton taking a fine catch off Wardle in the second innings. Although Holmes told the story wittily against himself, he and Robins perhaps combined resentment towards the north with a degree of envy towards Hutton.

The first phase of what Sheppard called a 'cloak-and-dagger' operation was a 'conspiratorial' approach by Aird, who took care the new candidate would not be seen anywhere near the MCC office:

> I got various mysterious messages from him,
> including one that I should come to a meeting at
> his house when, he said, 'I will leave the door open
> so that you can come straight in without too much
> chance of recognition.'

No doubt Aird was initially tasked with finding out whether Sheppard, who had suggested he might play 12 games for Sussex in the summer holiday, was actually available for the winter. Sheppard broke down the question into two parts: whether he should interrupt his vocational course for the ministry, and whether it was right to offer himself as a rival to a man who had helped him greatly on his first tour in 1950/51:

329

As I thought about the first question and discussed it with older friends, it seemed that, if I were to captain the side, this was an altogether different contribution to make to cricket than simply going as a member of a team ... Rightly or wrongly I decided that it would only be right to break my training if it was a question of the captaincy.

As to the even more sensitive second point, Sheppard sought guidance from Norman Sykes, Dixie Professor of Ecclesiastical History at Cambridge. Sykes, from Liversedge in the West Riding, also happened to have a keen academic interest in the Moravian religion. It had therefore been natural for Sheppard to have introduced Sykes to Hutton, and he now called for advice in the knowledge that the two Yorkshiremen had recently been in contact. Sheppard says Sykes 'encouraged' him to feel that Hutton would 'welcome' the chance to be released from the burden of leadership. Gibson, who had also been tutored by Sykes, vouched for the good faith of both men:

Sheppard, without for a moment considering
abandoning his call to the ministry, reasonably felt that
to set back his studies for six months or so, in order
to captain England in Australia, might be within God's
purposes. I say this entirely seriously. There has never
been any trace of the hypocrite about Sheppard.

Sheppard was now, however, put in a difficult position by the leak of his candidature. If asked whether he would tour under Hutton, he felt he could make no comment as this would reveal the condition on which he had made himself available. For his part Hutton, who otherwise adopted his usual approach that the 'best plan was to say nothing', was quickly reported by Yorkshire newspapers to have magnanimously made himself available as a player in Australia, even if he were to be overlooked as captain.

There is an interesting anomaly in the two accounts Sheppard gave of the affair. In the first, he recounts a conversation in Cambridge in 1952 where Hutton predicts to him that he will be offered the captaincy after Brown and gives Sheppard his blessing. In the second, a similar conversation moves to 1954: 'I think they're going to ask you to captain England in Australia ... I very much hope you agree and we'll tell you what to do.' The story has a nice ring with shades of the Yorkshire tale where Emmott Robinson told Major Lupton, the amateur captain before Sellers, not to pad up as the senior pro Rhodes had already decided to declare.

Hutton was in Cambridge playing for Yorkshire between 19 and 21 May 1954. The news of MCC's approach to Sheppard had broken on 17 May. The timing seems to fit, except that Sheppard had previously stated he had to rely entirely on Sykes for an interpretation of Hutton's position: 'Perhaps the simplest thing would have been to ask Len himself, but the opportunity did not present itself.' The suspicion has to be that in his second version of events Sheppard was salving his conscience rather than sharpening his memory.

Presumably Sheppard had received all the necessary clearances, whether from his scruples or his college, by the end of the month. For, on 31 May, the issue of the England captaincy was a matter of debate at a meeting of the full MCC Committee:

> After considerable discussion in which Mr. C.H. Palmer and Mr. R.W.V. Robins, members of the MCC Selection Sub-Committee, were invited to join, it was decided that no special instructions should be given to the MCC Selection Sub-Committee concerning the captaincy for the MCC tour to Australia, 1954/55.
>
> It was agreed that the Sub-Committee should be given a free hand to recommend the Captain considered by them to be the best fitted for the position and that should they recommend L. Hutton his selection would be approved by the MCC Committee.

The very fact this minute exists provides evidence that 'special instructions' were under consideration. Holmes attended the meeting. He and Robins presumably made the case that any repeat of the West Indies experience would be insupportable, and that a suitable young gentleman was now in place to take over. Who spoke up for Hutton is less clear. Perhaps it was Palmer, although he may have chosen to keep his head down. Perhaps it was Sir William Worsley, Baronet Hovingham. As an ex-Yorkshire captain, Worsley had taken the 'keenest interest' in Hutton's career and he is recorded as having come to London for the meeting.

This 'considerable discussion' may have established a slim majority view that Hutton should be allowed to continue if he proved fit to do so. But a selectors' meeting was still planned at the East India Club in mid-July 'for the purpose of considering the captaincy'. Hutton's critics continued to lobby long into the summer.

A sign of Hutton's concern is that he reached out to Swanton. Swanton's reply, written the day after the MCC Committee meeting, is the only part of the correspondence to have survived:

> You say you hope those in authority have still 'a little faith' in me. From all I know they have a great deal. I believe there may be some who wonder whether it is asking too much for you to get half the runs in Australia and run the whole show as well. I should say your Captaincy in England is automatic until '56 inclusive. As for the Australian Tour there is perhaps a case for and against. There is a good deal of heart-searching on the subject – and, I think, it is now realised belatedly by everyone that a great mistake was made in not sending to West Indies a strong manager who could have really helped you.
>
> Which ever way the decision goes (and I confess to an open mind about it, seeing the many points on both sides) I think *the knighthood* ought to be safe for about 1960!

There is a combination of self-satisfaction and sycophancy here but Swanton was essentially giving his honest assessment – except perhaps of his own position. He would outline the view of 'those in authority' more clearly in a *Telegraph* column six weeks later: 'The moral is the one that sticks out a mile to anyone who has played in or accompanied touring teams, that the jobs of England captain at home and abroad are quite different, and the qualities required are by no means identical.' Hutton's mind could hardly have been put at rest.

The affair seemed to generate a momentum of its own in June and July. This was partly because of Hutton's absences from the game. He ascribed his back trouble to a 'sharp change in climate' but it is perhaps significant that his first brief rest from county cricket, to take mud-bath treatments in Harrogate, came shortly after the Sheppard news broke. Hutton was clearly under severe stress. He had also been deeply affected by the recent death of his 'second father', George Hirst.

After emerging from Harrogate, Hutton made a duck in the rain-ruined first Test. Swanton launched his book on the West Indies tour during this game. While its assessment was by no means unsympathetic, a comment about Hutton being a 'Staff Officer' not a 'Battalion Commander' could certainly be read in parallel with Warner's recently republished essay on captaincy.

Hutton was also tiring of press articles which suggested 'that I should be relieved of the leadership so that I could "concentrate" on my batting'. His inverted commas indicate that this was an age-old euphemism when captains were sacked. The line of argument, alluded to in Swanton's private letter, seems at first sight to be absurd. Hutton had topped the batting lists in every series he had been captain and in his last three Tests abroad had averaged 149.33. By contrast, Sheppard's undergraduate back-lift had been exposed by Lindwall and Miller on the 1950/51 tour. Before returning for Sussex in June, he had being playing only occasionally in college cricket for Ridley Hall and club cricket for Little Shelford (because of his religious beliefs he would not play on Sundays). Even Aird, dealing with some correspondence the next winter, noted that 'on the evidence of the West Indies tour, the cares of captaincy did not prevent Hutton making runs'.

But runs were not the only issue. Some of the inner circle had convinced themselves that Hutton's defensive approach, often described by southerners as his 'native caution', was having a debilitating effect on the other batsmen. Perhaps it was during the Lord's Test, where the great and good of the game traditionally gathered, that Hutton was told to take these briefings against him seriously:

A former England captain told me of a move in the 'inner circle', who direct the policy of the game, towards a change of leadership. He made it clear to me that I was not everybody's choice as captain for the tour of Australia.

Yardley or Wyatt could have been Hutton's informant. There is also the intriguing outside possibility that his mole was Jardine, who resigned from the captaincy in 1934 in the knowledge that the inner circle was determined to take it off him. Although Jardine was never invited onto selection sub-committees, he was on the MCC sub-committee which dealt with the logistics of the Australia tour.

Hutton decided to act on this 'information' when Yorkshire came back to Lord's to play Middlesex the week after the first Test. He was dismissed cheaply in both innings by Alan Moss and *Wisden* records that he looked 'plainly out of form'. Hutton suggested this was mainly because he was concentrating on a visit to Aird's office 'to go frankly into the question with him'. Hutton reaffirmed that he wanted to captain MCC in Australia but that he would be 'equally pleased' to 'give my fullest support to whoever else was elected'. He later pointed out the considerable sacrifice he would be making, as he could earn £10,000 for covering the tour as a journalist.

Aird told Hutton to write a letter to this effect. He also insisted that, whatever had been said to question Hutton's position, 'its origin had not been the headquarters of MCC at Lord's'. We now see why Aird was so keen to meet Sheppard off MCC premises – so that he could avoid telling a barefaced lie. Certainly, the Church of England was still acting on the assumption that Sheppard would need to be released from his studies, the Archbishop of Canterbury giving his blessing in late June because of the 'crying need for someone to bring back into the higher ranks of English cricket a sort of moral decisiveness and discipline which has been slipping'. But it is possible that Aird sensed the Holmes-Robins conspiracy was not infecting enough key decision-makers.

Kilburn, admittedly always pro-Hutton, supplies an anecdote which supports this interpretation:

I can remember driving to one of the Essex grounds from our London hotel with Norman Yardley, who was then on the England Selection Committee and saying to him: 'Look are you going to make Leonard captain for Australia?' 'Oh yes, I think so, no question about it.' 'Well', I said, 'for God's sake tell him or you'll have him in a mental home. Put the chap out of his uncertainty.'

Yorkshire started a Championship game against Essex at Romford on 23 June, the day Hutton announced he was too unfit to be considered for the second Test. He would miss the Essex game and the next six county matches. When Sheppard was named as substitute captain, a few journalists noted the possible link with Bailey's disciplinary issues. But most saw confirmation of what Bray had called a 'long-term' plan for Australia. The *Express* and the *Mirror*, in a rare alliance, protested that the 'anti-Hutton brigade' at Lord's was knocking the 'first nail' in the coffin of professional captaincy.

David Kynaston has highlighted the 'undeniable class tincture' which increasingly coloured the debate. Alan Ross made a similar observation in 1955, adding a slap of sarcasm to drive home the point: 'The Press had made some play of the amateur *versus* professional aspect of the business, which no one but a complete moron could have supposed had anything to do with it whatsoever.' The two lobbies gathered their rhetorical forces as the cricketers gathered for the Gentlemen v Players match at Lord's. A traditional tour trial was now being viewed as a captaincy trial for Sheppard in Hutton's continued absence (Compton captained the Players).

Swanton affected to sit on the splice but drew a contrast between Hutton's 'strong accent on defence' and the qualities of Sheppard, 'a young cricketer of strong character and much determination to whom leadership comes naturally'. Sharing self-consciously 'mild thoughts' with readers of his *Cricketer* column, C.B. Fry mused that 'recent developments, of course, bring D.S. Sheppard into the picture'. Fry confined this comment to Sheppard's possible role as an opening batsman, and some of his other observations could even be construed as offering tacit support for Hutton. But Fry also emphasised the importance of 'temperament and character'.

A sentence on the motivations of the selectors smacked of Warner and seemed to be preparing the ground for a change: 'They do not disappoint expectation or shock "common sense" just for the sake of such futile results.'

Some of Hutton's supporters were now convinced that he would be removed. Ross Hall launched an embittered attack on the 'cant' of the 'influential majority' at Lord's who were about to stab Hutton in the back in order to appoint a public-school amateur: 'What bilge! What disgustingly outdated poppycock!'

The irony is that at the moment the debate reached its height – it was the main topic of discussion on BBC's *Sporting Questions* on 23 July – the decision had already been made, at least in principle. It has sometimes been surmised that it was influenced by Sheppard's double failure for the Gentlemen but in fact the selectors convened on 14 July, the first day of the Lord's trial. They recommended to the main MCC Committee, due to meet the following week, that Hutton should be made captain, subject to a 'final medical examination before sailing'.

As with Trueman's omission at a later meeting, there were differing accounts of the degree of consensus. *Wisden* reported in 1955 that Hutton had been recommended by 'only a single vote'. This assertion was retracted in the next edition of the Almanack at the request of MCC, who 'have stated that Hutton received a unanimous vote'. The make-up of the selection committee, with an even number of members, would have made a one-vote margin impossible unless someone abstained, or unless the chairman had used a casting vote. Palmer had 'no recollection' of a poll but was clear about his own preferences: 'I went for Hutton for the simple reason that I'd lived with him through thick and thin in the West Indies. As far as I was concerned David Sheppard was a budding Archbishop.' Yardley and Ames were almost certain to have remained loyal. It is safe to assume that Robins was in the Sheppard camp and that Allen would have joined him in any show of hands.

Altham therefore becomes a potentially pivotal figure. Allen had been instrumental in admitting him to the inner circle. Altham was also close to Aird, with whom he played for Hampshire in the 1920s, and Swanton, who assisted him in later editions of his *History of Cricket*. Altham proudly cited Sheppard – who would give the eulogy at his memorial service – as one of the four great examples of the post-war Oxbridge coaching system, along with May, Cowdrey and Dexter.

Whether Altham's specialisms as a technical coach, public-school housemaster and connoisseur of the golden age sharpened or softened his attitude to professionals is open to debate. But he seems to have been less bumptious than some in the inner circle. There are also signs he did not always see eye to eye with Allen about particular players, even if they collaborated on wider issues. Griffith, in one of several memos which record his increasing misgivings about Allen, described some inner-circle drinks on the eve of Hutton's departure to Australia: 'For once Gubby was in sparkling form and became involved in a series of heated arguments with the Treasurer – inevitably about cricket.'

Altham also had a personal motivation to be pragmatic. He was the only chairman of selectors in the history of that role without either Test-playing experience or experience as a county captain (even A.J. Holmes, who dropped Hutton in 1948, was thus qualified). In his daunting new role, it would have been natural for him to develop deeper personal relations with the incumbent skipper. According to Altham's grandson, Robin Brodhurst, he frequently corresponded with Hutton during the Australia tour and the two men always exchanged warm Christmas cards. Before the crucial selectors' meeting, it was Altham who had personally 'visited Sheffield and seen both L. Hutton and his doctor and had received a satisfactory report on Hutton's health'. Hutton's persistent 'physical and mental' issues in 1954 were genuine, but it may have been a characteristically shrewd move to remove himself from cricket while the debate was raging. Englishmen of the inner-circle type, to their credit, did not like to be seen kicking a man when he was down.

Furthermore, Altham would have been determined to mark his term in office with a win against Australia. The 1948 edition of his *History* (Hutton's desert-island book) had included a new final chapter which, for all its glorification of the amateur strain and the spirit of the game, concluded with a surprisingly strong endorsement of qualities Altham considered 'northern', especially the 'toughness of fibre' essential in international cricket: 'These are the armour for combat, and in them English cricket must clothe itself to command victory.' Perhaps Altham became persuaded that Hutton represented this 'integrity of cricket spirit', which in turn represented England's best chance of success in the Ashes.

Altham's role must remain a matter of conjecture. But Robins saw which way the wind was blowing when he breezed into Sheppard's hotel room during the second Test at Trent Bridge: 'I feel we've been unfair to Len. He was in a very difficult position in the West Indies.' This was not the last time Sheppard may have felt let down by Robins. In 1962, he decided to make himself available for the tour after next to Australia, at the behest of the new chairman of selectors. Robins waved cheerily in recognition of Sheppard's superb century for the Gentlemen – and then chose Dexter as captain for the tour.

The movement against Hutton survived Robins retiring from the fray. Ashton, for example, in an aside to Aird during the concurrent Bailey controversy, was still insisting that 'Sheppard with Hutton as V/Captain would be the better combination'. Holmes may have continued to whisper in private, especially as Hutton's continued tenure was contingent upon his fitness.

But, as Hutton himself later remembered, once his reappointment had been publicly announced 'the bottom fell out of the controversy'. He emerged from it all with a trace of deadpan: 'I'm relieved to know that the MCC selectors have thought I'm the right type of fellow to take the England team to Australia.' The rest is history.

Having hardly provided Hutton with unequivocal support as captain, MCC arguably provided him with less management support than was customary for expeditions down under. Of the twelve MCC tours to Australia between 1932/33 and 1974/75, which in those days were much longer than tours to the Caribbean, Hutton's was one of only three not to have two personnel officially sharing the burdens of management. Admittedly, Geoffrey Howard did not have the playing responsibilities of Palmer but he was otherwise on his own, and had to sort out all the finances himself because Lord's omitted to wire him funds: 'How much easier I would have found it to manage the tour if MCC had provided me with the two things I didn't have: help and money.'

Howard was a respected cricket administrator who had managed the MCC tour to India in 1951/52. Swanton still thought it 'lamentable' that Hutton was not given a 'distinguished player' with Test experience. He probably had in mind Brown (who followed the tour as a journalist) or Allen (who followed some of it as an observer). The inner circle did not appear to have followed through on Allen's suggestion to appoint a manager at 'a rather higher level'.

Nor did Lord's split the onerous dual role of 'scorer and baggageman' which Bill Ferguson had made his own since 1924/25: this was now assumed by George Duckworth. The presence of Harold Dalton suggested MCC had taken note of Hutton's recommendation after the West Indies that 'in future a masseur should accompany the team from England', but all tours to Australia since the war had been provided with one.

The support team certainly paled into insignificance compared with the tour of Australia in 2017/18, when England's Test party had more backroom staff than players. As well as a raft of specialist coaches and three personnel dedicated to fitness and conditioning, Joe Root had at his disposal an 'operations manager', an 'analyst', a 'performance psychologist' and a 'head of team communications'. But back in 1954/55, among their many other unofficial duties, Howard, Duckworth and Dalton respectively filled the first three of these roles and Hutton's favourite travelling journalist, Kilburn, filled the last. Much more by accident than design, the captain found the support he needed and would feel less isolated than in the West Indies. He had also, in his quiet way, absorbed important lessons from his experiences on and off the pitch the winter before.

Rather than a flight on a malfunctioning plane, MCC's party to Australia enjoyed a four-week passage on the SS *Orsova* which, according to Arlott, gave 'greater depth to many relationships'. This proved the point Palmer had made several times before the West Indies tour. Nor is it intended as a reflection on Palmer to quote Frank Tyson on Howard: 'A tour with Geoffrey as manager was certain to be enjoyable. He had in abundance that great quality of taking the trouble to do things well.'

According to Ross, 'there was a complete absence of managerial formality, at the same time a tacit insistence on the proper deference being paid by the players to the manager'. At the first team meeting, Howard laid down 'definite instructions about dress and the Press'; on the other hand, he thought of treats for the players such as oysters in Sydney and Davis Cup tickets in Melbourne. And, even though Howard found Hutton as much of an 'enigma' as everybody else, he arguably handled him better than anybody else.

Duckworth carried out his official duties impeccably. He seemed to have contacts everywhere in Australia, thanks to his three tours as a player with MCC and his Warrington rugby-league connections. Furthermore, as Swanton remembered, 'George was not to be confined by labels' and proved to be 'guide, philosopher and friend to all who had the sense to see the worth of his experience of cricket and Australia'. Hutton treasured Duckworth for being the quintessential Lancastrian. He savoured the irony – after an innings defeat in the first Test – of two men from different sides of the Pennines sitting together 'in the depths of gloom on a showboat' on the Brisbane River. At moments like this, Duckworth provided Hutton with the trusted sounding-board he could have done with in the West Indies.

On the grounds – or the pretext – that 'the scorer sees more than anyone', Duckworth was seconded to selection meetings. He may have been one of several influences behind the key adjustment of the tour: Tyson's reversion to the shorter run he had used in the Central Lancashire League. Duckworth certainly contributed to another big decision: he pointed out the unusual number of no-balls Bedser was bowling and, as a veteran of the Bodyline tour, probably reminded Hutton that Maurice Tate was sacrificed in a similar way in 1932/33. When his 'friend and counsellor' died in 1966, Hutton's tribute gave the scorer his true title: 'I was very lucky to have George as the assistant manager. His advice, I would say, was the vital factor in our success on that tour.'

Bailey had argued in *Playing to Win* that Dalton's 'capable services' should have been utilised more formally in the West Indies. His Essex colleagues had become accustomed to Dalton tending Bailey on the massage table 'with reverence'; in turn Bailey seemed to revere Dalton as a guru of mystical powers. Almost every other player agreed with Howard that the masseur was just a 'pseudo-medic' in a white coat, a verdict supported by Dalton giving Bedser extra massages instead of diagnosing shingles. But Hutton cherished him as much as Bailey:

> As the tour of Australia progressed, Dalton became as valuable to me as a non-playing vice-captain. Whenever I wanted to find out something about a player's physical or mental capabilities which was not obvious on the surface I consulted Dalton. Invariably he knew better than anyone. He proved an astute psychologist and welfare officer, as well as an excellent masseur.

Dalton's first task was to keep Hutton's two prize fast-bowling assets 'in top physical condition'. This involved characteristically unscientific methods. As well as intense courses of massage, Dalton gave Statham castor oil the night before Tests and fixed up Tyson at lunch and drinks breaks with a 'boost' of 'two raw eggs, beaten up in milk or orange juice, sometime spiked with a measure of sherry'. Dalton's tour diary reveals that his second role, traditional for masseurs in Yorkshire, was to serve as Hutton's 'timekeeper'. Twice Dalton records Tyson coming back to the hotel after midnight during State matches, and twice he goes on to note that Tyson 'bowled like a clot' the next day; he and Hutton combined to make sure the fast bowlers were in their rooms by ten for the Tests. Dalton's third and most important role was to act as welfare officer to Hutton himself. The captain often confided in him on the treatment table. After the nervous collapse in Melbourne – according to the masseur's diary at any rate – Hutton 'left it to me to get him right'. Dalton may well have been a quack. But his two VIP clients, Hutton and Bailey, believed in him.

Whereas eight pressmen had accompanied MCC to the West Indies, more than twenty were counted on the boat to Australia. Among them, as Wellings tartly observed, 'some of us could even claim to be trained journalists'. Hutton naturally gravitated towards those from his own county, none of whom had been in the West Indies: Bowes (who wrote for the *Yorkshire Evening News*), Kilburn (*Yorkshire Post*) and John Bapty (*Yorkshire Evening Post*). John Woodcock of *The Times* felt that these three figures were 'as close to him on that tour as anyone'. He had missed them the winter before.

But Hutton also shrewdly tickled the egos of Peebles – a close friend of Allen – and Brown – who had criticised him in an early tour article – by asking them to roll back the years and provide the team with practice against leg-spin. Hutton's invitation to the nets of a more occasional leg-spinner, Swanton, was probably more mischievous and was declined. But Swanton himself was to concede that in Australia Hutton 'developed the art' of keeping journalists happy by giving them copy, however 'Delphic'.

Kilburn revealed some time later that he had been informally appointed by the English press as 'a liaison man' with the players. Hutton therefore also 'knew where to come' for more general advice on handling the media. In the Caribbean, Hutton felt he had been 'let down' by several journalists who had pestered him after hours in the team hotel. He enquired in his captain's report as to the feasibility of MCC touring parties travelling separately from the press in future. It was Kilburn who persuaded him that 'if you give them something they'll forget about what it was they wanted to ask you'. Hutton set the tone in his opening press conference at Fremantle, a triumph of teasing understatement. Because he went to more trouble than in the West Indies to cultivate good press relations, he seemed to get away more easily with tactics like slow over-rates.

There were of course fewer 'incidents' to generate headlines in Australia apart from the cricket. Some of the MCC players visited an 'Aboriginal camp' during their stay but the indigenous population remained largely out of sight, and certainly out of mind, given the prevailing 'White Australia' policy. Australians were also far more likely than the white residents of the West Indies to identify with a professional captain. But, as one home journalist Johnny Moyes put it, Hutton 'was clearly anxious to please as well as to win'.

If Hutton improved his public relations, he also improved his internal relations. It must be pointed out immediately that he was, if anything, even more aloof and condescending to peripheral squad members than he had been in the West Indies. Keith Andrew found him the 'most remote of men'. To Reg Simpson, dropped after the first Test, he was a 'miserable bloody Yorkshireman'. Peter Loader remembered having one conversation with Hutton after the Tests began – in the gentlemen's toilets.

However, there were fewer cliques on the Australian trip. Trueman and Lock had been left at home. Compton and Evans – despite or because of the reintroduction of the third musketeer Edrich – managed to combine their extra-curricular activities with strong support for their captain. They helped get him out of bed in Melbourne and were at the crease to retain the Ashes in Adelaide, after Hutton had started worrying that 'the boogers have done us again'. Wardle was always a threat to team unity but behaved himself once he secured a Test place. His acts of tail-end piracy in Sydney and Melbourne justified Hutton's faith in him by themselves. Hutton also found in Appleyard not only a vital component of the bowling attack but a kindred spirit.

The 1954/55 triumph represented a changing of the guard. Men in their early twenties – Statham, May, Cowdrey and Tyson – made the most important contributions of all. The captain could always rely on Statham and thought May 'came back a 25 per cent better player' from the Caribbean. Crucially, Hutton took unusual care over the two maiden tourists who had been surprise selections. Allen rightly took the credit for advocating Cowdrey and Tyson in committee, although it may be worth remembering Swanton's remark that 'the easiest way to get a thing through' was to persuade Gubby 'it had been his own idea' – Hutton had also observed their potential. Cowdrey, who had to cope with news of his father's death early on the trip, always remembered his captain's 'kindness and consideration'. Tyson felt a natural loyalty, because of a shared 'Northern temperament', and grew to admire Hutton's 'superb psychology'.

The heavy defeat in the first Test at Brisbane was in many ways a re-run of the first Test in Jamaica, Hutton torturing himself even more because this was the Ashes and he had made a big mistake after winning the toss. But Tyson remembered that back at the hotel 'Len called for champagne all round'. Hutton had learned from the previous tour that he must keep heads up, however much his own was in a spin. This was also easier to do when someone else was paying: Bailey, incredibly, had won a prize of $100 for hitting the first six of the match and spent it on a bathful of bubbly.

Bailey was the last key ingredient. Benaud thought he acted as the 'perfect foil' to Tyson and Statham. Furthermore, at the moment in Sydney when Australia seemed to be cruising to a 2-0 lead, he made the vital breakthroughs through which the faster bowlers swarmed. He was the highest-scoring English batsman after May and Cowdrey, lending them support at crucial times. Miller, an all-rounder of greater ability, recognised that Bailey's 'psychological effect' upon the opposition and the crowd was fundamental to England's success.

All generals need to be lucky and Hutton had his fair quota in 1954/55. The team even had its American mascot, Henry Sayen, on hand for the comeback Test, where he doled out more prizes and reportedly danced a victory jig with Ronnie Aird. Perhaps Hutton's greatest piece of fortune was that his opposite number was not in the same league as Stollmeyer. Many in Australia believed Miller would have been a more dynamic leader than Ian Johnson. Arlott thought Johnson's appointment was partly inspired by the need for 'a fairly mild-tempered man' to lead Australia's upcoming tour to the West Indies.

Arlott was still sure that 'if one man is to take credit for the win, it must be Hutton'. Judges on both sides praised his cool 'resourcefulness', tactical 'mastery' and psychological 'edge'. Ray Robinson allowed himself a little dig at previous English regimes: 'By contrast with F.R. Brown's "ruddy dynamism", Hutton reminds me of a dog-car-driver constantly giving the reins little flicks, as much a reminder of his presence as a demand that the horse should quicken its gait.' Even Swanton, who had consigned Hutton to the rank of staff officer in the West Indies, praised his 'wise generalship'.

In Australia, Hutton melded the amateur and professional strains more successfully than anyone since Jardine. His first-choice bowling quartet were batsmen-hating northerners from relatively humble backgrounds. The two match-winning batsmen were products of Cambridge and Oxford. Hutton must have appreciated the tribute May and Cowdrey later paid him by modelling their own captaincy upon his.

Hutton became the first England captain to preside over a full Ashes-winning series at home and then retain the urn in the next series abroad. He was the only England captain to win a series in Australia between Jardine in 1932/33 and Illingworth in 1970/71. And unlike them, as he pointed out when confirming that 1954/55 was his greatest achievement, 'we won without leaving a smell'.

The inner circle's response to the triumph was generous. Aird, who had complimented the captain on a 'very fine job' on his own return from Australia, went to Hutton's cabin as soon as his ship had docked in Southampton to award him his MCC tie. Hutton was also given a vote of confidence without recent precedent by the new chairman of selectors Allen, who appointed him captain for the entire summer series against South Africa. MCC must also have been consulted about the knighthood conferred upon Hutton in 1956, an honour attained four years earlier than Swanton had predicted.

And yet Hutton's triumph was still qualified by tut-tutting at Lord's. In his public comments Warner concentrated on the young amateurs May and Cowdrey; in private he was still grumbling spitefully about Hutton. The MCC Cricket Sub-Committee mildly censured the captain for some minor incidents in the State matches. More significantly, 'Mr Allen reported on the tendency of the game as played by the MCC team to slow down.' Allen had calculated that Hutton's team averaged ten fewer eight-ball overs per day than the team he had captained to defeat in 1936/37, concluding that this 'not only deprived spectators of an hour's cricket but might well do grave harm to the game'.

Allen reappointed Hutton on the express condition that he would improve the over-rate and that any repeat offenders would be dropped. Such interference may have been a small factor in Hutton's protracted decision to retire in 1955. But there was a sense of inevitability given the burdens he had carried and the ambitions he had fulfilled. 'By the end,' Woodcock observed at Adelaide, 'Hutton was mentally spent and inwardly satisfied. The celebrations he left to younger men.' Hutton himself believed that the pressures of the West Indies tour had taken two years off his career. 'I'm surprised that he only said two' was Palmer's reaction.

Kilburn thought Hutton's intensity meant 'he missed some of the down-right joy of cricket and had to replace it with more secret satisfactions'. In Yorkshire, those satisfactions were perhaps as close as professionals could get to joy. It was Hutton's privilege, on his return, to present Wilfred Rhodes with the ball from the England victory at Melbourne 50 years before his own: 'A nice smile came across his fine face.' Hutton also treasured Rhodes' 'faraway look' as the all-rounder reflected upon other highpoints of his career with uncharacteristic feeling. After Hutton stopped playing, his own fine smile was more in evidence: 'It's all right this Sir Leonard business, but it's another ten shillings on the bill.' Our Len could also allow himself the occasional faraway look when recollecting the great triumphs of The Oval, Sabina Park and Adelaide.

Reverberations In The West Indies

CHAPTER 19

THE TRIALS OF THE THREE Ws

In an interview at the cusp of his retirement in 1963, Frank Worrell looked back on the decade since Hutton's tour to the Caribbean: 'This probably sounds unbearably egotistical but I went on fighting alone for ten years … There were principles involved.' It was rare for him to pass explicit comment on these principles, which included fairer pay and youth development but revolved around what, in this interview, he called 'the colour question'. It was also rare for Worrell not to acknowledge other contributions to the fight, especially by Weekes and Walcott, who he knew 'will stick by you and defend you through each and every crisis'.

The Three Ws had been born within about two miles and two years of each other, reportedly delivered by the same midwife. The social distance between them was originally wider. Worrell and Walcott both attended Combermere School, but one of the reasons they did not see eye to eye as teenagers may have been that Walcott's parents paid the fees for him to leave for the more exclusive Harrison College. Weekes left his elementary school at the age of 14. He remembered drily that the three of them realised, once they were in the Test team, that a 'merger' as the W-formation made 'good business sense'.

While remaining firm friends and allies, the Three Ws began to plough their own furrows soon after Hutton's tour. Walcott took up a post in British Guiana to run the Booker cricket development programme. Although Weekes went back to Bacup in 1956 and 1958, he had begun to concentrate on paid coaching roles in the Caribbean. Worrell remained in England. He still played some league cricket but his main focus was a sociology and administration course at Manchester University. Once graduated, he planned to work in further education back home.

In arguments about pay, conditions and status, the Board of Control did not often succeed in its attempts to divide the Three

Ws. Any tension between them probably arose from their all feeling well qualified to lead West Indies. The tensions within them were caused by the particular circumstances of the period, when Test cricket became a grind and the responsibilities of the popular hero a burden. On the field, they were sometimes torn between 'brighter' cricket and 'safety-first' cricket. On the wider stage, England was the place where they had sometimes made a home and made a living. But they agreed it was time for the British to go home, and it was through them that some nationalists were now trying to make a statement.

'Rites', Edward Kamau Brathwaite's great poem about Barbadian cricket, draws some of its detail from the MCC tours of 1947/48 and 1953/54. A trademark back-foot drive by Walcott inspires a moment of almost spiritual ecstasy in the Kensington Oval crowd 'as if was *they* wheelin' de willow | as if was *them* had the power'. Weekes sometimes experienced this feeling in the decade he played Test cricket between 1948 and 1958: he remembered generally 'uplifting times' when more people of his background were breaking through into first-class cricket and top-table politics.

But the message of Brathwaite's poem as a whole was that the emphasis should still be on the words *as if*. Walcott is deceived by Laker – as he was four times in 1953/54 – the home side falls apart and a fan who was baying for the Englishmen's blood must return to his day job, servilely 'lickin' gloy | pun de Gover'ment stamps'. In the late 1950s, the power wielded in Barbados and other islands by nationalist ministers was increasing, but British Governors still held ultimate sway. The Three Ws were also living in a limbo of *as if* in the Test team. They supplied most of the batting power, and a lot of the thinking power, but they were not in control of the side, having to serve under three light-skinned captains after Stollmeyer.

'What am I going to say to Frank Worrell?' This was Stollmeyer's reaction when the Board of Control told him in July 1954 that Worrell was to be replaced as his vice-captain by Atkinson for the first home series against Australia. Stollmeyer thought the decision was 'preposterous in any circumstances'.

348

The Board later tried to clarify that it was 'purely an experiment' because of the particular circumstances of the next West Indies tour, a 'development' series in New Zealand scheduled for 1955/56. Stollmeyer was unlikely to be available for business reasons, Worrell for academic reasons, and only two professionals could be taken for budgetary reasons. It was therefore sensible forward planning to secure the services of Weekes and Ramadhin as the pros and to name Atkinson captain. Worrell would in any case benefit from a rest after four years of 'continuous cricket'; Walcott could be put on stand-by should Weekes feel the same way. Atkinson was being given the vice-captaincy against Australia so that he could gain leadership experience, not because the Board had necessarily chosen him as Stollmeyer's long-term successor.

All this might have seemed reasonable enough given that the tour was designed to blood younger players before the visit to England in 1957. But the announcement came as a 'bombshell' even to conservative newspapers. In *The Gleaner*, Strebor Roberts saw sad confirmation that 'only people who meet certain conditions can ever hope to captain West Indies teams'. The Board's insistence that Worrell was still under consideration for captaincy in the future was treated with the same scepticism as MCC's protestations that Trueman was judged purely on his cricket. Certainly, the other leadership appointments for New Zealand – Pairaudeau as vice-captain and Goddard as player-manager – seemed to confirm Roberts' point about the 'conditions' for such roles. Roberts also noted that Atkinson was roughly a year younger than Walcott, two years younger than Weekes and three years younger than Worrell, all of whom had 'an ocean of ability and experience'.

Walcott felt it was 'much more likely' the Board had demoted Worrell because of his professional status than his black skin. In Walcott's experience, elite administrators were clinging to the 'old-fashioned precedent' of the amateur captain, which had 'its roots deeply laid in England' despite Hutton's appointment. Roberts dealt with this line of argument by suggesting that if the Board was so wedded to such a 'silly tradition' it could have appointed Rae, now working as a lawyer in Jamaica and still playing as an amateur.

But the irony was that Hutton, who had just caused so much offence to West Indians, was also providing them with an inspiring example. In *Colour Bar*, published soon after MCC's return from the Caribbean, Constantine suggested that his appointment as captain 'in the most conservative of all English sports' provided hope that the game, and perhaps the world, might one day function 'irrespective of colour' as well as class. James later reflected that the dignified rise of Hutton, a common man 'superior' to the officers, provided the 'framework' for his campaigns for Worrell's leadership. Nationalists were becoming more assertive: Norman Manley's PNP won the Jamaican general election in January 1955. His son Michael described the captaincy issue, which rumbled on through the Australia series, as 'a bone stuck in history's throat'.

West Indians had been relieved, given the widespread coverage given to the Bourda disturbance in 1953/54, that the Australians did not cancel their tour in 1954/55. At the same time, they were disappointed to learn that Bradman would not, as originally hinted, be accompanying the party. Bradman had at least been diligent in arranging a meeting between Ian Johnson, the Australian captain, and Palmer. The MCC manager 'spent two or three hours with Ian, telling him what the players should avoid doing and so on'.

When Johnson got to the Caribbean he 'went out of his way to be charming' – especially, it seems, to the administrators who had not warmed to Hutton. The tourists also mixed with opponents and supporters much more happily than the English. The Three Ws, who roomed together in Trinidad, fondly remembered an all-night card school with Keith Miller on the eve of the second Test – in a rare bright spot for the home side, Walcott and Weekes scored centuries the next day and Miller took one for 96. Generally, however, stung by their defeat at Hutton's hands, the Australians were typically uncompromising on the field. Sobers, who established himself during this series, summed it up succinctly: 'They let us have it.'

Hutton no longer needed to do any homework on the Australians and probably paid little attention as he wound down towards retirement. But he might have been forgiven for wondering why Bradman was not writing any critical articles about this tour. There were flashpoints in every Test. We have already noted that Ron Archer reacted to an umpiring decision in exactly the way which had brought such opprobrium upon Graveney. Miller's dissent was often nearly as flagrant. He was also roundly booed in Barbados for procuring a new ball by deliberately bowling wides – and then launching a ferocious barrage of bouncers with it.

Nevertheless, Walcott thought Miller's flashes of anger were 'occasional and short-lived', and held a widely shared view that the series against Johnson's men was 'singularly pleasant' in comparison with the one against Hutton's. Visiting journalists, who found their hosts still in 'sullen mood' about the events of the previous winter, made an effort to play down any incidents. Perhaps also, as Michael Manley observed, on-field needle caused less popular ill-feeling because Australia had never been 'the hub of an empire'. In any case, as the visitors amassed huge scores and slowly crushed the West Indies 3-0, local reporters were concentrating on their own side's internal conflicts.

Some of these reflected traditional insular rivalries. The Sabina Park crowd taunted the Guyanese Glendon Gibbs for the crime of dropping a catch; Trinidadians chanted 'Go Home McWatt'; Barbadians unfurled a placard saying 'Hang Holt – Save Hylton', a heartless allusion to the recent failures of a Jamaican batsman and the imminent execution for murder of a great Jamaican fast bowler, Leslie Hylton.

But the most divisive issue was Worrell's demotion, which Stollmeyer believed was 'the cause of much of the dissension and bad cricket played by our team in the series'. This became especially true because of Stollmeyer's own issues: he sprained a finger in practice before the series began and then injured his shoulder in BG. Atkinson was therefore placed in the invidious position of taking over as skipper for the first Test, being dropped from the team for the second, returning under Stollmeyer for the third and then assuming the captaincy again for the final two games with the Three Ws in the ranks.

After Stollmeyer's second injury, Ken Wishart, one of the Guyanese representatives on the Board, seems to have intervened on Worrell's behalf. He was reportedly never forgiven for questioning 'white supremacy' by dos Santos, who insisted that Atkinson lead the side in Barbados. In his home Test, Atkinson produced an extraordinary personal performance, saving the game with a double century.

Even so, Worrell's case had become such a cause célèbre that a protest meeting was held at Kingston Racecourse, threatening a boycott if he were not appointed captain for the final Test on his adopted island. Rumours spread, as in 1953/54 after the hounding of Stollmeyer, that the Board might switch the game from Jamaica to Trinidad. It went ahead at Sabina: Australia won by an innings and 82 runs. Roberts renewed his campaign for Worrell in *The Gleaner*, noting 'great indignation' about the way a 'perfect gentleman' had been treated and asking why the Board continued to 'force immaturity and imperfection among us'.

Michael Manley felt that the 'insult' of Atkinson's captaincy explained Worrell's 'increasing disconnection from the game locally between 1956 and 1960'. Relations were also deteriorating between the Board and Weekes. He felt compelled to deny rumours that he had been fined for showing dissent to umpire Gillette in the third Test. He noted that in New Zealand he was asked to carry 'additional responsibility with the bat, not the captaincy'. He was still 'determined' to do well – he averaged over 100 for the tour – but more for the missing 'Frank and Clyde' than the new leadership.

Walcott had made a gargantuan personal contribution against Australia – his aggregate of 827 runs is still a record for a series in the Caribbean – but strongly implied that the Three Ws had been demotivated by having to play under Atkinson. He also seemed to suggest the days of their deferring to white captains were over: even if Stollmeyer had been fit to lead throughout, 'his presence would not, I feel, have made too much difference'.

It was still assumed by many, and certainly by Stollmeyer himself, that he would be captain in England. He remembered an 'order' from the Queen to this effect, conveyed by Princess Margaret on her 1955 Caribbean tour, and it was his last remaining ambition in cricket to lead West Indies in the 'mother country'. Stollmeyer therefore travelled to British Guiana in the autumn of 1956 as Trinidad captain for a Quadrangular Tournament of the Big Four colonies, which doubled as an unofficial trial for the upcoming tour.

Hoping to 're-establish' his claims after a string of injuries, Stollmeyer felt he got a bad decision from umpire Kippins as Trinidad failed to progress from their semi-final. The Quadrangular instead became an advertisement for Walcott's leadership skills, and the work he was doing as head of the Booker cricket development programme. He captained the home side to deserved victories in their semi-final against Jamaica (led by Rae) and in the final against Barbados (led by Goddard).

The games featured centuries by the GCC player Pairaudeau and three products of the sugar estates, Kanhai, Solomon and Butcher, the first player of indigenous Amerindian heritage to play for West Indies. BG also had the best bowlers in the tournament: Lance Gibbs, an 'African' finger-spinner, and Ivan Madray, an 'Indian' wrist-spinner, were hailed as new spin twins. Under Walcott, the team was establishing itself as a major force more representative of the whole country, even if the country itself was becoming increasingly divided – the next year Jagan's faction of the PPP defeated Burnham's in a bitter general election.

During a break in the final, Stollmeyer took a stroll across the Bourda ground with Cecil de Caires, a Guyanese representative on the Board of Control who had broken the news of Worrell's demotion to him in 1954. De Caires again proved to be the bearer of bad tidings:

> 'Jeff, I have something to tell you.' 'What's that?' said
> I. 'The President has gone across to Barbados to ask
> John Goddard to captain the team to England.' For a
> moment I was literally stunned, then I turned to him
> and said, 'Cecil, I have played my last first-class match.'

Stollmeyer announced his immediate retirement the moment he set foot back in Trinidad. Andy Ganteaume, selected for the tour, believed his deposition marked the end of a long intra-island power struggle with dos Santos: 'As we say in Trinidad and Tobago, "Two man rat can't live in the same hole."' Stollmeyer certainly did not start playing an engaged part in West Indies cricket administration until dos Santos retired as president in 1960. Meanwhile, Jamaicans detected an inter-island alliance of convenience between dos Santos and Barbadian Board members. They understood Rae had been promised the captaincy, only for dos Santos to propose that Goddard, who initially seemed to be angling for the role of manager, should again lead West Indies in England.

The role of manager was instead split between the Guyanese de Caires and the Barbadian Tom Peirce. The failure to demarcate their duties, and their failure to get on, was one of several structural problems. Walcott had been promised the vice-captaincy, but the announcement was made clumsily on the boat to England with little sensitivity to the feelings of Worrell, waiting for the team in Manchester where he was sitting his exams. For Weekes, the passage over on the SS *Golfito* also revealed the 'race and class issues that got in the way of team unity': the white amateurs enjoyed the 'luxury' facilities in first while the black professionals were in steerage, 'like Jonah, in the bowels of the ship'.

On deck amongst the younger players, Atkinson was alleged to have briefed against the Three Ws for being more interested in money than the development of the game at home. As with Hutton's men, there is a risk of exaggerating the cliques within the squad: Weekes and Walcott happily formed a card school with Atkinson and the young white wicketkeeper Gerry Alexander. But Worrell later reflected on a tour of 'factions' with no 'unity of purpose', self-sabotaged by a 'lack of advice to young players', a 'lack of planning' and a 'lack of good administration'. If Swanton had been unhappy with the qualifications of the leadership team on MCC's 1953/54 tour, in 1957 Worrell was unhappy about joint-managers 'so unfamiliar with English conditions', and a captain who had more experience of those conditions 'without assimilating enough knowledge to do the team much credit'.

Nevertheless, West Indies came into the first Test unbeaten, and looked like winning it easily until the monumental May-Cowdrey pad-play partnership of 411. Walcott thought Cowdrey in particular enjoyed 'immunity' from lbw; Weekes joked bitterly he had contracted 'laryngitis' from all his unsuccessful appealing. Ramadhin bowled 774 balls in the match, still a Test record, and was broken for the rest of the series.

The familiar complaints about Goddard's overbowling of the spinners and underappreciation of tactics only increased as West Indies subsided shambolically, thrice beaten by an innings within three days. Walcott reflected that Test cricket was becoming 'ever more intense and hard', with a degree of sorrow that the emphasis on 'national prestige' was sucking enjoyment out of the game, but also a degree of anger that the amateurish organisation of West Indian cricket was not preparing its players properly for the heat of international competition.

In fairness, Goddard did not have any in-form fast bowlers: Anthonyson and Mason, still the victims of prejudice against the 'smaller' islands, had been among those left at home. The tourists were also beset by injuries, most significantly to all three Ws: Pairaudeau spent more time running for them than he did for himself. But, as the tour unravelled, Goddard became an ever more remote figure. Blanked by his captain in the team hotel, Ganteaume sarcastically wondered whether Goddard was 'preoccupied by strategy'. His only form study seemed to be of the racehorses he was buying to add to his string back in Barbados.

With Weekes beset by thigh, sinus and finger problems, and Walcott literally and metaphorically hamstrung, it was Worrell who provided what *Wisden* called 'unmistaken gifts of leadership'. Asked to open the batting and the bowling in the last three games, he carried his bat for 191 to help draw the third Test and took seven for 70 when England won by an innings in the fourth.

Like the body language of the players, whose fielding was notably shabby, the messages given out by the tour were in complete contrast to 1950. The disunity of the West Indies cricket team did not bode well for the West Indies Federation, whose first elections would be held across the Caribbean in March 1958. For the Windrush generation, the tour was more a reflection than a release of tension: 1958 would also be the year of 'race riots' in Nottingham and Notting Hill.

After two days under the cosh in the game with Surrey, Worrell and Walcott produced a match-winning partnership. They both claimed that they were subject to 'violent' racial abuse from some of the county's players. Ignoring his captain May's request to 'steady on', one fielder allegedly made a reference to the West Indians who formed the majority of the crowd: 'You would not have known those b____s were here yesterday, but listen to them now.' Whether the blank was to be filled in by the word 'blacks' or the word 'bastards', Worrell says he left The Oval 'a very sad man'.

By the time West Indies returned there for the final Test they had reached rock bottom. Goddard lost the toss on a wicket made for Laker and Lock. He then took to his bed with flu after Graveney scored a century on the first day. According to Ganteaume, 'opinion was divided' as to whether he covered up his illness in order to deny Walcott the honour of officially leading the side. In reply to England's 412, West Indies managed 89 and, following on, 86 (J.D.C. Goddard 'absent ill' in both innings).

A handicapped Weekes bagged a pair in his last Test in England, an exhausted Worrell's contribution amounted to four runs and no wickets, and a disillusioned Walcott had an impossible task as on-field captain. He too would not play a Test in England again. He composed himself to make a balcony speech of 'commendable good humour', looking back to the happier experience of 1950 in the hope that West Indies could come back as a stronger unit in 1963. Few journalists on either side believed this was possible after what one of them called an 'unconditional surrender'. As J.S. Barker put it, 'Goddard became a name associated both with West Indies' finest hour and also their most dismal failure'.

When the team returned home, with no crowds on the quayside and no public holidays declared, some members of the Board of Control defended Goddard and tried to blame the debacle on Walcott and Weekes. De Caires told journalists that both players 'did not bother much about getting fit' and half-repeated the insinuation of Goddard that they had applied themselves more on the town than at the crease.

Co-manager Peirce, Weekes's first Barbados captain, immediately rebutted these allegations. A more formal defence committee was then set up, with a view to legal action, by Errol Barrow, who had won a by-election the previous year and would oust the more conservative Adams in the Barbados general election of 1961. The committee was joined by other regional politicians, including Burnham, who had once served with Barrow on the Council of Colonial Students when they were studying law in London.

The shift in the use of cricket for political ends, already evident on Hutton's tour, was continuing apace. Whereas British Governors, conservative Board of Control members and even Bustamante had used the game to emphasise the links between mother country and colonies, nationalist politicians trying to sever those links were now tapping into the popularity of the players. Eventually, in the spring of 1958, a statement was extracted from the Board of Control expressing regret for 'certain references in the West Indian press regarding the physical condition of Clyde Walcott and Everton Weekes'.

By then they had announced their retirement from international cricket. In their last home series, against Pakistan, Sobers credited both men for their support at the crease when he broke Hutton's Test world record. They were now all playing under Alexander, who had been capped only twice when he was appointed captain. Many Jamaicans tolerated the decision, given that Alexander was the first from their island to lead the side since Headley. From Trinidad, Stollmeyer seemed to think the appointment of a wicketkeeper was an insult to the intelligence; from Barbados, the former Test player Foffie Williams considered it an insult to the captaincy credentials of Walcott and Weekes; from BG, the journalist Hank Harper thought it an insult to the whole of Caribbean sport: 'The time has come when these fossils who call themselves selectors must be given the boot.'

At the end of the series, few believed the explanation that Walcott and Weekes were retiring from Tests, at the ages of 32 and 33, so that they could concentrate on mentoring young players in the colony sides of BG and Barbados. All Weekes will say now is that dos Santos deserves some credit for the Board's decision to give him and Walcott £100 retirement cheques, a financial gesture he cannot remember any of the politicians making.

The next winter Alexander led West Indies to victory in India and defeat in Pakistan. Umpiring decisions were, as ever, a talking point. But the main controversy had involved the young Jamaican fast bowler Roy Gilchrist, like Trueman a popular hero with a temperamental streak. He had been sent home early for various episodes of alleged swearing and for deliberately bowling beamers at Swaranjit Singh. Opponents of the Board noted that Singh and Alexander were students at Cambridge together, and felt the example made of Gilchrist was yet another case of a high-caste captain destroying the career of one of their own. They also pointed to Worrell's more sympathetic handling of Gilchrist – when he stood in as captain for the indisposed Goddard and Walcott in minor games at the fag-end of the 1957 tour – and asked why he was still not in charge.

It was not quite so simple. The Board had already twice offered Worrell the captaincy. Barker leaked their 'confidential' approach for the home series against Pakistan. When the party was announced for India, Worrell was named to lead it (with Alexander as vice-captain) but too late for him to claim extended university leave. Worrell himself acknowledged that Alexander 'began to mould the team' into a better unit, dealing with the 'splinter groups' inherited from Goddard.

Another interpretation of the Gilchrist affair was provided by Basil Butcher. Rather than seeing Alexander as the Board's blue-eyed boy, he made the point that Alexander's family was considered 'high brown' in Jamaica. The Guyanese manager, Berkeley Gaskin, was the first black man to oversee an entire tour. Butcher believed the leadership team in fact felt under pressure from Board members who were ready to conclude that the side 'can't get along without a white boss'.

Furthermore, it emerged that Worrell had been approached during the 1957 tour of England to lead a West Indian team to South Africa in 1959, where they would play 'non-white' teams led by Basil D'Oliveira. Whether this well-intentioned initiative would expose or endorse apartheid sharply divided opinion in the Caribbean, Constantine eventually prevailing over his friend James in arguing for cancellation.

Officially, the Board of Control had no objection to what it called a 'private' tour. Worrell's ongoing recruitment of players, including Weekes, did not present quite the threat to its authority as Lloyd's recruitment on behalf of Packer in the late 1970s, if still provocative in the context of recent disputes about pay. The Board also felt entitled to ask – as it did not seem to be attending to the schedule of Worrell's university course – why he could find time to lead an unofficial team in South Africa but not the official Test side at home. The historian Woodville Marshall was an enthusiastic advocate of what he called the 'Worrell/Sobers revolution' in the 1960s. But his sense of the situation in the late 1950s was that 'people of my generation did not in general believe Worrell was getting a raw deal'. He even confessed that he had welcomed Goddard's recall in 1957.

Worrell did respond to the Board's request to play as vice-captain under Alexander in 1959/60, when MCC made their first visit since

Hutton's tour. The English suffered an early defeat by Barbados. The key contributions were by BCL products – Sobers, Seymour Nurse and Charlie Griffith – under what Swanton called the 'notably shrewd direction' of Weekes, who had replaced Goddard as colony skipper. Not required to bat, Weekes set up the victory by taking four wickets with his donkey-dropping leg-spinners. Whereas Barbados had not beaten MCC since 1925/26, they did so easily under their first black captain. Whereas BG had been thrashed by Hutton's men, Walcott led them to a comfortable draw and was persuaded to make a comeback in the final two Tests.

C.L.R. James drew an obvious inference after England's last four wickets put on 179 runs in the first Test: 'Everton Weekes wraps up the England tail. The England tail wraps up Alexander.' This was part of his 'Alexander Must Go' campaign, famously evoked – and a touch mythologised – in *Beyond a Boundary*. When James invited a comparison between his return to Trinidad and Headley's return to Jamaica, he was arguably exaggerating his own popularity and downplaying the efforts of local journalists such as Roberts, who had long been advocating Worrell's captaincy.

But his interventions, as editor of the PNM's weekly paper *The Nation*, were in some ways the culmination of what he had been writing throughout the decade about the go-slow on West Indian independence and the go-slow in modern Test cricket. The Federation had been functioning as an abstract political entity since 1958, with the Barbadian Adams as Chief Minister. Now the more difficult practical details were being negotiated, with squabbling between the larger islands and foot-dragging by the British. At a crucial moment for the future of the region, James was having doubts about the project, but none about the symbolism of the most qualified Caribbean cricketer still taking his orders from the white man. At the same time, he had been arguing, like Cardus, that a safety-first 'welfare state of mind' had plunged cricket into an unprecedented crisis. He saw in Worrell a figure who could not only give expression to a new 'national spirit' in the West Indies but also recover the spirit of the game worldwide.

After Hutton's retirement, May had led England to victory in six successive series. But his team juddered to a 4-0 defeat in Australia in 1958/59, a series marred by controversies about 'throwing' and painfully slow scoring. MCC reacted by appointing Robins as manager for the West Indies, and by purging the team of Lock and Bailey, whom Robins never forgave for the slowest half-century in Test history at Brisbane.

Swanton praised Robins profusely for maintaining 'the friendliest relations' with both the press and the hosts, implying that such an approach may have nipped some of the problems of Hutton's tour in the bud. The manager undoubtedly handled Trueman, who was in any case a riper character, more successfully than Palmer or Hutton. But other tourists suggested Robins 'had very little to do with the players and everything to do with the press'; even Swanton was forced to admit he was not '*en rapport* with all the senior members of the side'. The battle between hard cricket and brighter cricket, fought between Hutton and Lord's by telegram in 1953/54, took place in the MCC dressing room in 1959/60.

Lifeless pitches were a contributory factor in another attritional series, but the issues of slow over-rates, slow scoring and short-pitched bowling were again to the fore. Robins encouraged chivalrous gestures in some of the tour matches but May's controversial decision to refuse Kanhai a runner at Sabina Park – no doubt partly inspired by Holt's use of a runner at Bourda in 1953/54 – typified the spirit in which the Tests were played.

When May returned home injured, his stand-in Cowdrey was if anything even more determined not to squander a 1-0 lead, and the chance to win a series in the West Indies for the first time. On the final day of the final Test, Robins barged in to argue 'with his customary force' for a sporting declaration. Cowdrey refused point-blank. Trueman, now senior professional, is said to have escorted Robins out with a vigour reminiscent of Bustamante's entourage.

It still takes two not to tango. Alexander had played football and cricket with May at Cambridge but seemed to share his aversion to 'the old type of amateur outlook'. Just as May modelled his captaincy on Hutton, Alexander seemed to take his cue from Stollmeyer, not least in the time it took him to set his field.

From the radio commentary box, Stollmeyer praised England's go-slow tactics once they were ahead as 'good defensive cricket'. On the field, Worrell seemed in full agreement with the 'dog-in-the-manger attitude' which Alan Ross thought bedeviled the series.

He set the tone in the first Test at the Kensington Oval. Worrell's eleven-hour innings reminded Bray of 'Trevor Bailey at his worst'. Ross noted the theory that his refusal to speed up was part of 'a personal vendetta against the Barbados members for a long-standing social slight'. Even Worrell's admirers accepted that Alexander declared, when he was three short of a double century, more out of exasperation than malice.

At its annual meeting held after the bore-draw fourth Test in BG, the Board acceded to the popular demand that Worrell should captain West Indies on the forthcoming tour to Australia. Alexander was reported as saying he was 'so happy for Frank'. He also confessed he was more than ready to stand down, 'suffering from Worellitis' after the campaigns by the press and worn out by a 'war of attrition' on the field. Within a year, he would credit Worrell's captaincy for giving him the 'remarkable feeling' that cricket could be fun again.

CHAPTER 20

THE TRIUMPH OF WORRELL

Test Match cricket to-day is no sort of game. It is a
battle. And to win you need not only the strenuous
effort of individual players: the work of each player
must be backed by a sense of solidarity, of all the
others supporting him, not only actually but, so
to speak, in the spirit. The lack of this is the chief
weakness of the West Indies team in big cricket. We
have not been able to get together in the sort of
spirit which says, 'Look here, we are going out to-day
against those fellows and it is war to the knife!' ... Until
all members of a West Indies side realise that every
consideration must give way before the necessity of
uniting in spirit and in truth to win through a series of
Test Matches the West Indians will not play the cricket
that I know they can play. Much depends on the
players, much more depends on the leadership, which
must itself be above pettiness, sympathetic, and yet be
strong and command respect from all in the team.

These words could have been written by Worrell at virtually any
time after 1950. They were in fact written by Constantine in 1933,
just after the Bodyline series. The main 'consideration' he thought
had rotted 'the heart out of our cricket' – captaincy based on skin
colour – finally gave way at the beginning of the 1960s with Worrell's
appointment. Very soon, Worrell would fulfil Constantine's prophecy
that he that he would 'live to see a West Indian team, chosen on
its merits alone, captained by a black player, win a rubber against
England'. Worrell achieved this by following some of Constantine's
instructions to the letter, uniting the team in the spirit of 'Shannonism'
and rising above insular pettiness.

But perhaps the memory of a series almost as acrimonious as
Bodyline influenced a different emphasis in his approach. It was

against Hutton's men in 1953/54 that Headley, the other great West Indian pioneer, said (according to Trueman at any rate): 'This ain't cricket any more. This is war!' After three wars to the knife with England in the 1950s, Worrell made the important decision, with some help from the Australians, to play Test cricket as a game again.

Richie Benaud, who did so much to make the 1960/61 series one of the most compelling of all time, never detected 'resentment' in his opposite number about coming to the captaincy at the advanced age of 36: 'There was perhaps a calm shaking of the head as if to say, why are people so stupid.' As we have seen, the delay was partly caused by Worrell's own decision to become a mature student. It worked to his advantage in one sense because the advances in the region's cricket during the 1950s, which had more to do with local initiatives than the Board of Control, were now coming to fruition.

Seymour Nurse and Conrad Hunte, under the watchful eye of Weekes, had now followed Sobers from the BCL into the international side. The flowering of Guyanese cricket supervised by Walcott found full expression at Test level under Worrell's captaincy: at Adelaide, Gibbs took the first hat-trick against Australia in the 20th century, and Kanhai became the first West Indian to score a hundred in each innings of a Test down under; at Brisbane, the famous tie was achieved by Solomon, whose childhood target practice bringing down mangoes with marbles served him well when he had one stump to aim at from square leg.

Worrell observed that 'the experience of the 1957 tour served us in good stead on future tours'. Reacting against Goddard, he introduced a 'rota' system for State games so that the younger players were not discouraged and the senior players not burnt out. Anticipating Lloyd in a later era, he was determined to stamp out factional insularity: 'On previous tours Barbadians seemed to stick together, and so with players from Trinidad, Jamaica and British Guiana. We cut across all that. We were a team.'

The captain had an all-round cricketing intelligence which had been sharpened by his years as a Central Lancashire League professional. He also shrewdly recruited the Lancastrian Duckworth, his manager when he captained the Commonwealth in India, to reprise the role of baggageman/scorer/guru which Hutton had found so helpful in Australia.

Worrell added an emotional intelligence not always so associated with the north of England. Sobers thought the tour was 'a lesson in the art of cricket captaincy'. The skipper 'tore away' any sense of the leadership team being an unapproachable 'they', treating every member of the squad as an adult. But he was also prepared to crack 'a fair old whip over us' and to grasp selectorial nettles, dropping Ramadhin for Gibbs in the third Test, a particularly difficult decision as there would then be no Trinidadian in the eleven. And he did all this without ever losing his celebrated cool. Alexander was paying a compliment when he noted that Worrell, famous for taking naps in the dressing room, had 'a remarkable sedatory sort of influence on the boys' whenever they were boiling over.

Alexander, like Bailey in 1954/55, put away any personal disappointment to make an enormous contribution. Alan Davidson, Australia's man of the series, modestly considered him the most 'influential' player on both sides because of the 'ton of motor' he gave to the middle order and the fielding effort. As importantly, Alexander laid to rest the notion, once recorded by Constantine, that 'white players might be too self-conscious to do their best' under a black captain.

The more romantic of Worrell's advocates had hoped his tour manager might be Constantine (now Minister for Labour in the PNM government) or Headley (now Jamaica's national coach). Some also felt that Gaskin, who had expressed the wish to continue in the role, was unfairly overlooked. But it was generally agreed that Gerry Gomez played his part as manager, even on the field in three up-country games, with characteristic gusto. Several players remembered him 'screaming' with delight when Worrell played a copybook off-drive in an innings of 82 which helped win the third Test. Whether Worrell had Gomez with him by design or on sufferance – there is evidence both ways – captain and manager took the plaudits of the crowd together at the end of the tour, when 250,000 Melburnians turned out for a ticker-tape motorcade.

Worrell had arrived conscious of the responsibility of being the first black West Indies captain with tenure. He was also conscious of the need to re-establish West Indies prestige, after playing in four series in the 1950s where they had been ground into the dust by England and Australia. Against a strong Australian side who had recently thrashed England, he could have been forgiven for trying to 'do 'em' like Hutton in 1953/54, and for repeating his own approach in 1959/60. What he actually did, largely on his own initiative, was to cut through the impasse in international cricket for which he held Hutton partly responsible. Worrell told the press at the end of the tour that it was hard to know when an attritional mindset had prevailed in Tests 'but most cricketers feel Hutton was in it, and that Peter May picked it up from him'.

Hutton would argue that he picked it up from Bradman, who may have been a faster-scoring batsman but who gave the following instructions to Miller in 1948: 'When you get in front, nail 'em into the ground. When you get 'em down, never let up.' Yet Worrell's timing was perfect in that Bradman was increasingly anxious about the future of Test cricket after the negativity of the 1950s. The Don told the Australian players on the eve of the series that they should worry less about 'playing for the flag' and more about playing for the fans. Benaud remembered this team-talk 'caught everyone's attention', perhaps less because of Bradman's standing in the game than his influence as a Test selector.

The two captains therefore committed themselves to run-rates and over-rates which increased the level of entertainment and the likelihood of positive results. The series began with a tie and could have ended with one, Australia scraping home to win the series 2-1. In their first innings at Brisbane, West Indies scored twice the runs England had managed the previous winter in half the time. Fingleton credited Worrell with starting a revolution: 'From something which seemed inexorably headed for the textbooks of the antiquarians, international cricket emerged from that breathless, spine-tingling Test as a game that can be played as a game – for the enjoyment of the players themselves and the enormous delight of the cash customers.'

As well as better entertainment, Worrell wanted to reintroduce to Test matches a better spirit. Again, at the end of the tour, he drew a contrast between his approach and that of the English:

> The field with them is always a battleground. It's such
> a matter of national prestige to win and if not to win
> then at least draw. They must never lose. The English
> have lost their sense of humour. They never laugh on a
> Test field; they never see a joke.

Worrell did concede that England captains were under pressure from 'an army of popular Press ready to scream, to pounce, and to devour'. It was certainly easier for him to take a more gentlemanly approach on tour, away from equally intense media scrutiny in the Caribbean. It may also be unfair to draw conclusions from the extensive newsreel footage of the 1960/61 series compared with the snatched amateur cine film of 1953/54. But there is much more evidence of friendship, chivalry and laughter between the teams on the field in Australia.

Worrell expected his batsmen to walk and his bowlers to accept the umpires' decisions, instructions his players usually followed – even though some questionable calls at crucial moments arguably cost them the series. Wes Hall never wavered from the principle that bowling bouncers at tailenders was not 'the thing to do' – even when the No.11 Lindsay Kline held out with 'Slasher' Mackay for over a hundred minutes in the fourth Test to keep the series at one-all.

It is possible to be slightly cynical about the legend that has developed around the tour. Hall left his imprint on all the recognised batsmen – Mackay took the last ball of the fourth Test straight in the ribs – and was once warned by the umpires for intimidatory bowling. Nor was Worrell prepared to entertain at all costs. 'Frank conveyed to us,' Sobers remembered, 'gently and clearly, that aggressive cricket was wonderful and just what he wanted, but mixed with a good helping of discretion.'

One of several tactics Worrell picked up from Hutton (who had picked it up from Bradman) was to hold long conferences with his bowlers even if he had nothing to say, either to give them a breather or to convey the impression that a cunning plan was being put into operation. Benaud, otherwise unstinting in his praise for Worrell as 'a gentleman in every way', did imply that he was given a free pass when he tried to close the game down:

Occasionally we looked out when our chaps were
batting and saw bowling down the line of the leg
stump, to five men on the on-side...saw Wes Hall
taking six and seven minutes to bowl an over, with our
chaps' scoring rate behind the clock...and wondered.

And would so many have turned out for the West Indies
motorcade if they had won? Australians tend to have a soft spot for
touring captains so long as they are gallant losers: Freddie Brown,
a very different character from Worrell, was tremendously popular
in 1950/51.

But a country known for its parochialism had been entranced by
what Vaneisa Baksh calls Worrell's 'gracious persuasion'. The balcony
scene at Melbourne in February 1961 was arguably as symbolic
as the one at Lord's in 1950. The new perpetual trophy Worrell
handed over to Benaud had been named after him, in recognition
of the old-fashioned spirit he had revived and the world-record
attendances he had inspired. Men who would possibly not have
been allowed into Australia, had they not been playing cricket, left
the country as heroes. The myth that black men were not equipped
to lead had been scotched immediately one of them had been given
a proper chance to do so: 'We have gone far beyond a game ...
Clearing their way with bat and ball, West Indians at that moment
had made a public entry into the comity of nations.'

When C.L.R. James wrote these famous words, he knew there
would be no comity of Caribbean nations. In September 1961,
Norman Manley lost a Jamaican referendum on Federation. On
the grounds that 'one from ten leaves nought', Williams withdrew
Trinidad, leaving the eight smaller islands who had signed up for
a combination to fend for themselves. The very day, in late 1961,
that had been earmarked for the simultaneous independence of
West Indian islands in Federation marked the moment when the
project was officially declared dead. Jamaica and Trinidad gained
independence separately in 1962. The region had virtually nothing
to show for a decade of negotiations other than The University of
the West Indies. But there was still the cricket team.

'Cricket in 1963 was Frank Worrell!' Barker, the journalist who criticised Hutton so fiercely in Trinidad in 1953/54, reached this conclusion having followed Worrell's triumphant progress through England. He thought the tour had 'injected new life' into Test cricket there, after a 'Thirty Years' War of Negativity'.

Brighter cricket certainly remained one of Worrell's priorities after he had reluctantly agreed, despite feeling like the 'the world's oldest living cricketer', to lead his side for one last series. As his new vice-captain Hunte put it, 'our aim is to go all out to win and enjoy ourselves doing so'. The desire to entertain was linked to a second objective. Worrell wanted 'to give West Indian cricket equality with England and Australia'. He helped represent the Board of Control at a meeting of the ICC at Lord's that summer, when it argued that West Indies should be invited back to England earlier than their next scheduled visit in 1971. Thirdly, as Worrell reflected at the end of the series, 'my aim was always to see the West Indies moulded from a rabble of brilliant island individuals into a real team', something he felt even more strongly about now that the individual islands would not be teaming up in Federation. Finally, having tasted joy in 1950 and despair in 1957, he wanted to beat Ted Dexter's side. All these objectives were achieved.

The second Test at Lord's, when Cowdrey walked out for the last two balls with his arm in plaster to ensure a draw, was at least as exciting as the tied Test in Brisbane. The BBC interrupted a news broadcast to bring viewers coverage of the final over, more than six million calls were made to the UMP latest-score service during the series, and there were lockouts at most of the Test grounds for the first time since the Coronation Ashes.

The goodwill which the tourists generated – and the revenue that could be channelled back into county cricket – meant that the international schedule was indeed rejigged. Allen was credited with the idea of 'split' summers in England for the Test teams with less drawing power, and as early as 1966 West Indies came back for a full five-match series originally intended for South Africa.

Arlott ascribed the tour's 'dual success, in play and in public interest' to the support West Indies received from 'truly bipartisan crowds'. He also observed Worrell's side was devoid of 'the colour prejudice which in the past has impaired every aspect of West

Indian life', perhaps a polite way of pointing out that – for the first time – none of the senior leadership team was white. Worrell again had Duckworth carrying the bags, but Gaskin was back as manager and was praised by Arlott for his 'subtle part' in the triumph. The 'little pals' of 1950 were no longer in the Test side: Valentine was still a loyal Worrell lieutenant, captaining the tourists in some of the county games; Ramadhin was now landlord of the Horse & Hounds in Uppermill, Lancashire. But Sobers and Kanhai provided the same kind of symbolism when they combined brilliantly for the pivotal partnership of the series. Whereas the English selectors chopped and changed under the chairmanship of Robins, ten of Worrell's men played in every Test. Even the tinkering with the problematic opener position may have involved an attempt to ensure Jamaican representation in the team.

And West Indies won 3-1, taking the inaugural Wisden Trophy. If Lord's 1950 represented VE Day, the scenes at The Oval in 1963, after the tourists triumphed by eight wickets, reminded Ian Wooldridge of 'VE Night'.

John Clarke's book on the tour, *Cricket With a Swing*, noted that Worrell's side captivated 'the game's upper crust' as well as the 'man in the street'. Robins reportedly 'laughed his way home from Leeds', the West Indians' sparkling victory in the Headingley Test proving that he had been right to tell his own players 'time and time again that cricket does not belong to them but to the people out there'. Robins' critics suggested that he kept saying the game was more important than the result because, even as his selections gravitated more towards Yorkshire, he was not getting many results. But Worrell wrote to Robins expressing gratitude for MCC's recognition that it was now the West Indians who were on the civilising mission: 'We return to the Caribbean proud men, proud at the thought of having assisted the counties and England elevens in providing the spectators with the sort of cricket they desired.'

The inner circle had found in Worrell the kind of captain they had been looking for instead of Hutton in the early 1950s. R.C. Robertson-Glasgow, a journalist of authority, seemed to have Hutton in mind when he suggested that Worrell was the first Test captain in recent memory to show that cricket was 'a human game', a truth long hidden 'to the sort who say "*that's* not a business stroke"'.

369

J.L. Manning, the *Daily Mail* sports columnist, argued that if Hutton had been knighted despite leading such a divisive tour, Worrell should be knighted for leading such a harmonious one. The next year Worrell duly became the fourth cricketing 'Sir' after Hutton, Bradman and Hobbs.

However, West Indies were not always knights in shining armour in 1963. Worrell received a tremendous reception whenever he stepped on the field, but he took a notably long time to drag himself off it after a dubious decision in the third Test. The visitors did play what Willie Watson, now a selector, called 'Saturday-afternoon cricket' when they were well ahead, and in the one game they found themselves well behind. But, for the most part, Barker thought Worrell 'set out to play England at their own game', looking to grind out big scores if he won the toss and quickly resorting to defensive field-settings if not.

In the famous match at Lord's, Billy Griffith felt compelled to ring through from the MCC office to the press box, during Dexter's glorious innings of 70, to make sure journalists were aware that England were scoring their runs twice as quickly as West Indies. Ross noted that long spells by the pacemen, and time-wasting during England's run-chase, meant that the visitors bowled their overs at 14 per hour compared with England's 19: 'Hutton, I imagine, would have done the same as Worrell did, harnessing all that could be legally harnessed, giving nothing away.'

Godfrey Evans, watching Wes Hall and Charlie Griffith intimidate the home batsmen under Worrell's shrewd husbandry, was likewise reminded of the way Tyson and Statham got 'on top' of the Australians under Hutton. Griffith broke a few bones in the county games and his magnificent spells in the last two Tests finally broke England's spirit. Home journalists complained, if not as loudly as in the 1980s, about 'frightening blitzes' of bouncers. There were also what Barker called 'mutterings' about Griffith's action. Umpire Syd Buller, considered a 'hanging judge' on the issue of throwing, never called him but still annoyed the West Indians by repeatedly no-balling him for dragging (in the last series played under the back-foot no-ball law). At The Oval, Buller also issued two warnings for intimidatory bowling. He recalled 'Frank was very nice about it' when he gave the first caution; Griffith was less nice about it when he gave the second.

None of this could alter the feeling of English journalists that Worrell's cricketers were a 'popular and vital force' who had achieved something 'romantic and glorious'. For a future journalist growing up in Streatham, Simon Barnes, the 1963 series was a life-changing experience: 'The first impression was of the gravitas of Frank Worrell ... Here was a man who, just by saying good morning, could make you embarrassed that you ever watched *The Black and White Minstrel Show*.' The BBC ran that programme for another 15 years, so it is important to keep the impact of Worrell's tour in perspective. But Barnes was by no means alone in believing that this West Indies team, especially in the shape of Sobers, 'changed cricket's possibilities and, for so many people who watched, changed the way we saw ourselves and each other'.

'It was the first time in my life,' agreed the Yorkshire spinner Geoff Cope, 'I realised that it doesn't matter what colour you are.' As a 16-year-old colt, he had been chosen to help clean the kit in both dressing rooms at the Headingley Test. Whereas Cope was 'frightened' of a dismissive Dexter, he found Worrell 'so calm, honest, loving'. At a closing reception, the Lord Mayor of London credited Worrell for the fact 'a gale of change has blown through the hallowed halls of cricket'.

It would still take another two years for the Imperial Cricket Conference to rename itself the International Cricket Conference. Yet Worrell's timing was perfect again in that his approach, at the same time exciting and easy-going, chimed with what Barnes remembered as a 'new' feeling in Britain in 1963. Even the cricket journalists were distracted by the Profumo Affair, perhaps the clinching moment in the shift from deference to irreverence in attitudes towards the 'Establishment'. It was also the year of the Beatles' first LP, the year Philip Larkin thought 'sexual intercourse' began. So did the Gillette Cup.

Although Trueman disliked one-day cricket, he was more than ever a symbolic figure. He had threatened to make himself unavailable for the series, after having his good-conduct bonus – for Dexter's tour of Australia – withheld once more by MCC. But he emerged triumphant, taking twelve for 119 at Edgbaston and 34 wickets in total. He was now a master of his craft. But whereas Hutton had been idolised as the quintessential artisan, Trueman had become a quintessential modern celebrity. He was also now simply a cricketer. The distinction between Gentlemen and Players had, at last, been abolished by MCC in the winter of 1962.

Worrell's victory was one of the highpoints of the first short period of West Indies dominance in Test cricket between 1962 and 1967 (the second period under Lloyd and Richards lasted from 1976 to 1995). The captaincy was handed on to Sobers. Worrell was his team manager in 1964/65, when West Indies beat Australia for the first time to become undisputed, if unofficial, 'world champions'. Continuing as a Test selector, but concentrating on his role as Warden of the St Augustine campus of The University, Worrell usually kept his own counsel with the same dignity which had distinguished his playing career.

But he did object when Barbados, to celebrate its recently achieved independence, put on a 'Test' and a one-day game against The Rest of the World early in 1967. However strong the island's team under Sobers, Worrell felt the matches undermined West Indies cricket: 'The part must not be greater than the whole.' This was one of his last public statements. On the day Barbados lost the limited-overs game, Worrell died of leukemia at the age of 42. Sir Frank was the first sportsman to receive a memorial service at Westminster Abbey. Swanton gave the oration: 'He was a Federalist, nearest whose heart was the unity of the West Indian peoples in all their diversity ... Under the subtle knack of his personality differences of colour, island prejudices, seemed to melt away.'

When Sobers repeated Worrell's 3-1 win in England in 1966, his tour manager was Stollmeyer. They stood shoulder to shoulder in further controversies involving Griffith: the manager dealt with what he called an 'unrelenting and offensive' home press and strongly objected to the Board's withdrawal of the bowler's good-conduct bonus. Although they did not always see eye to eye in the 1970s, Sobers paid tribute to Stollmeyer's 'smiling, unruffled' part in the 1966 victory: 'I knew that here was a worthy successor to Sir Frank Worrell, which is one of the highest tributes I can pay any man.'

From 1974 to 1981, Stollmeyer served as the ninth president of the Board of Control. During his tenure, he saw West Indies win the first two World Cups but was also plunged into the Packer crisis – where he renewed acquaintance with Palmer, then MCC president. In 1981, Stollmeyer was succeeded by Rae, a proud nationalist but 'census white' under some local definitions, who in turn was succeeded by Walcott in 1988. It has often been remarked that it took three decades of Test cricket before a black captain was given permanent tenure of the West Indies team. As remarkably, it took nearly another three before a black president was elected by the Board.

One of Walcott's early duties was to give the oration at the funeral of one of his predecessors. In September 1989, Stollmeyer was murdered by armed robbers on his Mon Valmont estate. His contribution to West Indian cricket may not have been as game-changing as Worrell's but it was still, as Walcott recognised, important: 'I think the Caribbean as a whole has lost a great man.'

AFTERWORD

And what should they know of England who only
England know?
Rudyard Kipling, *The English Flag* (1891)

What do they know of cricket who only cricket know?
C.L.R. James, *Beyond a Boundary* (1963)

And so we return to the overwhelming question of *Beyond a Boundary*. As has often been noted, it alludes to a line of poetry from the days of Queen Victoria. Back then, Kipling was exhorting his complacent 'street-bred' countrymen to reflect upon the sacrifices made by their armed forces all around the globe, and to appreciate that they were nothing without their far-flung empire.

In 1963, James re-spun these old orthodoxies to bowl a couple of googlies. Whereas Kipling wanted his readers to consider the pervasive influence of the colonies on the mother country, James wanted his readers to consider the pernicious influence of the mother country on the colonies. Whereas Kipling derided, in another famous poem, 'flannelled fools' for treating the serious business of imperial government as a giant scheme of outdoor recreation, James believed cricket was at the heart of the British programme to instil its 'code' into its overseas subjects.

It is also possible that James was provoked by the fact a British cabinet minister had recently, on St George's Day 1961, quoted Kipling's question for the first line of a speech. This stirring piece of oratory looked back even further than the 'brash adventurous days of the first Elizabeth', which had been such a rallying point at the time of the Coronation. Instead, it argued that 'the homogeneity of England' stretched back to Anglo-Saxon times. In an observation which may have come as a surprise to Hutton and Trueman, this sense of Englishness was described as so profound and embracing that 'the counties and the regions make it a hobby to discover their differences and assert their peculiarities'. Now that the days of empire were 'plainly over', it should be a matter of pride that the homeland had never depended on its colonies for its unique character and strength: 'Perhaps after all we know most of England "who only England know."'

Beyond a Boundary confidently replies that West Indians know the English 'more sharply than they themselves'. There is a trace more anxiety in the book's insistence upon the ties between the Caribbean and Britain, and the parallels between self-realisation in cricket and self-realisation in politics. Now the old imperial power was leaving, the small nations of the West Indies might become yet more marginalised, and the West Indians living in Britain, like James himself, yet more demonised. The speech to which *Beyond a Boundary* seems to be responding was by Enoch Powell.

When, five years later, Powell reacted to winds of change by predicting rivers of blood, E.W. Swanton promptly wrote a letter to *The Spectator* condemning his 'twisted expression of national pride' and apparent hatred of 'fellow members of our Commonwealth'. Swanton and James shared a deep sense of cricket as an enduring Commonwealth institution which could break through the kind of barriers that Powell was seeking to erect. Swanton would also agree with the proposition of *Beyond a Boundary* that the English game profoundly changed the West Indies and that the West Indies profoundly changed the English game. Where the two men differed, generally speaking, was that Swanton believed cricket at its best was unsullied by politics, whereas James thought cricket at its best was drenched in it.

Swanton certainly treasured the way the game 'can reflect personality and individual idiosyncracy' but believed its role, especially on MCC tours, was 'to maintain an *ethos* which both influences and reflects the British character …, as it has done for the best part of a century'. James appreciated that, for better and for worse, cricket had helped suffuse this 'civilising' ethos throughout the English-speaking Caribbean. But he delighted in the paradox that, especially when West Indians were playing MCC teams, it powered 'dynamic explosions of individual and creative personalities expressing themselves to the utmost limit'. For Swanton, the game was akin to a religion whose best traditions had to be conserved. For James, it was an arena of conflict where the forces of history would prevail.

'To play it keenly, honourably, generously, self-sacrificingly, is a moral lesson in itself ... Foster it, my brothers ... protect it from anything that would sully it, so that it may grow in favour with all men.'

Lord Harris (1931), quoted in the introduction to Jeffrey Stollmeyer's *Everything Under the Sun* (1983)

I am sure that such figures as Lord Hawke and Lord Harris did much to set standards which the game will be ill advised to despise and ridicule as old-fashioned nonsense.

Len Hutton, *Fifty Years in Cricket* (1984)

Stollmeyer and Hutton both seemed to concur, in their mellow memoirs, with Swanton's view that Lord Harris was not a 'many-chinned blimp' but 'a universally respected man of awesome dignity'. Thirty years earlier, Swanton had criticised them both for not always fostering the spirit of the game nor goodwill across the Commonwealth. He was harsher on Hutton, playing cricket for money, but Stollmeyer was hardly playing it for fun.

If they were single-minded captains in 1953/54, Stollmeyer and Hutton came to appreciate, in the committee room and the press box, the importance of the 'standards' about which Harris and Swanton were so particular. The English gentleman's sense of cricket as more than a game had an unctuous whiff, whether invoked on the front foot as an integral part of the empire's cultural arsenal, or on the back foot as a bulwark against encroachment by pros and colonials. Yet, for all his vested interests, Harris sounded a prophetic warning that the game might matter less to people if the pursuit of victory by players, or profit by administrators, became the essential virtues. Any lover of cricket would sign up to the values at the core of his code: respect for teammates and opponents, for the laws and the umpires, for the need of the public to be entertained and of the next generations to be nurtured.

The inner circle of MCC could also contend that it tried to govern the game in the best interests of 'all men'. Without Harris's sly management of what he called 'the republic of cricket', the first-class game in England may well have split into two separate codes – rugby was the most obvious example of the many sports where amateur and professional became rigorously segregated. Without Warner's insistence that the omission of black and brown players from West Indies teams would be 'absurd', cricket at international level may have taken much longer to be multiracial – even if South Africa proved a difficult counter-example. Those nostalgic for the Corinthian spirit, once television money began to dominate the game more brazenly after Packer, included many retired professionals as well as Gubby Allen.

Swanton lived long enough to lament the transfer of power in cricket from Lord's mandarins to media moguls. The Packers, Murdochs and Modis may have less of 'the egoism of the patron' but, unlike Harris, Warner and Allen, they are in it only for themselves. Under their economic control, the lot of the elite cricketer has been vastly improved, the international game's survival in some form has arguably been ensured and the women's game is now being properly fostered. But cricket's traditions are not always protected, nor opportunities to learn it well diffused: there are more public schoolboys in the England team today than in 1953/54.

Because of his preoccupation with an individual's 'background', Swanton would have been comfortable enough with this. But he would have been saddened by the prospect of ancient counties with a heritage becoming city franchises without a soul. He would also have been saddened, as a lifelong enthusiast for Caribbean cricket, that no England touring side this century has played a Test series against West Indies taking in all of the Big Four venues. There may be justifiable reasons for the neglect of the traditional Test centres, other than Barbados. It still amounts – even if Swanton would not quite put it this way – to an act of cultural vandalism. His conserving spirit should never be despised.

> According to the colonial version of the code, you
> were to show yourself a 'true sport' by not making a
> fuss about the most barefaced discrimination because it
> wasn't cricket.
> C.L.R. James, *Beyond a Boundary* (1963)

By 'letting the side down' all you mean is that the nigger-driving sahib oughtn't to do anything that reveals that he shares a common humanity with the niggers he drives.

John Wain, *Hurry on Down* (1953)

Nevertheless, back in the 1950s, the MCC ethos was ever more subject to ridicule. The most obvious piece of hypocrisy, which in fact makes the inner circle seem more human, is that many of them – Harris, Hawke, Warner, Allen, Robins – were driven by a strong will to win which periodically caused them to countenance manoeuvres that were clearly 'not cricket' when it suited them.

More importantly, and more insidiously, MCC and the West Indies Board of Control proclaimed that class and race feeling had no place in the 'fellowship' of cricket only because their own social and racial attitudes were so embedded. Warner pretended to himself that MCC ruled with the 'consent of the governed', but that was because he cast beyond the pale anybody he decided was a 'cricketing Bolshevik', a phrase the Board of Control also used of Worrell.

When James said 'Worrell Must Captain' and 'Alexander Must Go', he knew he had to be almost as unfair to Alexander as the Board had been to Worrell. But he felt it was time to say a 'final goodbye', after decades of more patient protest, to the Harris code. Class discrimination in Britain may have seemed less barefaced than race discrimination in the Commonwealth, especially in Coronation year when the emphasis was on national communion. But an analogy was drawn that year in *Hurry on Down*, whose angry young hero lashes out against the values of a rugger-playing head boy. John Wain's first novel is one of the many ambivalent depictions of 'Us' against 'Them' in British and Caribbean literature after the war.

Working-class or peasant-class communities tend to be romanticised by the writers who leave them at the first opportunity. But in the 1950s, despite the social and geographical mobility being offered to eleven-plus children and Windrush children, those communities were still, like the county cricket of the period as remembered by Stephen Chalke, 'rich in craft skills and camaraderie'. That communal structure of feeling explains why it mattered to James that every hero from Constantine to Sobers remained to the core a West Indian cricketer 'not merely a cricketer from the West Indies', and why it mattered to Kilburn that 'Yorkshire cricketers' were more than 'cricketers from Yorkshire'.

For James, the spirit of 'Shannonism', of saying 'they are no better than we' while observing the valid parts of the code, reached its apotheosis in Worrell's triumphant captaincy. According to his wife Selma, James also took particular 'relish' in the way 'MCC, once it had been well and truly beaten, had gone to meet Hutton on his return at Southampton dock with an MCC tie'.

Hutton was ultimately more interested in beating Australia than MCC. He retired to Surrey not Yorkshire. But the Pudsey version of Shannonism suffused his cricket. He could relate to 'Us' against 'Them', even when the form of expression was more extrovert than his own. From the press box, Hutton well understood the meaning of swagger in the cricket of Viv Richards, describing him as a man 'descended from cane-cutters and slaves' who batted 'like a millionaire, as if he owned six sugar plantations'.

> They want to relax, and merely to watch … a game of
> skill and quality played hard and cleanly, not an all-in
> battle with propaganda accompaniment.
> E.W. Swanton, *West Indian Adventure* (1954)

> 'You hear the latest from British Guiana?'
> 'What, the strike still on?'
> 'Things really bad out there.'
> 'Man, go away, eh. We facing defeat and you want to
> talk politics.'
> V.S. Naipaul, 'The Test Match' (1963)

'If I knew that I was going to die today,' said the mathematician G.H. Hardy, 'I think I should still want to hear the cricket scores.' Swanton recognised that it might be 'a ludicrously old-fashioned view' to presume that people followed the game to take their minds off 'sterner realities', but the comments Naipaul overheard on Worrell's last tour gave it a ring of truth. Late in life, when his disciples came to his flat in Brixton to talk politics, James would sometimes put the cricket on and ask for a toasted crumpet.

He would still make the point that the entreaty to keep politics out of sport was itself a form of propaganda. In particular, local whites and English journalists had 'colossal nerve' when they accused West Indians of bringing racial feeling into the game. Swanton, never a bigot if always a snob, could respond that he condemned chauvinism on both sides in 1953/54, and that observers to his left became as uncomfortable about the cricket field being used as a political battleground. Alan Ross, a friend of the novelist Wain and an impassioned opponent of apartheid, described James as a 'malicious xenophobe' for his caricature of Alexander.

Constantine, Shannon's greatest son, went into politics to crusade against the negative stereotyping that denies human beings their full complexity, citing the objection that he was too immature and emotional to captain West Indies as an example of 'the black man being kept in his "place"'.

Yet it is part of the complexity of being human, and certainly part of being a sports fan, that we also fall back on stereotypes to take pride in our own place, pride that can carry its own embedded prejudices. The wonderfully stubborn and wonderfully mythologised exceptionalism of Yorkshire cricket, most obvious in the 'birthright' qualification that prevailed until 1991, has often festered into the racism displayed by Trueman and/or Wardle at Bourda in 1953/54. When Richards expressed his understandable pride in leading 'the only sporting team of African descent' that could beat all-comers, he was asked to think again by the Indian communities in Guyana and Trinidad.

> To grin at cricketers on equality's field day …
> Derek Walcott, 'Montego Bay – Travelogue 11', in *Poems* (1951)

> Old hanging ground is still green playing field – …
> Martin Carter, 'After One Year', in *Jail Me Quickly* (1964)

James's grand claim that cricketers played revolutionary 'representative roles' was open to probing from the Nursery End of Caribbean anti-imperialism as well as the Pavilion End of Swanton's Anglican conservatism. The first objection was that his romantic cultivation of cricketers as heroes provided only a mirage of freedom

Fourth Test bore-draw on the Port-of-Spain mat. Day 1: Weekes has edged Bailey behind – or so Spooner and Lock seem to think (as square-leg umpire Achong looks on). Reprieved on 43, Weekes made 206. Day 5: A clearer edge, into his face as he tried to hook a King bumper, felled Laker – who then zigzagged off the playing area with the assistance of the Trinidad Armed Police. These incidents typified the 'modern "battlefield" atmosphere' in which the match was played.

Fifth Test, Jamaica: England lost an apparently vital toss but Bailey's career-best seven for 34 opened up the game – he bowled Weekes for a duck. Bailey then played a crucial role as makeshift opener before providing Sobers with the opportunity to become the youngest wicket-taker in Test cricket – 'Silly little cut'.

Fifth Test, Day 3: Wardle (56*) and Hutton (205*), with Worrell and Stollmeyer behind, walking off at tea. Moments later, the England captain brushed aside Chief Minister Bustamante, a perceived snub which subsequent handshakes could not completely repair. Bustamante may have been seeking a photograph to add to his Coronation album: he was the only representative of a colony to make the shot of Commonwealth Prime Ministers (sixth from the left between Nehru and Churchill).

Left: Trueman and Bailey, sunbathing on the SS *Ariguani* on the passage home, oblivious to the shadow Lord's was about to cast over their careers. Right: D.S. Sheppard – opening for England with Hutton, L. – at a less sunny Old Trafford in 1952. A faction within MCC also conspired to install Sheppard as captain for the 1954/55 tour of Australia.

After the coup failed, the selectors posed for the cameras with the reappointed Hutton. From left to right: Allen, Robins (both pro-Sheppard), Hutton, Altham, Ames, Palmer, Yardley. The three figures on the right probably voted for Hutton, so the role of Altham as chairman of selectors became pivotal.

Altham came to see the players off at Tilbury. Three vital members of Hutton's backroom team were George Duckworth (standing extreme left), Harold Dalton (standing fourth left next to Hutton) and Geoffrey Howard (extreme right).

The other was Jim Kilburn, pictured with Hutton on their departure for a previous tour. Hutton's husbandry of the admirable Statham and Tyson was the main reason England retained the Ashes – they walk off after the win at Melbourne, with Evans behind, getting as close to a group hug as men of their temperament were able.

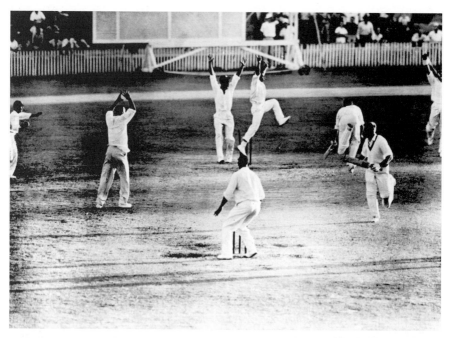

Two famous run-outs emblematic of the excitement Worrell's captaincy reinjected into Test cricket. Above: The last act of the tie at Brisbane in 1960/61 – Worrell covered the bowler's end as Joe Solomon (extreme left) threw out Ian Meckiff. Below: A footrace between two 38-year-olds in the last over of the 1963 Lord's Test – Worrell's dismissal of Derek Shackleton required Cowdrey, arm in plaster, to come out for the final two balls.

Two Queen's Park 'boss' men played their part in the 'Worrell/Sobers revolution' of the 1960s. Gerry Gomez, tour manager in 1960/61, was at Worrell's side on the team's motorcade through Melbourne. Five years later, Sobers and Stollmeyer returned together in triumph to Barbados, having stood shoulder to shoulder as captain and manager in England.

'Essential humanity': Worrell, Weekes, Ramadhin and Walcott, photographed in 1957; Hutton pictured in retirement by Jane Bown.

and progress for the people who worshipped them. Partly for the simple reason the islands are so small, the greatest West Indian cricketers have all left to make a living elsewhere, first in the northern leagues, then in the English counties, now in the T20 tournaments. In the 1950s, the Three Ws and the spin twins may, as James asserted, have filled 'a huge gap' in the 'consciousness' of people back home. But this did little to bridge the gap in circumstances, however admirable their service as educators whenever they returned.

The second and more historically complex objection was that cricket was too respectable a medium in which to seek reparation for plantation brutality. During Hutton's tour, a desire for truth before reconciliation was expressed by a radical in British Honduras (now Belize), who was happy to see more of his countrymen playing softball: 'I hate cricket and afternoon tea and all that bunkum.' But in the British West Indies, as James knew, cricket was too intimate a part of 'social and political life' for rejection of it to be a viable option. Even those who felt most strongly that the English 'code' was bunkum and sought to revive different traditions – Marcus Garvey, Cheddi Jagan, Walter Rodney – all seem to have been students of the game.

The Jamaican sociologist Orlando Patterson tried to encapsulate this 'double consciousness' in 1969, the year after a riot in the Test between West Indies and England at Sabina more violent than the disturbance at Bourda in 1954: 'Cricket is the game we love for it is the only game we can play well, the only activity which gives us some international prestige. But it is the game, deep down, which we must hate – the game of the master.'

This tension was still active in the era of 'Fire in Babylon', when for two decades a team drawn from a region of only six million people produced a distinctive brand of cricket which was too powerful for the rest of the world. Two historians, the Guyanese Clem Seecharan and the Antiguan Tim Hector, have celebrated in equal measure the achievements of the sides led by Lloyd and Richards. One has recognised it as a 'sociological miracle of the twentieth century'; the other has pointed out that, during this very period, all four of the traditionally strongest cricket territories suffered 'structural adjustment' by a new master, the International Monetary Fund.

Cricketers like the Constantines ... , George Headley and Frank Worrell ... were prepared to celebrate the glass as half-full rather than rage against its being half-empty. They were willing also to wait. It was thanks to their pride and forbearance that the next generation, ... Richards included, could triumph so memorably in what was able to be, by then, healthy competition between true equals.

Mike Brearley, 'Sir Donald Bradman Oration' (2013)

Steeped within the tradition of Constantine, Headley and Worrell, came the artistic genius of Sobers and the ideological radicalism of Richards ... It was politics, an ideological power struggle, and it was recognised by the world as such.

Professor Sir Hilary Beckles, 'The Radical Tradition in the Culture of West Indies Cricket' (1994)

These contrasting views of the development of West Indian cricket are not so far apart as selective quotation can make them appear. The speeches of Brearley and Beckles both recognise that any victim of injustice is involved in a psychological and historical process where submission and resistance are both in play. *Beyond a Boundary* is a book about these 'deep down' tensions.

The great line of Yorkshire professionals, less blatantly than the West Indian pioneers, were also victims of injustice. Their play said: we are the best men in the island, whether their pride was expressed through the yeomanry of Hirst, the polish of Sutcliffe or the theatricality of Trueman. English cricket's feudal system treated them as though they were not. It can be argued that their mildly subversive – and often highly amusing – grumbles about that system laid the best path for Hutton's quiet refusal to turn amateur, described by Michael Down as 'the most significant single event' in the 'emancipation' of the professional cricketer.

It can also be argued that the aggression Yorkshiremen displayed on the pitch against Middlesex at Lord's should have been directed at the MCC squires in the pavilion. Perhaps Powell had reason to assert that the forces of English patriotism and respectability reduced other loyalties to mere gesture. But pre-war professionals were not entirely taken in by the cant that a 'Bolshevist' uprising would let down the spirit of the English game. Perhaps they knew, whether by instinct or calculation, that the transfer of their labour from the counties was not worth ostracism by Lord's: the Lancashire League did not pay as well as Kerry Packer. Or perhaps they did not know themselves how much they were being forced to wait, and how much they were willing to wait.

As in the selection of cricket teams, it can be hard to find the right balance. Indeed, it is perhaps the best argument for cricket being able to teach moral lessons, or at least provide emotional consolations, that it holds so many things in balance. Despite what Constantine called its 'wars and inequalities', there is something special about the game for those who fall under its spell, with its dynamics – more ritualised, intricate and intense than in many pastimes – of playing for yourself and playing for the team, of setting yourself free and reining yourself in, of wanting badly to win without being a bad sport. As Weekes put it, sentimentally but still sagely, cricket is 'as sweet and painful as life itself'.

What Weekes said of his mentor Headley could also be said of Hutton: 'He spoke with precision, and no rancour. He would tell the harsh truth in a dignified sort of way.' For all the rancour of the 1953/54 series, what often shines through is the dignity of the cricketers, their pride and forbearance in the face of harsh truths often beyond their control.

Towards the end of his life, Hutton said he would like to start out in cricket all over again: 'But I don't want to know what I know now because there's a lot of fun finding out.' Like Weekes and Headley, he always liked to work things out for himself, while drawing on the accumulated wisdom of those who had gone before him. He can be censured, especially on the West Indies tour, for working people out only to exploit their weaknesses, and for concentrating his mind only on what was relevant to his profession. He did not always find the wider perspective that Swanton expected of an MCC captain. But he had discovered more by the time he and Bannister sat down to write *Fifty Years in Cricket*. In its understated way, that book – one of the main inspirations for this book – is full of the fun of finding things out. It is also full of love: for family, comrades, county, country and cricket.

There are many more important human activities which could be substituted in the question 'What do they know of cricket who only cricket know?' The game is lodged in the cultural cortex of a former empire, not an interconnected world, and it may seem 'old-fashioned nonsense' to those who legitimately rage about the glass still half-empty. But cricket is one of the activities where our different backgrounds and characters can come to life in a way which allows us to respect, and gently celebrate, what Arlott once called 'the essential humanity of the difference'.

STATISTICAL
AND
REFERENCE
SECTIONS

FIRST TEST

Sabina Park, Kingston, Jamaica   **15, 16, 18, 19, 20, 21 January 1954**

WEST INDIES – First Innings

			balls	mins	4s	6s	out at
M.C. Frederick	c Graveney b Statham	0	12	18	-	-	1/6
J.B. Stollmeyer *	lbw b Statham	60	180	249	6	-	2/140
J.K. Holt	lbw b Statham	94	285	358	9	-	4/234
E. de C. Weekes	b Moss	55	98	105	11	-	3/216
C.L. Walcott	b Lock	65	105	125	8	-	6/316
G.A. Headley	c Graveney b Lock	16	56	65	2	-	5/286
G.E. Gomez	*not out*	47	115	162	5	-	
C.A. McWatt +	b Lock	54	73	97	4	-	7/404
S. Ramadhin	lbw b Trueman	7	11	14	1	-	8/415
E.S.M. Kentish	b Statham	0	2	2	-	-	9/416
A.L. Valentine	b Trueman	0	1	2	-	-	10/417
Extras	*b 9, lb 4, w 1, nb 5*	19					
		417					

Runs per over: 2.68   Overs per hour: 15.34

WEST INDIES – Second Innings

			balls	mins	4s	6s	out at
M.C. Frederick	lbw b Statham	30	75	97	1	1	3/46
J.B. Stollmeyer *	c Evans b Bailey	8	24	34	-	-	1/28
J.K. Holt	lbw b Moss	1	12	17	-	-	2/31
E. de C. Weekes	*not out*	90	149	232	12	-	
C.L. Walcott	c Bailey b Lock	25	42	46	2	-	4/92
G.A. Headley	b Lock	1	2	2	-	-	5/94
G.E. Gomez	lbw b Statham	3	18	25	-	-	6/119
C.A. McWatt +	*not out*	36	82	109	4	-	
S. Ramadhin							
E.S.M. Kentish							
A.L. Valentine							
Extras	*b 10, lb 4, nb 1*	15					
	(for 6 wkts, declared)	**209**					

Runs per over: 3.12   Overs per hour: 14.01

ENGLAND BOWLING

Statham	36	6	90	4	17	2	50	2
Trueman	34.4	8	107	2	6	0	32	0
Moss	26	5	84	1	10	0	30	1
Bailey	16	4	36	0	20	4	46	1
Lock	41	14	76	3	14	2	36	2
Compton	2	1	5	0				

Toss won by West Indies
Umpires: P. Burke, T.A. Ewart

West Indies won by 140 runs

ENGLAND – First Innings

			balls	mins	4s	6s	out at
W. Watson	b Gomez	3	11	13	-	-	1/4
L. Hutton *	b Valentine	24	74	78	2	-	2/49
P.B.H. May	c Headley b Ramadhin	31	91	99	4	-	4/79
D.C.S. Compton	lbw b Valentine	12	24	20	2	-	3/73
T.W. Graveney	lbw b Ramadhin	16	48	44	3	-	5/94
T.E. Bailey	*not out*	28	189	159	1	-	
T.G. Evans +	c Kentish b Valentine	10	32	23	1	-	6/105
G.A.R. Lock	b Ramadhin	4	24	22	1	-	7/117
J.B. Statham	b Ramadhin	8	22	21	1	-	8/135
F.S. Trueman	c McWatt b Gomez	18	21	33	2	1	9/165
A.E. Moss	b Gomez	0	4	20	-	-	10/170
Extras	*b 9, lb 2, w 1, nb 4*	16					
		170					

Runs per over: 1.90   Overs per hour: 19.49

ENGLAND – Second Innings

			balls	mins	4s	6s	out at
W. Watson	c & b Stollmeyer	116	245	259	16	-	2/220
L. Hutton *	lbw b Gomez	56	132	138	6	-	1/130
P.B.H. May	c McWatt b Kentish	69	187	208	10	1	3/277
T.W. Graveney	c Weekes b Kentish	34	115	122	2	-	5/282
D.C.S. Compton	b Ramadhin	2	20	18	-	-	4/282
T.E. Bailey	*not out*	15	45	51	1	1	
T.G. Evans +	b Kentish	0	2	1	-	-	6/282
G.A.R. Lock	b Kentish	0	7	7	-	-	7/282
J.B. Statham	lbw b Ramadhin	1	8	5	-	-	8/283
F.S. Trueman	b Kentish	1	9	11	-	-	9/285
A.E. Moss	run out	16	8	14	3	-	10/316
Extras	*b 4, lb 1, nb 1*	6					
		316					

Runs per over: 2.44   Overs per hour: 18.46

WEST INDIES BOWLING

Kentish	14	5	23	0	29	11	49	5
Gomez	9.2	3	16	3	30	9	63	1
Ramadhin	35	14	65	4	35.3	12	88	2
Valentine	31	10	50	3	25	6	71	0
Headley					5	0	23	0
Walcott					2	1	4	0
Stollmeyer					3	0	12	1

SECOND TEST

Kensington Oval, Bridgetown, Barbados   6, 8, 9, 10, 11, 12 February 1954

WEST INDIES – First Innings			balls	mins	4s	6s	out at
J.K. Holt	c Graveney b Bailey	11	21	34	2	-	3/25
J.B. Stollmeyer *	run out	0	10	18	-	-	1/11
F.M.M. Worrell	b Statham	0	3	1	-	-	2/11
C.L. Walcott	st Evans b Laker	220	343	398	28	1	9/378
B.H. Pairaudeau	c Hutton b Laker	71	178	175	14	-	4/190
G.E. Gomez	lbw b Statham	7	25	31	1	-	5/226
D. St E. Atkinson	c Evans b Laker	53	106	112	9	-	6/319
C.A. McWatt +	lbw b Lock	11	47	41	2	-	7/352
S. Ramadhin	b Statham	1	11	16	-	-	8/372
F.M. King	b Laker	5	6	9	1	-	10/383
A.L. Valentine	*not out*	0	4	5	-	-	
Extras	*lb 2, nb 2*	4					
		383					

Runs per over: 3.06   Overs per hour: 17.26

WEST INDIES – Second Innings			balls	mins	4s	6s	out at
J.K. Holt	c & b Statham	166	271	284	27	1	2/273
J.B. Stollmeyer *	run out	28	64	68	4	-	1/51
F.M.M. Worrell	*not out*	76	221	234	9	-	
C.L. Walcott	*not out*	17	21	17	2	-	
B.H. Pairaudeau							
G.E. Gomez							
D. St E. Atkinson							
C.A. McWatt +							
S. Ramadhin							
F.M. King							
A.L. Valentine							
Extras	*b 4, nb 1*	5					
(for 2 wkts, declared)		**292**					

Runs per over: 3.04   Overs per hour: 19.01

ENGLAND BOWLING

Statham	27	6	90	3	15	1	49	1
Bailey	22	6	63	1	12	1	48	0
Lock	41	9	116	1	33	7	100	0
Laker	30.1	6	81	4	30	13	62	0
Compton	5	0	29	0	1	0	13	0
Palmer					5	1	15	0

Toss won by West Indies
Umpires: H.B. de C. Jordan, J.H. Walcott

West Indies won by 181 runs

ENGLAND – First Innings

			balls	mins	4s	6s	out at
L. Hutton *	c Ramadhin b Valentine	72	310	268	9	-	5/119
W. Watson	st McWatt b Ramadhin	6	35	50	-	-	1/35
P.B.H. May	c King b Ramadhin	7	27	20	1	-	2/45
D.C.S. Compton	c King b Valentine	13	75	61	1	-	3/70
T.W. Graveney	c & b Ramadhin	15	132	126	-	-	4/107
C.H. Palmer	c Walcott b Ramadhin	22	79	75	4	-	6/158
T.E. Bailey	c McWatt b Atkinson	28	127	100	2	-	8/176
T.G. Evans +	b Gomez	10	33	26	2	-	7/176
J.C. Laker	c Gomez b Atkinson	1	16	14	-	-	9/177
G.A.R. Lock	*not out*	0	45	37	-	-	
J.B. Statham	c Holt b Valentine	3	27	23	-	-	10/181
Extras	*b 2, lb 1, nb 1*	4					
		181					

Runs per over: 1.20   Overs per hour: 22.18

ENGLAND – Second Innings

			balls	mins	4s	6s	out at
L. Hutton *	c Worrell b Ramadhin	77	228	222	11	-	3/181
W. Watson	c McWatt b King	0	5	4	-	-	1/1
P.B.H. May	c Walcott b Gomez	62	107	104	11	-	2/108
D.C.S. Compton	lbw b Stollmeyer	93	223	193	14	-	4/258
T.W. Graveney	*not out*	64	187	172	10	-	
C.H. Palmer	c Gomez b Atkinson	0	7	3	-	-	5/259
T.E. Bailey	c sub (Hunte) b Stollmeyer	4	4	3	1	-	6/264
T.G. Evans +	b Ramadhin	5	41	33	1	-	7/281
J.C. Laker	lbw b Ramadhin	0	4	4	-	-	8/281
G.A.R. Lock	b King	0	22	24	-	-	9/300
J.B. Statham	b Gomez	0	10	12	-	-	10/313
Extras	*b 6, lb 1, w 1*	8					
		313					

Runs per over: 2.24   Overs per hour: 21.16

WEST INDIES BOWLING

King	14	6	28	0	18	6	56	2
Gomez	13	8	10	1	13.4	3	28	2
Worrell	9	2	21	0	1	0	10	0
Atkinson	9	7	5	2	23	10	35	1
Ramadhin	53	30	50	4	37	17	71	3
Valentine	51.5	30	61	3	39	18	87	0
Stollmeyer	1	0	2	0	6	1	14	2
Walcott					2	0	4	0

389

THIRD TEST

Bourda, Georgetown, British Guiana   24, 25, 26, 27 February, 1, 2 March 1954

ENGLAND – First Innings

		balls	mins	4s	6s	out at
W. Watson	b Ramadhin	12	76	76	-	-	1/33
L. Hutton *	c Worrell b Ramadhin	169	495	457	24	1	5/306
P.B.H. May	lbw b Atkinson	12	72	63	2	-	2/76
D.C.S. Compton	c Stollmeyer b Atkinson	64	264	228	8	-	3/226
T.W. Graveney	b Ramadhin	0	12	16	-	-	4/227
J.H. Wardle	b Ramadhin	38	84	91	4	-	6/321
T.E. Bailey	c Weekes b Ramadhin	49	155	141	7	-	9/412
T.G. Evans +	lbw b Atkinson	19	60	43	3	-	7/350
J.C. Laker	b Valentine	27	45	43	4	1	8/390
G.A.R. Lock	b Ramadhin	13	45	46	2	-	10/435
J.B. Statham	*not out*	10	14	13	2	-	
Extras	b 20, nb 2	22					
		435					

Runs per over: 1.98   Overs per hour: 21.46

ENGLAND – Second Innings

		balls	mins	4s	6s	out at
T.W. Graveney	*not out*	33	64	63	5	-	
P.B.H. May	b Atkinson	12	10	12	2	-	1/18
W. Watson	*not out*	27	47	49	1	1	
L. Hutton *							
D.C.S. Compton							
T.E. Bailey							
T.G. Evans +							
J.H. Wardle							
J.C. Laker							
G.A.R. Lock							
J.B. Statham							
Extras	b 3	3					
(for 1 wkt)		**75**					

Runs per over: 3.72   Overs per hour: 19.21

WEST INDIES BOWLING

Gomez	32	6	75	0	5	1	15	0
Worrell	15	4	33	0				
Ramadhin	67	34	113	6	4	0	7	0
Valentine	44	18	109	1				
Atkinson	58	27	78	3	7	0	34	1
Stollmeyer	2	1	3	0				
Walcott	2	0	2	0	2	0	6	0
Weekes					1.1	0	8	0
Christiani					1	0	2	0

Toss won by England
Umpires: E.S. Gillette, B. Menzies

England won by nine wickets

WEST INDIES – First Innings			balls	mins	4s	6s	out at
F.M.M. Worrell	c Evans b Statham	0	1	1	-	-	1/1
J.B. Stollmeyer *	b Statham	2	15	21	-	-	2/12
E. de C. Weekes	b Lock	94	180	166	14	-	6/134
C.L. Walcott	b Statham	4	6	6	1	-	3/16
R.J. Christiani	c Watson b Laker	25	62	71	2	-	4/78
G.E. Gomez	b Statham	8	34	49	1	-	5/132
D. St E. Atkinson	c & b Lock	0	16	24	-	-	7/139
C.A. McWatt +	run out	54	154	150	3	-	8/238
J.K. Holt	*not out*	48	150	166	5	-	
S. Ramadhin	b Laker	0	5	9	-	-	9/240
A.L. Valentine	run out	0	12	13	-	-	10/251
Extras	*b 8, lb 7, w 1*	16					
	251						

Runs per over: 2.37   Overs per hour: 18.30

WEST INDIES – Second Innings							
J.K. Holt	b Lock	64	152	159	11	-	3/120
J.B. Stollmeyer *	c Compton b Laker	44	104	108	8	-	1/79
F.M.M. Worrell	c Evans b Statham	2	19	20	-	-	2/96
E. de C. Weekes	c Graveney b Bailey	38	84	90	7	-	4/168
C.L. Walcott	lbw b Laker	26	91	101	4	-	6/200
R.J. Christiani	b Bailey	11	20	22	1	1	5/186
G.E. Gomez	c Graveney b Wardle	35	116	100	4	-	8/246
D. St E. Atkinson	b Wardle	18	75	71	2	-	7/245
C.A. McWatt +	*not out*	9	33	29	1	-	
S. Ramadhin	b Statham	1	8	11	-	-	9/251
A.L. Valentine	b Wardle	0	5	3	-	-	10/256
Extras	*b 2, lb 4, nb 2*	8					
	256						

Runs per over: 2.18   Overs per hour: 19.26

ENGLAND BOWLING

Statham	27	6	64	4	22	3	86	2
Bailey	5	0	13	0	22	9	41	2
Laker	21	11	32	2	36	18	56	2
Wardle	22	4	60	0	12.3	4	24	3
Compton	3	1	6	0				
Lock	27.5	7	60	2	25	11	41	1

391

FOURTH TEST

Queen's Park Oval, Port of Spain, Trinidad   17, 18, 19, 20, 22, 23 March 1954

WEST INDIES – First Innings			*balls*	*mins*	*4s*	*6s*	*out at*
J.K. Holt	c Compton b Trueman	40	88	106	6	-	2/92
J.B. Stollmeyer *	c & b Compton	41	69	87	5	-	1/78
E. de C. Weekes	c Bailey b Lock	206	292	354	25	-	3/430
F.M.M. Worrell	b Lock	167	389	438	23	-	4/517
C.L. Walcott	c & b Laker	124	180	211	18	1	6/627
B.H. Pairaudeau	run out	0	41	37	-	-	5/540
D. St E. Atkinson	c Graveney b Compton	74	93	116	9	3	8/681
C.A. McWatt +1	b Laker	4	15	14	-	-	7/641
W. Ferguson +2	*not out*	8	30	29	1	-	
S. Ramadhin							
F.M. King							
Extras	*b 6, lb 4, w 4, nb 3*	17					
(for 8 wkts, declared)		**681**					

Runs per over: 3.43   Overs per hour: 17.05

WEST INDIES – Second Innings			*balls*	*mins*	*4s*	*6s*	*out at*
B.H. Pairaudeau	hit wkt b Bailey	5	35	45	-	-	1/19
W. Ferguson +2	b Bailey	44	85	109	4	-	3/72
E. de C. Weekes	c sub (Suttle) b Trueman	1	2	6	-	-	2/20
F.M.M. Worrell	c sub (Moss) b Lock	56	78	84	6	2	4/111
C.L. Walcott	*not out*	51	78	93	6	-	
D. St E. Atkinson	*not out*	53	52	63	8	-	
J.K. Holt							
J.B. Stollmeyer *							
C.A. McWatt +1							
S. Ramadhin							
F.M. King							
Extras	*lb 2*	2					
(for 4 wkts, declared)		**212**					

Runs per over: 3.85   Overs per hour: 16.18

ENGLAND BOWLING

Statham	9	0	31	0				
Trueman	33	3	131	1	15	5	23	1
Bailey	32	7	104	0	12	2	20	2
Laker	50	8	154	2				
Lock	63	14	178	2	10	2	40	1
Compton	8.4	1	40	2	7	0	51	0
Graveney	3	0	26	0	5	0	33	0
Hutton					6	0	43	0

Toss won by West Indies
Umpires: E.E. Achong, K. Woods

Match drawn

ENGLAND – First Innings

		balls	mins	4s	6s	out at
L. Hutton *	c Ferguson b King	44	104	98	6	-	1/73
T.E. Bailey	c Weekes b Ferguson	46	167	182	8	-	2/135
P.B.H. May	c Pairaudeau b King	135	277	249	24	-	3/301
D.C.S. Compton	c & b Ramadhin	133	306	349	17	-	5/424
W. Watson	c Atkinson b Walcott	4	37	40	1	-	4/314
T.W. Graveney	c & b Walcott	92	198	215	15	1	6/493
R.T. Spooner +	b Walcott	19	99	91	2	-	7/496
J.C. Laker	*retired hurt*	7	56	58	-	-	*8/520*
G.A.R. Lock	lbw b Worrell	10	30	30	-	-	8/510
F.S. Trueman	lbw b King	19	32	42	2	-	9/537
J.B. Statham	*not out*	6	23	39	-	-	
Extras	b 10, lb 5, w 7	22					
		537					

Runs per over: 2.43   Overs per hour: 18.86

ENGLAND – Second Innings

		balls	mins	4s	6s	out at
W. Watson	c Ferguson b Worrell	32	32	31	5	-	1/52
R.T. Spooner +	c Ferguson b Ramadhin	16	37	36	1	-	2/52
P.B.H. May	c Worrell b McWatt	16	48	40	3	-	3/83
L. Hutton *	*not out*	30	55	51	6	-	
T.W. Graveney	*not out*	0	8	14	-	-	
D.C.S. Compton							
T.E. Bailey							
J.C. Laker							
G.A.R. Lock							
F.S. Trueman							
J.B. Statham							
Extras	lb 4	4					
(for 3 wkts)		**98**					

Runs per over: 3.27   Overs per hour: 20.22

WEST INDIES BOWLING

King	48.2	16	97	3				
Worrell	20	2	58	1	9	1	29	1
Ramadhin	34	13	74	1	7	4	6	1
Atkinson	32	12	60	0	4	0	12	0
Ferguson	47	7	155	1				
Stollmeyer	6	2	19	0				
Walcott	34	18	52	3				
Weekes					5	1	28	0
McWatt					4	2	16	1
Pairaudeau					1	0	3	0

FIFTH TEST

Sabina Park, Kingston, Jamaica   **30, 31 March, 1, 2, 3 April 1954**

WEST INDIES – First Innings

			balls	mins	4s	6s	out at
J.K. Holt	c Lock b Bailey	0	5	2	-	-	1/0
J.B. Stollmeyer *	c Evans b Bailey	9	27	37	-	-	3/13
E. de C. Weekes	b Bailey	0	12	16	-	-	2/2
F.M.M. Worrell	c Wardle b Trueman	4	12	18	-	-	4/13
C.L. Walcott	c Laker b Lock	50	106	140	9	-	7/110
D. St E. Atkinson	lbw b Bailey	21	80	84	2	-	5/65
G.E. Gomez	c Watson b Bailey	4	5	5	1	-	6/75
C.A. McWatt +	c Lock b Bailey	22	68	63	2	-	8/115
G.St A. Sobers	*not out*	14	32	44	2	-	
F.M. King	b Bailey	9	12	17	1	-	9/133
S. Ramadhin	lbw b Trueman	4	6	15	1	-	10/139
Extras	*lb 1, nb 1*	2					
		139					

Runs per over: 2.29   Overs per hour: 16.25

WEST INDIES – Second Innings

			balls	mins	4s	6s	out at
J.K. Holt	c Lock b Trueman	8	37	51	-	-	1/26
J.B. Stollmeyer *	lbw b Trueman	64	225	242	8	-	4/123
E. de C. Weekes	b Wardle	3	33	34	-	-	2/38
F.M.M. Worrell	c Graveney b Trueman	29	149	136	2	-	3/102
C.L. Walcott	c Graveney b Laker	116	234	262	20	-	8/306
G.E. Gomez	lbw b Laker	22	101	102	3	-	5/191
D. St E. Atkinson	c Watson b Bailey	40	94	100	7	-	6/273
C.A. McWatt +	c Wardle b Laker	8	14	17	1	-	7/293
G.St A. Sobers	c Compton b Lock	26	72	79	5	-	10/346
S. Ramadhin	c & b Laker	10	40	34	2	-	9/326
F.M. King	*not out*	10	27	21	2	-	
Extras	*b 4, lb 3, w 1, nb 2*	10					
		346					

Runs per over: 2.04   Overs per hour: 18.61

ENGLAND BOWLING

Bailey	16	7	34	7	25	11	54	1
Trueman	15.4	4	39	2	29	7	88	3
Wardle	10	1	20	0	39	14	83	1
Lock	15	6	31	1	27	16	40	1
Laker	4	1	13	0	50	27	71	4

Toss won by West Indies
Umpires: P. Burke, T.A. Ewart

England won by nine wickets

ENGLAND – First Innings

			balls	mins	4s	6s	out at
L. Hutton *	c McWatt b Walcott	205	489	534	23	1	7/392
T.E. Bailey	c McWatt b Sobers	23	111	121	3	-	1/43
P.B.H. May	c sub (P'deau) b Ramadhin	30	62	64	4	1	2/104
D.C.S. Compton	hit wkt b King	31	66	70	5	-	3/152
W. Watson	c McWatt b King	4	11	8	-	-	4/160
T.W. Graveney	lbw b Atkinson	11	18	25	2	-	5/179
T.G. Evans +	c Worrell b Ramadhin	28	149	141	3	-	6/287
J.H. Wardle	c Holt b Sobers	66	108	124	9	1	9/406
G.A.R. Lock	b Sobers	4	20	16	1	-	8/401
J.C. Laker	b Sobers	9	25	21	1	-	10/414
F.S. Trueman	not out	0	2	8	-	-	
Extras	lb 3	3					
		414					

Runs per over: 2.34   Overs per hour: 18.45

ENGLAND – Second Innings

		balls	mins	4s	6s	out at
T.W. Graveney	b King	0	5	4	-	-	1/0
W. Watson	not out	20	41	55	3	-	
P.B.H. May	not out	40	49	49	7	-	
L. Hutton *							
T.E. Bailey							
D.C.S. Compton							
T.G. Evans +							
J.H. Wardle							
G.A.R. Lock							
J.C. Laker							
F.S. Trueman							
Extras	b 12	12					
(for 1 wkt)		**72**					

Runs per over: 4.55   Overs per hour: 17.27

WEST INDIES BOWLING

King	26	12	45	2	4	1	21	1
Gomez	25	8	56	0				
Atkinson	41	15	82	1	3	0	8	0
Ramadhin	29	9	71	2	3	0	14	0
Sobers	28.5	9	75	4	1	0	6	0
Walcott	11	5	26	1				
Worrell	11	0	34	0	4	0	8	0
Stollmeyer	5	0	22	0				
Weekes					0.5	0	3	0

RESULTS OF TOUR MATCHES

(italics = not first-class)

First-class: Played 10   Won 6   Drawn 2   Lost 2

All matches: Played 17   Won 8   Drawn 7   Lost 2

December 16, 17   Somerset Cricket Club, Bermuda
Combined XI 73 (Wardle 4-16) & 104 (Laker 5-35)
MCC 205 (Laker 67, Graveney 52, Mulder 4-49)
MCC won by an innings and 28 runs

December 20, 21, 22   Somerset Cricket Club, Bermuda
MCC 148 (Woods 5-49, Symonds 4-29) & 166-6d
Bermuda 133 (Lock 8-54) & 90-6
Drawn

December 23, 24, 26   Somerset Cricket Club, Bermuda
Bermuda 133 (Lock 7-35)
MCC 135-1 (Hutton 67, Watson 55*)
Drawn

December 30, 31   Chedwin Park, Spanish Town, Jamaica
Combined Parishes XI 168 (Frederick 85, Lock 4-25) & 89-3
MCC 275-4d (Bailey 78, Compton 73)
Drawn

January 2, 3, 5, 6   Sabina Park, Kingston, Jamaica
Jamaica 266 (Rickards 75, Frederick 60) & 170 (Trueman 5-45, Statham 4-35)
MCC 457-7d (Watson 161, Graveney 82, Compton 56, Scarlett 4-155)
MCC won by an innings and 21 runs

January 8, 9, 11, 12   Melbourne Park, Kingston, Jamaica
Jamaica 187 (Frederick 58, Moss 4-47) & 328-4d (Holt 152, Rae 53, Headley 53*)
MCC 286 (May 124, Scarlett 4-69) & 34-1
Drawn

January 15, 16, 18, 19, 20, 21   Sabina Park, Kingston, Jamaica
First Test: West Indies beat England by 140 runs

January 25, 26   Recreation Ground, St John's, Antigua
Leeward Islands 38 (Wardle 5-7, Laker 4-29) & 167 (Compton 5-50)
MCC 261 (Hutton 82, Graveney 50)
MCC won by an innings and 56 runs

January 29, 30, February 1, 2, 3   Kensington Oval, Bridgetown, Barbados
Barbados 389 (Atkinson 151, Lock 4-119) & 179 (Lock 5-57, Laker 4-47)
MCC 373 (Suttle 96, Hutton 59*, May 57, Watson 53, Walcott 4-42)
          & 196-9 (Suttle 62, Goddard 5-43)
MCC won by one wicket

February 6, 8, 9, 10, 11, 12   Kensington Oval, Bridgetown, Barbados
Second Test: West Indies beat England by 181 runs

February 17, 18, 19, 20   Bourda, Georgetown, British Guiana
MCC 607 (Watson 257, Graveney 231)
British Guiana 262 (Christiani 75, Wardle 6-77) & 247 (Christiani 82)
MCC won by an innings and 98 runs

February 24, 25, 26, 27, March 1, 2   Bourda, Georgetown, British Guiana
Third Test: England beat West Indies by nine wickets

March 6,8   Queen's Park (Old), St George's, Grenada
MCC 205-7d (Hutton 82) & 177-3 (May 93, Wardle 66)*
Windward Islands 194 (Neverson 90, Trueman 7-69)*
Drawn

March 10, 11, 12, 13, 15   Queen's Park Oval, Port of Spain, Trinidad
Trinidad 329 (Gomez 91, Stollmeyer 89, Moss 4-63)
          & 232 (Asgarali 65, Trueman 4-47)
MCC 331-8d (Watson 141, Palmer 87, Ferguson 4-119)
          & 233-3 (Compton 90*, Bailey 90)
MCC won by seven wickets

March 17, 18, 19, 20, 22, 23   Queen's Park Oval, Port of Spain, Trinidad
Fourth Test: Drawn

March 26, 27   Jarrett Park, Montego Bay, Jamaica
MCC 135 (Bailey 55)
Jamaica Colts & Country XI 97-6
Drawn

March 30, 31, April 1, 2, 3   Sabina Park, Kingston, Jamaica
Fifth Test: England beat West Indies by nine wickets

TEST MATCH AVERAGES

ENGLAND

BATTING	M	I	NO	Runs	HS	Ave	100s	Balls
L. Hutton	5	8	1	677	205	96.71	2	1887
J.H. Wardle	2	2	-	104	66	52.00	-	192
D.C.S. Compton	5	7	-	348	133	49.71	1	978
P.B.H. May	5	10	1	414	135	46.00	1	930
T.E. Bailey	5	7	2	193	49	38.60	-	798
T.W. Graveney	5	10	3	265	92	37.85	-	787
W. Watson	5	10	2	224	116	28.00	1	540
R.T. Spooner	1	2	-	35	19	17.50	-	136
F.S. Trueman	3	4	1	38	19	12.66	-	64
T.G. Evans	4	6	-	72	28	12.00	-	317
J.C. Laker	4	5	1	44	27	11.00	-	146
C.H. Palmer	1	2	-	22	22	11.00	-	86
A.E. Moss	1	2	-	16	16	8.00	-	12
J.B. Statham	4	6	2	28	10*	7.00	-	104
G.A.R. Lock	5	7	1	31	13	5.16	-	193

Scoring rates of leading English batsmen *(runs per 100 balls)*

May	44.5	Watson	41.5	Hutton	35.9
Compton	35.6	Graveney	33.7	Bailey	24.2

BOWLING	Overs	Mdns	Runs	Wkts	Best	Ave	5wi
J.B. Statham	153	24	460	16	4-64	28.75	-
T.E. Bailey	182	51	459	14	7-34	32.78	1
J.C. Laker	218.1	84	469	14	4-71	33.50	-
F.S. Trueman	133.2	27	420	9	3-88	46.66	-
J.H. Wardle	83.3	23	187	4	3-24	46.75	-
G.A.R. Lock	292.5	87	718	14	3-76	51.28	-
A.E. Moss	36	5	114	2	1-30	57.00	-
D.C.S. Compton	27.4	3	144	2	2-40	72.00	-

T.W. Graveney 8-0-59-0   L. Hutton 6-0-43-0   C.H. Palmer 5-1-15-0

FIELDING

- 8 T.W. Graveney
- 6 T.G. Evans *(5 ct, 1 st)*
- 4 D.C.S. Compton, G.A.R. Lock
- 3 J.C. Laker, W. Watson
- 2 T.E. Bailey, J.H. Wardle
- 1 L. Hutton, J.B. Statham

A.E. Moss and K.G. Suttle each took one catch as a substitute fielder

WEST INDIES

BATTING	M	I	NO	Runs	HS	Ave	100s	Balls
C.L. Walcott	5	10	2	698	220	87.25	3	1206
E. de C. Weekes	4	8	1	487	206	69.57	1	850
J.K. Holt	5	9	1	432	166	54.00	1	1021
W. Ferguson	1	2	1	52	44	52.00	-	115
F.M.M. Worrell	4	8	1	334	167	47.71	1	872
D. St E. Atkinson	4	7	1	259	74	43.16	-	516
G.St A. Sobers	1	2	1	40	26	40.00	-	104
C.A. McWatt	5	8	2	198	54	33.00	-	486
J.B. Stollmeyer	5	9	-	256	64	28.44	-	718
B.H. Pairaudeau	2	3	-	76	71	25.33	-	254
G.E. Gomez	4	7	1	126	47*	21.00	-	414
R.J. Christiani	1	2	-	36	25	18.00	-	82
M.C. Frederick	1	2	-	30	30	15.00	-	87
F.M. King	3	3	1	24	10*	12.00	-	45
G.A. Headley	1	2	-	17	16	8.50	-	58
S. Ramadhin	5	6	-	25	10	3.83	-	81
A.L. Valentine	3	4	1	0	0*	0.00	-	22
E.S.M. Kentish	1	1	-	0	0	0.00	-	2

Scoring rates of leading West Indian batsmen *(runs per 100 balls)*

Walcott	57.9	Weekes	57.3	Atkinson	50.2	Holt	42.3
McWatt	40.7	Worrell	38.3	Stollmeyer	35.6	Gomez	30.4

BOWLING	Overs	Mdns	Runs	Wkts	Best	Ave	5wi
E.S.M. Kentish	43	15	72	5	5-49	14.40	1
G.St A. Sobers	29.5	9	81	4	4-75	20.25	-
C.L. Walcott	53	24	94	4	3-52	23.50	-
J.B. Stollmeyer	23	4	72	3	2-14	24.00	-
S. Ramadhin	304.3	133	559	23	6-113	24.30	1
F.M. King	110	41	247	8	3-97	30.87	-
G.E. Gomez	128	37	263	7	3-16	37.57	-
D.St E. Atkinson	177	71	314	8	3-78	39.25	-
A.L. Valentine	190.5	81	378	7	3-50	54.00	-
F.M.M. Worrell	70	10	193	2	1-29	96.50	-

W. Ferguson 47-17-155-1   C.A. McWatt 4-1-16-1   E. de C. Weekes 8-1-39-0
G.A. Headley 5-0-23-0   R.J. Christiani 1-0-2-0   B.H. Pairaudeau 1-0-3-0

FIELDING

8   C. McWatt *(7 ct, 1 st)*
4   F.M.M. Worrell
3   W. Ferguson, S. Ramadhin, E. de C. Weekes, C.L. Walcott
2   G.E. Gomez, J.K. Holt, F.M. King, J.B. Stollmeyer
1   D.St E. Atkinson, G.A. Headley, E.S.M. Kentish, B.H. Pairaudeau

B.H. Pairaudeau and C.C. Hunte each took one catch as a substitute fielder

TOUR AVERAGES IN ALL FIRST-CLASS MATCHES

BATTING

	M	I	NO	Runs	HS	Ave	100s	50s
L. Hutton	8	12	2	780	205	78.00	2	4
W. Watson	9	16	3	892	257	68.61	4	1
T.W. Graveney	8	14	3	617	231	56.09	1	3
T.E. Bailey	8	11	4	346	90	49.42	-	1
D.C.S. Compton	10	14	1	630	133	48.46	1	4
K.G. Suttle	4	7	1	251	96	41.83	-	2
P.B.H. May	10	18	2	630	135	39.37	2	3
C.H. Palmer	3	4	-	142	87	35.50	-	1
J.H. Wardle	5	5	-	130	66	26.00	-	1
J.C. Laker	7	9	1	123	33	15.37	-	-
F.S. Trueman	8	9	3	81	20	13.50	-	-
R.T. Spooner	5	8	1	93	28	13.28	-	-
G.A.R. Lock	9	12	2	105	40*	10.50	-	-
A.E. Moss	5	6	2	39	16	9.75	-	-
T.G. Evans	6	8	-	72	28	9.00	-	-
J.B. Statham	5	6	2	28	10*	7.00	-	-

BOWLING

	Overs	Mdns	Runs	Wkts	Best	Ave	5wi
J.B. Statham	194.5	35	541	22	4-35	24.59	-
A.E. Moss	161.5	38	490	18	4-47	27.22	-
T.E. Bailey	251.5	79	611	22	7-34	27.77	1
J.H. Wardle	240.3	77	569	18	6-77	31.61	1
F.S. Trueman	319.4	81	909	27	5-45	33.66	1
J.C. Laker	330.5	113	756	22	4-47	34.36	-
G.A.R. Lock	486.1	157	1178	28	5-57	42.07	1
D.C.S. Compton	81.4	16	325	6	2-40	54.16	-

C.H. Palmer 22-13-33-0   T.W. Graveney 16-6-71-0   L. Hutton 6-0-43-0

FIELDING

14 T.W. Graveney
9   T.G. Evans *(8 ct, 1 st)*
7   D.C.S. Compton, R.T. Spooner *(4 ct, 3 st)*, F.S. Trueman
6   G.A.R. Lock
5   J.H. Wardle
4   J.C. Laker, W. Watson
3   T.E. Bailey, K.G. Suttle
2   L. Hutton, A.E. Moss, J.B. Statham

Moss, Statham and Suttle also took one catch each as substitute fielders

FURTHER READING

A full bibliography and related material can be found at who-only-cricket-know.uk. My main primary sources have been newspapers, interviews and the MCC Archive. This list is intended to provide a flavour of the key secondary sources, good introductions to a theme and some of the writing I have found most rewarding or provocative. London is the place of publication unless otherwise stated.

INTRODUCTION

Monographs on the tour
BANNISTER, Alex. *Cricket Cauldron: With Hutton in the Caribbean* (Stanley Paul, 1954).
SWANTON, E.W. *West Indian Adventure: With Hutton's MCC Team, 1953/54* (Museum Press, 1954).

Other tour-related material
BAILEY, Trevor. Private cine film collection [kindly loaned by Justyn Bailey].
England's Finest: On Tour with Hutton's Men (MCC DVD, written and directed by Michael Burns; executive producer Adam Chadwick, 2009).
PALMER, Charles. *MCC Tour of West Indies, 1953/54* (VHS, Leicester: Welford Audio Visual, 2004).
PEEL, Mark. *Ambassadors of Goodwill: MCC Tours, 1946/47-1970/71* (Worthing: Pitch Publishing, 2018).
Wisden Cricketers' Almanack, 1955 (the tour section with a report by Reg Hayter is on pp.762-85; see also Arlott's 'Cricket Books, 1954', pp.991-92).

Colonial legacies in the Caribbean
HALL, Catherine. *Civilising Subjects: Metropole and Colony in the English Imagination, 1830-1867* (Cambridge: Polity, 2002).
JAMES, C.L.R. *The Black Jacobins: Toussaint L'Ouverture and the San Domingo Revolution*, ed. James Walvin (Harmondsworth: Penguin, 2001 [first published 1938]).
MINTZ, Sidney. *Sweetness and Power: The Place of Sugar in Modern History* (Harmondsworth: Viking, 1985).
MORGAN, Philip and HAWKINS, Sean (eds.). *Black Experience and the Empire* (Oxford: Oxford University Press, 2004).

WILLIAMS, Eric. *Capitalism and Slavery* (André Deutsch, 1964 [first published 1944]).

Cricket and empire

HARRIS, Lord. *A Few Short Runs* (John Murray, 1921).

SEECHARAN, Clem. *Muscular Learning: Cricket and Education in the Making of the British West Indies at the End of the 19th Century* (Kingston: Ian Randle, 2006).

STODDART, Brian and SANDIFORD, Keith (eds.). *The Imperial Game: Cricket, Culture and Society* (Manchester: Manchester University Press, 1998).

WARNER, P.F. *Cricket in Many Climes* (Heinemann, 1900); (ed.) *Imperial Cricket* (Subscribers' edition, 1912).

The sunset of empire

CANNADINE, David. 'James Bond & the Decline of England', *Encounter*, 53 (November 1979), pp.46-53.

Oxford History of the British Empire, general ed. Wm. Roger Lewis, 5 volumes (Oxford: Oxford University Press, 1998-99), volumes 4 and 5.

WAGG, Stephen (ed.). *Cricket and National Identity in the Postcolonial Age: Following On* (Routledge, 2005).

WARD, Stuart (ed.). *British Culture and the End of Empire* (Manchester: Manchester University Press, 2001).

CHAPTER 1

The 1950 series

ARLOTT, John. *Days at the Cricket* (Longmans, Green, 1951).

BABB, Colin. *They Gave the Crowd Plenty Fun: West Indian Cricket and its Relationship with the British-Resident Caribbean Diaspora* (Hertford: Hansib Publications, 2012).

KUMAR, Vijay. *Cricket Lovely Cricket* (New York: the author, 2000).

Radio and the Caribbean

MANDLE, Jay and MANDLE, Joan. 'Political Struggle and West Indies Cricket', *New West Indian Guide*, 70 (1996), pp.101-06.

RICHARDSON, Willy. 'The Place of Radio in the West Indies', *Caribbean Quarterly*, 7 (1961), pp.158-62.

RUSH, Anne Spry. *Bonds of Empire: West Indians and Britishness from Victoria to Decolonization* (Oxford: Oxford University Press, 2011).

Kitchener and calypso

BATEMAN, Anthony and BALE, John (eds.). *Sporting Sounds: Relationships between Sport and Music* (Routledge, 2009).

JOSEPH, Anthony. *Kitch: A Fictional Biography of a Calypso Icon* (Leeds: Peepal Tree, 2018).

London is the Place for Me, two-disc compilation (Honest Jon's Records, 1992).

ROHLEHR, Gordon. *Calypso & Society in Pre-Independence Trinidad* (Port of Spain: the author, 1990).

Constantine and 'race relations'

CONSTANTINE, Learie. [with C.L.R. James] *Cricket and I* (Philip Allan, 1933); *Cricket in the Sun* (Stanley Paul, 1946); *Colour Bar* (Stanley Paul, 1954).

HILL, Jeffrey. *Learie Constantine and Race Relations in Britain and the Empire* (Bloomsbury Academic, 2019).

PAUL, Kathleen. *Whitewashing Britain: Race and Citizenship in the Postwar Era* (Ithaca: Cornell University Press, 1997).

PEARSON, Harry. *Connie: The Marvellous Life of Learie Constantine* (Little, Brown, 2017).

Windrush Generation: some oral histories and literature

GRANT, Colin. *Homecoming: Voices of the Windrush Generation* (Jonathan Cape, 2019).

HINDS, Donald. *Journey to an Illusion: The West Indian in Britain* (Heinemann, 1966).

LAMBETH COUNCIL. *Forty Winters On: Memories of Britain's Post War Caribbean Immigrants* (The Voice Newspaper/South London Press, 1988).

LAMMING, George. *The Emigrants*; *The Pleasures of Exile* (both Michael Joseph, 1954; 1960).

PHILLIPS, Mike and PHILLIPS, Trevor. *Windrush: The Irresistible Rise of Multi-Racial Britain* (HarperCollins, 1998).

SELVON, Sam. *The Lonely Londoners* (Allan Wingate, 1956); 'The Cricket Match' [1957], anthologised in *The Bowling was Superfine* (see Chapter 3 below), pp.225-28.

Black Britain: some academic studies

BIDNALL, Amanda. *The West Indian Generation: Remaking British Culture in London, 1945-1965* (Liverpool: Liverpool University Press, 2017).

FRYER, Peter. *Staying Power: The History of Black People in Britain* (Pluto, 1984).

OLUSOGA, David. *Black and British: A Forgotten History* (Macmillan, 2016).

SCHWARZ, Bill (ed.). *West Indian Intellectuals in Britain* (Manchester: Manchester University Press, 2003).

TAJFEL, Henri and DAWSON, John (eds.). *Disappointed Guests: Essays by African, Asian, and West Indian Students* (New York: Oxford University Press, 1965).

CHAPTER 2

The Coronation and New Elizabethanism

GIBBS, Philip. *The New Elizabethans* (Hutchinson, 1953).

MORRA, Irene and GOSSEDGE, Rob (eds.). *The New Elizabethan Age: Culture, Society and National Identity after World War II* (I.B. Tauris, 2016).

SHILS, Edward and YOUNG, Michael. 'The Meaning of the Coronation', *Sociological Review*, 1 (1953), pp.63-81.

WEBSTER, Wendy. *Englishness and Empire, 1939-1965* (Oxford: Oxford University Press, 2005).

The summer of sport

RICE, Jonathan. *1953: The Crowning Year of Sport; Foreword by HRH The Duke of Edinburgh* (Methuen, 2003).

RICHARDS, Gordon. *My Story* (Hodder and Stoughton, 1955).

TOSSELL, David. *The Great English Final, 1953: Cup, Coronation & Stanley Matthews* (Durrington: Pitch Publishing, 2013).

WALTON, Theresa and BIRRELL, Susan. 'Enduring Heroes: Hillary, Bannister, and the Epic Challenges of Human Exploration', *Journal of Sport History*, 39 (2012), pp.211-26.

British society in the 1950s

HENNESSY, Peter. *Having it so Good: Britain in the Fifties* (Penguin, 2007).

KYNASTON, David. *Austerity Britain, 1945-51; Family Britain, 1951-57* (both Bloomsbury, 2007; 2009).

MARWICK, Arthur. *British Society since 1945* (Allen Lane, 1982); *Class: Image and Reality in Britain, France and the USA since 1930* (Collins, 1980).

VANSITTART, Peter. *In the Fifties* (John Murray, 1995).

The Coronation Ashes

ARLOTT, John. *Test Match Diary, 1953: A Personal Day-by-Day Account of the Test Series England v Australia* (James Barrie, 1953).

CARDUS, Neville. *Cardus in the Covers* (Souvenir Press, 1978).

The Final Test [1953], directed by Anthony Asquith, screenplay by Terence Rattigan (DVD Best of British Collection, 2006).

FINGLETON, J.H. *The Ashes Crown the Year: A Coronation Cricket Diary*, introduced by Michael Parkinson (Pavilion Books, 1986 [first published 1954]).

SWANTON, E.W. *The Test Matches of 1953* (Daily Telegraph, 1953).

THOMSON A.A. *Cricket My Happiness* (Museum Press, 1954).

WEST, Peter. *The Fight for the Ashes, 1953: A Complete Account of the Australian Tour* (Harrap, 1953).

CHAPTER 3

General studies of Caribbean society

BURTON, Richard. *Afro-Creole: Power, Opposition, and Play in the Caribbean* (Ithaca: Cornell University Press, 1997).

DABYDEEN, David and SAMAROO, Brinsley (eds.). *Across the Dark Waters: Ethnicity and Indian Identity in the Caribbean* (Macmillan Caribbean, 1996).

JOHNSON, Howard and WATSON, Karl (eds.). *The White Minority in the Caribbean* (Kingston: Ian Randle, 1998).

LEWIS, Gordon. *The Growth of the Modern West Indies* (MacGibbon & Kee, 1968).

LOWENTHAL, David. *West Indian Societies* (Oxford University Press, 1972).

Overviews of West Indies cricket

BECKLES, Hilary. (ed.) *An Area of Conquest: Popular Democracy and West Indies Cricket Supremacy* (Kingston: Ian Randle, 1994); (ed. with Brian Stoddart) *Liberation Cricket: West Indies Cricket Culture* (Manchester: Manchester University Press, 1995); *The Development of West Indies Cricket*, 2 volumes (Kingston: UWI Press, 1998); (ed.) *A Spirit of Dominance: Cricket and Nationalism in the West Indies* (Kingston: UWI Press, 1998).

BIRBALSINGH, Frank. (with Clem Seecharan) *Indo-Westindian Cricket* (Hansib, 1988); *The Rise of Westindian Cricket: From Colony to Nation* (St John's: Hansib, 1996).

BROWN, Stewart and McDONALD, Ian (eds.). *The Bowling was Superfine: West Indian Writing and West Indian Cricket* (Leeds: Peepal Tree, 2012).

COZIER, Tony. *The West Indies: Fifty Years of Test Cricket* (Angus and Robertson, 1978).

JAMES, C.L.R. *Beyond a Boundary* (Hutchinson, 1963); *Cricket*, ed. Anna Grimshaw (Allison & Busby, 1986).

MANLEY, Michael. *A History of West Indies Cricket* (André Deutsch, 1988).

Period literature and travelogues

FERMOR, Patrick Leigh. *The Traveller's Tree: A Journey through the Caribbean Islands* (John Murray, 1950).

FIGUEROA, John (ed.). *Caribbean Voices: An Anthology of West Indian Poetry*, 2 volumes (Evans, 1966-70).

MITTELHOLZER, Edgar. *With a Carib Eye* (Secker and Warburg, 1958).

NAIPAUL, V.S. *The Middle Passage: Impressions of Five Societies – British, French and Dutch – in the West Indies and South America* (André Deutsch, 1962).

RAMCHAND, Kenneth. *The West Indian Novel and its Background* (Faber and Faber, 1970).

WALCOTT, Derek. *Collected Poems, 1948-1984*; *What the Twilight Says: Essays* (both Faber and Faber, 1992; 1998).

Headley

BURROWES, S.I. and CARNEGIE, J.A. *George Headley* (Thomas Nelson, 1971).

LAWRENCE, Bridgette. *Masterclass: The Biography of George Headley* (Leicester: Polar, 1995).

WHITE, Noel and HEADLEY, George. *George 'Atlas' Headley* (Kingston: Institute of Jamaica, 1974).

CHAPTER 4

The inner circle and England selection

BROWN, F.R. *Cricket Musketeer* (Nicholas Kaye, 1954); 'Batsmen Must be Bold: Forward Play the First Essential', in 1954 *Wisden*, pp.87-91.

HOWAT, Gerald. *Plum Warner* (Unwin Hyman, 1987); *Cricket's Second Golden Age: The Hammond-Bradman Years* (Hodder and Stoughton, 1989).

RENDELL, Brian. *Gubby under Pressure: Letters from Australia, New Zealand and Hollywood, 1936/37*; *Walter Robins: Achievements, Affections and Affronts* (both Cardiff: Association of Cricket Statisticians, 2007; 2013).

SWANTON, E.W. *Sort of a Cricket Person* (HarperCollins, 1972); *Gubby Allen: Man of Cricket* (Hutchinson/Stanley Paul, 1985).

SYNGE, Allen. *Sins of Omission: The Story of the Test Selectors, 1899-1990* (Pelham, 1990).

WARNER, Pelham. *Cricket between Two Wars* (Chatto & Windus, 1942); *Long Innings: The Autobiography* (Harrap, 1951); 'Twilight Reflections', in 1955 *Wisden*, pp.95-104.

The English Gentleman
COLLINS, Marcus. 'The Fall of the English Gentleman: The National Character in Decline, c.1918-1970', *Historical Research*, 75 (2002), pp.90-111.
MANGAN, J.A. *Athleticism in the Victorian and Edwardian Public School: The Emergence and Consolidation of an Educational Ideology* (Cambridge: Cambridge University Press, 1981).
RAVEN, Simon. *The English Gentleman: An Essay in Attitudes* (Anthony Blond, 1961).
WILKINSON, Rupert. *The Prefects: British Leadership and the Public School Tradition* (Oxford University Press, 1964).

CHAPTER 5

The Stollmeyer family in Trinidad
DE VERTEUIL, Anthony. *The Germans in Trinidad* (Port of Spain: Litho Press, 1994).
STOLLMEYER, C.F. *The Sugar Question Made Easy* (E. Wilson, 1845).
STOLLMEYER, Hugh. 'Literary Clubs and Art', 'The Time has Come!', 'India's Dilemma', 'The Calypso and Politics', in facsimile reprints of *The Beacon, 1931-39*, compiled by Reinhard Sander (Millwood: Kraus Reprint, 1977).
STOLLMEYER, Jeffrey. *Everything Under the Sun: My Life in West Indies Cricket* (Stanley Paul, 1983); *The West Indies in India, 1948/1949: Jeffrey Stollmeyer's Diary*, ed. Kenneth Ramchand with Yvonne Teelucksingh (Macoya: Royards Publishing, 2004).

Trinidad background
BRERETON, Bridget. *Race Relations in Colonial Trinidad, 1870-1900* (Cambridge: Cambridge University Press, 1980).
CAMPBELL, Carl. *The Young Colonials: A Social History of Education in Trinidad and Tobago, 1834-1939* (Barbados: UWI Press, 1996).
JAMES, C.L.R. *The Life of Captain Cipriani...; with the Pamphlet The Case for West-Indian Self Government*, introduced by Bridget Brereton (Durham: Duke University Press, 2014 [first published 1932 and 1933]).
SINGH, Kelvin. *Race and Class: Struggles in a Colonial State, Trinidad, 1917-45* (Calgary: University of Calgary Press, 1994).

WOOD, Donald. *Trinidad in Transition: The Years after Slavery* (Oxford: Oxford University Press for the Institute of Race Relations, 1986).

Cricket background

GANTEAUME, Andy. *My Story: The Other Side of the Coin* (St James: Medianet, 2007).

THOMSON, Philip. *Ramblings from the Distant Past* (Port of Spain: GTM Fire, 1996).

CHAPTER 6

Hutton

HOWAT, Gerald. *Len Hutton: The Biography* (Heinemann Kingswood, 1988).

HUTTON, Len. [with Thomas Moult] *Cricket is My Life* (Hutchinson, 1949); [with Reg Hayter] *Just My Story* (Hutchinson, 1956); [with Alex Bannister] *Fifty Years in Cricket* (Stanley Paul, 1984).

KITCHIN, Laurence. *Len Hutton* (Phoenix House, 1953).

THOMSON, A.A. *Hutton and Washbrook* (Epworth Press, 1963).

TRELFORD, Donald (ed.). *Len Hutton Remembered* (H. F. & G. Witherby, 1992).

A Tribute to Leonard Hutton (Yorkshire CCC DVD, directed by Mike Hooper with interviews by Stephen Chalke, 2007).

The Yorkshire milieu

BENNETT, Alan. 'A Day Out' [1972], collected in *Objects of Affection and Other Plays for Television* (BBC, 1982).

HATTERSLEY, Roy. *A Yorkshire Boyhood* (Chatto & Windus, 1983).

HOGGART, Richard. *The Uses of Literacy: Aspects of Working-Class Life, with Special References to Publications and Entertainments* (Chatto & Windus, 1957).

HUTTON, J.E. *A History of the Moravian Church* (Moravian Publication Office, second edition, 1909 [first published 1895]).

THOMSON, A.A. *The Exquisite Burden* (Herbert Jenkins, 1935).

Yorkshire cricket

CHALKE, Stephen. (with Derek Hodgson) *No Coward Soul: The Remarkable Story of Bob Appleyard*; *A Summer of Plenty: George Herbert Hirst in 1906*; *Five Five Five: Holmes and Sutcliffe in 1932* (all Bath: Fairfield Books, 2003; 2006; 2007).

HAMILTON, Duncan (ed.). *Sweet Summers: The Classic Cricket Writing of JM Kilburn* (Bradford: Great Northern Books, 2008); *Wisden on Yorkshire: An Anthology* (Wisden, 2011).

KILBURN, J.M. *A History of Yorkshire Cricket*; *Thanks to Cricket* (both Stanley Paul, 1970; 1972).

Old Ebor: Cricket from the Dim and Distant Past (website): see especially the five-part blog on 'Herbert Sutcliffe and the Yorkshire Captaincy in 1927'.

WOODHOUSE, Anthony. *The History of Yorkshire County Cricket Club, with a Personal View by Sir Leonard Hutton* (Christopher Helm, 1989).

England cricket, 1938-52

BLUNDEN, Edmund. *Cricket Country* (Collins, 1944).

FINGLETON, J.H. *Brightly Fades the Don*; *Brown and Company: The Tour in Australia* (both Collins, 1949; 1951).

FOOT, David. *Wally Hammond: The Reasons Why* (Robson Books, 1996).

KNOX, Malcolm. *Bradman's War: How the 1948 Invincibles Turned the Cricket Pitch into a Battlefield* (Robson Books, 2013).

WILDE, Simon. *England the Biography: The Story of English Cricket, 1877-2018* (Simon and Schuster, 2018).

Amateur and professional; north and south

BIRLEY, Derek. *The Willow Wand: Some Cricket Myths Explored* (Queen Anne Press, 1979); *A Social History of English Cricket* (Aurum, 1999).

DOLLERY, H.E. (Tom). *Professional Captain* (Stanley Paul, 1952).

HILL, Jeffrey. 'The Legend of Denis Compton', *The Sports Historian*, 18 (1998), pp.19-33.

HOLT, Richard. *Sport and the British: A Modern History* (Oxford: Clarendon Press, 1989).

MARSHALL, Michael. *Gentlemen & Players: Conversations with Cricketers* (Grafton Books, 1987).

MIDWINTER, Eric. *'Class Peace': An Analysis of Social Status and English Cricket, 1846-1962* (Cardiff: Association of Cricket Statisticians, 2017).

WAGG, Stephen. '"Time gentlemen please": The Decline of Amateur Captaincy in English County Cricket', *Contemporary British History*, 14 (2000), pp.31-59; (ed. with Dave Russell) *Sporting Heroes of the North: Sport, Religion and Culture* (Newcastle Upon Tyne: Northumbria Press, 2010).

Bailey

Autobiographies: *Playing to Win* (Hutchinson, 1954); *Trevor Bailey's Cricket Book* (Frederick Muller, 1959); *Wickets, Catches and the Odd Run* (Collins, 1986).

Biographies by: Jack Bailey (Methuen, 1993); Alan Hill (Durrington: Pitch Publishing, 2012).

Compton

Autobiographies: *Playing for England* (Sampson Low, 1948); *In Sun and Shadow* (Stanley Paul, 1952); *End of an Innings* (Oldbourne, 1958).

Biographies by: E.W. Swanton (Sporting Handbooks, 1948); Ian Peebles (Macmillan, 1971); Peter West (Stanley Paul, 1989); Tim Heald (Pavilion, 1994).

Evans

Autobiographies (all published by Hodder and Stoughton): *Behind the Stumps* (1951); *Action in Cricket* (1956); *The Gloves are Off* (1960).

Biography by: Christopher Sandford (Simon & Schuster, 1990).

Graveney

Autobiographies: *Cricket through the Covers* (Frederick Muller, 1958); *Tom Graveney on Cricket* (Frederick Muller, 1965); *Cricket over Forty* (Pelham, 1970); *The Heart of Cricket* (Arthur Barker, 1983).

Biographies by: Christopher Sandford (H.F. & G. Witherby, 1992); Stephen Fay (Methuen, 2005); Andrew Murtagh (Pitch Publishing, 2018).

Laker

Autobiographies: *Spinning Round the World* (Frederick Muller, 1957); *Over to Me* (Frederick Muller, 1960); (with Pat Gibson) *Cricket Contrasts: From Crease to Commentary Box* (Stanley Paul, 1985).

Biographies by: Don Mosey (Queen Anne Press, 1989); Alan Hill (André Deutsch, 1998); Brian Scovell (Stroud: History Press, 2006).

Lock

Autobiography: *For Surrey and England* (Hodder and Stoughton, 1957).

Biographies by: Kirwan Ward (Adelaide: Rigby, 1972); Alan Hill (Stroud: History Press, 2008).

May

Autobiographies: *Peter May's Book of Cricket* (Cassell, 1956); [with Michael Melford] *A Game Enjoyed: An Autobiography* (Stanley Paul, 1985).

Biographies by: Robert Rodrigo (Phoenix House, 1960); Alan Hill (André Deutsch, 1996).

Palmer

MILLER, Douglas. *Charles Palmer: More Than Just A Gentleman* (Bath: Fairfield Books, 2005).

Statham

Autobiographies: *Cricket Merry-Go-Round* (Stanley Paul, 1956); *Flying Bails* (Stanley Paul, 1961); *His Own Story: A Spell at the Top*, ed. Peter Smith (Souvenir Press, 1969).

Biographies by: Tony Derlien (Derby: Breedon, 1990); Malcolm Lorimer (ed.) (Manchester: Parrs Wood Press, 2001).

Trueman

Autobiographies: *Fast Fury* (Stanley Paul, 1961); *The Freddie Trueman Story* (Stanley Paul, 1965); *Ball of Fire: An Autobiography* (J.M. Dent, 1976); (with Don Mosey) *Fred Trueman Talking Cricket: With Friends Past and Present* (Hodder and Stoughton, 1997); *As It Was: The Memoirs of Fred Trueman* (Macmillan, 2004).

Biographies by: John Arlott (Eyre & Spottiswoode, 1971); Don Mosey (Kingswood Press, 1991); Chris Waters (Aurum Press, 2011).

Wardle

Autobiography: (as told to A.A. Thomson) *Happy Go Johnny* (Robert Hale, 1957).

Biography by: Alan Hill (Newton Abbot: David & Charles, 1988).

Watson

Autobiography: *Double International* (Stanley Paul, 1956).

Biography by: Frank Garrick (Cheltenham: Sportsbooks, 2013).

CHAPTER 7

Bermuda background

BROWN, Walton. *Bermuda and the Struggle for Reform: Race, Politics and*

411

Ideology, 1944-1998 (Bermuda: Cahow Press, 2011).

HODGSON, Eva. *Second-Class Citizens; First-Class Men*, (Bermuda: Writers' Machine, second edition, 1988 [first published 1963]).

JOEL, Stanhope. (as told to Lloyd Mayer) *Ace of Diamonds: The Story of Solomon Barnato Joel* (Frederick Muller, 1958).

MANNING, Frank. 'Celebrating Cricket: The Symbolic Construction of Caribbean Politics', *American Ethnologist*, 8 (1981), pp.616-632.

CHAPTERS 8 AND 9

Jamaica: general background

BRATHWAITE, Edward. *Folk Culture of the Slaves in Jamaica* (New Beacon, 1970).

CURTIN, Philip. *Two Jamaicas: The Role of Ideas in a Tropical Colony* (Cambridge, MA.: Harvard University Press, 1955).

PATTERSON, Orlando. *The Sociology of Slavery: An Analysis of the Origins, Development and Structure of Negro Slave Society in Jamaica* (MacGibbon & Kee, 1967); *The Confounding Island: Jamaica and the Postcolonial Predicament* (Cambridge, MA.: Harvard University Press, 2019).

THOMSON, Ian. *The Dead Yard: A Story of Modern Jamaica* (Faber and Faber, 2009).

Jamaica: period background

HALL, Stuart. (with Bill Schwarz) *Familiar Stranger: A Life between Two Islands* (Allen Lane, 2017).

HENRIQUES, Fernando. *Family and Colour in Jamaica* (Eyre & Spottiswoode, 1953).

KERR, Madeline. *Personality and Conflict in Jamaica* (Liverpool: Liverpool University Press, 1952).

MACMILLAN, Mona. *The Land of Look Behind: A Study of Jamaica* (Faber and Faber, 1957).

PARKER, Matthew. *Goldeneye: Where Bond Was Born: Ian Fleming's Jamaica* (Hutchinson, 2014).

Jamaica: cricket background

BERTRAM, Arnold. *Jamaica at the Wicket: A Study of Jamaican Cricket and its Role in Shaping the Jamaican Society* (Kingston: Research and Project Development, 2009).

MOORE, Brian and JOHNSON, Michele. 'Challenging the "Civilising Mission":
Cricket as a Field of Socio-Cultural Contestation in Jamaica, 1865-1920', in
In the Shadow of the Plantation: Caribbean History and Legacy, ed. Alvin
Thompson (Kingston: Ian Randle, 2003), pp.351-75.

CHAPTERS 10 AND 11

Barbados: general background

BECKLES, Hilary. *A History of Barbados: From Amerindian Settlement to
Nation-State* (Cambridge: Cambridge University Press, 1990).

CHAMBERLAIN, Mary. *Empire and Nation-Building in the Caribbean:
Barbados, 1937-66* (Manchester: Manchester University Press, 2010).

HOYOS, F.A. *Grantley Adams and the Social Revolution: The Story of the
Movement that Changed the Pattern of West Indian Society* (Macmillan,
1974).

Barbados: period background

COZIER, E. L. *Caribbean Newspaperman – an Autobiography: The Life and
Times of Jimmy Cozier* (Bridgetown: Literary Features Caribbean, 1985).

LAMMING, George. *In the Castle of My Skin* (Penguin Classics, 2017 [first
published 1953]).

LEWIS, Gary. *White Rebel: The Life and Times of T.T. Lewis* (Barbados: UWI
Press, 1999).

MARSHALL, Paule. *Brown Girl, Brownstones* (Virago, 1980 [first published
1959]).

Barbados: cricket background

SANDIFORD, Keith. *Cricket Nurseries of Colonial Barbados: The Elite Schools,
1865-1966* (Kingston: UWI Press, 1998).

STODDART, Brian. 'Cricket, Social Formation and Cultural Continuity in
Barbados: A Preliminary Ethnohistory', *Journal of Sport History*, 14 (1987),
pp.317-40.

CHAPTERS 12 AND 13

Guyana: general backgound

ATHERTON, Mike. 'Guyana: Green and Troubled Land', *Intelligent Life* (Spring
2009), pp.117-20.

NEWMAN, Peter. *British Guiana: Problems of Cohesion in an Immigrant Society* (Oxford University Press, 1964).

ROSE, James. *British Colonial Policy and the Transfer of Power in British Guiana, 1945-1964* (King's College London PhD thesis, 1992).

SEECHARAN, Clem. *Sweetening 'Bitter Sugar': Jock Campbell the Booker Reformer in British Guiana, 1934-1966* (Kingston: Ian Randle, 2005).

SMITH, Raymond. *British Guiana* (Oxford University Press, 1962).

Guyana: period background

BIRBALSINGH, Frank. *The People's Progressive Party of Guyana, 1950-1992: An Oral History* (Hansib, 2007); *Guyana and the Caribbean* (Chichester: Dido, 2004); *Guyana: History and Literature* (Hertford: Hansib, 2016).

CARTER, Martin. *University of Hunger: Collected Poems and Selected Prose*, ed. Gemma Robinson (Tarset: Bloodaxe, 2006).

PEREIRA, Joseph 'Reds'. (with Katherine Atkinson) *Living My Dreams* (Bloomington: AuthorHouse, 2011).

SIMMS, Peter. *Trouble in Guiana: An Account of People, Personalities and Politics as they were in British Guiana* (Allen & Unwin, 1966).

Guyana: cricket background

KANHAI-GIBBS BENEFIT COMMITTEE. *Kanhai, Gibbs: A Tribute to Two Outstanding West Indians* (Port of Spain: The Committee, 1974).

MOORE, Brian. 'Colonialism, Cricket Culture, and Afro-Creole Identity in the Caribbean after Emancipation: The Case of Guyana', *Journal of Caribbean History*, 33 (1999), pp.54-73.

SEECHARAN, Clem. *From Ranji to Rohan: Cricket and Indian Identity in Colonial Guyana, 1890s-1960s*; *Hand-in-Hand History of Cricket in Guyana*, volume one 1865-1897, volume two 1898-1914 (all Hertford: Hansib, 2009; 2016; 2018).

CHAPTERS 14 AND 15

Further Trinidad background

GOMES, Albert. *Through a Maze of Colour* (Port of Spain: Key Caribbean Publications, 1974).

MENDES, Alfred. *Autobiography*, ed. Michèle Levy (Barbados: UWI Press, 2002).

RICHARDSON, Bonham. *Igniting the Caribbean's Past: Fire in West Indian History* (Chapel Hill: University of North Carolina Press, 2004).

RYAN, Selwyn. *Race and Nationalism in Trinidad and Tobago: A Study of Decolonization in a Multiracial Society* (Toronto: University of Toronto Press, 1972); *Eric Williams: The Myth and the Man* (Kingston: UWI Press, 2009).

WILLIAMS, Eric. *History of the People of Trinidad and Tobago* (André Deutsch, 1963 [first published in Port of Spain, 1962]).

CHAPTER 16

Fifth Test

CHANDLER, Martin. 'Trevor Bailey 16-7-34-7', in *Supreme Bowling: 100 Great Test Performances*, eds. Patrick Ferriday and Dave Wilson (Brighton: Von Krumm, 2016), pp.203-10.

SAYEN, Henry. (as told to Gerald Brodribb) *A Yankee Looks at Cricket* (Putnam, 1956).

Paths to independence

FOOT, Sir Hugh. *A Start in Freedom* (Hodder and Stoughton, 1964).

GRAY, Obika. *Demeaned but Empowered: The Social Power of the Urban Poor of Jamaica* (Kingston: UWI Press, 2004).

MAWBY, Spencer. *Ordering Independence: The End of Empire in the Anglophone Caribbean, 1947-1969* (Basingstoke: Palgrave Macmillan, 2012).

CHAPTER 17

Some fictional 'cocks of the north'

BRAINE, John. *Room at the Top* (Eyre & Spottiswoode, 1957).

SILLITOE, Alan. *Saturday Night and Sunday Morning* (Allen, 1958); *The Loneliness of the Long Distance Runner and other stories* (Allen, 1959).

STOREY, David. *This Sporting Life* (Longmans, 1960).

Trueman, Bailey and MCC

BAILEY, Trevor. 'Drama on the Cricket Field by the Iron Man of the Test Matches', *The People*, 16 May 1954, p.9; *Playing to Win* (Hutchinson, 1954).

HUTTON, Len. Captain's Report 1953/54, extracts reproduced in *The Cricketer* (May 1998), pp.28-29.

WILLIAMS, Jack. '"Fiery Fred": Fred Trueman and Cricket Celebrity in the 1950s and early 1960s', *Sport in Society*, 12 (2009), pp.509-522.

CHAPTER 18

The attempted coup against Hutton

ALTHAM H.S. (with E.W. Swanton) *A History of Cricket* (fourth edition, Allen & Unwin, 1948): see especially the new Chapter 32; *The Altham-Bradman Letters*, ed. Robin Brodhurst (Newnham-on-Severn: Christopher Saunders, 2020).

The Cricketer, Volume XXXV (1954): Sir Pelham Warner, 'Some Thoughts on Captaincy', 1 May & 15 May, pp.106, 153-54; W[ilf] Wooller, 'A Question of Psychology', 15 May, p.158; C.B. Fry, 'The Selectors' Task', 10 July, p.293.

GIBSON, Alan. *The Cricket Captains of England: A Survey* (Cassell, 1979).

HOLMES, E.R.T. *Flannelled Foolishness: A Cricketing Chronicle* (Hollis & Carter, 1957).

SHEPPARD, David. *Parson's Pitch* (Hodder and Stoughton, 1964).

MCC in Australia 1954/55

ARLOTT, John. *Australian Test Journal: A Diary of the Test Matches* (Phoenix Sports, 1955).

MOYES, A.G. *The Fight for the Ashes, 1954/55: A Critical Account of the English Tour in Australia* (Harrap, 1955).

PEEBLES, Ian. *The Ashes, 1954/55* (Hodder and Stoughton, 1955).

ROSS, Alan. *Australia 55: A Journal of the MCC Tour* (Michael Joseph, 1955).

TYSON, Frank. *In the Eye of the Typhoon: Recollections of the MCC Tour of Australia, 1954/55* (Manchester: Parrs Wood, 2004).

Hutton's support team

CHALKE, Stephen. *At the Heart of English Cricket: The Life and Memories of Geoffrey Howard* (Bath: Fairfield Books, 2001).

DALTON, Harold. Tour Diary and Scrapbook [private collection].

KILBURN, J.M. *Cricket Decade: England v Australia, 1946-1956* (Heinemann, 1959).

MIDWINTER, Eric. *George Duckworth: Warrington's Ambassador at Large* (Cardiff: Association of Cricket Statisticians, 2007).

CHAPTER 19

Weekes and Walcott

BRATHWAITE, Edward. 'Rites' [first published 1967], collected in *The Arrivants: A New World Trilogy* (Oxford: Oxford University Press, 1973).

WALCOTT, Clyde. *Island Cricketers* (Hodder and Stoughton, 1958); (with Brian Scovell) *Sixty Years on the Back Foot: The Cricketing Life of Sir Clyde Walcott* (Gollancz, 1999).

WEEKES, Everton with BECKLES, Hilary. *Mastering the Craft: Ten Years of Weekes, 1948-1958* (Barbados: Universities of the Caribbean Press, 2007).

Test series of the 1950s

HARRIS, Bruce. *West Indies Cricket Challenge* (Stanley Paul, 1957).

LANDSBERG, Pat. *The Kangaroo Conquers: The West Indies v Australia, 1955* (Museum Press, 1955).

ROSS, Alan. *Through the Caribbean: The MCC Tour of the West Indies, 1959/1960* (Hamish Hamilton, 1960).

SWANTON, E.W. *West Indies Revisited: The MCC Tour, 1959/60* (Heinemann, 1960).

CHAPTER 20

Worrell

EYTLE, Ernest. *Frank Worrell* (Hodder and Stoughton, 1963).

JAMES, C.L.R. 'Sir Frank Worrell', in *Cricket: The Great Captains*, ed. John Arlott (Pelham, 1971), pp.135-52.

PILGRIM, Torrey. *The Sir Frank Worrell Pictorial* (New York: Creation/Innovation Services, 1992).

TENNANT, Ivo. *Frank Worrell: A Biography* (Cambridge: Lutterworth Press, 1987).

1960/61 in Australia

BENAUD, Richie. *A Tale of Two Tests: With Some Thoughts on Captaincy* (Hodder and Stoughton, 1962).

Calypso Summer (ABC documentary series, directed by Lincoln Tyler, 2000).

FINGLETON, J.H. *The Greatest Test of All* (Collins, 1961).

ROBERTS, L.D. *Cricket's Brightest Summer* (Kingston: the author, 1961).

1963 in England

BARKER, J.S. *Summer Spectacular: The West Indies v England, 1963* (Collins, 1963).

BARNES, Simon. 'The Making of the Man', *The Nightwatchman*, Barbados special edition (2016), pp.48-53.

CLARKE, John. *Cricket with a Swing: The West Indies Tour, 1963* (Stanley Paul, 1963).

NAIPAUL, V.S. 'The Test', anthologised in *The Bowling was Superfine* (see Chapter 3), pp.316-24.

ROSS, Alan. *The West Indies at Lord's* (Eyre & Spottiswoode, 1963).

WOOLDRIDGE, Ian. *Cricket, Lovely Cricket: The West Indies Tour, 1963* (Hale, 1963).

AFTERWORD

Beyond a Boundary

CUDJOE, Selwyn and CAIN, William (eds.). *C.L.R. James: His Intellectual Legacies* (Amherst: University of Massachusetts, 1995): see, in particular, the essay 'Keeping a Straight Bat' by Mark Kingwell.

FEATHERSTONE, David, GAIR, Christopher, HØGSBJERG, Christian and SMITH, Andrew (eds). *Marxism, Colonialism and Cricket: C.L.R. James's Beyond a Boundary* (Durham: Duke University Press, 2018).

WESTALL, Claire. 'What They Knew of Nation and Empire: Rudyard Kipling and C.L.R. James', in *Kipling and Beyond: Patriotism, Globalisation and Postcolonialism*, eds. Kaori Nagai and Caroline Rooney (Basingstoke: Palgrave Macmillan, 2010), pp.165-84.

What should they know of England

FAY, Stephen and KYNASTON, David. *Arlott, Swanton and the Soul of English Cricket* (Bloomsbury, 2018).

FEATHERSTONE, Simon. *Englishness: Twentieth Century Popular Culture and the Forming of English Identity* (Edinburgh: Edinburgh University Press, 2009); 'Late Cuts: C.L.R. James, Cricket and Postcolonial England', *Sport in History*, 31 (2011), pp.49-61.

HARRIS, Trevor (ed.). *Windrush (1948) and Rivers of Blood (1968): Legacy and Assessment* (Routledge, 2020).

POWELL, Enoch. Speech to the Royal Society of St George, 22 April 1961 (the original manuscript is accessible on enochpowell.info).

Who Only Cricket Know

BECKLES, Hilary. 'The Radical Tradition in the Culture of West Indies Cricket', in *An Area of Conquest* (see Chapter 3), pp.42-54.

BREARLEY, Mike. *On Cricket: A Portrait of the Game*; *The Spirit of Cricket* (both Constable, 2018; 2020).

CHALKE, Stephen. *Through the Remembered Gate* (Bath: Fairfield Books, 2020).

LISTER, Simon. *Fire in Babylon: How the West Indies Cricket Team Brought a Nation to its Feet* (Yellow Jersey Press, 2015).

PATTERSON, Orlando. 'The Ritual of Cricket', originally published in *Jamaica Journal*, 3 (1969), collected in *Liberation Cricket* (see Chapter 3), pp.141-47.

ACKNOWLEDGEMENTS

I would first like to thank my wife Mariya and our daughters, Frankie and Freya, for their love and support. Living with a writer can be as difficult as living with a cricketer - and they still have to put up with both on Sundays in the summer.

My greatest debt is to Stephen Chalke, who has been guide, philosopher and friend to *Who Only Cricket Know*. He took it on as he neared retirement, tended it with care, intelligence and patience and then ensured a seamless handover to the new curators of Fairfield Books. Stephen has in abundance that great quality of taking the trouble to do things well. His own body of work at Fairfield, rich with the humanity of cricketers, is a publisher's dream. For me and many other writers, he has also been a dream publisher.

Matt Thacker and Wildfire Sport, who produce *The Nightwatchman* quarterly, have done another great service to cricket by continuing the Fairfield imprint. They have done me a great service by taking on this project, putting their trust in it and their energy into improvements of content and form. I would like to thank Matt and his team, especially the designer Rob Whitehouse, for their hard work bringing the book to press and the website into existence.

As a fan of the Villa and the obituaries section of *Wisden*, I was already familiar with the quality of Richard Whitehead's writing. I can now testify to his qualities as an editor. I could not have asked for a more sympathetic, inspiring and eagle-eyed companion during the final stages of the project.

I first met Lancashire member Nigel Llewellyn by chance at a Lord's Test match when he overheard me pontificating about I forget what. Nigel read a first draft of each chapter and was still prepared to read them all again. The narrative voice of *Who Only Cricket Know* owes more to him than anyone. Nigel has been an enormous influence on the book and we have had enormous fun.

Gloucestershire member Hugh Johnstone was my roommate on a tour of Barbados, where he did a better impression of Laker than I did of Hutton. Hugh has kindly read and improved several versions of the text, as have my brother Jonty and my mother Melba (both Worcestershire). My friend Rebecca Lea Williams (rebsville.com) has provided one of her beautiful maps.

I owe a great debt to the cricketers who, despite their advanced years, went to considerable trouble along with their families or secretaries to grant me interviews: Alan and Sonia Moss, Bruce and Gillian Pairaudeau, Calvin and JeanMaire Symonds, Sir Everton Weekes and Carole Burnett. Their memories rarely failed and their kindness never. I have also been touched by the generosity and patience of those I approached for Caribbean background: Colin Babb, Vaneisa Baksh, Frank Birbalsingh, Bridget Brereton, Lance Neita, Robin Wishart.

I'd like to thank the staff of the MCC Library at Lord's (especially Robert Curphey), the London Library and the British Library. All three institutions can be proud of the service they provide and the culture they preserve.

I'd also like to thank the following for responding to queries, reading sections, making suggestions, making introductions or otherwise providing help and support:

Ben Adams, the Amin Cup group, Justyn Bailey, Arnold Bertram, Robin Brodhurst, Anthony Brooke, Duncan and Gordon Burles, Eric and Karen Caines, Martin Chandler, Richard Clayton, Hubert Devonish, Martin Eales, David Frith, Gardeners CC, David Gleave, Rich Guy, Peter Hayter and Sally Davies, Sam Hayward, Simon Hooper, Ludovic Hunter-Tilney, Richard Hutton, Tom Leahy, John Leigh, Lexi, Nick Mays, Douglas Miller, the North v South teams, Old Robsonians FC, George Pagliero, Orlando Patterson, Hristo and Petko Petkov, Jonathan Pritchard, Tatiana Prokayeva, Craig Ramadhin and the late Sonny Ramadhin, Mike Richards, Michael Roberts, David Robertson, Samantha Robinson, Clem Seecharan, Micky Stewart, the late Peter Stormonth-Darling, John and Will Sutton, Katarzyna Tomczak, Paul Warburton, Tim Webb, Giles Wilcock, Anika Woodhouse, Jim Wynn, Noel Young Wines.

INDEX

Dates of birth and death are provided for the 18 West Indians who appeared in the 1953/54 Test series, and for the 16 MCC tourists.

The Oval 35-6, 90, 356
Baldwin, S. – 150
Bannister, Alex (*Daily Mail*)
   assessment of tour in *Cricket
      Cauldron* 12-13
   Bermuda, in situ in 120
   critiques West Indian hosts 218, 222,
      253-4, 268, 272, 296
   defends MCC players 121, 184, 220,
      240, 244, 253-4
   ghosts Bradman 121; and Hutton 81,
      383
   his impressions of local whites 148, 184
   other citations 100, 121 (pen-picture),
      122, 141-2, 149, 151-2, 155, 163,
      182, 186, 207, 224, 236-8, 246, 258,
      263-4, 273, 285, 287, 289-90, 315
Bannister, R.G. – 96
Bapty, John (*Yorkshire Evening Post*)
   – 341
Barbados Advocate – 184; *see also*
   Coppin
Barbados background
   cricketing 48-50, 98-9, 103, 106, 109,
      177-8, 181, 203, 359, 363
   environmental **43**, 178, 182
   social and political 25, 126, 177-80,
      183-5, 213-4, 255, 348, 361, 372
Barbados Labour Party (BLP) – 177-8,
   255
Barbados Regiment – 38
Barker, J.S. (*Trinidad Guardian*) – 109-
   10, 257, 260, 264-5, 268, 270, 272,
   356, 358, 368, 370
Barnes, Natasha – 73
Barnes, Simon – 371
Barrow, Errol – 24, 178, 356
Barrow, Llewelyn – 26
Basdeo, Sonny – 228
Beacon, The (Trinidad journal) – 75, 256
Beckles, Professor Sir Hilary – 28,
   155, 382
Bedser, Alec – 12, 31, 64-6, 91, 98, 113,
   175, 196, 220, 234, 312, 314-15, 340
Bedser, Eric – 65
Belafonte, Harry – 146
Benaud, Richie – 99, 279, 343, 363,
   365-7
Benn, Anthony Wedgwood – 17

Bennett, Don – 116
Bermuda
   Allied Powers conference 129, 131
   complicated cricket politics 130-1
   'Cup Match' 130
   Hotel Keepers' Act 129-30
   peripheral to British West Indies and
      cricket 39
   permanent military base winding
      down 129
   persuades MCC to add leg of tour 39,
      129
   See also race and colour
Bermuda Sports (magazine) – 132
Berry, Scyld – 93, 192-3
Bertram, Arnold – 150
Binns, Alfie – 104, 138
Birbalsingh, Frank – 109, 230, 237
Birley, Derek – 97, 142
Blackett, Fitz – 74
Blake, Evon – 130
Blunden, E.C. – 83
Blythe, Colin – 207
Blyton, Enid – 57
Bodyline tour, and 'spectre' of –
   12-13, 15, 30, 56, 90, 95-6, 178, 272,
   309, 322, 325, 340, 362
Botham, Ian – 93-4, 323
Bourda (Georgetown)
   covers, improvised 236
   crowd behaviour 218, 230-1, 238-9,
      244, 245-52
   Headquarters of 'boss' club 227, 250-1
   pitch 230-1, 236, 242, 251
   press box 233
   stands and enclosures: College 248;
      members' 225, 239, 251; popular
      246, 251
   wire fencing 218
Bowes, Bill – 85, 96, 121, 320, 341
boycotts by
   Bermudan whites 131
   BG: Cricket Association 39; crowds
      220 (both threatened)
   Jamaica: crowds 171, 352 (threatened);
      journalists 108
Bradman, Don – 31, 36, 83-6, 90-1, 93,
   111, 121, 137, 176, 216, 234, 264,
   271, 288, 350, 365-6, 370

Bradmanesque averages
Ganteaume (112.00) – 49
Hutton (149.33) – 333
V.H. Stollmeyer (96.00) – 78
Walcott (82.70) – 352
Weekes (121.12) – 108
Worrell (147.00) – 98
Bramall Lane (Sheffield)
barracking 86, 329
cushion-throwing 77
luncheon-room (Swanton/Hutton meeting) 59-60
Brasher, C.W. – 96
Brathwaite, Edward Kamau – 348
Bray, Charles (*Daily Herald*) – 118, 120 (pen-picture), 121, 123, 157, 159, 162, 204, 210, 241, 262, 270, 289-90, 327-8, 335, 361
Brearley, Mike – 137, 292, 382
Britain, Great
interchangeability with 'England' 10, 56, 164, 179, 185, 251, 257, 303, 348, 374-5
national communion 29-30, 35-6, 374-5, 378
regional differences 18, 36, 81-4, 86, 93, 223, 311, 329, 337-8, 343-4
post-war austerity 14, 29-30, 34, 304
post-war societal shifts 35-7, 69, 91-7, 117, 119, 149, 371
British Broadcasting Corporation (BBC)
radio 22, 32, 38, 121, 163, 336 (*Sporting Questions*)
television 29, 31, 34, 307, 368, 371
British empire
becoming interchangeable with Commonwealth 17, 30, 36, 102, 134, 375-6 (*but see* colonies)
loyalty of local whites to 17, 149-50, 174, 178, 227, 249, 256
'sub-Kiplingesque' attitudes to 143-4
sunset of 16-17, 28, 130, 374-5 (*see also* Egypt, Hong Kong, Kenya, Malaya)
See also cricket: game of empire
British Guiana (or BG, now Guyana)
background
cricketing 49-50, 79-80, 103-4, 109, 225-8, 251-2, 353, 363

environmental **43**, 217, 221, 235-6
social and political 14, 50, 133-4, 217-20, 226-8, 249-52, 353
British Guiana Volunteer Force – 38, 50
British Honduras (now Belize) – 381
British West Indies and British Guiana Sugar Association – 24
British West Indies Federation
aspirations for 16, 24, 27, 52
inception and quick collapse of 18, 355, 359, 367-8
Brock, Edwin ('The Year Before the War') – 37
Brodhurst, Robin – 337
Brogan, Colm – 215
Brown, F.R. (Freddie)
captain of 'ruddy dynamism' 55, 59, 62, 66, 325, 339, 344, 367
chairman of 1953 home selection panel 55, 58-9, 328
member of West Indies sub-committee 55, 62, 97
undermines Hutton 58-9, 97, 216, 342
unfavourably compared with Hutton 344
See also tours and Tests: MCC to Australia 1950/51
Bruce, General C.G. – 30
Buller, Syd – 370
Burke, Perry – 159-60, 164-6, 226, 291
Burnett, H.J.B. – 269
Burnham, Forbes – 24, 218-19, 228, 250-1, 353, 356
Bustamante, Alexander – 44, 174, 294-5, 299-303, 356-7, 360; *see also* incidents
Butcher, Basil – 221, 353, 358
Butler, Uriah (Buzz) – 126

Calthorpe, Hon. F.S.G. – 303
Campbell, J.M. (Jock) – 219
Cardus, Neville (*Manchester Guardian*) – 29, 32, 34, 82, 84, 96-7, 117, 359
Carter, Martin – 380
catches, easy or costly, dropped by
Bailey 158
Compton 238
Evans 158, 196 (*and* 207 for missed stumping)

424

as MCC assistant secretary 64, 260,
   307, 317, 321-2, 337, 370
as MCC tourist 60-1, 148, 260
Griffith, Teddy – 104
Guiana Graphic editorial on riot – 249
Guinness, Alec – 239

Haigh, Gideon – 51
Hailsham, first Lord (Hogg, Douglas
   McGarel) – 177-8
Hall, Ross (*Daily Mirror*) – 122 (pen-
   picture), 162, 166, 169, 198, 204,
   206-8, 214-15, 241, 263, 268, 272,
   285, 293, 297, 336
Hall, Stuart – 143-4
Hall, Wes – 103, 366-7, 370
Hammond, Walter (W.H. from 1938) –
   90-1, 93, 114, 200, 217, 225-6, 264,
   292
Hardstaff, Joe (junior) – 61
Hardy, G.H. – 379
Harland, Professor S.C. – 71, 75
Harmison, Steve – 234
Harper, Henry (Hank) – 357
Harris, third Lord (George Francis
   Robert) – 15, 70
Harris, fourth Lord (George Robert
   Canning) – 15, 50, 56, 73, 94, 376-8
Harvey, Bagenal – 122
Harvey, Neil – 33, 85, 118
Hassett, Lindsay – 36
Hattersley, Roy – 86
Hawke, Lord (Martin Bladen) – 35, 39,
   56, 89, 92, 95, 280, 376, 378
Hawkins, Jack – 239-40
Hayter, Reg (Reuters/*The Times*) – 14,
   122 (pen-picture), 160, 170-1, 291,
   298
Hazlitt, William – 107
Headley, George (1909-83)
   *pen-picture: still scoring heavily in
      Birmingham League 102*
   'Atlas' and 'Black Bradman': symbolic
      status as 22-3, 51-3, 146
   captain of: West Indies (1948) 45, 52,
      214; Jamaica (post-war) 103, 357;
      Combined Parishes (1953/54) 140
   disciples: *see* Gomez, Stollmeyer,
      Weekes

Jamaica: adopted son 23, 39, 44, 51,
   146; national coach 364; returning
   prophet 51-3, 359
injuries 45, 78, 103, 140
league cricket 23, 47, 52-3, 102
mastery, tactical 77-9, 152
method and waning powers 53, 100,
   122, 140, 147
Nethersole, sponsored by 45, 52-3,
   152
Nunes: record partnership 50, 210;
   strained relationship 50, 53
selection controversies: for Jamaica
   53; for West Indies 140-1, 152, 164,
   174, 195
swansong in first Test 11, 152, 155-7,
   160, 162, 164, 166-7, 170, 189, 363
rancour, absence of 77-8, 382-3
returns to Dudley 284
See also incidents
Hector, Richard – 221
Hector, Tim – 381
Hendren, Patsy – 118, 269, 322
Hennessy, Peter – 36
Henriques, Fernando – 145
Hesketh, Clifford – 309
Hill-Wood, W.W.H. – 129
Hirst, George Herbert – 88, 95, 333, 382
Hobbs, Jack – 96, 322, 370
Hobson, Harold – 14
Hodgson, Eva – 130
Hoggart, Richard – 83, 143
Holding, Michael – 151
Hole, Graeme – 33
Holmes, Group Captain A.J. – 86, 337
Holmes, Major E.R.T.
   barracked in Sheffield 86, 329
   conspires in London 328-9, 331-2, 334,
      338
Holmes, Percy – 98
Holt, John (senior) – 102, 159-60
Holt, John (junior) (1923-97)
   *pen-picture: father and son more
      famous 102*
   1953/54 series
   century for Jamaica in tour match 141,
      267
   first Test 153-5, 159-60, 162, 165-6, 226
   second Test 195-6, 207-8, 210

430

on management of cliques and men
140, 142, 187-9, 315
on umpiring 166, 181
on win-at-all-costs policy 136, 140
on wives joining tour 281
reputations as: dryly humorous
181, 188, 239, 277, 281; tartly
undeferential 115, 206, 321
wood over Walcott (at some expense)
201, 243, 273, 299, 348
Lamming, George – 27-8, 51
Lara, Brian – 70, 273
Larbey, Bob (*A Month of Sundays*) – 57
Larkin, Philip ('Annus Mirabilis') – 371
Larwood, Harold – 56-7, 96, 119, 309
Lawrence, D.H. – 83
leagues, local
Barbados Cricket (BCL) 48-9, 106, 107,
359, 363
Birmingham 47, 52-3, 102, 284
Bradford 81-2, 114, 204, 269
Central Lancashire 47, 99, 123, 340, 363
Lancashire 23, 47, 52, 102, 105, 107,
147, 383
Somers Isles (Bermuda) 130
Lee, General Robert – 325
Lee Kow, Eric – 245, 256
Legall, Ralph – 104
Lewis, A.R. – 223
Lewis, Professor Gordon – 40, 48, 178
Lillee, Dennis – 142
Lindwall, Ray – 31, 34, 67, 85, 108, 114,
118, 119, 137-9, 176, 262, 275, 288,
333
Livingstone, David – 17
Lloyd, Clive – 20, 72, 99, 252, 358, 363,
372, 381
Loader, Peter – 65-6, 311-12, 342
Lock, Tony (1929-95)
*pen-picture: dart-throwing, spine-
bending 'stormy petrel' 111*
1953: Coronation Ashes 31, 33, 35-6,
115; selection for tour 64
1953/54 series
first Test 152, 154-5, 157-8, 162-3,
165-7, 173, 175
second Test 196, 198, 201, 205-8
third Test 229, 234, 237-9, 242-3
fourth Test 265, 270-1, 273, 276-7

fifth Test 284-6, 296, 298-9, 301
tour matches, functions and travel
128, 132, 137, 141-2, 181-3, 304
1954/55: eliminated 312-13, 315
1957: eleven for 48 v WI at Oval
355-6
1959/60: eliminated again 360
Bourda: fears number is up 245;
names house after 250
called for throwing: loudly by fans
166-7; privately by players 38, 166,
182; publicly by umpires 115, 166,
175, 181-2, 226
feels senior players leave him: out in
cold 187-8, to carry the can for lift
incident 199-200
histrionics 141-2, 182, 207, 229
miscellaneous citations 11, 118
neutered without faster ball 183, 198
pulls through to contribute to
comeback 250, 273, 286
Lord Beginner (Egbert Moore,
calypsonian) – 21
Lord Kitchener (Aldwyn Roberts,
calypsonian) – 21, 26-7
Lord Mayor of London (Sir James
Harman, property developer) – 371
Lord Radio (Oliver Broomes,
calypsonian) – 76
Lord's cricket ground
archives and library 13, 18, **127**, 307,
326
'Headquarters', spiritual home of
cricket 20, 28, 89, 333
Long Room 14, 55
pavilion and dressing rooms 22, 24, 92
Robins memorial bench 57
stands: Allen and Warner 57; 'G' (now
Compton) 26
secretary's office 329, 334, 370
Tavern 125
See also balcony scenes, Imperial
Memorial Gallery, MCC
Louis, Joe – 218
Luckhurst, Brian – 32
Luke, Sir S.E.V. – 183
Lupton, Major A.W. – 331
Lyttleton, Sir O. (soon to be Viscount
Chandos) – 130

434

435

437

pyramid, essential white-brown-black 48-9, 51
stereotypes, racial 23, 79, 143, 147, 247, 326, 380
race discrimination legislation: Barbados (1956) 178; Britain (1965) 26
racial harmony and integration 15-16, 23-5, 30, 44, 75-6, 256, 377
racial tension and violence 26-7, 133, 217, 355
racism: overt 26-7, 71, 73, 75, 147, 178-9, 375; 'sedimented' 27, 72, 143-5, 378, 380
Rae, Allan – 23, 46, 53-4, 72, 105, 138, 283, 349, 353, 373
Ragbeer, Seegobin – 251
Rait-Kerr, Diana – **127**
Rait-Kerr, Colonel R.S. – 308-9
Ramadhin, Sonny (1929-2022)
  pen-picture: dynamo with a 'doosra' 105
  1950: hero of tour to England 11, 21, 23, 25, 27, 67, 75, 100
  1951/52: hiccups in Australia 76, 105
  1953: availability for selection 47, 50, 54
  1953/54 series
  first Test 159, 161-3, 166, 172-3
  second Test 201-5, 210-11, 213
  third Test 230-1, 233-4, 239, 241, 243, 245, 248
  fourth Test 275-6
  fifth Test 286, 290-1, 293, 299
  1957: broken by pad-play 225, 354
  1956-63: involvement (and non-involvement) in later series 349, 354, 364, 369
  recalls MCC non-fraternisation policy 135
  spells cast over English batsmen 67, 105, 204-5, 230-1, 233
  subject of English comments or complaints 138, 166, 182-3
  unorthodox deliveries 202, 203, 275
Rana, Shakoor – 159
Ranjitsinhji, K.S. – 22
Rattigan, Terence – 31, 36
Razack, Shan – 239, 246
Redoubtables Ladies CC (Purley) – 220

Rhodes, Wilfred – 34, 115, 119, 207, 331, 345-6
Richards, Sir Gordon – 30, 92
Richards, Viv – 52, 277, 372, 379-82
Richardson, Willy – 38
Rickards, Ken – 52
riots (at cricket grounds)
  Bourda (1953/54) 238-41, 245-52
  Queen's Park Oval (1959/60) 245
  Sabina Park (1967/68) 381
riots/disturbances (other)
  Enmore (1948) 218
  Fyzabad (1937) 126, 256
  Kingston (1968) 133
  Nottingham/Notting Hill (1957) 355
  Port of Spain (1903) 255
Roberts, Andy – 52
Roberts, Strebor (*Gleaner*) – 50, 108-9, 157, 295, 349, 352, 359
Robertson-Glasgow, R.C. – 369
Robins, Penny – 62-3, 184
Robins, R.W.V.
  background and cricket career 55, 57, 67, 83, 89, 269
  broadcasts on BBC 163, 321
  England/MCC selector 55, 57-8, 86, 369
  inner-circle administrator 55, 93-5, 129, 176, 216, 312, 321, 378
  MCC tour manager 360-1
  peripheral role in Bailey controversy 316
  prime role in conspiracies against Hutton 93, 328-31, 334, 336, 338
  warned off golf course by Enid Blyton 57
Robinson, Emmott – 331
Robinson, Ray – 106, 246, 344
Rodney, Walter – 250, 381
Rollox, Alwyn (Toby) – 222, 227-8
Root, Joe – 339
Rosebery, sixth Earl of (Albert Edward Harry Meyer Archibald Primrose) – 307, 326
Ross, Alan – 115, 121, 152, 335, 339-40, 360-1, 370, 380
Rostron, Frank (*Daily Express*) – 122 (pen-picture), 123, 139, 162, 186, 210-11, 215, 229, 232, 234-5, 261, 277, 285, 291, 297

445

447